Anarchists of the Caribbean

Anarchists who supported the Cuban War for Independence in the 1890s launched a transnational network linking radical leftists from their revolutionary hub in Havana, Cuba to South Florida, Puerto Rico, Panama, the Panama Canal Zone, and beyond. Over three decades, anarchists migrated around the Caribbean and back and forth to the United States, printed fiction and poetry promoting their projects, transferred money and information across political borders for a variety of causes, and attacked (verbally and physically) the expansion of US imperialism in the "American Mediterranean." In response, US security officials forged their own transnational antianarchist campaigns with officials across the Caribbean. In this sweeping new history, Kirwin R. Shaffer brings together research in anarchist politics, transnational networks, radical journalism, and migration studies to illustrate how men and women throughout the Caribbean Basin and beyond sought to shape a counter-globalization initiative to challenge the emergence of modern capitalism and US foreign policy while rejecting nationalist projects and Marxist state socialism.

KIRWIN R. SHAFFER is Professor of Latin American Studies at Pennsylvania State University, Berks College. He is the author of *Anarchist Cuba* (2019), *Black Flag Boricuas: Anarchism, Antiauthoritarianism, and the Left in Puerto Rico, 1897–1921* (2013), and co-editor of *In Defiance of Boundaries: Anarchism in Latin American History* (2015), which was the winner of the 'Outstanding Academic Title' award by *Choice* in 2016.

Global and International History

Series Editors:
Erez Manela, *Harvard University*
John McNeill, *Georgetown University*
Aviel Roshwald, *Georgetown University*

The Global and International History series seeks to highlight and explore the convergences between the new International History and the new World History. Its editors are interested in approaches that mix traditional units of analysis such as civilizations, nations and states with other concepts such as transnationalism, diasporas, and international institutions.

Titles in the Series

Stephen J. Macekura and Erez Manela, *The Development Century: A Global History*

Amanda Kay McVety, *The Rinderpest Campaigns: A Virus, Its Vaccines, and Global Development in the Twentieth Century*

Michele L. Louro, *Comrades against Imperialism*

Antoine Acker, *Volkswagen in the Amazon: The Tragedy of Global Development in Modern Brazil*

Christopher R. W. Dietrich, *Oil Revolution: Anti-Colonial Elites, Sovereign Rights, and the Economic Culture of Decolonization*

Nathan J. Citino, *Envisioning the Arab Future: Modernization in U.S.–Arab Relations, 1945–1967*

Stefan Rinke, *Latin America and the First World War*

Timothy Nunan, *Humanitarian Invasion: Global Development in Cold War Afghanistan*

Michael Goebel, *Anti-Imperial Metropolis: Interwar Paris and the Seeds of Third World Nationalism*

Stephen J. Macekura, *Of Limits and Growth: The Rise of Global Sustainable Development in the Twentieth Century*

Anarchists of the Caribbean

Countercultural Politics and Transnational Networks in the Age of US Expansion

KIRWIN R. SHAFFER
Pennsylvania State University, Berks

CAMBRIDGE
UNIVERSITY PRESS

CAMBRIDGE
UNIVERSITY PRESS

University Printing House, Cambridge CB2 8BS, United Kingdom

One Liberty Plaza, 20th Floor, New York, NY 10006, USA

477 Williamstown Road, Port Melbourne, VIC 3207, Australia

314–321, 3rd Floor, Plot 3, Splendor Forum, Jasola District Centre,
New Delhi – 110025, India

79 Anson Road, #06-04/06, Singapore 079906

Cambridge University Press is part of the University of Cambridge.

It furthers the University's mission by disseminating knowledge in the pursuit of education, learning, and research at the highest international levels of excellence.

www.cambridge.org
Information on this title: www.cambridge.org/9781108489034
DOI: 10.1017/9781108773706

© Kirwin R. Shaffer 2020

This publication is in copyright. Subject to statutory exception and to the provisions of relevant collective licensing agreements, no reproduction of any part may take place without the written permission of Cambridge University Press.

First published 2020

Printed in the United Kingdom by TJ International Ltd. Padstow Cornwall

A catalogue record for this publication is available from the British Library.

Library of Congress Cataloging-in-Publication Data
Names: Shaffer, Kirwin R., author.
TITLE: Anarchists of the Caribbean : countercultural politics and transnational networks in the age of US expansion / Kirwin R. Shaffer, Pennsylvania State University, Berks.
DESCRIPTION: Cambridge, United Kingdom ; New York, NY : Cambridge University Press, 2020. | Series: Global and international history | Includes bibliographical references and index.
IDENTIFIERS: LCCN 2019052442 (print) | LCCN 2019052443 (ebook) | ISBN 9781108489034 (hardback) | ISBN 9781108733304 (paperback) | ISBN 9781108773706 (epub)
SUBJECTS: LCSH: Anarchism–Caribbean Area. | Cuba–History–1810-1899.
CLASSIFICATION: LCC HX860 .S53 2020 (print) | LCC HX860 (ebook) | DDC 335/.830972909034–dc23
LC record available at https://lccn.loc.gov/2019052442
LC ebook record available at https://lccn.loc.gov/2019052443

ISBN 978-1-108-48903-4 Hardback

Cambridge University Press has no responsibility for the persistence or accuracy of URLs for external or third-party internet websites referred to in this publication and does not guarantee that any content on such websites is, or will remain, accurate or appropriate.

For Mom and Dad

Contents

List of Figures		*page* ix
Acknowledgments		xi
List of Abbreviations		xiii
	A Biographical Prologue: The Transnational World of José María Blázquez de Pedro	1
	Introduction: An Antiauthoritarian Cartography of the Caribbean	11
1	Anarchist Straits: Cuba's War for Independence and the Origins of the Caribbean Network	42
2	Anarchists versus *Yanquis*: The Anarchist Network Resists US Neocolonialism, 1898–1915	64
3	*¡Tierra y Libertad!*: Caribbean Anarchists and the Mexican Revolution, 1905–1930	125
4	The Caribbean *Red* during the Red Scare: Anarchists and the Bolshevik Revolution, 1917–1924	155
5	Anarchists versus *Yanquis* II: The Canal, the Great War, Puerto Rico's Status, and Banana Republics, 1916–1926	186
6	*Bolivarianismo anarquista*: Anarchist Pan-Americanism in the Heart of the Hemisphere	214

7 Down but Not Out: Confronting Socialists, Communists,
   and Tropical Fascists, 1925–1934   252
   A Literary Epilogue: Marcelo Salinas and Adrián del
   Valle, 1920s–1930s   273

Bibliography   291
Index   307

Figures

P.1 José María Blázquez de Pedro as a twenty-year-old
Spanish soldier in Cuba in 1895   *page* 2
P.2 The Blázquez de Pedro family grave in Amador Cemetery
(Panama City) with the original cross removed   8
I.1 Map of the anarchist Caribbean   12
1.1 Enrique Creci, a leading anarchist in Cuba in the 1890s
who found refuge in Florida before joining a military
expedition in 1896 to cast off Spanish colonial rule from
the island, dying soon after   43
2.1 Luis Barcia: Tampa's leading anarchist in the post-Cuban
War years   80
2.2 ¡Tierra! (1903, 1905, 1913): the longest-running anarchist
newspaper in Cuba (1902–1915) and the key Caribbean
regional information source with brief iterations in the
1920s and 1930s   87
3.1 Mug shots of Marcelo Salinas and Maximiliano Olay in
Tampa after being arrested for "conspiring" to assassinate
President Madero of Mexico in January 1913   136
3.2 Adrián del Valle's *De maestro a guerrillero* and his ode to
revolutionary violence for anarchist justice during the
Mexican Revolution, though written in the late 1920s
when Cuba was ruled by the dictator Machado – perhaps
a larger call to anarchists to resist the dictatorship   138
3.3 Juan Francisco Moncaleano, a stalwart example of anarchist
transnationalism, with activism in Colombia, Cuba, Mexico,

	and the United States, until the transnational network outed him as a potential child molester	148
4.1	Antonio Penichet, anarcho-syndicalist author, labor leader, pro-Bolshevik, and all-around bad-ass	163
4.2	Launched on May Day 1920 in the midst of growing worker radicalism, the Bayamón-based *El Comunista* was the longest-running anarchist newspaper in Puerto Rico until it was closed under US government repression in early 1921	171
5.1	José María Blázquez de Pedro in 1913 on the eve of leaving for Panama	188
5.2	Víctor Recoba from Peru (seated on the left) began his transnational anarchist activism in the Canal Zone in 1914, led the first general strike against the Canal Zone in 1916, and ventured around the Americas in the following decade, including Cuba, Mexico, Peru, and the United States	190
6.1	Joseph Calleia as "Vasquez" – an anarchist on the run from Panama, caught in the United States, deported to Panama, and leader of plane crash survivors in a Latin American jungle in the 1939 movie *Five Came Back*	215
6.2	The anarchist Pan-American magazine *Cuasimodo: Magazine Interamericano* published in Panama City, complete with Cuasimodo ringing the steeple bell overlooking the Panama Canal, 1920	223
6.3	In 1919, Argentinean anarchist Julio Barcos arrived in Panama and published *Cuasimodo*	224
6.4	The anarchist–Marxist led FORP launched *El Obrero* in 1921 in Panama City. It included advice for workers to look to the IWW and radical workers rising up in the United States	226
6.5	The Mexican-born José C. Valadés joined with Julio Díaz from Argentina to coordinate a 1925 anarchist conference in Panama with the cooperation of the Blázquez de Pedro brothers	240
E.1	Marcelo Salinas (circa 1928 with the publication of *Alma Guajira*). He and Adrián del Valle (in the late *machadato* years) enjoyed literary success at the very moment their comrades in Cuba were under threat by the Machado government	274

Acknowledgments

❋

This book has been a long time in the making, and as such many people have helped to shape it. I wish to thank the ever-growing cohort of scholars who research the history of anarchism around the world, especially Steven Hirsch and Geoffroy de Laforcade – key ringmasters in the Latin American Anarchist Circus that has globetrotted to conferences around the United States, Latin America, and Europe this past decade-plus. Many other historians focusing on the Greater Caribbean Region have helped me shape this book and its arguments, including Evan Daniel, David Díaz-Arias, Amparo Sánchez Cobos, Barry Carr, Chris Castañeda, Montse Feu, Mario Castillo, and Jorell Meléndez-Badillo. Raymond Craib, Constance Bantman, Davide Turcato, Carl Levy, José Moya, David Struthers, Kenyon Zimmer, Jesse Cohn, Sonia Hernández, Jim Baer, and the late (and desperately missed) Bert Altena have been invaluable over the years with stimulating discussions, tips, leads, and insights, and not the occasional cold beer.

Over the past twenty-five years, I've had the great privilege of working in some mighty fine libraries and archives in Puerto Rico, Panama, Cuba, the United States, and the Netherlands: the Biblioteca Nacional de Puerto Rico, the Archivo Nacional de Puerto Rico, the CDOSIP at the University of Puerto Rico-Humacao, the University of Puerto Rico-Río Piedras, the Center for Puerto Rican Studies at Hunter College, the New York Public Library, the US National Archives, the Instituto de Historia de Cuba, the Instituto de Literatura y Lingüística de Cuba, the Museo Municipal de Regla (Cuba), the Archivo Nacional de Panamá, the Biblioteca Nacional de Panamá, and the International Institute of Social History (Amsterdam). I offer my heartfelt appreciation to all those academics, librarians, and archivists who helped me find what I was looking for, brought things I didn't know I wanted (put actually needed), and expressed profound apologies for not being able to locate what I thought was there. So it goes. But, as always, I must offer my most gracious thank you to Mieke IJzermans, the former information director at the International Institute of Social History. Over the decades – beginning with my first research trip to the IISG as a Ph.D. student in 1995 – Mieke has been an ever-present supporter of my work, always curious about what I found, and a friend.

I offer a special thank you to my editor, Debbie Gershenowitz. From the beginning, she saw promise in this project and has helped me steer what was once a nearly 200,000-word manuscript into something far leaner and better ... I hope. The staff at Cambridge University Press is superb and have held my hand through my many questions and concerns. The Interlibrary Loan staff at the Penn State University Berks College library has been fantastic in acquiring almost everything that I requested, and I'm especially thankful to the library heads for keeping around that old clunker of a microfilm reader tucked away in the corner of the library – even if that reader is responsible for my now questionable eyesight. My division heads Ken Fifer and Belén Rodríguez-Mourelo, my academic affairs chairs Paul Esqueda and Janelle Larson, and my Global Studies colleague Randy Newnham have been generous in awarding me conference and research money over the years and as such probably deserve more thanks than this one line.

Finally, family. Over the course of this project, life took some sharp turns: divorce, marriages, children graduating high school and college, grandchildren – you know, life. Here's to my children Sarra, Nathaniel, Imane, Hannah, and Malick – and to my amazing grandchildren Kilian, Zeno, Lucía, Harper, and all those still to come. But, of course, the greatest thanks can never be truly and fully expressed for that is to my adored and adorable wife and partner, Zohra. Thank you, gracias, merci, shukran.

Abbreviations

ACP	American Communist Party
AFL	American Federation of Labor
ALC	Asociación Libertaria de Cuba (Libertarian Association of Cuba)
ANERC	Asociación de Nuevos Emigrados Revolucionarios de Cuba (Association of New Revolutionary Emigrants from Cuba)
CDOSIP	Centro de Documentación Obrera Santiago Iglesias Pantín, Humacao, PR
CES	Centro de Estudios Sociales (Social Studies Center)
CGT	Confederación General de Trabajadores (General Confederation of Workers), Mexico
CMIU	Cigar Makers International Union (aka The International)
CNOC	Confederación Nacional de Obreros Cubanos (National Confederation of Cuban Workers)
CNT-FAI	Confederación Nacional del Trabajo – Federación Anarquista Ibérica (National Confederation of Work – Iberian Anarchist Federation), Spain
Comintern	Communist Third International
CPAS	Comité Pro-Acción Sindical (Pro-Action Union Committee), Guatemala
DASC	Diego Abad de Santillán Collection
DOJ	United States Department of Justice
FGAC	Federación de Grupos Anarquistas de Cuba (Federation of Cuban Anarchist Groups)
FII	Federación Individualista Internacional (International Individualist Federation)

FLT	Federación Libre de Trabajadores (Free Federation of Workers), Puerto Rico
FOH	Federación Obrera de la Habana (Havana Workers Federation)
FORA	Federación Obrera Regional Argentina (Argentina Regional Workers Federation)
FORP	Federación Obrera de la República de Panamá (Workers Federation of the Panamanian Republic)
FRT	Federación Regional de los Trabajadores (Regional Federation of Workers), Puerto Rico
ICC	Isthmian Canal Commission
IISG	Intenationaal Instituut voor Sociale Geschiendenis (International Institute of Social History), Amsterdam
IWW	Industrial Workers of the World
JdI	Junta de Inquilinato, Panama
MTW	Marine Transport Workers
PCC	Partido Comunista Cubano (Cuban Communist Party)
PLM	Partido Liberal Mexicano (Mexican Liberal Party)
PRC	Partido Revolucionario Cubano (Cuban Revolutionary Party)
RG	Record Group
SGT	Sindicato General de Trabajadores (General Trade Union of Workers), Panama
SLP	Socialist Labor Party of the United States
UNIA	Universal Negro Improvement Association
USNA	United States National Archives
USSR	Union of Soviet Socialist Republics

A Biographical Prologue

The Transnational World of José María Blázquez de Pedro

We asked, "Dr. [Blázquez de Pedro], you never wear a hat. Why not?" And he quickly replied emphatically, as if expecting the question: "No. I never wear a hat since above my head is THE WORLD."[1]

As war raged on the distant island of Cuba in 1895, the Spanish government increasingly sent young men to the Caribbean to suppress a rebellion that had been joined by anarchists in Cuba, Florida, and New York. For Cuban nationalists who represented propertied interests, this was a war to liberate Cuba and become an independent, capitalist, Catholic country. For the anarchists who joined the rebellion, this was an anticolonial social revolution that would liberate Cuba from Spanish tyranny, create decentralized control, abolish capitalism, and destroy clerical influences.

One of the young Spaniards sent to suppress the Cuban rebellion was a twenty-year-old from the western Spanish town of Béjar – José María Blázquez de Pedro, who fought in Cuba from September 1895 to December 1898 (Figure P.1).[2] Spain's 1898 defeat in the Caribbean against combined Cuban and US forces, and the loss of most of its remaining

---

[1] Nicolas Justiniani, "Recuerdos imborrables Don José María Blásquez de Pedro y el Dr. José Llorent," *Revista Lotería* (Panama), 186, May 1971, 69–70.
[2] Ignacio C. Soriano Jiménez and Miguel Íñiguez, *José María Blázquez de Pedro: anarquista de ambos mundos (en Béjar, Panamá y Cuba)* (Vitoria: Asociación Isaac Puente, 2017), 27–28; Hernando Franco Muñoz, *Blázquez de Pedro y los orígenes del sindicalismo panameño* (Panama City, Panama: Movimiento Editores, 1986), 163; *La Revista Nueva*, January 1918, 16; and, *Nueva Luz*, October 16, 1923, 7.

1

FIGURE P.1 José María Blázquez de Pedro as a twenty-year-old Spanish soldier in Cuba in 1895

global empire, shocked the Spanish population. For some soldiers who were sent to Cuba, the experience led to a fundamental reevaluation of their beliefs and principles. Blázquez de Pedro returned to Spain thoroughly disillusioned by the war. He soon rejected militarism, patriotism, and nationalism when he encountered Spain's fervent anarchist movement.[3] He created a library in his home, wrote for the Spanish anarchist press, published books of poetry, and in 1910 organized the anarchist group "Los Autónomos."[4]

Cuba had noticeably impacted the young anarchist – an impact seen in one of his poems, "De Antaño y Ogaño" (From Olden Times and Our Times). He wrote the first half while fighting in Cuba. It praises Spain and the quest to put down the Cuban insurrection; however, the second half

---

[3] Franco Muñoz, *Blázquez de Pedro*, 164.
[4] Jiménez and Íñiguez, *José María Blázquez de Pedro*, 15–16.

of the poem, written in 1904, presents disparaging images of the arrogant, overbearing Spain, while praising Cuba.[5] He further rejected Spanish imperialism and nationalist wars in his "La agonía del repatriado. Poema-monólogo" (The Agony of the Repatriated. Poem-Monologue). A soldier returning to Spain describes his deployment to Cuba and "being overwhelmed listening to the insults / enduring the insults / from those who should be thanking you / for your help, kindness, and care."[6] But the soldier then comes to understand why the people he's there to "help" would behave with such disrespect as he sees the senseless death, destruction, and bloodshed during the war. "That noble Spain / unfortunate and beautiful, / ... / look how they've turned me / into a violent soldier, / martyr of the country."[7] The returning veteran channels this disillusionment into a broader hatred of all those who he believes profited from the war: "Damn my country ... those who enjoy life but don't work ... who suffer but don't protest ... avarice ... those who exploit ... pray ... the slave who doesn't rebel ... all countries ... war ... Damn a thousand times the God of those with too much / the God of the nationalists / and the God of those who rule."[8]

Blázquez de Pedro's anarchism and his turn against God had repercussions. He labeled all religions as "stultifying and contrary to human dignity," but the Catholic Church as "the worst and most absurd of all of them." Church leaders demanded his imprisonment, prompting his arrest in Madrid in 1905, when he was sentenced to jail for nine months for his antireligious pronouncements. In fact, he was regularly jailed between 1904 and 1908.[9]

Many anarchists understood that any future revolution needed its seeds planted in the youth of today. For anarchist thinkers on education, like Spain's Francisco Ferrer y Guardia and Blázquez de Pedro, youth were naturally free and antiauthoritarian. As Blázquez de Pedro put it:

---

[5] José María Blázquez de Pedro, "De Antaño y Ogaño," in *Sangre de mi sangre (Poesias). Sin Ajena prologación* (Panama City, Panama: Impreso Talleres Gráficos "La Unión," 1924), 116–118. The poems in the collection appeared in 42 newspapers and magazines in Spain and the Americas before he combined them into a book while in Panama.

[6] José María Blázquez de Pedro, *La agonía del repatriado. Poema-monólogo* (Lisbon: Typographia do Commercio, 1910), 8.

[7] Ibid., 11–12.

[8] Ibid., 14–15. Throughout Spain and Cuba, anarchist newspapers sold his books. See, for instance, *¡Tierra!*, August 10, 1907, 4, which sold his poetry collection *Rebeldías Cantadas*.

[9] José María Blázquez de Pedro, *Pensares* (Barcelona: Imprenta de Cuesta, 1905), 33; Jiménez and Íñiguez, *José María Blázquez de Pedro*, 14.

"Observe children and you will see how they are naturally rebellious, how with the most ingenuous and simplistic spontaneity they reject all authority, all imposition."[10] However, contemporary education destroyed spontaneity, liberty, and rebellion in children. Education especially crushed a child's imagination, "castrating him morally and intellectually, killing or atrophying his impulses and energies – the essence of wellbeing that was given the child by nature."[11] It did not help that the parents acquiesced in the destruction of their children's freedom. They accepted the status quo of education without thinking of the myriad alternatives that children could experience: "they persist in the idea that their children do everything with the right hand only. As if there were no left hand! The true education is ambidextrous."[12] And so Blázquez de Pedro advocated the importance of both physical and intellectual education – the very philosophy advocated by his better-known contemporary, Ferrer y Guardia.

Blázquez de Pedro also wrote about labor, but just as importantly he wrote about what life one's labor should create. In the spirit of labor activists of the day, he called on workers to demand an eight-hour day: "don't ask the bourgeoisie or authorities or gods, because if you ask them, they won't give it to you." Then, after winning the eight-hour day, the workers had to "continue afterwards conquering and conquering always until you have won Pleasure." And pleasure – enjoying life – was key to all labor conquests for Blázquez de Pedro. "Work is not dishonorable but working to excess is."[13] Working was not something to be idolized. "You work more than is necessary, much more than you ought to, much more than should be possible, much more than is just because you consent to it with a meek stoicism and an inconceivable resignation." One shouldn't display their calloused hands as some "noble flag of pride but instead as flagrant and irrefutable proof of your deformation, of your slavery." In fact, he concluded, "those broken hands are the gravest and most irrefutable accusation against the present society of privilege, wrong, and violence."[14] The ultimate goal was not a better job, but enjoying pleasures away from one's job. In verse, he continued this theme: "Enjoying life is no crime / ... / Enjoying life is human, natural, and beautiful / it degrades nobody and delights everyone."[15] And there was no higher pleasure, he

---

[10] Blázquez de Pedro, *Pensares*, 42.   [11] Ibid., 42.   [12] Ibid., 22.

[13] José María Blázquez de Pedro, *El derecho al placer* (Barcelona: Biblioteca Vertice, 1906), 9–12.

[14] Ibid., 3–6.

[15] José María Blázquez de Pedro, *Rebeldías Contadas* (Béjar: Tipografía Silverio Sánchez, 1905), 11.

noted, than "perpetuating life through the sexual act of reproduction."[16] Publicly, anarchists were prudish and denounced workers who spent time drinking and playing cards or billiards. But here, alas, was an anarchist publicly reveling in pleasure and getting laid.

Spain, though, was not enough for him. Or, perhaps it was too much, with two sisters and both parents dying between 1909 and 1913. In 1914, he moved with his two brothers and a sister to Panama at the invitation of a long-time anarchist activist in the Canal Zone. He went with the grand idea to use the Panamanian isthmus as a geographical point to unite anarchists throughout the Americas. Upon arriving in the Caribbean port of Colón, Blázquez de Pedro embarked on a regular writing schedule with anarchists in Havana and Spain. In mid-1915, he left Colón and relocated to the Pacific port of Panama City with his siblings, where he began to shift his focus to more militant labor-based anarchism, publishing *Himnos anarquistas* (Anarchist Hymns) and forming a new "Los Autónomos" group with the Peru-born anarchist Víctor Recoba and twenty-two others.[17]

In October 1916, upwards of 10,000 workers walked off the job to protest wages and conditions on the Panama Canal.[18] Blázquez de Pedro was one of the multinational leaders of the new Maritime Workers Union, speaking at rallies where he called on strikers to persuade those still working to stop and join the strike while condemning American control of the canal.[19] Following the strike, Blázquez de Pedro – though regularly labeled a "radical" and a "socialist" by US informants – worked and agitated openly in Panama City for the next nine years. During that time, he published periodic columns in the city's mainstream and progressive papers as well as the anarchist-edited *Cuasimodo: Magazine Interamericano* and

---

[16] Blázquez de Pedro, *Pensares*, 23–24.
[17] Franco Muñoz, *Blázquez de Pedro*, 173; Jiménez and Íñiguez, *José María Blázquez de Pedro*, 17, 31, 33, 230, 243; *¡Tierra!*, July 16, 1914, 2 and July 23, 1914, 2; *Tierra y Libertad*, May 3, 1916, 4. In early 1915, Blázquez de Pedro sent nearly weekly columns to the Barcelona newspaper *Tierra y Libertad*. Copies were then mailed back to readers in the Caribbean. These columns helped to keep anarchists in Panama linked to the outside world. Money often accompanied these columns, most of it collected by Blázquez de Pedro. See, for instance, *Tierra y Libertad*, December 29, 1915, 4.
[18] Michael Conniff, *Black Labor on a White Canal: 1904–1981* (Pittsburgh: University of Pittsburgh Press, 1985), 50–53.
[19] Memorandum for Captain Mitchell, October 4, 1916; Letter from Resident Engineer to Acting Governor, October 5, 1916; and, Re: Maritime Union Society, October 9, 1916 in RG185 Isthmian Canal Commission Records. 1914–1934 (hereafter cited as ICC 1914–1934), 2-P-59.

his own magazine, *El Cabellero Andante*. He worked to create a cultural center promoting the free exchange of ideas and collaborated with other leftists in Panama to create rationalist education. As he noted in the opening editorial of *El Cabellero Andante*, "We are knights errant of all generous ideals, of all redemptive ideals, of all ideals for improvement ... Our ideal can be reduced to three words: Freedom, Love, Beauty."[20]

Culture and aesthetics were important to the middle-aged anarchist, and Panama City lacked both. He decried the state of disrepair of Panama City's Lesseps Park and the Paseo de las Bóvedas, the lack of trees and flowers in the Plaza de Herrera, the poorly attended public classical music performances, the ghastly yellow-painted façade of the Municipal Palace, and the architectural blasphemy behind someone painting the old, historic stone towers of the Panama Cathedral – which might have been the site of religious fanatics, but that was no reason not to appreciate the beauty of the building constructed by working people.[21]

Added to this were his fervent denunciations of republican democracy. As a good anarchist, he mistrusted all government initiatives.[22] Not only was individual initiative superior to governmental initiative, but states – even republican ones – were themselves anti-individual. Ultimately, he suggested that people would do well to understand that democracy was not the most progressive political development in human history, nor the end of historical development. "After absolute monarchy, there was constitutional monarchy. After constitutional monarchy, there was the democratic republic. After the democratic republic, there will be syndicalism, state socialism, and anarchism ... The children of good democrats ought to be syndicalists, socialists, and anarchists."[23] He tried to get his readers to see that democracy was really just a bunch of legislators passing laws for their own interests, and "returning to the People" their own natural rights, customs, and aspirations that they never lost in the first place. "Individualism," he concluded, "is not, nor can it be democratic, aristocratic, monarchic, theocratic, or plutocratic, but simply and solely anarchic, or better said, anarchist."[24]

---

[20] José María Blázquez de Pedro, *Observaciones de un andariego en Panamá: crónicas y artículos, sin prólogo ajeno* (Panama City: Talleres Gráficos de "El Tiempo," 1922), 176–178.

[21] *La Revista Nueva*, June 1917, 446–448; September 1917, 204–207; Blázquez de Pedro, *Observaciones*, 21–25 and 26–27.

[22] Blázquez de Pedro, *Observaciones*, 133–134.   [23] Ibid., 56–58, 144, 147.

[24] Ibid., 28–29; 54–55, 63.

As for capitalist Panama, Blázquez de Pedro was true to his anarchist roots. Capital was not preserved for those who produced it, but controlled by "a parasite, far removed from production, by an idle *señor*, backed up by laws and by all of the armed forces," taking from the true producers and "giving back in exchange a salary INFERIOR to the value of what they produced ... Let every capitalist disappear and Humanity will not suffer in the least; let every worker disappear, and the most chaotic disorder will ensue without delay."[25] The first nationwide labor organization in Panama since the 1916 general strike emerged in 1921, and Blázquez de Pedro played a decisive role. Workers created the Federación Obrera de la República de Panamá (Workers Federation of the Panamanian Republic, or FORP) and its newspaper *El Obrero*. Blázquez de Pedro was elected to the FORP's Central Executive Committee. That July, he and his comrades formed a separate entity known as the Grupo Comunista. Weekly, the group met in Blázquez de Pedro's Panama City home.[26] They opposed all politics and capitalism, declared themselves followers of communism, and viewed the Bolshevik government as the best and most practical contemporary expression of their own ideals.[27] By 1925, the Grupo Comunista formed a new union – the Sindicato General de Trabajadores (General Trade Union of Workers, or SGT). The SGT members then formed the Liga de Inquilinos y Subsistencias (Tenants and Basic Necessities League, aka the Liga), which protested soaring rents and living costs in Panama.

Through its newspaper, *El Inquilino*, the Liga organized a campaign to empower renters to resist rent increases. On October 1, some 4000 people of multiple nationalities in Panama City went on strike, refusing to pay rent. At the same time, Blázquez de Pedro and his brother Martín were coordinating the first Inter-Continental Congress of Anarchists, scheduled for early November and with delegates from throughout Latin America pledging to attend. But the United States and Panama repressed the strike and detained anarchists arriving for the congress.[28] The government deported Blázquez de Pedro, who disembarked in Havana, where he lived

---

[25] *Cuasimodo*, April 1920, 40–43.
[26] Memorandum for the Governor from Inspector George Vraff, November 17, 1921, in RG185 ICC 1914–1934, 2-P-8.
[27] Marco A. Gandásequi, *Las luchas obreras en Panamá (1850–1978)* (Panama City: Talleres Diálogo, 1980), 35, 52, 58–59; Ricaurte Soler, *Panamá: historia de una crisis*. Panama City: Siglo XXI, 1989), 50–51; Franco Muñoz, *Blázquez de Pedro*, 176.
[28] Letter dated November 4, 1925, Diego Abad de Santillán Collection (hereafter referred to as DASC), Correspondence. IISG, Amsterdam, the Netherlands.

FIGURE P.2 The Blázquez de Pedro family grave in Amador Cemetery (Panama City) with the original cross removed.
Author's personal collection

until his death a year and a half later at the age of fifty-two to thirty-two years since he first saw Cuba as a Spanish soldier.[29] Still, José's journey was not over. Even in death he continued as a migrating anarchist. In 1929, comrades shipped his remains to Panama City and buried them in Amador Cemetery. Oddly, someone erected a cross over this anti-clerical man's grave – a cross that (appropriately) was removed decades later (Figure P.2).[30]

Blázquez de Pedro is not a member of the anarchist canon. Few people today have heard of him, but this Spanish-born radical played a crucial role in Panama and linking the isthmus to the wider Caribbean anarchist world – a role that many other migrating anarchists from Spain, Cuba, Puerto Rico, and Peru played throughout the region. Blázquez de Pedro was the best-known and longest working of a wide-ranging group of migrant anarchists in Panama. His writings to colleagues in Spain and

---

[29] US State Department Weekly Country Report from Panama for 10/31 to 11/7 on Communist Leanings of Inquilinos with Enclosures, November 14, 1925, 819.00B. RG59 General Records of the Department of State. Internal Affairs of Panama. General Conditions (hereafter referred to as RG59 Panama). US National Archives, College Park, MD.

[30] I cannot say when the cross was removed, but when I found the grave in summer 2015 the cross was no longer there.

Cuba, his transnational communiqués, and his activities with anarchists throughout the Caribbean Basin also illustrate his importance in larger transnational anarchist networks. Blázquez de Pedro functioned as a "middle-man" of sorts in the networks. As the leading anarchist voice in Panama, his writings to Cuba and Spain helped to showcase Panamanian politics and culture to his colleagues abroad. In another sense, Blázquez de Pedro was greatly concerned with the development of culture (literature, arts, schools, etc.) in Panama. At the same time, he was an essayist and poet – a creator of anarchist cultural productions that appeared in Panama, Cuba, and Spain. Thus, when he wrote about his wartime experiences in Cuba, prison in Spain, rent strikes in the canal, or Pan-Americanism and cultural debates in Panama, he was translating the local for global consumption as well as applying the global for local interpretation.[31]

José María Blázquez de Pedro's story is one of several anarchist biographies in this book. Or, maybe biography is not quite the right term because we rarely have full-scale biographical profiles of these men and women. Rather, we usually have brief encounters and episodic meetings. We see them here and there, or maybe just for an instance and then they are gone. So, what we really have are mini-memoirs that enable us to unravel anarchist networks by tracing people's physical movements, actions, influences, and both the ideological and geographical trajectories of their writings. Networks did not just appear. They were coordinated by anarchist agency to resist and subvert authoritarian institutions. Some of these people were well known, others were blips on the historical record. As Constance Bantman and Bert Altena note in their volume on transnational anarchist history, "individuals ... are like cities, the 'nodes' in the networks, and they provide an insight into the latter."[32]

Through coordinated actions of workers from different countries; through fundraising campaigns abroad for local use or local fundraising for use abroad; through transfers of newspapers, books, journals, and

---

[31] On the role of individuals as cultural "go betweens" and as people who help us unravel the networks, see Constance Bantman, "The Militant Go-Between: Émile Pouget's Transnational Propaganda (1880–1914)," *Labour History Review* 74, no. 3 (2009): 274–287; and Davide Turcato, "Italian Anarchism as a Transnational Movement, 1885–1915," *International Review of Social History* 52 (2007): 407–444.

[32] Constance Bantman and Bert Altena, "Introduction: Problematizing Scales of Analysis in Network-Based Social Movements," in *Reassessing the Transnational Turn: Scales of Analysis in Anarchist and Syndicalist Studies*, eds. Constance Bantman and Bert Altena (Oakland, CA: PM Press, 2017), 4.

articles; and, through the movement of flesh and blood between nodes – through all of these "transtemporal transfers" of ideas, money, migrations, and even memories – anarchists forged networks as a way to bring forth a new anarchist dawn.[33] To be sure, Caribbean anarchists were not alone. Anarchists elsewhere in the Americas likewise created and benefited from such networks. Steven Hirsch notes how Peruvian radicals joined anarchist migrants and communicated with anarchist organizations in Chile and Argentina.[34] The Buenos Aires Federación Obrera Regional de Argentina was "regional," not national, as it organized workers along the waterways linking and transgressing the political borders of Argentina, Uruguay, and Brazil to create "anarchist federative networking throughout the region," in the words of Geoffroy de Laforcade.[35] Caribbean anarchists worked in similar ways. From Spain to Cuba to Spain to Panama to Cuba to Panama, José María Blázquez de Pedro's story almost perfectly "bookends" the high era of Caribbean anarchism. He was the most important voice in the Panamanian node of a series of networks that linked the Caribbean to South America, Central America, New York, and Spain. His story is one of dozens of well-known (at the time) and less well-known anarchists who moved around the Caribbean network, published criticism and propaganda, communicated with their radical brethren in the network and beyond, and helped to create a Caribbean anarchist presence to counter priests, politicians, capitalists, and American imperialists in the three decades following the Cuban Independence War.

---

[33] I wish to acknowledge Achim von Oppen and Christine Hatzky, who offered these ideas about transtemporal transfers and network intentions respectively in their closing remarks at the "Entangled Spaces in the Americas: Concepts and Case Studies" workshop at Bielefeld University in Bielefeld, Germany, April 2014.

[34] Steven Hirsch, "Peruvian Anarcho-Syndicalism: Adapting Transnational Influences and Forging Counterhegemonic Practices, 1905–1930," in *Anarchism and Syndicalism in the Colonial and Post-colonial World, 1870–1940: The Praxis of National Liberation, Internationalism, and Social Revolution*, eds. Steven Hirsch and Lucien van der Walt (Leiden: Brill Academic Publishers, 2010), 267.

[35] Geoffroy de Laforcade, "Federative Futures: Waterways, Resistance Societies, and the Subversion of Nationalism in the Early 20th-Century Anarchism of the Río de la Plata Region," *Estudios Interdisciplinarios de América Latina* 22, no. 2 (2011): 91.

Introduction

An Antiauthoritarian Cartography of the Caribbean

> The network is stretched out, and in it will fall the fat Levites, the feathered, and the crowned.
> R. Huerta, Havana, 1914

By the early 1900s, anarchists penetrated the far corners of the Western Hemisphere. In Cuba, Florida, Puerto Rico, and Panama, activists – like their comrades everywhere – struggled to create their own anarchist visions of a free, egalitarian society for all, regardless of race, ethnicity, nationality, or gender.[1] To accomplish this, they challenged the power structures of society in international and domestic capitalism, religion (especially Catholicism), and the state. These men and women always thought of themselves as internationalists. They rejected nationalist and patriotic rhetoric they believed falsely divided humanity for the material and political interests of a few elites. They saw their local and national struggles as part of a regional Caribbean antiauthoritarian network linked to a larger global movement (Figure I.1).

Now, some may see the anarchists as unimportant and marginal in the region before the 1930s. After all, they did not achieve (nor even seek) state power. They did not believe in governments, though some modified this view when the Bolshevik Revolution emerged. Thus, some readers

---

[1] For an overview of Latin American anarchist historiography, see Geoffroy de Laforcade and Kirwin Shaffer, "Introduction: The Hidden Story Line of Anarchism in Latin American History," in *In Defiance of Boundaries: Anarchism in Latin American History*, eds. Geoffroy de Lafordade and Kirwin Shaffer (Gainesville: University Press of Florida, 2015), 1–22.

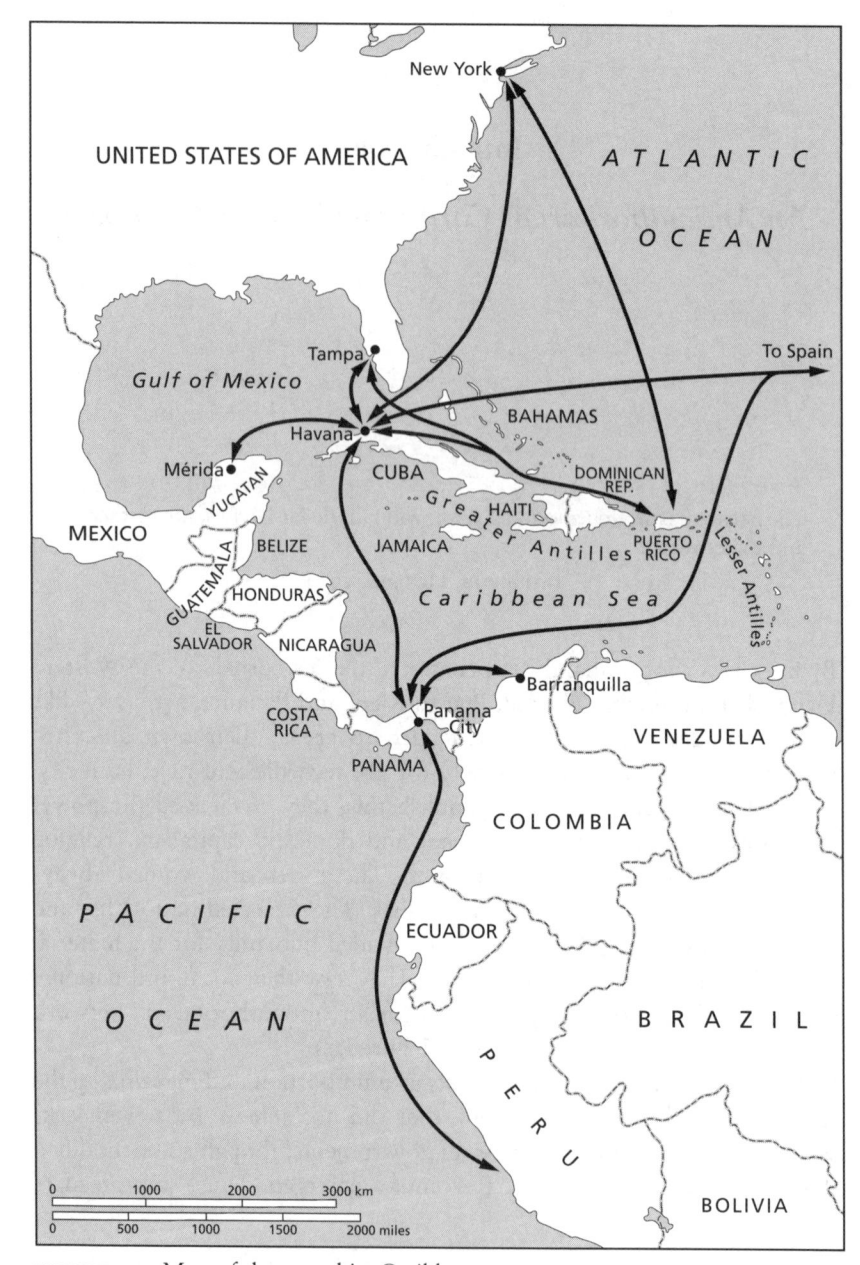

FIGURE 1.1 Map of the anarchist Caribbean.

could be skeptical about the significance of anarchists. One could argue that if they were not part of the political competition, then they were irrelevant. Or, maybe some readers who know leftist history would argue that they traveled a "misguided" path. Certainly, Marxist historians of the Caribbean have devalued anarchists and the history of anarchism. However, the surge in histories of anarchism in the past twenty years clearly shows that such previous interpretations are misguided.

There are numerous reasons to reevaluate the history of anarchism in the Caribbean. First, when we examine the emergence of left-wing politics in the region, traditional historiography tends to focus on Marxism, whether seen in terms of Socialist Parties, Communist Parties, or Marxian anti-imperialist leagues. But the anarchists were the original leftists in the region. In the first decades of the twentieth century, these men and women *were* leftist politics in the Caribbean (and most of Latin America) before the emergence of Socialist Parties in the 1910s and Communist Parties in the 1920s and 1930s. In Cuba, anarchists existed for some 25 years before the emergence of a Socialist Party and 40 years before the creation of the Communist Party. In Puerto Rico, while Socialists and anarchists coexisted after 1898, the Socialist Party of the island was not created until 1915 and the Communist Party until 1934. In Panama, anarchists were in the isthmus from 1905 onward. No Marxist party existed until the late 1920s, even though Marxists and anarchists worked together in the Communist Group in the early 1920s – a group that idolized the Industrial Workers of the World, that is, anarcho-syndicalism. Thus, anarchists were the first to attack the spread of global capitalism and the growing imperial presence of the United States in the Caribbean. Second, in an era of new "independent" entities like Cuba, Puerto Rico, and Panama, anarchists were the rare activists in the region to oppose nationalism and nationalist movements as they advocated non-nationalist, non-Marxist alternative futures for the Caribbean. A third compelling reason for the importance of anarchists in the Caribbean is what anarchists created: a substantial, regionwide transnational network to coordinate communications and organizations, bring down US-backed capitalist politics, and illustrate their internationalist as opposed to nationalist agendas. They were enough of a threat that intelligence agencies launched their own coordinated transnational surveillance system and repression measures, seeing anarchists and their feared networks as legitimate targets of a regional anti-Red campaign that began decades before what we know as the post-1917 Red Scare in the United States.

Anarchists, of course, were not the only entities to operate transnationally in the Caribbean. Numerous forces also crossed geopolitical borders in the region. Freemasons established lodges as early as the 1700s throughout the islands, and masonic lodges communicated with one another over the centuries. By the late 1800s, political figures seeking independence from Spain emerged in Puerto Rico and Cuba, but with supporters from elsewhere in the Caribbean Basin. In fact, Caribbean governments and leaders regularly aided various independence causes in Cuba and Puerto Rico in the nineteenth century.[2] As modern capitalism spread throughout the Caribbean, people traveled in its wake to work in factories, fields, and construction projects. In the first decades of the twentieth century, Antillean migration spread to Venezuela, Panama, Cuba, and more. As Antillean women and men moved across national and colonial borders, they established local but transnationally linked communities and organizations that created what Lara Putnam calls a "racial brotherhood."[3] As she writes, "the extensive circulation of people combined with an extensive circulation of media, making it possible for individual experiences in the far-flung locales to add up to cohesive intellectual and cultural movements."[4] One well-known example concerns Marcus Garvey, who organized the first Universal Negro Improvement Association (UNIA) chapter in Jamaica in 1914. Over the next decade, Garvey relocated its headquarters to New York City, while chapters flourished throughout the Caribbean, with branches in Cuba, Jamaica, Costa Rica, and Panama. As Jossiana Arroyo puts it in her study of Caribbean freemasonry, such transnational actors created "cross-national dialogues and connections" in their work "for similar ends."[5]

US-headquartered agribusiness firms also became transnational entities throughout the region after 1898. The American Tobacco Corporation

---

[2] For a splendid transnational discussion of this, see Dalia Antonia Muller, *Cuban Émigrés & Independence in the Nineteenth-Century Gulf World* (Chapel Hill: University of North Carolina Press, 2017).

[3] Lara Putnam, "Nothing Matters but Color: Transnational Circuits, the Interwar Caribbean, and the Black International," in *From Toussaint to Tupac: The Black International since the Age of Revolution*, eds. Michael O. West, William G. Martin, and Fanon Che Wilkins (Chapel Hill: University of North Carolina Press, 2009), 108–109.

[4] Lara Putnam, *Radical Moves: Caribbean Migrants and the Politics of Race in the Age of Jazz* (Chapel Hill: University of North Carolina Press, 2013), 5.

[5] Jossiana Arroyo, *Writing Secrecy in Caribbean Freemasonry* (New York: Palgrave Macmillan, 2013), 70–71; P.C. Emmer, Bridget Brereton, B.W. Higman, eds., *General History of the Caribbean: Caribbean in the Twentieth Century* (London: UNESCO Publishing, 2004), 238.

dominated tobacco growing and cigar making in Cuba, Florida, and Puerto Rico. The United Fruit Company so dominated tropical-fruit-for-export production that one automatically associates this massive transnational corporation with the image of a banana republic in the Caribbean. Milton Hershey had his own sugar plantation and town in Cuba to fuel a growing cheap chocolate craze in the United States. The spread of transnational agribusiness coincided with the spread of other US economic enterprises in the region. US-based tram, railroad, and electric companies poured in to develop modern infrastructure. At the same time, the United States built (with public funds, privately produced materials like steel and concrete, and a multinational workforce) the Panama Canal for transoceanic military and economic transport.

The expansion of regular commercial and passenger shipping across the Caribbean, between the Caribbean and the US eastern seaboard, across the Atlantic, and after 1914 along the Pacific coast of Latin America via the Panama Canal helped make all this possible. Within the Caribbean, dozens of ships plied the waters connecting any number of ports. In 1888, the US-based *Olivette* and *Mascotte* both began carrying passengers and freight between Tampa, Key West, and Havana, and did so until at least 1918 when the *Olivette* sank in the waters between Key West and Havana. Not only were the ships crucial in the growing movement of tobacco workers between Cuba and Florida, but also in 1898 Washington requisitioned the ships to transport US troops to Cuba. By 1911, these two ships played another key role in the advancing age of globalization: Both housed wireless telegraph stations.

Numerous companies over the decades established regular sailing services to ports throughout the Caribbean. In 1911, the Ward Line's *Monterey*, *Mexico*, *Esperanza*, and *Morro Castle* ships ran regular services linking New York, Havana, and the Mexican ports of Progreso and Veracruz. Its ships the *Saratoga* and *Havana* ran regular services between New York and Havana. By 1916, the Clyde Steamship Company's Mallory Line linked New York with Key West and Tampa, while its Porto Rico Line had three ships plying the waters between New York and San Juan, with stops in Ponce and Mayagüez. Known mainly for its agribusiness exploits in the region, the United Fruit Company's Great White Fleet carried people as well as bananas. By 1916, it had four ships carrying passengers between New York, Havana, Cristóbal, Bocas del Toro, and Puerto Limón.

According to the *International Shipping Digest* in August 1919, fifty companies sailed ships to the Caribbean and Central America from US ports alone.[6] In the early 1920s, the New York and Cuba Mail Company had taken over many of the Ward Line's ships and routes from a decade earlier while adding routes linking New York, Nassau, Havana, and the Mexican ports of Progreso, Veracruz, and Tampico. Not only US-based ships sailed these waters of course. For instance, in 1912, the German-owned Hamburg–America Line controlled different shipping companies, including the Compañia Sud Americana de Vapores, the Pacific Steam Navigation Company, the Compañia Peruana de Vapores, and the Pacific Mail Steamship Company. All serviced passenger routes between Peru and Panama during construction of the Panama Canal. By the early 1920s, the UK-based Pacific Line to South America sailed two passenger ships from New York to Havana, through the Panama Canal, and south along the Pacific coast with stops in Callao, Peru and Valparaiso, Chile.[7] Shipping lines were so important that daily newspapers in the region published full-page daily schedules.[8]

Anarchists joined in these cross-border movements. The emergence and development of Caribbean anarchism in this transnational setting was linked to four historical developments. First, Benedict Anderson noted, "anarchists were [quick] to capitalize on the vast transoceanic migrations of the era."[9] Radicals from Europe as well as European workers who would become radicals in the Americas sailed to join home-grown anarchists born in the Caribbean and Latin America. Spanish, Cuban, and Puerto Rican anarchists arrived in Florida when cigar factory owners moved production there from a turbulent Cuba. In Puerto Rico, some global anarchists joined Puerto Rico-born anarchists, and these Boricua anarchists joined others when they migrated to Cuba, Florida, and New York. In Cuba, ever-new waves of Spanish-born anarchists joined Cubans and together the two transferred ideas, money, news-papers, and even themselves throughout the region. One of their landing spots was Panama, where anarchists from Spain, Cuba, Argentina, Colombia, and Peru arrived to build the canal or work in either the zone or the cities of the republic.

Anarchists and their adversaries made use of the ships in more ways than just transportation. For instance, anarchists took advantage of

---

[6] *International Shipping Digest*, August 1919, 26 and 41.
[7] For examples of shipping timetables worldwide from the 1800s to the 1950s, see "Maritime Timetable Images": www.timetableimages.com/maritime.
[8] For example, see the *Star and Herald* of Panama City.
[9] Benedict Anderson, *Under Three Flags: Anarchism and the Colonial Imagination* (New York: Verso, 2005), 2.

rather captive audiences to spread the word and raise funds. This was the case in April 1914, when Vicente Allegue sailed from Florida to Havana. While on board the *Mascotte*, he raised money from sixteen men willing to have their names published in Cuba's leading anarchist weekly newspaper *¡Tierra!*.[10] Governments also employed ships to deport radicals. Manuel María Miranda, an anarchist born in Cuba, was arrested in 1896 during the Cuban War for Independence and put on a ship to Puerto Rico with other persons that the Spanish colonial government in Cuba found dangerous. He then sailed on the *Ciudad de Cádiz* to Spain, spending fourteen days crossing the choppy, rough December Atlantic Ocean. Then, Miranda, 90 Cubans, and 200 Filipinos were crowded onto the steamship *Larache* for the three-day voyage from Cádiz to the Canary Islands and another long trip on the *Larache* ultimately to the political prisoner island of Fernando Póo off the current Equatorial Guinean coast.[11] Authorities likewise deported people like Nicolás Gutarra. In 1924, after he led a rent strike in Colombia, the government loaded him on a ship and sent him to Panama, where he spoke with anarchists just beginning to organize renters for an upcoming strike. Thus, governments – usually acting in what they deemed their national interests – sometimes facilitated the anarchist networks through deportations on these ships to other countries where they could interact with a new anarchist cohort or become inspired to rewrite, rethink, and expand on their ideas of social revolution.[12]

A second factor in the rise of Caribbean anarchism can be found in Spanish migration, which fundamentally shaped anarchism in the region. Between 1902 and 1915, 369,466 Spaniards legally immigrated to Cuba. Over three-quarters were day laborers, peasants, farm laborers, or had no stated occupation – the very populations from which anarchists emerged and which anarchists targeted with their propaganda.[13] Some of these migrants were either committed anarchists or had been exposed to a long

---

[10] *¡Tierra!*, April 23, 1914, 4.
[11] Manuel M. Miranda, *Memorias de un deportado* (Havana: Imprenta la Luz, 1903), 13–25.
[12] The historian Kenyon Zimmer makes similar points in his research on Red Scare-era deportations.
[13] Kirwin R. Shaffer, *Anarchism and Countercultural Politics in Early Twentieth-Century Cuba* (Gainesville: University Press of Florida, 2005), 73; Dominga González, "La inmigración española en Cuba," *Economía y Desarrollo* 1 (1988): 105; Consuelo Naranjo Orovio, "Trabajo libre e inmigración española en Cuba, 1880–1930," *Revista de Indias* 52, no. 195/196 (1992): 790.

tradition of anarchist activity in Spain. Not all stayed in Cuba; many boarded ships and migrated throughout the Caribbean in search of work and activism. The earliest destination for Spaniards and Cubans was the tobacco factories of Florida. In 1890, 233 Spaniards and 1313 Cubans were officially registered as working in Tampa alone. By 1900, nearly 1000 Spaniards joined 3533 Cubans in Tampa's workforce. By 1910, some 2337 Spaniards and 3859 Cubans worked in the city.[14] Meanwhile, similarly large numbers of Spaniards migrated to the Panama Canal Zone. Between 1904 and 1912, only eighty-seven Cubans and forty-one Puerto Ricans officially migrated to the zone, but 4012 Spaniards traveled there mainly as construction workers – and none of this includes those who just went on their own without an official contract.[15] Thus, Spanish anarchists sometimes dominated embryonic anarchist movements, as in Panama, and other times supplemented Caribbean-born anarchists, as in Cuba and Florida.

The development of a strong anarchist presence in Havana served as a third factor in the rise of Caribbean anarchism. A network was only as good as its nodal cities – especially the node that functioned as its revolutionary hub city. As Barry Carr puts it, "the exiles and revolutionary diasporas in these hub cities were one link in an expanding transnational network of radical activists and insurgent intellectuals who practiced a form of contentious politics in which they journeyed across national boundaries, driven by state repression, ideological fervour, and the desire for revolutionary adventure."[16] In the Caribbean, Havana was

---

[14] G. R. Mormino and G. E. Pozzetta, "Spanish Anarchism in Tampa, Florida, 1886–1931," in *"Struggle a Hard Battle": Essays on Working-Class Immigrants*, ed. Dirk Hoerder (Dekalb: Northern Illinois University Press, 1986), 177.

[15] Julie Greene, *The Canal Builders: Making America's Empire at the Panama Canal* (New York: Penguin Press, 2009), 396–399.

[16] Key works for thinking about nodal cities in radical networks include: Ilham Khuri-Makdisi, *The Eastern Mediterranean and the Making of Global Radicalism, 1860–1914* (Berkeley: University of California Press, 2010); Kenyon Zimmer, "A Golden Gate of Anarchy: Local and Transnational Dimensions of Anarchism in San Francisco, 1880s–1930s," in *Reassessing the Transnational Turn: Scales of Analysis in Anarchist and Syndicalist Studies*, eds. Constance Bantman and Bert Altena (Oakland: PM Press, 2017), 100–117; and David Struthers, *The World in a City: Multiethnic Radicalism in Early Twentieth-Century Los Angeles* (Urbana: University of Illinois Press, 2019). For the Caribbean Basin, see Barry Carr, "Pioneering Transnational Solidarity in the Americas: The Movement in Support of Augusto C. Sandino 1927–1934," *JILAR* 20, no. 2 (2014): 141–152; Kirwin Shaffer, "Havana Hub: Cuban Anarchism, Radical Media, and the Trans-Caribbean Anarchist Network, 1902–1915," *Caribbean Studies* 37, no. 2 (2009): 45–81, and "Latin Lines and Dots: Transnational Anarchism, Regional Networks, and

the primary hub for migrants and exiles who founded radical organizations, published the majority of the newspapers, and coordinated much of the networking. Havana was also where most of the region's anarchist schools were created. In addition, Havana's anarchists led health campaigns by launching their own healthcare facilities and vegetarian restaurants.[17] Thus, Havana was the political and cultural hub of regional anarchism. But it should also be noted that in years when Cuban anarchism was under greater assault than normal, the press could not publish, and schools did not function, then often it was New York City or Tampa or even Bayamón, Puerto Rico that became a hub where Caribbean anarchists went to work, agitate, and continue the network's operation. Even Colón, Panama became the leading global site for the International Individualist Federation (FII) in 1911.

Finally, the spread of US economic, military, and political influence throughout the Caribbean Basin in the early twentieth century facilitated the spread of Caribbean anarchism. Whereas most of Spanish America had thrown off colonial rule by the 1820s, in the early twentieth century Cuba, Puerto Rico, and Panama were just becoming free from political control by other countries: Cuba and Puerto Rico from Spain (1898) and Panama from Colombia (1903). However, these societies proved to be anything but independent, as the United States either controlled or strongly shaped all three. Between 1898 and 1902, the US military occupied Cuba until the military government handed political authority to Cubans in May 1902 after the Cubans agreed to insert the Platt Amendment into the Cuban Constitution. Besides authorizing creation of a US naval base (Guantánamo Bay), the amendment allowed the United States to militarily intervene should Washington deem Cuba to be unstable and thus a threat to US interests. Meanwhile, Puerto Rico became a noncolony "colony" of the United States after the US Supreme Court upheld the island's unique status in 1901 by declaring that Puerto Rico belonged to the United States but was not part of the United States. In 1917, Puerto Ricans gained US citizenship, allowing them unfettered mobility between the island and the US mainland, especially New York City, but the island remained in political limbo in relation to its status with Washington. In 1903, the United States encouraged and orchestrated the independence of Panama from Colombia with the intention of building a transisthmian

---

Italian Libertarians in Latin America," *Zapruder World: An International Journal for the History of Social Conflict* 1 (2014), www.zapruderworld.org/?s=latin+lines+and+dots.

[17] See Shaffer, *Anarchism and Countercultural Politics*.

canal. Following independence, the United States gained control of the ten-mile-wide Canal Zone from the Caribbean to the Pacific that ran through the middle of Panama. Similar language as that in the Platt Amendment was inserted into the 1903 treaty with Panama that created the Canal Zone. The Panamanian Constitution also allowed US military intervention into the republic should instability arise. These political developments resulted in the expansion of various North American sectors into the Caribbean Basin after 1898. US companies spread North American capitalism, political and military advisers advocated the institutions of republicanism, North American churches arrived, and the non-revolutionary American Federation of Labor (AFL) developed affiliated unions.

As anarchists spread on the backs of US expansion, they also attacked that expansion. Global anarchists did not lack an anti-imperialist message. As Lucien van der Walt and Steven Hirsch clearly illustrate, the heyday of global anarchism occurred as Europe was carving up large swaths of the globe. Anarchist movements both in the colonies and in the metropoles placed anticolonialism central to their agendas.[18] But in turn-of-the-century Latin America – a region largely freed from Spanish colonial rule since the early 1800s – such direct imperial control only existed in the Caribbean Basin – first by Spain and then by the United States.

Thus, Caribbean anarchists faced a unique situation compared to anarchists in other parts of Latin America: having to operate within the realm of US oversight. As a result, anarchists joined their antipolitics, anticapitalist agendas with an anti-imperialist challenge to the United States. They confronted US-based industrial capital in places like the Cuban and Puerto Rican sugar and tobacco export sectors. In Panama, the massive canal project brought anarchists into direct conflict with US canal operators. Besides these struggles against capital, they also confronted the antianarchist AFL, which anarchists believed favored white US workers and business interests. Anarchists also attacked the emergence of US-style representative democracy, which they saw as deceptive: The masses supposedly had a voice, but the elite ran these places for their own interests and the interests of the US political and economic overlords. Finally, they criticized Caribbean governments' collusion with the United States, decried US military interventions and militarism in general, and challenged US concepts of Pan-Americanism.

---

[18] Lucien van der Walt and Steven Hirsch, "Rethinking Anarchism and Syndicalism," in *Anarchism and Syndicalism in the Colonial and Postcolonial World*, eds. Steven Hirsch and Lucien van der Walt (Leiden: Brill, 2010), lv–lxii.

By the 1920s, anti-imperialist movements across the political left emerged to challenge the spread of US influence in the Caribbean. Certainly, anti-imperialist forces had no shortage of targets ranging from US control in Cuba and Panama, US ownership of Puerto Rico, US occupations of Haiti and the Dominican Republic, and US military interventions in many of these countries, as well as Mexico and Nicaragua. Following the 1917 Bolshevik victory in Russia, the Communist International (aka, the Comintern) began to link emerging Communist parties and organizations throughout the Caribbean and Central America to challenge US expansion.[19] Transnational solidarity in Latin America and the Caribbean was especially rich after 1927 as anti-imperialist organizations emerged to support Augusto César Sandino's struggle against US Marines in Nicaragua.[20] But such anti-imperialist movements were not just Soviet-fueled. Anarchists established some of the first transnational anti-imperialist solidarity networks in the Caribbean years before any orders to do so arrived from Moscow.

HOW ANARCHIST NETWORKS FUNCTIONED IN THE CARIBBEAN BASIN

Several years ago, many historians began to think that the nation-state framework for the study of anarchism was misplaced. After all, anarchists did not consider themselves as citizens of nation-states, so why should historians limit their focus on them as such? So, I began to write a history of Caribbean anarchism that privileged networks over nations. But, in turn, tracing networks without local and national contexts became a rather unsatisfying practice. Too often transnationalism seemed to privilege the connections between locations over the vital importance of the local and national. To this point, Davide Turcato reminds us that "[a]bandoning a national framework of analysis does not necessarily mean abandoning a national perspective but rather a territorial scope of analysis. Anarchists fought against states, not against nations."[21]

---

[19] Ricardo Melgar Bao, "Cominternismo intellectual: Representaciones, redes y practicas político culturales en América Central, 1921–1933" *Revista Complutense de Historia de América*, 35 (2009): 140–147.
[20] Carr, "Pioneering Transnational Solidarity," 143–144.
[21] Davide Turcato, "Nations without Borders: Anarchists and National Identity," in *Reassessing the Transnational Turn: Scales of Analysis in Anarchist and Syndicalist Studies*, eds. Constance Bantman and Bert Altena (Oakland: PM Press, 2017), 41.

Thus, one needs to study these networks both in specific places and between those places. That means developing "the local" and "the national" while simultaneously tracing the establishment and maintenance of linkages. In short, anarchists did not live and work daily on the linkages that connected one city or country to another. If we think of networks as "dots" connected by "lines," people lived, worked, and agitated on the dots.[22] Anarchists had to live daily under the economic realities of local and international capitalist investment, the laws of local and national governments, and the challenges arising from a diverse array of actors: local bishops and police, national intelligence officers, mainstream editorial writers, nationalist trade union leaders, and Socialist Party bosses in the local union halls.

Nodal cities like Havana, Panama City, and Tampa were key for these regional linkages. Cities had long been important in anarchist organizing. In port cities especially we can trace the movement of sailors, workers, intellectuals, refugees, and more as they traveled between ports and then sometimes went inland. What we are looking at is a regional network linked together mostly by port cities. But these cities were also points that linked anarchists in towns and cities throughout a country and then linked countries transnationally. Havana was the nodal port city that linked Regla, Cruces, Santiago, and more in Cuba. San Juan linked to Bayamón and Caguas in Puerto Rico. Panama City linked towns throughout the Republic of Panama and the Canal Zone. Thus, the port cities served as the contact points for the regional network, coordinated groups in their respective countries, and then linked each other. In this way, one can think of Bayamón, Puerto Rico linked to Cruces, Cuba and Gatún, Panama Canal Zone via the nodal port cities of San Juan, Havana, and Panama City, respectively.

Each locality was influenced by other localities, whether it was the men and women who traversed between places, the money they transferred from one city to another to buy newspapers or finance local and international causes, or the communiqués and letters published from abroad in various newspapers that inspired, challenged, or helped to raise the international consciousness of readers. Transnational transfers influenced local and national events and conditions. Networks could also provide havens for anarchists needing to escape a local situation, whether due to police harassment or, as sometimes happened, to personality or

---

[22] See Shaffer, "Latin Lines and Dots."

ideological conflicts between anarchists in a city. Thus, in my mind one must spend equal time on the nodes as well as the linkages between them. Not forsake one for the other, not drop our focus on the national for the transnational, but instead develop them as thickly and simultaneously as possible.

In addition, anarchists operated in several realms of activism simultaneously – the individual, the local, the national, the transnational, the regional, the transregional, and even the hemispheric. In their collection of essays on "reassessing the transnational turn" in anarchist histories, Bantman and Altena stressed the importance of using multiple scales of analysis to do transnational research – scales that range from the individual biography to local, national, and regional levels. "Different scales of analysis often need to be applied simultaneously and can also change over time," they write. "[T]hey should be regarded as fluid and continuous rather than as discrete levels of analysis."[23] In a study of anarchism in Central America, José Julián Llaguno Thomas emphasizes that multiple scales of analysis are key to "understand[ing] the rise of movements more completely" as anarchists functioned in one locale but interacted regionally and globally.[24]

Thus, we should explore the interplay between individual anarchist biographies, the larger regional and hemispheric dimensions, and every level in between that ties all this together. This book, therefore, is a regional study linking activists across borders, mainly through movement between port cities, and incorporates multiple scales of analysis from individual memoirs to hemispheric organizations. And because this is a study of multiple nodes, this also becomes a comparative study of how anarchists in different cities in the network interacted with their local realities, the presence of US entities, competing unions, the Mexican Revolution, the Great War, the Bolsheviks, the rise of Communist Parties, and the emergence of tropical fascists.

So, how did these anarchist networks function? Let me outline four features: the work and impact of traveling "celebrity" anarchists; the multiple roles of "rank-and-file" migrants; the impact on and of anarchist novels, plays, poetry, and short stories; and, the role of the anarchist press.

---

[23] Bantman and Altena, "Introduction: Problematizing Scales of Analysis," 12–13.
[24] José Julián Llaguno Thomas, "Acción Local y Auditorio Global: La Presencia Anarquista en América Central Según sus Fondos Documentales entre 1910 y 1930," *Diálogos* 17, no. 2 (2016): 38–39.

ANARCHIST MIGRANTS IN THE CARIBBEAN BASIN

Caribbean-born anarchists built and developed anarchist groups in Puerto Rico and Cuba. In fact, anarchism in Puerto Rico was almost entirely homegrown, but its adherents regularly migrated between Puerto Rico, Cuba, and the United States. At the same time, in Florida and Cuba anarchist migrants arriving from Italy, Spain, or other American countries complemented native-born anarchists. Amparo Sánchez Cobos has shown the Cuban movement's heavy (though by no means exclusive) dependence on fresh waves of anarchists from Spain.[25] In Panama, migrant anarchists were central to the origins and development of local anarchism. There appears to have been no anarchist presence in the Panamanian isthmus before the United States began to build the Panama Canal in 1904. Only then did anarchists migrate to the Canal Zone and launch the isthmus's first anarchist groups. Thus, depending on the specific network node, migration played either almost no role, a complementary role, or the central role in developing anarchism.

At times, migrating anarchists moved with the intention of starting new organizations. Sometimes, like itinerant preachers, they traveled to spread the word of a new day before moving on to their next stop. Often they moved for work opportunities, then used their free time to organize groups and communicate with the network. Sometimes they were forced to move due to deportation; other times out of fear for their lives. But those who fled usually went to cities where they found fellow anarchists, enabling them to share in solidarity and information. As Raymond Craib puts it, anarchists created urban "transnational communities" comprised of anarchists who were locally born, had moved from the countryside or other communities in the nation-state, or migrated from abroad, and in these communities they "forged translocal linkages and connections with counterparts" from around the world.[26] David Struthers makes a similar point about Industrial Workers of the World (IWW) activists in the United States–Mexico borderlands. There was both interaction across borders and "local internationalism" of multiethnic, multilingual radicals

---

[25] See Amparo Sánchez Cobos, *Sembrando ideales: Anarquistas españoles en Cuba (1902–1925)* (Madrid: Consejo Superior de Investigaciones Científicas, 2008).

[26] Raymond Craib, "Sedentary Anarchists," in *Reassessing the Transnational Turn: Scales of Analysis in Anarchist and Syndicalist Studies*, eds. Constance Bantman and Bert Altena (Oakland: PM Press, 2017), 141; and *The Cry of the Renegade: Politics and Poetry in Interwar Chile* (New York: Oxford University Press, 2016), 12.

working together in one locale.[27] These "proletarian globetrotters," as Barry Carr has called people like them, were the flesh and bones of Caribbean anarchism.[28]

TRAVELING "CELEBRITY" ANARCHISTS

Prominent men and women traveled across extensive networks promoting the anarchist ideal, and in doing so were often afforded celebrity status by locally based anarchists wherever they ventured. The first of these celebrity visits occurred in early 1900 when Errico Malatesta visited Cuba at the invitation of his old comrade Adrián del Valle, whom he had met in exile in London in the early 1890s – Malatesta from Italy, Del Valle from Spain. As seen in Chapter 2, Malatesta's visit scared US and Cuban authorities, who tried to prohibit him from speaking. His international celebrity status drew large audiences and raised money for the newspaper *El Nuevo Ideal*, which could then continue to spread not only among readers in Cuba but also to the important anarchist enclave of southern Florida. Malatesta's visit helped to solidify the anarchist presence in Cuba and beyond.[29]

Thus, when someone like Pedro Esteve traveled from New York to Tampa to give talks and to help organize an IWW branch in the city or Malatesta ventured to Havana or fellow travelers like the freethinker Belén de Sárraga toured the Americas in the 1910s giving talks attacking the Catholic Church, these visits were covered and editorialized in the local anarchist press in the same way that mainstream newspapers would cover a visiting foreign dignitary.[30] Because anarchist press coverage of these visits was exported across the networks, readers in the far-flung

---

[27] David Struthers, "IWW International and Interracial Organizing in the Southwestern United States," in *Wobblies of the World: A Global History of the IWW*, eds. Peter Cole, David Struthers, and Kenyon Zimmer (London: Pluto Press, 2017), 74.
[28] Barry Carr, "'Across Seas and Borders': Charting the Webs of Radical Internationalism in the Circum-Caribbean," in *Exile & the Politics of Exclusion in the Americas*, eds. Luis Roniger, James N. Green, and Pablo Yankelevich (Brighton: Sussex Academic Press, 2014), 218.
[29] Kirwin Shaffer, "An Anarchist Crucible: International Anarchist Migrants and Their Cuban Experiences, 1890s–1920s," in *Handbook on Cuban History, Literature, and the Arts*, eds. Mauricio Font and Araceli Tinajero (Boulder: Paradigm Press, 2014), 81–84.
[30] For discussions of Belén de Sárraga's tour in the Caribbean, see her book *El clericalismo en América a través de un continente* (Lisbon: José Assis & A. Coelho Dias, 1915); and Kirwin Shaffer, *Black Flag Boricuas: Anarchism, Antiauthoritarianism, and the Left in Puerto Rico, 1897–1921* (Urbana: University of Illinois Press, 2013), 99–104.

reaches of the Americas could read about the visits. When they toured the networks, the visits generated enthusiasm and funds for anarchist projects, reinvigorated anarchist mobilization wherever they went, and reinforced in local anarchists' minds that what they were doing was important.

RANK-AND-FILE MIGRANT ANARCHISTS

Unlike the handful of celebrity anarchists who stayed for short periods of time, rank-and-file migrant anarchists were central to long-term nodal and network organization. These were the anarchist men and women who streamed back and forth across the Atlantic, the Caribbean, and the Florida Straits. They played numerous roles as foreign correspondents, fundraisers for political causes, subscribers to and distributors of international newspapers, and cultural brokers who helped native-born and immigrant anarchists work in common cause while making international anarchism relevant to local populations.

As "foreign" correspondents, anarchists traveled the networks and wrote letters back to other network sites. These letters described local conditions and political realities for readers based elsewhere. Once published in newspapers in Cuba, these newspapers were then sent across the networks. For instance, writers in Panama would analyze their local Panamanian contexts, publish these abroad, receive these published accounts a couple of weeks later, and then sell or give away those very copies of the newspaper with their analyses.

When rank-and-file men and women migrated, they often wrote or spoke about their experiences in two or more countries, educating people in their new resident cities about life and politics abroad. For instance, when the anarchist educator Julio Barcos left Argentina in 1919, he traveled to Puerto Rico, the United States, and throughout Central America. In Panama, he joined forces with a friend from Puerto Rico and José María Blázquez de Pedro in literary and educational endeavors. He helped Panamanian education reformers to navigate educational issues based on controversies that he had encountered in Argentina.[31] Sometimes Caribbean migrants ventured beyond the extended Caribbean. Around 1905, for instance, the Cuba-based anarchist Miguel Albuquerque "became quite prominent in Ecuador," where he had gone

---

[31] On this pan-leftist interaction and the writings of the Argentine anarchist Julio Barcos, see the Panama City, Panama magazine *Cuasimodo* that he helped to run from 1919 to 1920.

years earlier "seeking assistance for the independence war in his country but stayed as he became involved in Ecuadorean social and political struggles."[32] It also was possible for rank-and-file anarchists to become celebrity anarchists – people like Marcelo Salinas, who grew up in the new Cuban republic, was a rank-and-file operator in Havana and Tampa during the 1910s and rose to celebrity status by the 1930s thanks to his prize-winning play and novel.

We also should not discount the importance of linguistic connections and their central roles in these networks of rank-and-file anarchist migrants. The vastness of the Caribbean Basin geographically was made somewhat smaller by the fact that the majority of anarchists spoke Spanish – something that also facilitated the constant renewals of local movements when anarchists arrived from Spain. As Bantman and Altena note, "language was usually the most determinant criterion for international sociability while abroad."[33] Spanish was the *lingua franca* of this network and the overlapping networks that linked the Caribbean with anarchists in the United States, Latin America, and Spain. Yet, anarchists in the nodes often spoke more than Spanish. In Florida and Panama, one found Italian speakers. As a result, the press in Florida published articles in Italian while strike speeches in Panama could be in Italian as well. English-language columns and speeches were also important in reaching out to potential Anglo and African American workers in Florida or to the large British West Indian community in the Canal Zone and Panama. In addition, Spanish-speaking anarchists worked in US-based labor groups, which in places like Philadelphia had large Antillean workforces. While such multilingual efforts existed, it was nevertheless Spanish-speaking anarchists who linked the network.

ANARCHIST COUNTERCULTURE AND TRANSNATIONAL ANARCHISM

As Jesse Cohn writes, fiction illustrates how "anarchist politics have historically found aesthetic expression in the form of a 'culture of resistance.'" This resistance culture "had to somehow *prefigure* a world of freedom and equality" that also "meant nothing less than *cultivation* of

---

[32] Ángel Cappelletti, *El anarquismo en América Latina* (Caracas: Biblioteca Ayacucho, 1990), CXLV.
[33] Bantman and Altena, "Introduction: Problematizing Scales of Analysis," 15.

resistant bodies and souls."[34] This anarchist resistance culture – or counterculture – challenged the hegemony of the state–capital–religion unholy trinity. It also educated and raised consciousness in followers and potential fellow travelers, notes Sergio Grez Toso.[35] The US-based anarchist Jaime Vidal emphasized the importance of anarchist culture in a 1913 column in the bilingual (Spanish and Italian) anarchist newspaper *Risveglio* (Awakening) in Tampa. "If we intend to revolutionize the world and to create peace on earth; if we seek to organize the great masses of slaves with the end of emancipating them, we ought not to neglect cultural work because no movement nor individual or collective action will truly triumph if the minds of the fighters have not been cultivated and initiated with the principles of true social justice."[36] Anarchists targeted multiple audiences with their countercultural productions: women and children who attended performances, working-class and peasant men and women who read anarchist fictional scenarios, and workers in specific industries like tobacco. For instance, as Jorell Meléndez-Badillo notes, anarchists targeted "progressive elements in the Puerto Rican and Cuban artisan sector that fought against proletarianization." In cigar factories, *lectores* (readers) were agents of dissemination.[37]

From the late 1920s to early 1930s, the world's anarchists published 650 short Spanish-language novels written by authors based in Spain and Latin America. The La Novela Ideal and La Novela Libre series were published in Spain, then sold and distributed across the American networks. The first of each series was written by the Havana-based Adrián del Valle.[38] These stories – and the dozens of long and short works of fiction published by anarchists from the early 1900s onward – sometimes explored universal themes like capitalist greed, exploitation of women

---

[34] Jesse Cohn, *Underground Passages: Anarchist Resistance Culture, 1848–2011* (Oakland: AK Press, 2014), 4, 16–17, 58; italics in the original.

[35] Sergio Grez Toso, "Resistencia cultural anarquista: Poesía, canto y dramaturgia en Chile, 1895–1918," in *Cultura y política del anarquismo en España e Iberoamérica*, eds. Clara E. Lida and Pablo Yankelevich (Mexico City: El Colgio de México, 2012), 261.

[36] *Risveglio*, June 1913, 1.

[37] Jorell A. Meléndez-Badillo, "Interpreting, Deconstructing and Deciphering Ideograms of Rebellion: An Approach to the History of Reading in Puerto Rico's Anarchist Groups at the Beginning of the Twentieth Century, 1899–1919," in *Without Borders or Limits: An Interdisciplinary Approach to Anarchist Studies*, eds. Jorell A. Meléndez-Badillo and Nathun Jun (Cambridge: Cambridge Scholars Publishing, 2013), 63–67.

[38] See Adrián del Valle, *Mi amigo Julio* (Barcelona: La Revista Blanca, n.d.) for the La Nueva Ideal series and *Todo lo vence el amor* (Barcelona: La Revista Blanca, n.d.) for the La Novela Libre series.

and children, the noble work of prostitute heroines or revolutionary mothers, the hypocrisy of the Catholic Church, and the celebration of strikes and revolutionary uprisings. Such topics could be read and understood by followers wherever they were sold and distributed. Less frequent were works set in specific locations. For instance, Cuba-born anarchist Antonio Penichet published novels set in Cuba in the decades following Spanish rule, but the themes that emerge tackled universal anarchist themes of exploitation, corrupt politicians, repression of strikes, and antimilitarism – themes relevant to readers throughout the networks, regardless of their knowledge of Cuban history.[39]

Some anarchist literature not only inspired anarchists but also riled authorities. US entry into the Great War and the Bolshevik Revolution of 1917 brought forth massive US governmental efforts to suppress radicals and radical literature in the network. Anarchists, true to their strident antimilitarism, created anti-war fiction like Del Valle's *Jesús en la Guerra*. In Penichet's *El soldado Rafael*, Cubans emulated the Bolshevik Revolution when workers and soldiers joined forces for justice. Both the US and Cuban governments went to great transnational efforts to suppress its distribution.

Anarchists also created imagery and commentary through poetry. Newspapers regularly published poems by the region's anarchists. Blázquez de Pedro's poems from Panama appeared in Cuban papers and his poetry collections were sold in Havana. Tampa-based Cuban anarchist Marcelo Salinas's poetry on the Mexican Revolution could be found in Cuban papers as well. Anarchists throughout the network read these poems and others. In addition, some poems were recited by activists – or often their children – during weekly meetings or at labor and political rallies.

While reading literature was mainly an individual activity – except in cigar factories, where *lectores* read aloud to the workers – theater was public and community-oriented. Radical theater was popular throughout the anarchist world, especially during weekly social gatherings. Anarchists staged plays written by anarchists as well as liberals, republicans, and freethinkers. Adrián del Valle wrote his 1898 play "Fin de fiesta" in New York. The play centers on a young woman who defies her father's arranged marriage plans for her. She falls in love with a labor leader who leads a strike against her father's factory. When the workers storm the family residence to demand concessions, the father/factory owner

---

[39] Antonio Penichet, ¡*Alma Rebelde!, novela histórica* (Havana: El Ideal, 1921) and *La vida de un pernicioso* (Havana: Avisador Comercial, 1919).

points a gun at the strike leader/boyfriend. Our heroine dives in front of the bullet, dying from her father's hand while saving her labor-leader lover. The plot was simple and nonspecific enough to be performed anywhere. In fact, not only was it regularly staged in Cuba, but also San Francisco, Puerto Rico, and Chile – and not just by anarchists but sometimes labor progressives and Socialists.[40] One play written by a Caribbean anarchist was even successful with mainstream audiences. Marcelo Salinas received a Cuban national literary prize in 1928 for his play "Alma Guajira." It became a silent film in 1929.[41]

ANARCHO-JOURNALISM AND RADICAL NETWORKS

If migrating anarchists were the networks' flesh and bones, and literary works were the conscience to illustrate correct behavior and interpretations, the newspapers were the cerebral cortex – key to perception, consciousness, communication, and memory retention. Anarchists primarily used their newspapers to disseminate ideas and news with anarchist critiques for local and national readers. Some newspapers were equally transnational networking tools that anarchists used to frame the meaning of "Cuban" or "Puerto Rican" anarchism, whereby international anarchism was hybridized to fit local and national realities.[42] As such, they used the press to frame a Caribbean anarchist identity and to create a geopolitical imaginary of the Caribbean.

This was done not only by movement leaders and newspaper editors, but also everyday movement followers and readers of radical media. These men and women were not just consumers of the radical agenda, but also helped to create the agenda through their own columns and correspondence. They wrote the news about the news that they made. As Chris Atton concludes, radical media provide spaces for the voiceless to have a voice, where average people "might present accounts of their own experiences and struggles," "make their own news," or create "news themselves that is relevant to their situation" – a process of "native

---

[40] Palmiro de Lidia (Adrián del Valle), "Fin de fiesta, cuadro dramático" (New York: n.p., 1898). See discussions of non-Cuban performances in Shaffer, *Black Flag Boricuas*, 43–45, 50, 81; *Doctrina Anarquista Socialista*, March 30, 1905, 64; and, Grez Toso, "Resistencia cultural," 277.

[41] Alfonso J. García Osuna, *The Cuban Filmography: 1897 through 2001* (Jefferson: McFarland and Company, 2003), 21.

[42] For a discussion of anarchism, culture, and hybridization, see Shaffer, *Anarchism and Countercultural Politics*, 33–35.

reporting" and "witness activism."[43] As average people did basic organizing and writing, the "previously invisible base militants" became "visible as important historical actors," as Andrew Hoyt puts it.[44]

Radical media likewise unite disparate people and groups. As John Downing points out, social movements utilize their media to create global communication networks where people with like-minded ideas and goals unite across political frontiers. They form what he calls "cross-frontier migrant media" linking different locales into a regional network. By following a movement's financial information published in this media, we can use what Hoyt calls a "propaganda outward" approach where such financial information reveals the voiceless. We see these anonymous actors "enter the historical record" and communicate their "belonging" to an anarchist community that allowed them to stay in touch across vast distances.[45]

Between 1892 and 1929, Caribbean anarchists published over sixty newspapers and magazines that were entirely anarchist in orientation or contained significant amounts of anarchist influence either in articles, editing, or both. These papers were not only anarchist tools; they also serve as the single most important source for historians recreating these histories. Most newspapers were in Cuba. The others were evenly distributed between South Florida, the Panamanian isthmus, and Puerto Rico, with additional papers appearing in Colombia, Costa Rica, and New York. Much of the anarchist press in the Caribbean lasted only a few issues. These tended to be small, largely polemical papers that mainly reprinted anarchist tracts. While their long-term impact was undoubtedly limited, the fact that small groups of anarchists were able to cobble

---

[43] Chris Atton, "Green Anarchist: A Case Study of Collective Action in the Radical Media," *Anarchist Studies* 7 (2002): 493–497. For discussions on radical imaginaries, see Olaf Kaltmeier, "Inter-American Perspectives for the Re-thinking of Area Studies," *Forum for Inter-American Research* 7, no. 3 (2014): 171–182; and Eric Selbin, "Spaces and Places of (Im)possibility and Desire: Transversal Revolutionary Imaginaries in the Twentieth Century Americas," *Forum for Inter-American Research* 9, no. 1 (2016): 19–40.

[44] Andrew Hoyt, "Uncovering and Understanding Hidden Bonds: Applying Social Field Theory to the Financial Records of Anarchist Newspapers," in *Historical Geographies of Anarchism: Early Critical Geographers and Present-Day Scientific Challenges*, eds. Federico Ferretti, Gerónimo Barrera de la Torre, Anthony Ince, and Francisco Toro (London: Routledge, 2018), 29.

[45] John Downing, *Radical Media: Rebellious Communication and Social Movements* (Thousand Oaks: Sage, 2001), 83–94; Andrew Hoyt, "And They Called Them 'Galleanisti': The Rise of the *Cronaca Souversiva* and the Formation of America's Most Infamous Anarchist Faction (1895–1912)" (PhD dissertation, University of Minnesota, 2018), 24–25.

together limited resources to create these newspapers speaks to their efforts and dedication.

Some newspapers lasted longer but also tended to be more pan-sectarian than strictly anarchist. While anarchists played key roles in their development, the papers also published works by non-anarchist leftists that spoke to the anarchists' general belief in freedom of speech and hearing multiple voices. For instance, in Cuba, the freethinking journal *El Audaz* was published from 1912 to 1913 and linked anarchists with liberals and Socialists to promote the free thought cause. Similarly, in Panama from 1919 to 1920, the anarchist-edited *Cuasimodo: Magazine Interamericano* published non-anarchist left-wing authors.

Another type of newspaper was linked to a specific union. Here we can see how anarchists in Puerto Rico published radical critiques in newspapers that belonged to the AFL-associated Federación Libre de Trabajadores (Free Federation of Workers, or FLT). In Florida, anarchists often published columns in the AFL-affiliated *El Internacional*. In Panama, *El Obrero* in the early 1920s played this role. In Havana, anarcho-syndicalists who dominated the restaurant and café workers union published the long-running weekly newspapers *La Voz del Dependiente* and *El Dependiente*. All these newspapers – the short-lived ideological ones, the pan-sectarian ones, and those dominated by a union – tended to focus on local and national issues.

Then, there was ¡*Tierra!*. In the Caribbean network, ¡*Tierra!* was for over a decade (1902–1915) the key newspaper due to its regularity, longevity, and global reach. There were brief second and third iterations of the newspaper in the 1920s and 1930s. From its first issues, the newspaper's editors operated out of small offices in the heart of Havana's working-class district, publishing weekly editions except during the occasional political disturbance (such as the outbreak of the 1906 Civil War) when the paper missed a publication date or when it ran up so much debt that the printer refused to publish an edition. Correspondence to ¡*Tierra!* informed readers of events taking place throughout the Caribbean and beyond. Everyday people who were politically active wrote to the paper to describe their concerns and local issues. In so doing, these "native reporters" framed the larger movement to reflect local concerns while readers gained important national and international insights by reading these columns. In addition, anarchists from Cienfuegos, Cuba or Caguas, Puerto Rico or Gatún, Panama wrote about Cuban, Puerto Rican, and Panamanian issues respectively. Their articles were published in Havana one week and read by their comrades around Cuba, Puerto Rico,

Panama, or wherever else the newspaper was mailed or shipped in the suitcases of migrating anarchists. In this way, the paper generated both local and transnational knowledge, understanding, and consciousness, making ¡Tierra! not just a "Havana" newspaper but also a "Caribbean" newspaper. Just as cities or individuals could be network nodes, so could a newspaper – a sort of "pub as hub," if you will.

While ¡Tierra! played this transnational role, a few other papers did so as well – just for much shorter durations. The first of these were *El Productor* from Havana, *El Despertar* and *El Rebelde* from New York City, and *El Esclavo* from Tampa. All four were published in the 1890s, linked especially to the role of anarchists in the Cuban War for Independence. From 1911 to 1912, a rival anarcho-individualist network developed between the Canal Zone, Cuba, and Spain. The Canal Zone magazine *El Único* commented on global events, raised money for a printing press in Spain, and financed the newspaper *Vía Libre* in Havana to rival ¡Tierra!. By 1912, anarchists from Puerto Rico began to redirect their transnational communications toward the United States. As more Puerto Rican workers migrated to New York City, Puerto Rico-oriented articles began to appear in New York City's *Cultura Obrera*, while anarchists still on the island sent ever-larger amounts of money to purchase the paper. When ¡Tierra! folded in early 1915, *Cultura Obrera* became the international mouthpiece of the Puerto Rican anarchists.[46] Another newspaper played a key role in this history. A group of long-time anarchists like Emiliano Ramos in the cigar-rolling city of Bayamón published *El Comunista* in 1920 and 1921. The activists among the Bayamón bloc turned *El Comunista* into a propaganda organ distributed throughout the Caribbean and across the United States.[47]

Ultimately, anarcho-journalism provided a space for average people to have a voice. Just as importantly, it should be noted that not everyone could speak with their pen. Columns and letters sent from across the network often included money. Frequently, one person collected those financial contributions in the name of a local anarchist group, and the names of individual contributors were published. The published names allow us to trace movements of anarchists across the region. The names and money listed also provide insight into the numbers of people willing to forsake a bit of their already small wages to finance a newspaper with whose ideals they agreed. It is important to be cautious here, though.

---

[46] ¡Liberación!, October 19, 1912, 4; Shaffer, *Black Flag Boricuas*, 160–161.
[47] Shaffer, *Black Flag Boricuas*, 141–166.

Sometimes one contributor would use several different *noms de guerre*. For instance, M. D. Rodríguez in Panama could often be found on lists of Canal Zone-based anarchists, but other names he agitated under (Intransigente and Bernardo Pérez) could also appear on the list – making the number of activists seem a bit larger than it really was. Nevertheless, sometimes the money sent to a newspaper hundreds of miles away by average working people spoke just as loudly for them. They may have lived days away by steam ship, but they saw these "foreign" newspapers as their own.[48] It comes down to this: The anarchist press was central to creating a regional anarchist community – an anarchist identity that linked disparate individuals by political creed across the Caribbean regardless of their race, gender, or country of birth.[49]

COLONIALISM, NEOCOLONIALISM, POSTCOLONIALISM, AND CARIBBEAN ANARCHISM

It is impossible to explore anarchist politics in the Caribbean without putting it in the context of US foreign policy after 1898. The concept of an anarchist regional network was not unique in most of global anarchism. As mentioned earlier, what is unique is that, unlike anarchists elsewhere in Latin America, Caribbean anarchists (and their linked colleagues in Mexico and Central America) had to fight an encroaching imperial power. From the 1890s, Caribbean anarchists battled first Spanish and then US imperialism.

In a so-called postcolonial world, old colonial processes and mentalities linger even after the colonial power has been defeated. New political powers emerge that continue to emphasize a top-down, state-controlled society, an economy of capitalist "accumulation by dispossession" (as Maia Ramnath puts it), and the use of military and police services to reinforce the power of those in control.[50] Ramnath illustrates how, around the non-Western world, anarchists encountered such postcolonial societies that were further characterized by a formal independence that "fell almost immediately under the shadow of new forms of empire" where the new governments colluded; anarchists and syndicalists spread

---

[48] On how this worked in the Caribbean Basin, see Shaffer, "Havana Hub."
[49] For more on the press and community building, see Putnam, *Radical Moves*, 123–151; Hoyt, "And They Called Them," 30; and Kenyon Zimmer, *Immigrants against the State: Yiddish and Italian Anarchism in America* (Urbana: University of Illinois Press, 2015), 4.
[50] Maia Ramnath, *Decolonizing Anarchism: An Antiauthoritarian History of India's Liberation Struggle* (Oakland: AK Press, 2011), 28.

to these new postcolonial realms either via migration or along the great shipping routes then being established; and urban radicals found complementary comrades in rural agricultural and mining sectors, "which, given the ethnic make-up of the peasantry, drew strongly on indigenous traditions." As a result, anarchist anticolonial positions transitioned to cries for total decolonization not only of postcolonial mentalities and structures but also of neocolonial rule.[51]

Much of this occurred in the early twentieth century in Puerto Rico, Cuba, and Panama. Postcolonial traits could be found in all three: Economic, military, police, and political structures that benefited those in power were nominally different than those in existence during Spanish or Colombian rule, but they nevertheless served to benefit those in political and economic control. Such postcolonialism was then recentered to support US imperial expansion – an expansion facilitated by local colluders in the governments, the business communities, the police forces, and sometimes even the labor unions. Anarchists and syndicalists did in fact migrate around the Caribbean Basin, back and forth between locations, and along the US eastern seaboard. Shipping helped to spread such migrants, but the ships also became venues for radical seamen to spread anarchism.

However, we must interject a bit of nuance into Ramnath's outline. For instance, in Puerto Rico and especially Cuba, rural and urban radicals did forge alliances to tackle the unholy quaternity of state, capital, religion, and imperialism. However, the Florida and Panama anarchists were mostly urban, working in factories, ports, construction, and the like. In addition, there was no indigenous tradition in Florida, Cuba, Puerto Rico, or Panama upon which anarchists drew. Indigenous populations had been obliterated during Spanish rule, except in Panama where anarchists ignored indigenous groups and their plights. One should also note that Panama was not technically a colony of Colombia before its 1903 independence. This complicates things a bit; however, certainly the independence movement (no matter how Washington manipulated it for the United States's own ends in building a canal) saw itself as a victim of Bogota's despotism, thus justifying in their minds the push for territorial liberation. Further complicating Ramnath's point is the case of Puerto Rico, which never achieved independence following Spanish rule.

---

[51] Maia Ramnath, "Non-Western Anarchism and Postcolonialism," in *The Palgrave Handbook of Anarchism*, eds. Carl Levy and Matthew S. Adams (London: Palgrave Macmillan, 2019), 680 and 689.

Ultimately, I am not entirely comfortable talking about the region in "postcolonial" terms. Rather, after 1898 and 1903 respectively, Puerto Rico and the Panama Canal Zone were completely US territories – that is, colonies. Cuba and Panama were US protectorates in which the constitutions of each allowed Washington to intervene whenever it felt like it. In fact, the United States had military installations in Cuba and along the borders with Panama. In short, while there were postcolonial mentalities and structures, Cuba and Panama were in fact neocolonies – or maybe a protectorate is in fact a colony. "Neo" doesn't really mean much here except to signal degrees of political autonomy in both countries. As a result, anarchists throughout the region fought for total decolonization. They did not just attack the economic, political, military, and carceral structures of the new local and national rulers. They also attacked the imperial force that they served: the United States.

THE BOOK AHEAD

I have been asked over the years whether anarchists "intentionally" built this network. In short, the answer is "sort of." There was no Comintern-like organization that said, "if you build it, the authoritarians will fall." No marching orders went out from a central body. No one reported to higher-ups on the successes or failures of network development. Rather, the network grew organically from people moving for work, activism, refuge – or all three. Over the years, their daily activities and interactions forged and expanded the network. So, its origins were organic, but anarchists labored to grow and maintain the network that continued to offer opportunities for migrant anarchists to build anarchism in Washington's backyard.

As the reader contemplates the antiauthoritarian topography uncovered in the following pages, it is worth recalling just what geography is at play here and what we should consider "the Caribbean." The anarchist network focused on sites in Cuba, Puerto Rico, Florida, Panama, and the US-controlled Panama Canal Zone. But the reader will find other regional sites in these pages. Yucatán Mexico is here, as well as different cities in Colombia. The Central American countries of Guatemala, El Salvador, and Costa Rica make occasional appearances in these pages too, as do Colombia and Venezuela. Finally, while geographically speaking one might not think of New York City as part of the Caribbean – few university undergraduates are booking a flight to spend Spring Break on the beaches of Long Island – but culturally and politically, yes, New York City was (and still is) very much a Caribbean city where anarchists who agitated in Panama, Puerto Rico, Florida, and Cuba traveled to exile, for work, or as part of a grand circular migration that combined both. In fact, at times New York – just as much as Havana, Tampa, or Panama City – was where anarchists could meet fellow Caribbean radicals, as well as anarchists from around the world who organized in the city in numerous languages. Further, when the Havana hub was under severe repression as it was in the mid-1910s and again after 1925, the New York anarchists and their press became a way to link "otherwise geographically poorly interconnected fragments."[52]

So, our understanding of "the Caribbean" must extend beyond the islands, whose cities themselves are not necessarily on the Caribbean Sea. After all, as Barry Carr reminds us, Havana is not on the Caribbean Sea. Neither is Tampa nor Panama City nor San Juan. But all of these are connected as "the Caribbean" by historical dynamics – dynamics of migration, capitalist economic penetration, US military expansionism, and anarchists communicating with one another across what Carr calls the "Continental Caribbean."[53] Thus, this book is mainly about the three nodes of Panama, Puerto Rico, and Florida linked to the central hub of Havana. Yet, when anarchists in this extended Caribbean cartography communicated from Mexico, Guatemala, El Salvador, Costa Rica, Colombia, Venezuela, or especially New York, I show them as well.

One will notice, though, that the British and French West Indies mostly are absent from this study. This is because there seems to have been no history of anarchism in either. That said, West Indians did work with anarchists in Cuba, the Panamanian isthmus, and in places like the docks of Philadelphia. One will also notice the virtual absence of another important transnational entity during the late 1910s and 1920s: Marcus Garvey's Universal Negro Improvement Association. While the UNIA has been seen by supporter and foe alike as a "radical" organization, anarchists wanted nothing to do with it. To understand this, we have to see the UNIA through an anarchist lens: It promoted racial separatism (anarchists rejected this as a violation of anarchist universal humanism); it was a capitalist entity run like a corporation (anarchists hated capitalism); and it was a pro-Christian organization that wanted to promote the religion to the world's black peoples (in short, a Christian missionary society or – put

---

[52] Carr, "Across Seas and Borders," 228. Putnam makes a similar point about New York's Harlem being the northern point of the Caribbean. See *Radical Moves*, 128.

[53] Carr, "Across Seas and Borders," 222.

another way – a racialist, capitalist, Christian imperialist organization). You can see why anarchists kept their distance.

The following chapters take a broadly chronological approach to reading this historical map of anarchism. Where to begin? In his groundbreaking work *Under Three Flags* (republished as *The Age of Globalization* shortly before his death in 2015), Benedict Anderson wrote that "one could open the study of this vast rhizomal network anywhere," but he chose to open it in the Philippines.[54] Arguably one could ask the same about the Caribbean network. Where did it start? Where do we start? Barcelona in the early 1890s? London, where Spanish anarchist exiles like Pedro Esteve and Adrián del Valle interacted with other anarchists before heading to New York and Havana respectively? In Cuba itself with the first anarchist organizations and newspapers in the 1880s?

I begin this study not in one country. Rather, it begins on both sides of the Florida Straits as Cuba devolved into intertwined pillars of violence: colonial repression – revolution – more colonial repression – even more revolution. Chapter 1 focuses on the Cuban War for Independence in the 1890s. As Anderson noted, the war in Cuba itself was linked to global resistance in Puerto Rico, the Philippines, and even Barcelona. But this chapter focuses on the particular roles of anarchists in Florida and the connections between them and their comrades in Havana. The side of the Florida Straits you were on could make a world of difference. While Havana's anarchists faced severe repression by late 1896, anarchists in Florida operated in a climate of almost benign imperial neglect as Washington gave anarchists the space to support the war against Spain with supplies, men, and money. This trans-Strait symbiotic relationship gave birth to the Caribbean network, which came to be centered mostly in Havana after the war, but of which Tampa played an enormous role during the war and in the first years of Cuban political independence after 1902.

Chapter 2 explores the decade and a half following the Cuban war, noting how anarchists emerged and evolved across the region. In Cuba, the visit by Errico Malatesta and the creation of *¡Tierra!* helped anarchists build Havana into the network hub. Meanwhile, anarchists in Florida and Puerto Rico developed dual relationships by working with the anti-anarchist AFL unions on the ground while communicating with and funding *¡Tierra!* as their newspaper. By the early 1910s, anarchists in

---

[54] Anderson, *Under Three Flags*, 4.

Florida abandoned the AFL associations and forged the first IWW locals in the network. In Panama, anarchists migrated to the construction project shortly after it began, organized anarchist groups throughout the Canal Zone, linked themselves with Havana, and in 1911 created the isthmus's first anarchist publication. Throughout all of this, anarchists – no matter where they were – attacked US intervention, capitalism in the region, oversight of the canal, and US-designed political systems then being developed across the Caribbean.

Chapters 3 and 4 bring anarchists into armed conflict and revolution again. While the Cuban war was key to developing anarchist transnationalism, as Llaguno Thomas reminds us, the Mexican Revolution did the same.[55] Caribbean anarchists closely followed and engaged with the Mexican Revolution of 1910. They published manifestos from the Partido Liberal Mexicano (Mexican Liberal Party, or PLM) and raised money for the *magonistas*. Yet, the revolution also revealed fissures in the regional anarchist network as individualists and communists waged a global war (literally) on each other over whether the PLM was truly an anarchist group. As conflicts over what to do about Mexico settled down, anarchists then had to face the ramifications of the 1917 Russian Revolution. The revolution shaped the next decade and a half of anarchist agitation in the region as radicals attempted to figure out not only how to engage the new Communist state in Moscow but also how to interact with Marxists with whom anarchists worked and lived side by side. The post-1917 era also forced anarchists to confront the spread of US-backed anti-Communist surveillance. US intelligence agencies with their Caribbean partners tracked down and tried to suppress radicalism by expanding the Red Scare's surveillance and repression into the Caribbean and targeting Caribbean anarchists who, from the heights of officialdom, were now seen as "Bolshevikis."

Chapter 5 examines anarchist assaults on US neocolonialism from the eve of the Great War to the mid-1920s. In 1916, anarchists launched the first general strike against the US-controlled Panama Canal. Several months later, both Panama and Cuba declared war on Germany within hours of President Wilson's war declaration. Cuba developed a military draft modeled on the US draft. Puerto Rico's residents acquired US citizenship in early 1917, and thus the island's male population became eligible for the draft. Anarchists throughout the network emerged to

---

[55] Llaguno Thomas, "Acción Local," 39.

challenge this new wave of regional militarism. Around the same time in Puerto Rico, a pro-independence movement began forming. Anarchists debated the meaning of the island's independence from the United States, asking just how free and independent could a nation be in the "American Mediterranean"? Finally, anarchists began a campaign to counter the growing US friendship with dictators who ruled so-called banana republics for the benefit of US corporations. As such, anarchists continued their long critique of US expansionism in the Caribbean, reflecting their long role as anti-imperialist actors in Latin America.

Chapter 6 focuses on Panama and Pan-Americanism. US-based ideas of Pan-American unity rivaled a more Latin American ideal founded by Simón Bolívar in the 1820s. Yet, both were premised on the concept of nation-states cooperating to achieve particular ends. Anarchists envisioned a hemisphere-wide anarchist Pan-Americanism that functioned below the nation-state level and which they witnessed daily in Panama as multinational radicals from around the Americas traveled to work on the canal. But here the twin demons of Pan-American state repression (the Panamanian and Canal Zone governments) thwarted a leftist-inspired rent strike and anarchist efforts to launch the first hemisphere-wide anarchist congress.

In Chapter 7, the anarchist drama turns savagely to tragedy with still growing repression by Latin American governments and the United States to crush radicalism. Yet, all was not lost. Anarchists continued to work in their communities while maintaining transnational linkages, especially with the Spanish-language press in New York City. Long-time anarchists in Cuba and Puerto Rico, exiles in Mexico City, small groups and individuals in Panama City, Guatemala, and Colombia, a newspaper in Costa Rica, and others struggled in the early years of the global Great Depression to keep alive traditional anarchist critiques while confronting what they saw as the latest threats to humanity: Socialist parties, Stalinist Communist parties, and fascism – both European and tropical varieties.

As readers travel around this Caribbean circuit, I hope they will find interesting parallels between anarchist attempts to check the globalization efforts of the early 1900s with similar movements struggling against early twenty-first-century neoliberal globalization. In fact, the surge in studies of global anarchism and the emergence of transnationalism as a tool to write these histories seems in part a positive and contextual response to the hyper-globalized world that shapes our lives in the opening decades of this millennium. Possibly contemporary activists can learn a thing or two from their predecessors a century earlier as both groups seek and sought to check the forces of unrestrained capital and financial expansion, as well as the governments that have historically facilitated such expansion often under the guise of progress, modernization, and democratization.

One hundred years ago, people traveled to and throughout the Caribbean to fight for the anarchist cause against capitalist globalization backed by a militaristic foreign policy. Anarchists had another kind of globalization in mind, and as such often ran into government officials who arrested them and put them on trial if they were lucky; deported or even murdered them if they were not. What follows is a critical evaluation of these men and women who rose to stifle what they saw as unnatural and antihuman actions of corporations, governments, and US-based labor unions. Through their actions, the words they spoke and printed, the plays they performed, the newspapers they published and circulated widely and the money they sent to all parts of the network, anarchists joined forces not only to attack but also to create what Carr – building on Anderson – refers to as "oppositional 'imagined communities.'"[56] They fought for truly democratic, decentralized societies that prized freedom not for one country but for all peoples. They prioritized humanity over the divides created by political boundaries in newly liberated countries suddenly under the sway of an expanding US juggernaut and where both dictators and democratically elected governments did the United States's bidding by punishing those who challenged their power. Perhaps historians Peter Linebaugh and Marcus Rediker said it best at the end of their 2000 book, *The Many-Headed Hydra*: "The globalizing powers have a long reach and endless patience. Yet the planetary wanderers do not forget, and they are ever ready from Africa to the Caribbean to Seattle to resist slavery and restore the commons."[57] This book is about some of those planetary wanderers traveling throughout the Caribbean a century ago, who dedicated their lives and resources to thwarting authoritarianism and restoring that commons. Cheers!

---

[56] Carr, "Across Seas and Borders," 231.
[57] Peter Linebaugh and Marcus Rediker, *The Many-Headed Hydra: Sailors, Slaves, Commoners, and the Hidden History of the Revolutionary Atlantic* (Boston: Beacon Press, 2000), 353.

I

Anarchist Straits

Cuba's War for Independence and the Origins of the Caribbean Network

> The flag of independence that waves in the countryside is not just the flag of one determined party; it does not represent only the protest against Spanish domination. Rather, it represents the virile protest of all tyrannized and exploited people who make a supreme effort to attain their freedom.
>
> *El Esclavo*, Tampa, March 7, 1895

When the anarchist newspaper *El Esclavo* published these words, Cuba's anticolonial war versus Spain was only two weeks old. Over the coming months, the fight for independence did not go as well as Cuban rebels had hoped. Just months after the war began, Spaniards killed rebel leader José Martí. More broadly, Spanish troops were holding their own against the guerrillas. The rebel army needed help, which increasingly came from the anarchist-led working class across the Florida Straits in Key West and Tampa. Small waves of Florida-based freedom fighters picked up guns, invaded Cuba, and fought for its liberation. Enrique Creci (Figure 1.1) was one of them. In early 1896, he stood on the shores of Matanzas Province, east of Havana. He was not some average rebel soldier. As a Cuban-born cigar roller and anarchist agitator, he had published the anarchist *Archivo Social* in which he openly called for rebellion against the Spanish Crown. When war broke out, he relocated to Tampa.[1] Soon, he joined the independence forces, became a captain in a column led by rebel General Enrique Collazo, and in 1896 participated in an assault on Matanzas from a base of operations in Key West.

---

[1] Olga Cabrera, "Enrique Creci: un patriota obrero." *Santiago* 36 (December 1979): 146.

FIGURE 1.1 Enrique Creci, a leading anarchist in Cuba in the 1890s who found refuge in Florida before joining a military expedition in 1896 to cast off Spanish colonial rule from the island, dying soon after.
Author's personal collection

However, in a battle shortly after arriving in Matanzas, Spanish forces captured and executed him.[2]

Over the following years, Creci became an anarchist martyr. In May 1897, Tampa's anarchists memorialized his death. In the same issue of *El Esclavo* in which they commemorated the eleventh anniversary of the Haymarket Square bombing in Chicago, the editors recalled Creci's valiant efforts and the way he died: "Our sick comrade, found prostrated and in pain lying in a bed in one of the revolutionaries' rural field hospitals, was attacked and murdered by a gang of paid assassins like the kinds of dogs that [Spanish officials] Weyler and Cánovas set upon the people who want to shake off their brutal and degrading yoke."[3] Creci's armed actions and then his death became part of the anarchist propaganda campaign in Florida and Cuba as anarchists rallied to support a war to free the island.

---

[2] Shaffer, *Anarchism and Countercultural Politics*, 43–44; Joan Casanovas Codina, *Bread, or Bullets! Urban Labor and Spanish Colonialism in Cuba, 1850–1898* (Pittsburgh: University of Pittsburgh Press, 1998), 227.

[3] *El Esclavo*, May 19, 1897, 4; *Risveglio*, June 1913, 2–3.

Caribbean anarchism was transnational from its birth. The trans-Straits alliance that anarchists mobilized during the war had been forged over the previous decades. It emerged in the labor organizations of Cuba and southern Florida during the 1870s and 1880s. By 1873, Key West had become the most important manufacturing city in Florida, producing 25 million cigars per year largely using migrant labor from Cuba. Industrial Florida expanded in 1886 when cigar factory owner Vicente Martínez Ybor relocated his production facilities from Havana and Key West to the outskirts of Tampa. Martínez Ybor hoped to escape the growing labor movement that anarchists increasingly influenced. To this end, he negotiated a land deal with the Tampa Board of Trade to create a new company town, Ybor City, and began hiring Spanish, Italian, Cuban, and US tobacco workers.[4] But apparently Martínez Ybor had not counted on the fact that among the throngs of migrating workers would come the very anarchist agitators from whom he had sought to escape in the first place. In 1887, anarchists Enrique Messonier and Creci successfully organized workers in Key West. By 1888, the recently formed, anarchist-influenced Alianza Obrera (Labor Alliance) based in Havana began to organize tobacco industry workers throughout Tampa and Key West. In Cuba, anarchist cigar makers Messonier and Enrique Roig San Martín established a school for workers. By the 1880s, anarchists centered in Cuba's tobacco industry dominated leadership positions in the island's labor movement. They launched the weekly newspaper *El Productor*, which had correspondents from around metropolitan Havana as well as Key West and Tampa.[5] Then, anarchist-led strikes erupted in 1889, including a general strike that October in Key West that resulted in the owners agreeing to a pay raise for tobacco workers. In the early 1890s, anarchists from Spain and Cuba further organized radical activities and institutions in Havana and Florida.[6]

Thus, the rise of Florida's anarchist movement mirrored its rise in Havana. This only made sense considering the constant circular migration of workers, anarchists, and anarchist newspapers between the two cities. The Havana-based *El Productor*, *El Obrero*, and *Archivo*

---

[4] Mormino and Pozzetta, "Spanish Anarchism in Tampa," 175–177.
[5] Evan Matthew Daniel, "Cuban Cigar Makers in Havana, Key West, and Ybor City, 1850s–1890s: A Single Universe?," in *In Defiance of Boundaries: Anarchism in Latin American History*, eds. Geoffroy de Laforcade and Kirwin Shaffer (Gainesville: University Press of Florida, 2015), 30.
[6] Frank Fernández, *Cuban Anarchism: The History of a Movement* (Tucson: Sharp Press, 2001), 21–23; Daniel, "Cuban Cigar Makers," 33–44.

Social commented on issues central to workers in both Cuba and Florida. In 1894, Tampa's anarchists began publishing their first newspaper, *El Esclavo*, which found readers from New York to Havana. Anarchists published the paper almost weekly from June 1894 to March 1898. The paper sought to be "the defender of workers' interests, with no regard to workers' origins" and became a favorite to be read by the *lectores*.[7]

In this chapter, we see how *El Esclavo* played a key role in the emerging anarchist network around three important themes in the 1890s: the US labor scene, US politics for an audience with almost no experience in political republican democracy, and Cuba's independence struggle against Spain. This Florida experience would teach anarchists much about the postwar Caribbean, in particular the dilemmas of cross-ethnic unionization, their rejection of representative democracy as little more than a neocolonial tool for the elite to retain power, and their belief that political independence had to follow, not precede, a workers-based social revolution.

MIGRANT ANARCHISTS AND US LABOR

Anarchists launched *El Esclavo* in 1894 during a cigar worker strike at the Cheroots factory in Tampa. Shortly after the strike, an anonymous author suggested that the effectiveness of this labor action would be a bellwether for future labor actions, "not in Tampa, nor in Florida, rather for *habano* cigar rollers all over the United States ... and Havana."[8] As one of *El Esclavo*'s early writers, Maximino Goicoitía, reminded readers, "All of us are brothers in nature, and therefore we hate and want to obliterate frontiers" that divide workers.[9] With this internationalist sentiment, Tampa's anarchists began to interpret the North American labor scene for workers arriving from Cuba and Spain.

The first US labor issue for Tampa's anarchists was the Pullman Strike, initiated in May 1894 just as they launched the newspaper. Pullman, Illinois was a company town like Ybor City. While Ybor was built on the outskirts of Tampa, Pullman was built adjacent to Chicago. By July, federal troops had intervened on behalf of the Pullman Palace Car Company, breaking the strike. US government actions also helped to break the

---

[7] Gerald Poyo, "The Anarchist Challenge to the Cuban Independence Movement, 1885–1890," *Cuban Studies* 15, no. 1 (1985): 35; *El Esclavo*, June 9, 1894, 4.
[8] *El Esclavo*, June 13, 1894, 2.   [9] Ibid., June 20, 1894, 1–2.

American Railway Union led by Eugene V. Debs. Tampa's anarchists quickly responded. J. Cerraí celebrated the intensity of the strikes but also urged anarchists to note that the very Americans who wanted slavery's abolition had in many cases become the same ones who wanted to enslave workers into conditions worse than those of the United States's southern slaves: "Workers that speak our language, are, without doubt, those who ought to learn from the observed conduct of the federal government of this nation."[10]

This dismal picture of the United States grew bleaker when combined with an understanding of labor conditions that workers faced there. "Souveraine" portrayed the treatment of poor Spanish-speaking female workers in New York. He claimed that *despalilladoras* (female de-stemmers of tobacco leaves) were being forced to submit to every bestial whim of shop owners and managers, such as how, in one factory, the owner's son assaulted a young married female worker. When the woman's husband attacked him, the manager beat up the husband and both lost their jobs.[11]

Of course, it was horrendous that an Anglo boss's son could rape your wife, but the overall workplace and living conditions themselves were health hazards for all workers. Ybor City's boosters promoted it as a rationally planned city, but by 1894 little existed to support that image. The factories were the community's center. Around these factories, workers found flimsy, small wooden houses clustered together or took shelter in boarding houses. As one depiction of the city's early days concluded, Ybor City's first decade of existence "reflected the rawness of a mining camp and the dangers of a frontier presidio."[12]

Before the discovery of mosquitoes serving as vectors for the transfer of diseases like malaria, few people understood the health concerns surrounding large, stagnant sources of water. But some anarchists had their suspicions. In June 1894, one anonymous writer to *El Esclavo* noted how Ybor City was full of canals, which the writer suspected had something to do with disease and illness in the city. So, the writer asked rhetorically, if there were such a connection, then why not drain the canals and nearby swamps? He answered his own question by repeating a rumor: Doctors and pharmacists did not want to drain the canals, swamps, and lagoons because to do so would put them out of the business of treating the sick.

---

[10] Ibid., July 24, 1894, 1.   [11] Ibid., July 31, 1894, 2.
[12] Mormino and Pozzetta, "Spanish Anarchism in Tampa," 176–178.

Such claims were common in anarchist critiques of health and medicine in the early twentieth century.[13]

Anarchists also painted an unsavory picture of life inside American factories. Every day, hundreds of tobacco workers labored side by side in a factory, sorting, de-stemming, and rolling tobacco leaves. They often drank from the same single water source – maybe even the same cup. Such conditions favored the spread of diseases like tuberculosis. Since people from fourteen to seventy years old, male and female, worked in the factories, a wide stratum of the population was vulnerable to the spread of disease in the workplace. In addition, factories kept their doors and windows closed during the workday, exacerbating the hot, sweaty, closed confines of the factories.[14]

Medical costs like those for doctors and medicines were generally beyond the reach of an average worker; thus, working-class mothers frequently worked outside the home to earn money not only for food and housing, but also healthcare. This could have disastrous effects on children. Goicoitía cited an unnamed study that found infant mortality rose from 152/1000 to 195/1000 when the mother worked outside the home.[15] While not couched as a critique of working mothers – though to be sure it did assume a certain patriarchal, *machista* quality – Goicoitía was suggesting that if males' wages were higher, then fathers would earn enough money to pay medical expenses while mothers stayed home with their children. In essence, he and other anarchists charged that by paying workers low wages, Martínez Ybor and the other factory owners were responsible for child death.

From October 1894 to February 1895, tobacco workers and anarchists from Havana to New York conducted a series of labor actions to improve wages and conditions. Spanish and Cuban workers in Florida regularly donated money to a tobacco worker strike in New York in January 1895. In the week before war began in Cuba, tobacco workers at Tampa's La Rosa and Monné factories went on strike. The "Manifesto to Tobacco-Working People in General," published at the same time as *El Esclavo* was serializing Peter Kropotkin's *Conquest of Bread*, promised workers that "our triumph is the triumph of all workers in Florida, of all workers in the United States."[16]

---

[13] *El Esclavo*, June 28, 1894, 4; July 12, 1894, 2; July 18, 1894, 3. For the anarchist critique of health in Cuba, see Shaffer, *Anarchism and Countercultural Politics*, 107–161.
[14] *El Esclavo*, July 24, 1894, 3–4.   [15] Ibid., August 8, 1894, 2–3.
[16] Ibid., February 21, 1895, 2–3.

El Esclavo sought to take the gleam off what many migrant workers might have thought the United States represented. Such depictions of labor conditions in Florida helped anarchists frame their image of the international struggle so that whether in Spain, Cuba, the United States, Puerto Rico, or elsewhere, workers should understand that their true allies were each other no matter where they worked or where they were born. The American workplace was no better than any other capitalist factory in Cuba, Puerto Rico, or Spain. Workers across the Straits needed to aid each other, and in Florida that meant transnational tobacco workers had to wage economic warfare against "American" capitalists – whether those capitalists were Anglo Americans or Spanish migrants from Cuba.

MIGRANT ANARCHISTS AND US DEMOCRACY

For anarchists arriving from monarchial traditions in Spain and colonial despotism in Cuba, US republican democracy could hold a certain allure – at least initially. American rhetoric and mythology promoted the ideal of the common man playing a valuable, vital, and honored role in the political development of the United States. Whether it was Jeffersonian notions of a yeoman democracy or a constitution that protected free speech and assembly, Spanish and Cuban anarchists initially were attracted to a country and a system that appeared so radically different than their despotic homelands. When the Statue of Liberty was dedicated in 1886 – just eight years before the founding of *El Esclavo* – anarchist immigrants could be forgiven for thinking that the United States was a place where working men and women from around the world could come, unite, and work for a better collective future full of freedom. Of course, reality cut through the mythology, as anarchists soon discovered. Republicanism might give average men a political voice, but it could also be a tool to deceive those very people and maintain the capitalist status quo. After all, if 1886 was the year of the Statue of Liberty's dedication, it was also the year of the Haymarket Square Affair in Chicago.

An anonymous writer perhaps best expressed this conflicted image of the United States in June 1894. In a column titled "Una ilusión desvanecida" (The Faded Illusion), the author noted that to some anarchists, representative government could be a viable mechanism for people to govern themselves. This was impossible in the Europe that they knew, so "we then cast our gaze toward America, toward the virgin America, young and beautiful in whose breast those hungry and tyrannized

Europeans fled to find refuge ... The American land was the most propitious to establish and practice the principles of republicanism in all its purity." But after they arrived in the United States, they saw how the government "of the people" always sided with the minority bourgeoisie against the working majority. The government truly was of the rich, and for them as well. The fact that workers could vote "is a great farce that only serves to clinch tighter the workers' own chains." "Revolutionary socialism," i.e., anarchism, was the only answer.[17]

A central tenet of the American democratic mythology is that there is no class warfare in the United States. Every person who is willing to work can aspire to their goals. The United States provides everyone an equal opportunity. As a result, rigid, generational class structures are a throwback to Europe. Or, if there are examples of class conflict, they are not symptomatic of the overall American capitalist democracy. It did not take long for anarchists in Tampa to attack this myth, too.[18] J. C. Campos, an anarchist who could be found at various times in Tampa, New York, and Havana – and whose writings introduced Spanish-speaking anarchists to the Haymarket Affair years earlier – expressed profound shock at how workers' lives in the United States hung precariously on the whims of the wealthy and powerful, thus undermining the republican ideals of equal justice. Campos had traveled around the United States, witnessing the contradiction. He had seen a great abundance of food and an equally great abundance of starving people. He saw previously independent people being forced to work for wages as the industrial revolution spread its tentacles from artisans' shops in towns and cities to farms throughout the countryside. The great inventions that could make life better for the masses were being monopolized by the few so that they could grow ever richer. Great wealth from the government was being spent on weapons and a navy. Ultimately, in the United States – as everywhere in the world – the "government is nothing else but the arm that helps the bourgeoisie to subjugate the worker." In such an environment, Campos asked, were workers under Spanish imperial and colonial rule that much worse off than their North American counterparts?[19]

---

[17] Ibid., June 13, 1894, 1–2.   [18] Ibid., June 28, 1894, 4.
[19] Ibid., March 18, 1897, 1–2; see also Susana Sueiro Seoane, "Prensa y redes anarquistas transnacionales: El olvidado papel de J.C. Campos y sus crónicas sobre los mártires de Chicago en el anarquismo de lengua hispana," *Cuadernos de Historia Contemporánea* 36 (2014): 259–295.

July Fourth – American Independence Day – was a favorite time to question the ideals and realities of the US political system. In summer 1895, *El Esclavo* published "El 4 de Julio." An anonymous writer told a tale of how in the beginning of the American republic, all had looked good for the average man. However, in the past century, the nation's leaders "had done nothing more than follow in the footsteps of the old European and Asian states." Like those predecessors, the US republic was controlled by capital, worker exploitation increased daily, and free speech was for a select few and designed "to sustain bourgeois institutions."[20] As a result, any politics celebrating the working-class electorate would always be a sham as long as a real social revolution remained unfulfilled.

Tampa's anarchists continued this message in their analysis of the Socialist and Populist movements in the United States. Cerraí praised the idea of working people demanding to be heard. They symbolized for Cerraí "the first step toward revolution in the future." Still, he remained skeptical about a Populist or Socialist movement that had as its crowning achievement electoral political power.[21] Cerraí noted to his readers that both Socialists and anarchists "seek to abolish private property and government. The only real difference between one and the other is the methods that both employ to bring about social change" – Socialists choose to use government, which anarchists reject. What if Socialists could win elections? While a Socialist-led government would strive to implement its goals, there would remain a governmental structure. This would provide an avenue for the previous powerholders to block necessary reforms. Just as dangerous, it would create a system of power and control that could be too enticing for Socialist lawmakers to ever eliminate.[22] Meanwhile, Populists fared poorly in the 1894 US congressional elections. In the wake of the elections, one anarchist writer suggested that part of this lackluster performance could be attributed to things like voter fraud. This raised a serious question about whether a candidate with a radical democratic agenda could ever be elected in the United States. If the Populists could be disenfranchised, then why not Socialists as well? As the writer concluded, it should be clear by now that revolution and not election was the only viable route.[23]

Thus, any anarchist flirtations with democratic electoral politics were dashed by what anarchists in Florida witnessed firsthand. This would be an important lesson for anarchists after 1898, when the United States

---

[20] *El Esclavo*, July 9, 1895, 1.   [21] Ibid., July 31, 1894, 1.
[22] Ibid., August 22, 1894, 1–2.   [23] Ibid., November 21, 1894, 4.

began to impose its political system in places like Cuba, Puerto Rico, and Panama. So, when moderate, bourgeois Cuban *independentistas* proposed a representative government for post-independence Cuba, one can understand why anarchists said no. Republican democracy was not the answer nor what workers wanted. The revolution must not be replaced by any government. After all, if the United States was the best example of republicanism – and anarchists saw how poorly that was working out for the laboring classes – then the Americans could keep it.

ANARCHISTS AND THE RUN-UP TO WAR IN CUBA

In January 1892, the Junta Central de Trabajadores de la Región Cubana (Central Junta of Workers from Cuba) issued the "Manifiesto del Congreso Obrero de 1892" (Manifesto of the 1892 Labor Congress) that called for independence from Spain. Anarchists argued that for a social revolution to emerge on the island, Cuba first needed to break its colonial shackles. Anarchists in Cuba, Tampa, and beyond would no longer object to a "national liberation" movement; rather, collective freedom of a people was perfectly in line with the goal of social revolution and individual freedom.[24] Three-and-a-half months later, on May Day, *Hijos del Mundo* – the anarchist newspaper in Guanabacoa (across the bay from Havana) – printed a "Manifiesto á los trabajadores cubanos" (Manifesto to Cuban Workers). Commemorating the Haymarket martyrs of Chicago, the authors listed governmental abuses in North America and Europe, turning specifically to Spanish Prime Minister Antonio Cánovas del Castillo: "And Cánovas, who longs to bathe himself in the blood of workers, who cowardly garrotes our *compañeros* from Jerez and incarcerates countless distinguished by their ideas for freedom," should "be loathed with every energy in our souls for his profound wrongs." The manifesto called on workers to rise against the Spanish state: "Working people on their knees, we implore you to struggle for its [the revolution's] immediate arrival. Workers: long live Anarchy!"[25]

In an 1894 article titled "Lucharemos juntos" (We Will Fight Together), Cerraí praised the anarchists and separatists who "will struggle together"

---

[24] *El movimiento obrero cubano: documentos y artículos*, Vol. 1. (Havana: Editorial de Ciencias Sociales, 1975), 81.
[25] "Manifiesto á los trabajadores," *Hijos del Mundo* (Guanabacoa), May 1, 1892. Max Nettlau Collection. Regions and Countries. Central and South America. Other Countries. Cuba, 1892–1928, Folder 3404, International Institute of Social History, Amsterdam; Poyo, "The Anarchist Challenge," 41.

and be the key to a true independence for the island.[26] "Souvarine" urged Spanish workers to join the cause and to remember that even if not born in Cuba they could help those who were to free their homeland since everyone should have the right "to love the small corner where we have been born."[27] By the last half of 1894, with the outbreak of war imminent, Tampa's anarchists became more vitriolic and rancorous. For instance, the editors of *El Esclavo* published articles with titles like "They want war; they got it" and "Death to the bourgeoisie" that, among other things, described how to make dynamite and other useful explosive devices.[28]

In the meantime, Cerraí attacked those who sought independence for Cuba but refused to accept the necessity for revolutionary social change to accompany the change in political status. Such people favor "the political revolution that will only provide emancipation from Spain without achieving any benefit that will better the sad condition of the workers."[29] In an open letter to Cuban separatists in the United States, a columnist celebrated the approaching struggle. Yet, he warned freedom fighters who pick up a gun to gain their freedom to be careful, to know against whom they were fighting and why. Don't just fight to free the island only to have a new set of the bourgeoisie take over. Be sure, he warned, to "cast aside 'those men' who want to enslave you in the factories of your 'fellow countrymen.'"[30] Independence would be a launch pad for social revolution that would transform the island, not an end in itself that would substitute one bourgeois ruling elite for another and where "Cuban" workers would be exploited by "Cuban" owners.

Most anarchists in Cuba supported independence, viewing the conflict as an anticolonial struggle for freedom against Spanish imperial tyranny. Cuban anarchists joined José Martí's Partido Revolucionario Cubano (Cuban Revolutionary Party, or PRC). They hoped to push the independence movement away from its bourgeois leadership based in New York City and, upon freeing the island from colonial rule, initiate a revolutionary transformation. They agitated among workers and even Spanish troops. One such agitator was José García, who traveled throughout eastern Cuba during the war, seeking to convert Spanish soldiers to the independence cause.[31]

---

[26] *El Esclavo*, September 5, 1894, 1–2.   [27] Ibid., September 12, 1894, 2.
[28] Ibid., September 26, 1894, 3–4.   [29] Ibid., August 15, 1894, 1–2.
[30] Ibid., November 7, 1894, 1.
[31] Casanovas Codina, *Bread, or Bullets!*, 226; Shaffer, *Anarchism and Countercultural Politics*, 44.

Secundino Delgado, one of *El Esclavo*'s editors, provides a clear example of anarchist pro-independence support. Born in 1867, Delgado grew up on the Canary island of Tenerife. At fourteen, he joined other Canarians crossing the Atlantic to find work in Cuba's cigar factories. Some time later, he moved to Tampa, helped edit *El Esclavo*, threw his support behind the anticolonial struggle, and urged Canarian conscripts in the Spanish army to change sides. Delgado then left Tampa, traveling first to Key West and then Havana. Following a crackdown on Havana's anarchists in 1896, he fled Cuba, returning to the Canary Islands. Then, Delgado had to flee his homeland once again (this time heading to Venezuela) when Cuba's Captain General Valeriano Weyler accused him of being a Florida-based radical who orchestrated an assassination attempt. This native of the Canary Islands eventually returned and became one of the most well-known anarchist proponents of Canary national identity, and an outspoken anarchist supporter for the islands' independence from Spanish rule – a political cocktail he first tasted in Tampa during Cuba's independence war.[32]

However, not all anarchists supported the Cuban rebellion. Some anarchists in Cuba and New York City urged anarchists to avoid becoming involved in what they saw as largely a bourgeois affair. War critics like Pedro Esteve (at least initially) and Cristóbal Fuente urged neutrality. Beyond fear of replacing one government with another, they suspected that any overt anarchist support for the Cuban cause could result in a new wave of repression against anarchists in Cuba and Spain. In addition, some anarchists in Cuba feared that if they openly aided the rebellion, then Spanish workers seeking to remain loyal to the homeland could attack them; likewise, if anarchists in Cuba opposed the rebellion, then they faced potential retribution from pro-independence Cuban workers. So, anarchist neutrality was best.[33]

---

[32] See these excellent analyses of Delgado: Enrique Galván-Álvarez, "Anarchism and the Anti-colonial Canarian Imagination: The Missing Flag," *History Workshop Journal* 83, no. 1 (April 2017): 253–271; Juan José Cruz, "You Can't Go Home, Yankee: Teaching U.S. History to Canary Islands Students," *The History Teacher* 35, no. 3 (2002): 343–372; Casanovas Codina, *Bread, or Bullets!*, 227.

[33] Casanovas Codina, *Bread, or Bullets!*, 223–226; Christopher J. Castañeda, "Times of Propaganda and Struggle: *El Despertar* and Brooklyn's Spanish Anarchists, 1890–1905," in *Radical Gotham: Anarchism in New York City from Schwab's Saloon to Occupy Wall Street*, ed. Tom Goyens (Urbana: University of Illinois Press, 2017), 88; Zimmer, *Immigrants against the State*, 122.

To counter those radicals who questioned anarchist support for Cuba's independence struggle, *El Esclavo* published J. Raices's four-part article "La revolución social advanza" (The Social Revolution Advances). The last installment was published on February 6 – just days before the rebellion began. Raices concluded that workers had to fight for the revolution against Spain. Freedom for Cuba was morally correct and would lead to a new, just revolutionary society. By doing so, workers "can win from this a powerful moral influence that will give us at the same time all of the material force that we need in order to establish there [in Cuba] the true revolutionary socialism."[34]

ANARCHISTS DURING THE WAR FOR INDEPENDENCE

Just weeks following the outbreak of war in February 1895, anarchists in the United States cast the anticolonial rebellion in Cuba in broad global and historical terms. *El Esclavo* published the front-page manifesto "¡Obreros de Cuba!" (Cuban Workers!): "The flag of independence that waves in the countryside is not just the flag of one determined party; it does not represent only the protest against Spanish domination of Cuba. Rather, it represents the virile protest of all tyrannized and exploited people who make a supreme effort to attain their freedom."[35] Palmiro de Lidia – then in exile in New York City – put Cuba in the historical context of great revolutionary movements. He praised the American and French Revolutions for "illuminating the intelligences and burning the sacred flame of rebellion in the breasts of oppressed peoples" by their propaganda. However, as freedom spread in the nineteenth century, Cuba remained subjugated. It was time for Cuba to rise to the level of freedom that the Americas had long symbolized to the Old World.[36]

While focusing on the global importance of the war, anarchists also refocused attention on possible local conflicts in Tampa, where they regularly worried about possible divisions between Cuban and Spanish workers, fearing that either or both could lapse into a patriotic jingoism for or against the rebellion. For Cubans this could result in detesting all things Spanish, including potential working-class allies. For Spaniards in Tampa, this could mean falling back on some patriotic sense of nationalism as put forth by Madrid. Consequently, in the war's first year, Tampa's anarchists regularly encouraged workers of different nationalities to

---

[34] *El Esclavo*, February 6, 1895, 1–2.   [35] Ibid., March 7, 1895, 1.
[36] Ibid., August 21, 1895, 1–2.

support a working-class internationalist position. Based in Key West, Roque Morera reminded Spaniard and Cuban alike "that the Cuban people rarely talk of the Cuban republic and always of *Cuba libre* and independent Cuba." Such terms were important because a free Cuba was to be a bastion of freedom for all, not just Cubans. In addition, the paper called on Iberian workers not to volunteer or allow themselves to be sent to Cuba.[37]

Palmiro de Lidia also spoke directly to his fellow Spaniards while trying to humanize the war. While always a supporter of Cuban independence, he rejected how some separatist leaders painted the Spanish forces with broad strokes of savagery. He urged readers to remember that Spanish mothers – just like Cuban ones – cried and lamented their sons going off to Cuba "to defend the right of conquest." The letter caused a stir among some separatists in Cuba. The Havana-based anarchist "Perseverante" thought that de Lidia was being too soft on Spain. As is true in warfare throughout time, each side found it useful to stereotype, debase, and dehumanize their opponents, as many Cuban separatists did in order to fight Spain. But such demonization countered the spirit of internationalism. De Lidia reminded readers that most Spanish soldiers sent to Cuba were merely poor men pressed into service to fulfill the visions of grandeur of some general, some priest, some royal.[38]

In the end, violence was the order of the day. In December 1894, *El Esclavo* had praised the coming violent upheaval on the island and its implications: "Cuban workers, we are going to be the first to raise the red flag and show the entire world by example and soon it will be inclined to follow our lead."[39] In August 1895, *El Esclavo* praised the level of the violence that the rebel forces were waging throughout the island. As rebels destroyed fields and factories alike, many in the bourgeoisie complained about the cost of the war to their bottom lines. Anarchists wore such complaints as badges of honor. "Hurray for dynamite! Let the spirit of destruction guide the revolutionaries' paths," proclaimed one columnist.[40]

Meanwhile, anarchists joined the violence. They placed bombs throughout Havana, blowing up bridges and gas lines. The most celebrated bombing occurred in spring 1896. With the war entering its second year, Captain General Weyler arrived in Cuba to suppress the rebellion.

---

[37] Ibid., May 1, 1895, 1–2; May 15, 1895, 1.
[38] Ibid., September 4, 1895, 1; October 2, 1895, 1–2.   [39] Ibid., December 19, 1894, 1.
[40] Ibid., August 28, 1895, 1–2.

Planned in Florida with poor-quality dynamite, anarchists bombed the Palace of the Captains-General and destroyed the latrines – which actually was the target since the idea was to blow up the toilet when Weyler came to move his bowels. But, with his hemorrhoids, he rarely used the john and instead kept a chamber pot nearby.[41] In Tampa, though, anarchists celebrated the bombing for its symbolic importance as the paper urged people to produce "similar explosions!"[42] They also urged anarchists on the island to increase violence against Spanish targets in order "to teach the people who their true enemies were: the clergy, the bourgeoisie, and the military that sustains them."[43]

The violence got Weyler's attention, and the ramifications were immense. Weyler attacked Havana's labor organizations and banned the *lectores*. In October, the government began arresting radicals and closed *El Productor*. Weyler had help, and some of that help apparently came from a handful of Havana anarchists who continued to reject the idea of Cuban independence. One victim of this anarchist-on-anarchist intrigue was the prominent writer and spokesperson Manuel María Miranda. As Miranda told readers after the war, that October several tobacco workers "who had declared themselves anarchists since 1885, converted themselves into ferocious reactionary oppressors who applauded and congratulated that executioner of the Cuban people, General Weyler, for his cruel extermination policy." These anarchists began collecting money in the factories to support Spanish troops against the rebels. Miranda and other anarchists who worked at the Don Quijote de la Mancha factory rose up, spoke out, and protested the fundraising campaign. Some weeks later, Miranda learned that officials wanted to talk to him. Fearing the worst, he fled into hiding in Guanabacoa with plans of joining a wave of independence supporters streaming to Mexico. An unemployed *lector* took a job with the secret police and tracked down Miranda. He convinced Miranda to travel to Regla and board a banana boat sailing to the United States. Once in Regla, though, the police sprang their trap, arrested Miranda, and took him to Havana.[44] At the end of November, authorities charged him with being an anarchist and deported him to Spain's African prison colony on Fernando Póo.[45]

---

[41] Casanovas Codina, *Bread, or Bullets!*, 227. See also Frank Fernández's colorful description in *La Sangre de Santa Águeda: Angiolillo, Betances, and Cánovas* (Miami: Ediciones Universal, 1994), 22.
[42] *El Esclavo*, May 19, 1896, 3.   [43] Ibid., July 8, 1896, 3–4.
[44] *El Nuevo Ideal*, January 5, 1900, 4; Muller, *Cuban Émigrés*, 37.
[45] *El Nuevo Ideal*, January 12, 1900, 4.

The crackdown also shaped the workers' movement in Puerto Rico. Santiago Iglesias Pantín lived in Havana from 1888 to 1896. He worked with Havana's *El Productor* and the anarchist-led Workers Circle as its secretary just as the Circle solidified its support for independence. In December 1896, authorities raided his Havana home, confiscated his books and documents, and issued an arrest warrant. Fearing for his safety, he boarded a ship bound for London. But first the ship stopped in San Juan, Puerto Rico, where Iglesias Pantín disembarked and in early 1897 began a life of labor activism on that island.[46]

The war also had broad global support, with international anarchists pledging to come and fight. For instance, Argentinean and Spanish anarchists supported the war. Some Argentineans supposedly were preparing to embark for Cuba, while Spanish anarchists were volunteering for Cuban duty to spread propaganda among the soldiers.[47] Meanwhile, real-life internationalism was at work in the polyglot enclave of Tampa. Reflecting the large Italian anarchist support for the war, a few Italians joined armed expeditions with their Spanish-speaking comrades as they crossed the Straits to fight. Most expeditions arrived in western Cuba, especially the important tobacco-growing area around Pinar del Río. It was there that in late May 1897 a pair of Italian anarchists – Guglielme Petriccione and Orestes Ferrara – arrived with arms and men.[48]

By February 1896, fully a year into the war, there were at least five separate anarchist groups operating in Tampa and West Tampa. These groups, with names like La Alianza (The Alliance), El Hambre (The Hungry), El Despertar (The Awakening), Vigilante, and Sociedad de Propaganda Obrera (Society of Worker Propaganda), raised funds to launch more expeditions, send supplies to the front lines, and support families left behind in Cuba after anarchist husbands were deported.[49] Yet, the ability to raise money became a problem. The spreading

---

[46] Santiago Iglesias Pantín, *Luchas emancipadoras (Crónicas de Puerto Rico)*, Vol. I (San Juan: Imprenta Venezuela, 1929/1958), 17–19, 31–33; Igualdad Iglesias de Pagán, *El obrerismo en Puerto Rico: Época de Santiago Iglesias (1896–1905)* (Palencia de Castilla: Ediciones Juan Ponce de León, 1973), 22.

[47] *El Esclavo*, October 28, 1895, 4.

[48] Ibid., June 5, 1897, 4; Anderson, *Under Three Flags*, 190. See Chapters 3 and 7 in this book on the deradicalization of Ferrara from 1900 to the 1920s. *La Questione Sociale* in Paterson, New Jersey supported the war and anarchist Harry Kelly saw five Italian anarchists in Florida heading to Cuba. See Zimmer, *Immigrants against the State*, 121–122.

[49] Casanovas Codina, *Bread, or Bullets!*, 205–206, 227; *El Esclavo*, January 22, 1896, 1 and 4; February 20, 1896, 4; January 13, 1897, 2; February 24, 1897, 4.

conflagration on the island disrupted the key economic engine of Florida and Cuba: tobacco. Scorched earth policies waged by both sides laid to waste vast tobacco fields. As a result, less leaf arrived in Florida factories, and demand for workers slowed. Since anarchists relied on workers' contributions to support their activities and to aid in the war effort, the spreading of the conflict meant less money available to finance the rebellion. Plus, as people fled the conflict, they often found themselves in Florida looking for work, meaning that just when there was less work available, more workers were looking for jobs and driving down wages. So, although anarchists earlier had praised the violent destruction of the Cuban economy as a legitimate tactic in the war effort, they soon faced unforeseen consequences of that celebrated strategy.

Yet, in response to the war, decreased exports of tobacco leaf from the island to Florida factories, and increased intimidation from Florida factory owners, workers rose up rather than cowered. The effects of the war helped to inspire a growing sense of working-class consciousness. One writer warned the factory owners that they ought to be cautious about carrying their exploitations to the extreme because "modern ideas and the Cuban war have taught the workers to have *less respect for property* and to successfully master the torch and dynamite."[50] This actually encouraged anarchist agitation as workers continued their long tradition of clearing a factory with the simple cry of "¡Para las calles!" (To the streets!).[51]

As a result, labor actions surged throughout Tampa in 1895 and 1896. Several strikes emerged as economic pressures on workers increased. In September 1896, for instance, workers at the González Mora workshop struck to protest wage cuts. One anarchist considered the strike as a spark to increase worker consciousness, merging the labor strike with the imagery of the war: "To the struggle, then! To combat! And let the chips fall where they may!" By October, workers had gone on strike at other tobacco factories, including Los Cabezones and Ortiz. By winning those strikes, they were energized to go after more factories, including the most prominent: the Martínez Ybor factory itself. By December 1896, workers had won that strike too. In fact, strike activities in the last third of 1896 so embroiled Tampa's working class that *El Esclavo* abandoned almost all its coverage of the 1896 US presidential elections and the war in Cuba.[52]

---

[50] *El Esclavo*, June 24, 1896, 1. Italics in original.
[51] Mormino and Pozzetta, "Spanish Anarchism in Tampa," 188.
[52] *El Esclavo*, September 23, 1896, 1; October 7, 1896, 1; December 2, 1896, 1.

Anarchists on both sides of the Florida Straits were largely responsible for bringing workers to the separatist cause. There was no larger symbol of the separatist cause overall than José Martí. While Martí was known for advocating social reforms for a post-independence Cuba, one must wonder if the anarchists actually believed him. In nearly four years of publishing a weekly newspaper, Tampa's anarchists paid almost no attention to Martí and his copious writings. In the heady first year of its publication, in fact, not once did *El Esclavo* mention Martí, though they did make a couple of references to fellow independence leader Antonio Maceo.

While it was one thing to ignore Martí, just as odd was the paper's lack of focus on the US government and growing cries by some in the United States to take a stand against Spain in the war. Only once – in early 1897 – did US government actions draw the editors' attention. In 1896 the US Congress passed a resolution supporting Cuban independence, but President Cleveland did not act on the resolution, as a way of avoiding war with Spain. The incoming McKinley administration feared that the rebellion, now two years old, was destroying the Cuban economy and harming US investments. To the Tampa anarchists, any US governmental or military action would be self-serving and run against the interests of a free people on the island. "If the North American Senate and Congress advocate recognizing Cuban independence," they argued, "it is not for the affection and friendship that they have for the Cubans but because the capital investments they have there are in danger, and they hope that with an independent Cuba they will gain commercial monopolies that today they lack."[53]

Meanwhile, the US government generally turned a blind eye to the Tampa anarchists during the war. Anarchists were not arrested for their political activities regarding Cuba and there appears to have been no efforts by the US government to prevent anarchists from sending aid, supplies, and fighters from the Florida coast to the island. In addition, for most of its run, *El Esclavo* avoided censorship or suppression. However, that changed as anarchists stepped up their violence in Spain. During 1897, Spanish officials intensified their crackdown on anarchists in Cuba and Spain. Out of the mix emerged the very non-anarchist Puerto Rican Ramón Emeterio Betances. In 1871, Betances had moved to France – arriving just eight months after the fall of the Paris Commune. Many of

---

[53] Ibid., February 24, 1897, 2–3.

his friends over the years were anarchists and former *communards* like Élisée Reclus, Louise Michel, and Charles Malato. By 1896, Betances was such a recognized supporter of Cuban independence that he became the chief diplomat for the Cuban independence cause in Paris. In 1897, Betances met the Italian anarchist Michele Angiolillo and the two spoke of exacting revenge on the Spanish monarchy. While Betances hated Prime Minister Cánovas del Castillo for allowing Weyler carte blanche to butcher Cubans, Angiolillo equally hated the Spanish prime minister for authorizing the execution of anarchists at the Barcelona prison of Montjuïc. That summer, Angiolillo traveled to the resort of Santa Águeda, where Cánovas del Castillo was vacationing. As the prime minister rested outside the hotel, Angiolillo walked up to him and fired three bullets into the Spanish leader.[54]

Anarchists around the world celebrated the assassination of the man who had presided over massive atrocities committed by his forces in Spain and Cuba. In September, *El Esclavo* published two front-page columns praising Angiolillo's actions. One column concluded: "It was about time." In the other column, J. C. Campos likewise praised the assassination but lamented that in the name of the cause a hero like Angiolillo had to be sacrificed when Spanish officials arrested and then executed him.[55] But not all was good news for the anarchists. US authorities were appalled by anarchist praise of assassination and closed *El Esclavo*. The newspaper reemerged in February 1898 and published for only one more month. In that final issue, the editors sold portraits of Angiolillo for ten cents each as a fundraiser. US officials ordered the paper closed again. Both times the US government shut down the paper because it publicly celebrated assassinating a world leader.[56] And for someone like Manuel Miranda, stranded in a Spanish detention facility in Fernando Póo, the joy of Angiolillo's actions was tempered when the governor of the island refused to put Miranda's name on a general amnesty list of political prisoners because, as Miranda put it, "on my police record I was identified as an anarchist, and because the author of Cánovas del Castillo's death was also an anarchist ..." He did not need to complete the thought – guilt by ideological association.[57] Miranda would not go home until the war's end.

---

[54] Anderson, *Under Three Flags*, 184–194; Richard Bach Jensen, *The Battle against Anarchist Terrorism: An International History, 1878–1934* (New York: Cambridge University Press, 2014), 38; Fernández, *La sangre de Santa Águeda*, 16.
[55] *El Esclavo*, September 24, 1897, 1.   [56] Ibid., February 11, 1898; March 23, 1898.
[57] Miranda, *Memorias de un deportado*, 48.

CONCLUSION

In April 1898, the United States declared war on Spain and invaded Cuba, Puerto Rico, and the Philippines. Anarchists feared entrance of the United States into the war. As Kenyon Zimmer writes, US entry "placed anarchist backers of Cuban independence in an untenable position, as they could not in good conscience support the openly imperialist motives of the United States."[58] By the end of the year, Spain had surrendered to Washington and the United States began a four-year military occupation of the island. Any anticipated postwar anarchist social revolution was crushed.

In 1899, with the war over, anarchists brought Enrique Creci's remains to Havana for reburial. When his body arrived in Havana, men and women gathered at the Workers Center for commemorative and propaganda speeches, but the police broke up the event. In defiance, the crowd regathered and silently marched Creci's coffin to the cemetery, led by the editorial staff of Cuba's first post Spanish–era anarchist newspaper *El Nuevo Ideal*. In Guanabacoa, Jaime Mayol Martínez published his poem "Enrique Creci," addressing the anarchist: "you left behind a luminous footprint / like that of the sublime martyr of Judea."[59] As anarchists would come to see it, the war had been lost – no social revolution would emerge in Cuba – but those who sacrificed themselves and their efforts on both sides of the Florida Straits would be remembered for showing the path forward and for dying the martyr's death.

But if the war had been lost, a new regional anarchist network had been forged. The years preceding Spain's defeat in 1898 witnessed the emergence of two prominent and influential anarchist movements on opposite sides of the Straits – one in Havana and another mainly in Tampa. Both cities' movements were co-dependent on income, media, propaganda, and recruits. Before 1898, both Tampa and Havana had thriving anarchist presses that fed off one another. During the war, as state repression in Cuba surged, Tampa's anarchists became even more vital. After the US invasion in 1898, and as US military and economic interests spread throughout Cuba in the following years, anarchists would expand this network across the island.

The war was instrumental for the development of labor and anarchist politics in Puerto Rico and Panama too. Puerto Rico was Spain's other

---

[58] Zimmer, *Immigrants against the State*, 122.
[59] Jaime Mayol Martínez, "Enrique Creci," *Vibraciones* (Guanabacoa, Cuba, 1899), n.p; *Risveglio*, June 1913, 2–3.

sole colony in the Western Hemisphere by 1895. While some Puerto Ricans sought political independence or autonomy, the political atmosphere on the island was very different than in Cuba. There was no armed independence movement and organized labor with a radical consciousness was embryonic at best, with only a smattering of anarchist activists. But from this environment emerged an anarchist escapee from the Cuban war and Spanish repression on the island. When he fled Cuba and landed in Puerto Rico, Santiago Iglesias Pantín brought with him some serious anarchist credentials. While he would soon abandon anarchism, his arrival in San Juan not only gave anarchists and other labor radicals there a needed jolt, but also created the initial link between Puerto Rico and the growing anarchist network.

Cuba's war for independence also illustrated to US foreign policy experts specifically and expansionists in general that they needed a canal through Central America in order to expedite military transit, as well as trade, between the Pacific and Atlantic Oceans. Political intrigue resulted in creation of the independent Republic of Panama in November 1903. From 1904 to 1914, the United States oversaw and financed one of the world's great engineering feats by building the Panama Canal through the heart of the new republic. Of course, it was the tens of thousands of workers from Spain, Italy, and the West Indies who mostly built the canal. And among these workers were the first anarchists to organize in Panama, anarchists who would develop the western link of the Caribbean network – and all because Washington wanted a canal as a result of the Cuban war.

The war did more than launch US and anarchist expansion around the region. The war, and anarchist experiences in Florida especially, left lasting impressions on activists who were intent on creating anarchy in the Caribbean. Anarchists learned the importance of multiethnic organizing with cooperation between Cubans, Spaniards, Italians, and more. Anarchists also learned that representative democracy was little, if any, better than other forms of government, and as Washington came to spread democratic political institutions to Cuba, Puerto Rico, and Panama, anarchists were there with ample critiques learned firsthand in Florida. Finally, anarchists came to understand the dangers of supporting nationalist independence struggles. Here, it is worth considering that those anarchists who were skeptical of the war might have been correct. It sounds weak and lacking in a certain order of courage, but many had a valid concern. It was only reasonable that a post-independence capitalist class would want a government that passed laws to preserve bourgeois property. Anarchist war critics had every reason to believe that the bourgeoisie and wealthy would renege on promised social reforms and land redistribution for the thousands of working-class and peasant soldiers fighting for independence. After all, when did anarchists take the bourgeoisie at their word anyway? Though anti-war anarchists lacked crystal balls and were in the anarchist minority by not supporting the war, ultimately they would be proven right in terms of what followed the war and why supporting political independence struggles was fraught with danger.

2

Anarchists versus *Yanquis*

The Anarchist Network Resists US Neocolonialism, 1898–1915

> Today, Cubans aspire to be liberated from the intervention of the American government that, under the lying mantle of liberator, has come to dictate and tyrannize as in a country under conquest. Just and holy is their aspiration. But this will not be realized either by the rich class that needs American protection in order to be able to safely exploit the energetic Cuban worker or by the merchants of patriotism who beg their share of the interventionists' spoils.
>
> Errico Malatesta, Havana, March 1900

Between 1898 and 1903, three Caribbean nations became free of former rulers. The US invasion of Puerto Rico and Cuba in 1898 wrested the islands from Spanish ownership, but they then fell under US military occupation. The United States granted nominal independence to Cuba in 1902, after the Cubans formally adopted the Platt Amendment to their Constitution – an amendment written in Washington that granted the United States the right to invade Cuba when Washington deemed it necessary. Puerto Rico came to occupy a political no-man's land – neither independent nor an official US colony nor a US state, but nevertheless ruled by the United States. Meanwhile, the war proved to pro-expansionist politicians that if the United States were to become a major economic and military player on the world stage, it needed to move more quickly between the Pacific and Atlantic Oceans. President Roosevelt encouraged and aided pro-independence forces in the Colombian province of Panama to revolt against Bogota in 1903. The new country declared its independence, quickly won recognition from

Washington, and sold the United States a swath of land through central Panama. Immediately, the United States began construction of the Panama Canal. Cuba and Puerto Rico in the eastern Caribbean would serve as important defensive posts for the US Navy to guard entrance to the Caribbean and thus protect merchant and military transit through the canal.

These were neocolonial societies whereby the United States either controlled or strongly shaped all of them. Yet, while the new American empire tried to consolidate control in the Caribbean Basin, their empire was more porous than they would have liked. Despite efforts to prevent anarchists migrating to and through the region, anarchists arrived. Now, anarchists faced not just their traditional foes at the local and national levels, but also US political and military authorities. As a result, the anticolonialist message generated against Spanish rule during the Cuban independence war now took on an anti-imperialist tone regionwide as Caribbean anarchists became the first global anarchists to confront US foreign policy.

But anarchist organizing differed in strength across the Caribbean. In Cuba, where the largest anarchist presence existed, they were able to act autonomously without the need to work with non-anarchist unions. Outside Cuba, where the movement was smaller, anarchists sometimes fought against and other times worked with non-anarchist entities like Marxists, other progressives, and especially American Federation of Labor (AFL) affiliated unions. Yet, even while working with non-anarchists, they maintained important financial and communication linkages with the anarchist network hub in Havana.

In this chapter, we explore anarchist organizing and anti-American oppositional politics around the Caribbean in the two decades following the Cuban War for Independence, beginning with the arrival of celebrity anarchist Errico Malatesta in Havana in 1900. Then we turn to the challenges that Caribbean anarchists experienced in the decade and a half after the Cuban War: the dilemmas anarchists faced working with non-anarchist unions, how these dilemmas led to the origins of the first Latin Industrial Workers of the World (IWW) unions in the network, and how anarchists began to confront American authorities in US-controlled territories from Tampa to Panama. Throughout, we see the emergence of the newspaper ¡Tierra! in Havana in 1902 and how anarchists across the region began to use the newspaper as their key network propaganda and organizing tool.

THE POSTWAR STRAITS: MALATESTA AND ANARCHIST BUBIS IN CUBA

War's end in late 1898 ushered in a fluid political environment in Cuba in which various social sectors competed not only for the spoils of war but also to put their stamp on what a future, independent Cuba would look like. However, the United States was in no hurry to leave as debates raged in Washington on what to do with the new territories it had just acquired from Spain. The air of imperialism hung heavy in Havana over the coming years as US military governments controlled Cuba, while Cuban civil authorities and police did their bidding – usually to the detriment of workers generally and anarchists specifically.

While those working for the United States or supporting the occupation pointed to largely successful efforts to eradicate malaria and yellow fever, clean up Havana, and create a new education system, anarchists were less complimentary. By January 1899, Luis Barcia and Adrián del Valle had returned to Havana after spending the war in New York writing for the anarchist press. They immediately began publishing the newspaper *El Nuevo Ideal* just as the US occupation began in earnest. Del Valle and Barcia wasted no time attacking the United States. In the first issues of the newspaper, they decried occupation, with Barcia declaring Washington and President McKinley to be "the new tyrants." Both men compared Cuba with the Philippines, where Aguinaldo's armed insurrection continued fighting to liberate the archipelago from US rule.[1] Barcia suggested that forceful resistance was exactly the answer. After all, he noted, "if the Filipinos would have adopted a similar theory [be quiet, don't complain], the Americans by now would be in possession of every city on the archipelago, like in Cuba, yet now [thanks to Aguinaldo's resistance] the Americans only control the city of Manila." For Cubans who thought they could benefit from US control or at the very least should not do anything to antagonize the Americans, Barcia urged them to consider US history. North Americans had thirsted for new territories like California and Texas, while Anglos set about to "exterminate the red skins" in their quest for new lands. He warned that this would be Cuba's fate if people did not resist.[2]

Barcia reflected a growing theme in anarchist writing about the United States at the beginning of the twentieth century: For all its claims as a

---

[1] *El Nuevo Ideal*, February 4, 1899, 2; August 24, 1899, 2.   [2] Ibid., February 2, 1899, 1.

"model republic" whose systems should spread throughout the Americas, the United States was anything but friendly to – let alone a model for – the hemisphere's working masses. Del Valle repeatedly made this point, calling Washington "the false liberators" and stating that the "American republic, personification in principle of the democratic right that inspired the political radicalism of our age, today nourishes in its breast the same morbid passions as the European nations, with their thirst for territorial enlargement and wars of repression and conquest."[3]

Though Washington soon rejected efforts to annex Cuba, the continued presence of the US military, the growing investment of North American capital, and the increasing arrival of US culture troubled anarchists. Barcia charged that Cubans did not want a republic like the United States, where far too many workers had traveled to work, only to see how the American governing and business elite treated workers. Jovino Villar echoed Barcia's sentiments: "And this Republic called humane, civilized! ... Lies: How does it respond to these vain and lying praises? Chicago, yesterday [the Haymarket Affair]; today, the Philippines and Tampa; tomorrow...who knows what people, what class or what *raza*; and always, the black and the red skin, exterminated by the cruelest means ... the lynchings and other cruel punishments ... Humane republic!" J. Alonsín summed up: The United States's false image of liberty and democracy were truly represented by the Statue of Liberty – a statue that despite its symbolism "is hollow and lacks feeling."[4]

Y. A. Miqué's 1900 poem "Guajiro escarmentado" (Wary Guajiro) reflected the overall anarchist sentiment about the island in the first year of occupation. In the first stanza, Miqué assumes the point of view of the rural Cuban war veteran who sees the world from an anarchist perspective: "I am a Cuban *guajiro* / who yearns for freedom / and who fought to see my native land / free from all tyranny." But with a new imperial power in control and still no promise of land or social reform, he turns away and directs his attention toward social revolution: "With the machete in my hand / I fought day in and day out / and today it agonizes me to see / that those who rose to power have left me behind; / I will no longer struggle for them / but from this day on I will fight for Anarchy."[5]

On February 27, 1900, Italian anarchist Errico Malatesta arrived in Havana for a series of talks. His old friendship with Adrián del Valle,

---

[3] Ibid., March 25, 1899, 1.
[4] Ibid., February 11, 1899, 1–2; July 21, 1899, 1; February 2, 1899, 1.
[5] Ibid., January 26, 1900, 2. A *guajiro* was a rural peasant in Cuba.

whom he knew from meetings in Barcelona and London, paved the way for his trip to Cuba. The day after arriving, Malatesta attended a meeting of the Círculo de Trabajadores (Workers Circle), giving an interview to the press. The next night, minutes before his scheduled talk to a packed meeting hall at the Círculo, US military governor General Leonard Wood ordered civil governor Emilio Núñez to prohibit the anarchist from taking the stage. In a curious act of partial defiance to Wood, Núñez offered to withdraw the prohibition if Malatesta promised not to mention "anarchism" in his talks.[6] He agreed. He spoke about anarchism, but never uttered the word that night.

During his talks in Havana and Regla in March, Malatesta reinforced *El Nuevo Ideal*'s critiques of the United States as a model republic. He concluded his March 1 talk by reminding the audience that to understand the current Cuban climate, one had to look at more than just the US occupation. Cubans had thrown out the Spanish government but now "Spanish capitalists are still here exploiting the Cubans, and if [the Spanish capitalists] are thrown out, nothing will prevent Cubans from continuing to be subjugated by other capitalists – Cubans, Americans, or whatever nationality." *Cuba libre* in this postwar era "is not for Cubans but for the privileged who possess all of the wealth."[7] Two nights later, Malatesta returned to the Círculo podium where he spoke even more explicitly about the state of *Cuba libre*. "Here, in Cuba, there will be no shortage of men who will seek power, saying that they aspire to this position in order to help Cuba become independent and to do good for the people. These men will deceive the people," and only work for their own interests once in power. "The work of civilization and of freedom is not the work of governments but of the people, bolstered by conscientious minorities. Governments – defenders of privileged class interests – are, on the contrary, the main obstacles that systematically are opposed to the development of civilization and freedom."[8]

US and Cuban authorities were not amused. Malatesta had remained true to his word and not mentioned "anarchism," but Núñez could not overlook the thrust of his message. Malatesta clearly suggested the need to resist those who were taking power on the island. Next, Malatesta was

---

[6] *La Revista Blanca*, December 1, 1932, 1. This account draws from Adrián del Valle's thirty-two-year-old remembrance of Malatesta's visit. See also, *El Nuevo Ideal*, March 22, 1900, 1; Fernández, *Cuban Anarchism*, 42–43; and, Davide Turcato, "The Hidden History of the Anarchist Atlantic: Malatesta in America, 1899–1900," paper delivered at the European Social Science History Conference, Ghent, Belgium, April 2010.

[7] *El Nuevo Ideal*, March 9, 1900, 1–2.   [8] Ibid., March 29, 1900, 1; April 6, 1900, 1.

scheduled to speak on the origins and consequences of crime, but Núñez stepped in and prohibited the talk. This time he claimed that Malatesta had not obtained official permits to speak. To get around this ban, Malatesta attended labor meetings, and during the question period rose to speak.[9] On March 10, Malatesta left Cuba and traveled to New York, but he left behind several open letters, including one 'To the Cuban Workers' that appeared in *El Nuevo Ideal*. In one letter, Malatesta addressed both the Cuban civil and American military governments on the island as well as the class struggle unfolding whereby the rich were reaping the spoils of war. Noting that workers made up the bulk of the independence forces, he wrote how "it would be sad, profoundly sad if so much heroism and sacrifice will only serve to simply produce a change of masters, as has happened in other countries" and then to discover "that their own country's tyrants are as evil as the foreigners. And this is precisely the danger threatening Cuba, if the Cuban worker does not work quickly to stop it." In short, bourgeois Cubans were selling out the promised revolution.

Malatesta specifically warned about two types of Cubans of which to be wary. One was Cuban workers who believed that Spanish workers were stealing "Cuban" jobs. This was increasingly the line promoted by nationalist elements within the Cuban labor movement led by the prewar anarchist Enrique Messonier. "Guard yourselves against those Cuban workers who fall into the trap" of promoting nationalism, Malatesta warned. "The Spanish worker, who due to poverty or persecution had to abandon his country of birth, has the same reason to hate the Spanish government as the most persecuted Cubans; and, today he has as much interest in putting the brakes on bourgeois exploitation as any worker born in Cuba." The other Cubans to avoid were those seeking political office under American oversight. "Tomorrow, Cuban leaders will sweep aside the interests of their own children, as occurs in all 'independent' countries." Malatesta then foresaw the protectorate role that the United States would play in Cuba over the next thirty years, whereby the rich and political class "needs American protection in order to be able to safely exploit the energetic Cuban worker."[10]

There was only one path for Cuba, concluded Malatesta: "In order truly to be free, it is necessary to abolish not only this government or that,

---

[9] *La Revista Blanca*, December 1, 1932, 400–401.
[10] *El Nuevo Ideal*, March 22, 1900, 1. See also Fernández, *Cuban Anarchism*, 42–43 and Turcato, "The Hidden History of the Anarchist Atlantic."

but the institution of government itself." For those who asked, "how could we live without a government?" Del Valle responded in an adjacent column that such a question was often asked by "a poor man who by living *with* government lives *without* a shirt, working like a mule and usually going hungry." For those who would argue that without government there would be crime, hunger, poverty, etc., well, didn't all those things exist in societies *with* governments?

In the heady days of 1900, with various camps positing their own visions of Cuba's future, perhaps it was Manuel Miranda who offered up one of the most intriguing anarchist visions. After being deported to Fernando Póo in 1896 following General Weyler's crackdowns, Miranda devoted considerable time to studying the native Bubis on the island. Miranda described Bubi culture that – with a few exceptions – epitomized many anarchist romantic ideals of living cooperatively in nature. The Bubis did not punish their children. They grew simple foods and ate most of what they grew. They made oil that they traded to Europeans. "They worked the land communally, under the direction of the most intelligent." Polygamy was widely practiced, but adultery was severely punished with amputation of a hand. Meanwhile, all went about nude and in harmony with the elements. Solidarity seemed to reign among the Bubis; when Miranda gave a cookie to one Bubi, he proceeded to break it into little pieces to distribute evenly to all his friends. When Miranda told him that the cookie was his, the Bubi gathered all the pieces, gave them back to Miranda, and explained that the Bubis "could not eat or drink something alone without sharing it with all who were present." While all of this – except punishments for adultery – might have found sympathy in an anarchist worldview, the political dynamics were also appealing. There was only minimal government, and the king – a nominal figure – lived far removed from the population. Thus, Miranda concluded for his Havana readers, the Bubis who still lived in the forest were a people apathetic toward politics and lived a life of moderation with no hint of egoism, no thirst for becoming property owners, nor for "the vices that consume those rogues educated by the priests."[11] In short, the Bubis lived in solidarity, with no private property, limited or no government, and devoid of the poisons perpetrated by the Church. Could Cuba be Bubified?

---

[11] *El Nuevo Ideal*, April 20, 1900, 4. Miranda published the Fernando Póo columns from *El Nuevo Ideal* as the book *Memorias de un deportado* in 1903. Unfortunately, not long after writing these columns in early 1900, Miranda and his *compañera* Elena Peñalver lost their infant daughter to an undisclosed illness. *El Nuevo Ideal*, June 14, 1900, 2.

No, probably not, but resistance had to continue, nonetheless. Anarchists observed no shortage of problems that they often linked with the military occupation. In the countryside, waves of banditry swept through the island in the years immediately following the war. Some who fought for Cuba's freedom had expected material benefits in the form of land. Others expected their efforts would be rewarded with a social revolution. When neither materialized, some turned to banditry either to make a living, as a political statement to bring pain to those who violated promises of land reform and social revolution, or both.[12] Cuba's mainstream press condemned the return of bandit groups. But anarchists urged caution and to think carefully about the government's and the media's choice of words. "Careful, colleagues. Remember that bandits are what those who first rose in arms against Spain were called, and they were slandered. Will history repeat itself?"[13] What was a bandit and what was a rebel? These were not criminals, *El Nuevo Ideal* insisted. These "bandits" in Santiago de Cuba, Holguín, and Havana Province were pushed to violence by hunger. Palmiro de Lidia concluded that, "for my part, I frankly declare that between the beggar who begs and the *bandolero* who demands, I'm with the latter."[14]

Hunger was not the poor Cuban's only concern. In the cities, there was a shortage of adequate, affordable housing. In June 1899 – just six months into the occupation – anarchists called for a rent strike. They demanded revamped interior spaces, a new coat of whitewash every six months to clean and disinfect, showers installed, lights in corridors and patios for protection, windows for air, and more. With those reforms, people would return to paying rent.[15] A year later, no progress had been made so anarchists revised their demands to include a 35 percent rent reduction, abolishment of the practice of having to come up with the first month's rent and a rent deposit, for all repairs to be made to residences, for every renter to have a key to the front door leading onto the street, abolishment of the practice of locking the doors after 11 p.m. to prevent residents from leaving or entering, and outfitting of all residences with bathrooms, kitchens, and sufficient water.[16] But nothing seems to have transpired. Two years after the initial demands for change and threats of a

---

[12] For an excellent overview of Cuba's bandit history during these years, see Rosalie Schwartz, *Lawless Liberators: Political Banditry and Cuban Independence* (Durham, NC: Duke University Press, 1989).
[13] *El Nuevo Ideal*, April 8, 1899, 3.   [14] Ibid., April 22, 1899, 1.
[15] Ibid., June 2, 1899, 1; June 9, 1899, 2.   [16] Ibid., July 20, 1900, 1; July 27, 1900, 2.

rent strike, anarchists proposed another solution. They claimed that workers in the Cuban communities of Bejucal and Santiago de las Vegas, as well as in Tampa, were building comfortable, hygienic houses themselves. Maybe it was time for Havana's workers to do the same – a suggestion that seems to have fallen on deaf ears.[17]

Cuba gained formal political independence on May 20, 1902. However, political chaos returned in 1906 when the Liberal and Conservative parties rose up in civil war. Invoking the Platt Amendment, the United States invaded and ran Cuba again until 1909. During the three-year military occupation, anarchists derided the Cuban government's "democratic" pretenses, portraying politicians as conniving to win workers' votes and then turning their backs on those workers. Combined with a critique of Cuba's independence and self-rule, this portrayal of Cuban republicanism was also a critique of the United States since it had been the model for the political system. Anarchists on the island drew from the earlier critiques of American democracy enunciated by their comrades in Tampa in the 1890s. All it took was a brief violent episode to usher in US forces to illustrate how frail that system was and who held real power. Politicians who deceived the Cuban people for their votes were the same politicians whose actions brought forth the US invasion. The Cuban masses who had fought for true independence and social revolution found neither.[18]

During the second occupation, American authorities intensified surveillance and repression against anarchists. For instance, relying on a growing number of Havana police informants, occupation authorities feared that anarchists were responsible for new waves of agitation and planned bombings. American authorities were concerned about anarchists who they saw as taking Cuban jobs, sowing dissent in the working class, and creating instability for employers. Also, US occupation officers and their Cuban colleagues temporarily thwarted an islandwide anarchist propaganda tour when authorities arrested Marcial Lores and Abelardo Saavedra, who had just arrived from Spain. In response, anarchists condemned the military government of Charles Magoon, comparing him to former military governor Leonard Wood, who had restricted Malatesta's speaking engagements in 1900. In fact, Magoon had just arrived

---

[17] Ibid., June 26, 1901, 183.
[18] ¡Tierra!, November 10, 1906, 3; Kirwin Shaffer, "Contesting Internationalists: Transnational Anarchism, Anti-imperialism, and US Expansion in the Caribbean, 1890s–1930s," *Estudios Interdisciplinarios de América Latina y el Caribe* 22, no. 2 (2011): 22.

in Cuba after successfully overseeing the early years of the Panama Canal's construction, where he had worked to keep anarchists out of the Canal Zone.[19]

Throughout the first decade of Cuba's post-Spanish era, North American agribusiness spread across the island. The increase brought new workers from throughout Cuba, Spain, and the Caribbean to work in agriculture. Cuba's rural areas grew faster than its cities.[20] As a result, anarchists moved to these new economic zones and began organizing. For instance, in 1910, Saavedra moved his paper ¡Rebelión! from the port city of Regla to the central Cuban city of Cruces. There, in the heart of US sugar plantations, he established a Workers Center and disseminated anarchist propaganda. At the same time, Havana-based anarchists believed that these expanding areas were ripe for agitation. Soon, large amounts of money poured into Havana from rural-based radicals in sugar mills or from interior cities in the sugar and tobacco regions.[21]

By mid-1914, President Mario Menocal hoped to quiet growing anarchist radicalism with a series of labor laws, a government-sponsored labor congress, and a committee designed to explore labor problems. Anarchists rejected these piecemeal reforms as mere ploys to gain working-class votes just when anarchist labor activism seemed to be making progress. Menocal was in a bind. On one hand, workers demanded better conditions and wages. On the other hand, North American capitalists demanded that the government clamp down on radicals. If he did nothing – or too little – then Washington could invoke the Platt Amendment, invade again, and suspend his government. If he used violence, he could be accused of being a North American lackey. By late summer 1914, Menocal acted. The army moved against anarchists in Cruces and Havana. Included in this round-up and deportation were Saavedra, Vicente Lípiz, and Juan Tur, the editor of the anarchist weekly

---

[19] Letter from Inspector General of Jails, Penitentiary & Charitable Institutions to Gov. Magoon on Detention of Marcial Lores García and Abelardo Saavedra, May 5, 1907; Memo to the Chief of Staff from Captain John Furlong, December 28, 1907; Memo to the Chief of Staff on Havana Strike Conditions from Captain John Furlong, December 20, 1907. All from Record Group 199, Records of the Provisional Government: "Confidential" Correspondence, 1906–1909, National Archives, Washington, DC; ¡Tierra!, December 15, 1906, 1; June 12, 1907, 1; Shaffer, "Contesting Internationalists," 22.
[20] Mark Smith, "The Political Economy of Sugar Production and the Environment of Eastern Cuba, 1898–1923," *Environmental History Review* 19, no. 4 (1995): 39–45; Louis A. Pérez, *Cuba: Between Reform and Revolution* (New York: Oxford University Press, 1988), 225; Shaffer, *Anarchism and Countercultural Politics*, 73 and 150–153.
[21] Shaffer, "Havana Hub," 57–60.

newspaper *¡Tierra!*. In January 1915, they were deported to Spain, and with their departures *¡Tierra!* closed.[22]

With the deportations of anarchists and the government's closure of *¡Tierra!*, Cuba's anarchists found themselves in difficult circumstances. The anarcho-syndicalist *El Dependiente* and naturist journal *Pro-Vida* continued publishing. But a year into the repression, anarchists still lamented the Cuban "Crusade against the Anarchists" rooted in some trumped-up nationalism. "The black ghost of foreignism, conveniently planted by the bourgeoisie, is one of the greatest difficulties that trips up the advance of new ideas. Everyone who tries to spread propaganda for freedom and says 'Rebel,' is met by a son of the old exploiters of labor who replies with satisfaction: 'We are in *Cuba libre*,'" so why do we need to rebel? We're already free. It was no different when an anarchist tried to organize workers only to be confronted by "that stupid mass [who shouts] 'To Spain, to Spain with him where he can fix that part of the world because here [in Cuba] we have fixed ourselves!' and they tranquilly returned to their work, so happy and satisfied" as if no crimes had been committed since the days of colonial tyranny under General Weyler. After all, they continued, this is *Cuba libre* and we have elections and we have a regular change of government. But, concluded the anarchist F. Iglesias, "in no other place is changing the government so demonstrably useless as in Cuba." Were US-style republican politics really any better than a monarchy? Wasn't Cuba still little more than a colonial outpost but this time in a new US empire? The same tyranny, the same unthinking people. As Iglesias lamented, "Cuba has retreated to colonial times."[23]

LUIS BARCIA AND *LA RESISTENCIA* IN TAMPA

While anarchists in Cuba dealt with repeated US military occupations, anarchists in Florida had different concerns – how to work for improved working-class conditions as foreign workers in *Yanquilandia*. Of course, as anarchists migrated back and forth across the Straits, they were moving back and forth between a neocolonial setting in Cuba and what to many

---

[22] Amparo Sánchez Cobos, *Sembrando Ideales: Anarquistas españoles en Cuba (1902–1925)* (Madrid: Consejo Superior de Investigaciones Científicas, 2008), 281. The Puerto Rico-born anarchist Luisa Capetillo was in Havana at this time and was rounded up with her colleagues; however, she escaped deportation, which allowed her to continue to agitate for anarchism in the city.

[23] *Voluntad*, January 17, 1916, 1–2. For a similar critique of those who thought *Cuba libre* meant all was well, see *Voluntad*, March 13, 1916, 1.

amounted to internal colonialism in Florida. In the first three years following the US victory against Spain in 1898, two great labor conflicts erupted among the peninsula's tobacco workers: the 1899 Huelga de Pesa (Strike of the Scales) and a series of strikes in mid-1901. At the end of the nineteenth century, most Ybor City cigar makers remained unorganized. In 1899, managers at the Martínez Ybor factory tried to increase their control over the production process by limiting a specific weight of leaf used to roll a specific number of cigars. Workers interpreted the new weight measures as an attack on their skill, custom, and artisanship. The new policy also undermined cigar rollers' practice of rolling extra cigars for their own enjoyment. This was about power and autonomy in the workplace. When owners rebuffed workers' demands for more leaf, the cigar makers went on strike, demanding the scales be removed.[24]

The strike reflected broader, trans-Straits solidarity that anarchists in Florida and Cuba had forged during the war. Luis Barcia helped to spearhead this effort. By March 1899 he had left Havana and settled in Tampa, working for the Sociedad General de Trabajadores (General Society of Workers). By April, most of the money that funded Havana's *El Nuevo Ideal* that he and Adrián del Valle founded earlier that year came from Tampa thanks largely to Barcia's organizing efforts.[25] Barcia then called on Cuban workers to raise money to help Tampa strikers. "For now, our resources are enough to take care of necessities; but, if the situation becomes graver ... we will need the effective assistance of our Cuban brothers," urged Barcia.[26]

In July, owners throughout Tampa locked out some 4000 tobacco workers. At del Valle's urging, Havana painters, carpenters, and members of other unions joined tobacco workers throughout Cuba to raise thousands of dollars for a strike fund.[27] While the Spanish and American factory owners united to lock out the tobacco workers in Tampa, and while they had the full backing of the city's Chamber of Commerce and the Anglo establishment, the trans-Straits anarchist propaganda and revenue raising showed owners that the nearly four-month-old strike could continue indefinitely. Clearly, the owners had underestimated these transnational workers' power. Instead of breaking

---

[24] Durward Long, "'La Resistencia': Tampa's Immigrant Labor Union," *Labor History* 6 (1965): 195; Mormino and Pozzetta. "Spanish Anarchism in Tampa," 188.
[25] *El Nuevo Ideal*, April 8, 1899, 6.
[26] Ibid., May 20, 1899, 4. For similar language, see *El Nuevo Ideal*, July 28, 1899, 1.
[27] Ibid., July 14, 1899, 1; July 21, 1899, 1 and 3; August 17, 1899, 3; August 24, 1899, 3.

the workers, the lock out energized them, and workers held the line. In August, the owners conceded. They removed the scales, established a uniform pricing system for cigars, and allowed workers to have representative committees in each factory. Thus, victory relied significantly on Barcia and del Valle's anarchist efforts to get workers throughout Cuba to aid *compañeros* in Florida.

The victorious workers immediately formed La Sociedad de Torcedores de Tampa (The Tampa Cigar Rollers Society – aka, La Resistencia).[28] The union organized cigar industry workers, bakers, restaurant workers, porters, and laundry workers – in short, anyone who needed to stand up to their bosses to improve their conditions. The union published *La Federación* from April 1900 to August 1901, usually in Spanish, but sometimes with columns translated into English and Italian, reflecting the union's multiethnic make-up.[29] While 1058 Cubans, 455 Spaniards, and 289 Italians were members in April 1900, these figures grew to 1558, 550, and 310, respectively, by November. The union's membership lists also included workers from the United States, Mexico, Puerto Rico, the Canary Islands, the Dominican Republic, England, and Germany.[30] Yet, some Cuban workers in Tampa felt threatened by the large presence of non-Cubans. While worker solidarity may have been strong enough to help win the 1899 strike, some workers consistently fell back on nationalistic sentiments and intraclass antagonisms. In February 1900, some Cubans at the Martínez Ybor and Manrara factories left La Resistencia and formed the rival union La Liga Obrera de Tampa (The Tampa Labor League) to organize only Cubans in Florida.

Into this growing schism arrived Errico Malatesta on his way to Havana. Delaying his departure to Havana, Malatesta extended his stay in Tampa to help resolve the conflict between La Resistencia and La Liga as well as the related ethnic tensions between Cuban and Spanish cigar rollers. As Davide Turcato writes, Malatesta concluded that Tampa's workers "displayed a remarkable combativeness, but their effectiveness was hindered by political and patriotic divisions." As Malatesta left, La Resistencia renewed its closed-shop initiative, further straining relations

---

[28] Long, "'La Resistencia,'" 195–196; Mormino and Pozzetta, "Spanish Anarchism in Tampa," 189.
[29] See copies of *La Federación*, whose subtitled name was "Official Organ of the Cigar Rollers, Strippers and Sectors of Tampa," despite its efforts to appeal to non-tobacco workers.
[30] For the April figures, see *La Federación*, April 27, 1900, 2–4; for November, see Mormino and Pozzetta, "Spanish Anarchism in Tampa," 189.

with La Liga.[31] La Resistencia urged workers of all nationalities to see that La Liga's Cuban-only organizing was undermining the growing power of the union movement. *La Federación* advised former belligerents in the recent war "to unchain themselves from those former passions abroad." This meant not fighting for crumbs that the capitalists give "in order to take advantage" of you but instead to fight the capitalist "who has no other country than his coin purse."[32]

While La Resistencia appealed to Spanish and Cuban workers in Tampa to work together, it also tried to strengthen ties to the workers' movement in Havana. In 1893, anarchists in Havana and New York had jointly chosen and funded two delegates for an international anarchist conference in Chicago with the expectation that delegates would reflect the interests of all anarchists in those cities. Because anarchists tended to move back and forth between these two cities, the selection of joint representation made sense.[33] Anarchists planned another conference, this time in Paris in mid-1900. Building on the 1893 precedent, *La Federación* urged workers in Havana and Tampa to choose a common delegate and recommended Manuel María Miranda, who had recently returned to Cuba from Fernando Póo.[34] Consequently, just as some Cubans were causing trouble by forming La Liga and other disputes were blamed on lingering Cuban–Spanish animosity, *La Federación* urged all workers across the Straits to rally around a Cuban anarchist hero from the war years as the international representative of the region's tobacco workers to the Paris conference.

Nevertheless, attempts to calm the conflict went unheeded. In March 1900, *La Federación* accused La Liga's leaders of being agents in the service of factory owners. If true – or even possible, warned *La Federación* – then La Liga's members would have to make a choice: "To one side the honorable, and to the other the depraved!"[35] Then in April, all but twenty-nine workers who wanted to join La Liga walked out of the La Rosa Española factory. Anarchists warned dissenters that refusing to join the strike played into owners' hands. In manifestos, they urged La Liga supporters to drop their nationalistic pro-Cuban sentiment and join the

---

[31] Davide Turcato, *Making Sense of Anarchism: Errico Malatesta's Experiments with Revolution, 1889–1900* (New York: Palgrave Macmillan, 2012), 206–208.

[32] *La Federación*, February 16, 1900, 2.

[33] See Pedro Esteve, *Memoria de la conferencia anarquista internacional: Celebrada en Chicago en septiembre de 1893. A los anarquistas de España y Cuba* (Paterson, NJ: El Despertar, 1900).

[34] *La Federación*, February 16, 1900, 3.   [35] Ibid., March 16, 1900, 1–2.

strike.[36] As the newspaper put it: "There are no longer any Cubans, Spaniards, Italians, Americans, but only workers united in resistance societies willing to defend together the principle that is common to all."[37] By mid-May, tensions eased when La Liga and La Resistencia members signed a joint manifesto to end the dispute. They were "alarmed by the dismal future that workers can expect in this locality if they continue this division between brothers who suffer equally the exploitations of capital." The unions then merged.[38]

The anarchists had won. Or so it seemed, because soon a new labor feud erupted – this time between La Resistencia and a third union in Tampa: the Cigar Makers International Union (aka the CMIU or simply the International). La Resistencia and the CMIU formally had agreed to not recruit members away from each other. However, the CMIU began recruiting La Resistencia tobacco leaf strippers in the Argüelles factory. La Resistencia declared that the CMIU had broken the pact and urged all workers to support La Resistencia. A battle then engulfed the factories as neither union permitted its members to work next to the other's members, each urged employers to fire workers from the other union, and La Resistencia threatened to call a general strike.[39]

In November, Tampa's anarchists began to publish a second newspaper, *La Voz del Esclavo*. Both anarchist newspapers charged CMIU with complicity with factory owners and the police. *La Voz del Esclavo* offered evidence in December when it commented on a letter from a CMIU local that had been published in a recent edition of the socialist *Daily People*. The letter proclaimed the CMIU to be a "'conservative organization,' whereas La Resistencia is depicted as a revolutionary affair, a body of 'malcontents.'" The CMIU consisted of "'American workingmen'" and "'the La Resistencia body consists of non-American workingmen [and] imported agitators.'" The CMIU letter concluded that it was a better union for employers because it required a national vote of members before going out on strike, thus the CMIU "'is a better friend to

---

[36] "Gremio de Torcedores de Tampa: Manifiesto." Tampa, April 11, 1900; and "Los obreros huelguistas del taller de Ellinge. A LOS TRABAJADORES," Tampa, May 13, 1900. Max Nettlau Collection. Regions and Countries. North America. United States of America, folder 3385 (hereafter referred to as Nettlau-North America). International Institute of Social History, Amsterdam.

[37] Quoted in Long, "La Resistencia," 198.

[38] "OBREROS DE LA. 'Sociedad de Torcedores' y de 'La Liga Obrera' DE TAMPA." Tampa, May 17, 1900. Nettlau-North America.

[39] Long, "La Resistencia," 199–200.

you than a local Union like La Resistencia,' which 'can vacate your tables on an instant's notice' and thus 'damage your best interest.'" While the evidence was certainly slim, *La Voz del Esclavo*'s point was made: the CMIU was run by "the Labor Lieutenants of Capital" willing to undermine fellow workers to gain the good graces of the bosses.[40] Its leaders temporarily chagrined by the damning letter, the CMIU backed down in December, and La Resistencia expanded its membership drives to Key West and Havana.[41] However, this temporary victory lasted less than a year before Tampa's Anglo business and political establishment attacked the anarchist union head-on.

SHANGHAIING ANARCHISTS

Like most of Anglo America, Tampa's white elite feared foreign anarchists at the turn of the century. Anarchists, some of whom had lived and worked in their midst, plotted to assassinate General Weyler in Cuba during the war. The Italian anarchist Michele Angiolillo, who killed Cánovas del Castillo, had links to anarchists in New York and New Jersey. Anarchists targeted prominent businessmen in the United States, like Henry Frick, chair of the Carnegie Steel Company, who survived an assassination attempt by Alexander Berkman in 1892. That La Resistencia was also an immigrant union composed of foreigner anarchists further made Tampa's elite squeamish. In addition, anarchists preached cross-national and cross-racial unity, making appeals to people of color. White elites felt threatened by this, especially as efforts to enforce racial segregation gained speed in Tampa.[42] It should come as no surprise, then, that the city fathers' nativist agendas often found expression in physical assaults; anarchists frequently suffered the brunt of these attacks.

In May 1901, La Resistencia led a successful strike that forced city elders to establish a new streetcar line and repair an unsafe bridge linking Ybor City and West Tampa. Emboldened by their success, the union

---

[40] *La Voz del Esclavo*, November 17, 1900, 2; *La Federación*, December 14, 1900, 4. Some years later, Julián González, a Cuban-born cigar roller who went to Tampa in February 1896, remembered these two unions. He called the CMIU a highly centralized, anti-Latin, "American," and "practical" union that opposed the "Latin" and "radical" decentralized La Resistencia. Julián González, *El tabaquero en Tampa: Impresiones personales* (Havana: Rambla y Bouza, 1907), 1–14.
[41] Long, "La Resistencia," 202.
[42] For a brilliant and insightful look at conflicting issues of race, class, gender, and ethnicity in Tampa, one should consult N. Hewitt's *Southern Discomfort: Women's Activism in Tampa, Florida, 1880s–1920s* (Urbana: University of Illinois Press, 2001).

FIGURE 2.1 Luis Barcia: Tampa's leading anarchist in the post-Cuban War years. Centro Asturiano (Tampa)

declared a general strike on July 26 to stop owners from building branch factories in Jacksonville and Pensacola. That touched a nerve among community elites. Who were these foreigners to tell Americans what to do with their property? The leading newspaper *Morning Tribune* opined that it was time for citizens to stand up against the foreigners. An Anglo-led Citizens Committee soon emerged to remove agitators from the city.[43] The Citizens Committee's most notorious act targeted the most prominent anarchist in Florida: Luis Barcia (Figure 2.1).

For nearly forty years, Barcia was a mainstay on the Latin anarchist circuit between Havana, Florida, and New York. In 1879, the thirteen-year-old Barcia arrived in Havana from his home in Spanish Galicia. For years he wondered around the island working as a store clerk, a printer, and a cigar maker. His itinerant labor experience led him to lament the state of workers in colonial Cuba – a state that he claimed after working for poverty wages as a *dependiente* (store clerk) "was total slavery, worse, even, to what the poor negroes had. At least the negro slaves could rest at night and during holidays, and they also enjoyed special days."[44] Soon he

---

[43] Long, "La Resistencia," 202–206; "A LOS TRABAJADORES," May 24, 1901, Nettlau-North America; Hewitt, *Southern Discomfort*, 127–128; Mormino and Pozzetta, "Spanish Anarchism in Tampa," 190.
[44] Luis Barcia Quilabert, "Autobiography of Luis Barcia Quilabert" (unpublished manuscript), University of South Florida Special Collections Department. Tampa, Florida, 5–14, typed, handbound book.

moved to Havana, where he worked as a typesetter and began to read anarchist literature. For a short time, he worked as a cigar roller, where he heard more anarchist literature read aloud on the factory floor. By early 1891, Barcia had moved to New York and was one of the original nine members who founded the Grupo Parsons, one of the city's few Spanish-speaking anarchist groups that took its name from Albert Parsons, a Haymarket Martyr. Along with anarchists Manuel Martínez Abello and J.C. Campos, Barcia and the group launched *El Despertar*, the first Spanish-language anarchist newspaper in the United States, with Barcia and Campos as editors.

Once his New York City employers discovered they had a foreign anarchist agitator in their midst, they fired him. On December 19, 1891, Barcia boarded the *Alexandria* with several friends and steamed back to Havana.[45] From Cuba, he sent reports on the status of the Cuban independence movement.[46] When hostilities erupted in February 1895, Barcia was working in Tampa with *El Esclavo*, which he typeset. In 1896 he served on the Central Strike Committee that targeted the Martínez Ybor factory in Tampa, once again placing himself front-and-center in the anarchist cause among the immigrant workers and radicals.[47] In March 1898, Barcia met up with his old friend, the anarchist writer Adrián del Valle, in New York City. The two had known each other and worked together at *El Despertar* in 1891 and again in Cuba before the outbreak of war. With the war entering its third year, del Valle and Barcia launched another anarchist newspaper, *El Rebelde*, that condemned US imperialism after Washington declared war on Spain in April 1898. At war's end, in November 1898, Barcia left for Havana with his daughter and his pregnant wife Carolina. Del Valle soon followed.[48] Once in Havana, the two created the anarchist *El Nuevo Ideal*.[49] Unlike del Valle, who remained in Cuba until his death in 1945, Barcia soon returned to Tampa. In 1900, he was a printer for *La Federación* and began writing for *La Voz del Esclavo*.[50] In the eyes of Tampa's Anglo establishment, here was a

---

[45] *El Despertar*, August 1, 1891, 1; January 1, 1892, 1. For an overview of the paper's early years and beyond, see Castañeda's "Times of Propaganda and Struggle" and Barcia's "Autobiography of Luis Barcia," 25–26.
[46] *El Despertar*, January 15, 1892, 1–2.
[47] *El Esclavo*, March 16, 1895, 2; *El Despertar*, November 20, 1896, 4; "Autobiography of Luis Barcia," 30.
[48] *El Rebelde*, November 19, 1898, 2; "Autobiography of Luis Barcia," 32–33.
[49] Shaffer, *Anarchism and Countercultural Politics*, 45.
[50] *La Voz del Esclavo*, August 23, 1900, 1.

foreign anarchist linked to two local anarchist newspapers and writing for a third in Havana. Tampa's elite said enough was enough. As La Resistencia launched its July 1901 general strike, the city elders sprang into action with the intention of ridding the city of radicals – especially Barcia – once and for all.

Ten days into the strike, the Central Committee met at the Union Commercial Company building. Without warning, Tampa police and the Citizens Committee swooped into the meeting, seized a large amount of strike funds, and beat committee members. Other police threw stones at the leaders' homes, breaking windows and causing general pandemonium.[51] Tampa officials then closed the striking workers' soup kitchens. Merchants refused credit and raised the prices of goods. Union funds deposited in a local bank were frozen. When someone tried to withdraw strike funds, the bank notified police, who arrived to arrest the man. Workers began to leave the city in search of work in New York, New Orleans, Key West, and Havana. The future looked particularly bleak when the Liga de Trabajadores de Cuba (Cuban Workers League) in Havana refused to loan money to the strikers.[52] Were this not enough, the police then apprehended thirteen union leaders, and, without charging them with a crime, put the men on board the ship *Marie Cooper*. Besides Barcia, some of the deported included the Puerto Rican union leader Pedro Casellas, African American worker Charles Kelly, and José Fueyo, soon to be a regular columnist in the Havana anarchist press.[53]

Letters about the persecutions and deportations arrived in Havana, including one to Adrián del Valle informing him of the Anglo treachery. Havana's Comité de Auxilios (Support Committee), which had raised money for the 1899 Tampa strike, held a rally at which twenty anarchists spoke against the abuses and deportations.[54] That same month, del Valle and others embarked on a propaganda tour across Cuba to raise money for Tampa's strikers and for the families of those deported.[55] Meanwhile, La Resistencia redoubled its efforts, and *La Federación* went on the offensive. In a column addressed to "the citizens of Tampa," *La Federación* portrayed Tampa as "the dregs of the United States, and in her the

---

[51] *El Despertar*, September 1901, 1.
[52] Long, "La Resistencia," 207–209; "Autobiography of Luis Barcia," 52.
[53] Hewitt, *Southern Discomfort*, 128; *La Federación*, "Suplemento a La Federación de Tampa, Fla.," September 10, 1901 (note that the supplement says "10 agosto 1901," which is impossible because it contains some of the deported men's letters dated August 16, 1901).
[54] *El Nuevo Ideal*, August 14, 1901, 228–229.   [55] Ibid., August 21, 1901, 239.

barbarians of the North rule." Then the paper warned the city's elite to return "our *compañeros* healthy and safe"; otherwise, Tampa's workers would leave, and the bourgeois economy would collapse.[56] Not a bad threat if you could pull it off.

After almost a month, details of the deported radicals' fate began to emerge. Tampa businessmen who helped to coordinate and fund the Citizens Committee had paid $10,000 to the police to kidnap the men and pay for the ship to carry them away from the United States.[57] Then on September 10, the world heard from the deported workers for the first time in a series of letters written in mid-August and published in a special four-page supplement printed by *La Federación*. The editor introduced the letters by noting that now Tampa could join Barcelona (Montjuïc) and Chicago (Haymarket), where the state committed egregious abuses against workers.

A police squad had surrounded Barcia's house at 2:00 a.m. on August 5, beat on the door, and ordered him to come out. He refused. The police again knocked on the door, and this time Barcia said that if they wanted him they could wait until it was light out. Right then he was lying with his wife, who had given birth just three days earlier. As he recalled decades later, the baby "according to Carola [Carolina] had to be fed with her breast milk poisoned by the so-called citizens of Tampa." If the police wanted him at that moment, they would have to break down the door. "And that's what they did," Barcia noted. "They grabbed me to which I protested in the name of the Constitution and the human rights, which were ignored by the assassins and their masters." They put him in a carriage, and then the squad traveled to Fueyo's home and locked him up in a separate carriage. During daylight hours, Fueyo, Barcia, and other detainees were secured in an abandoned rail car.

Under cover of darkness, police took the detainees to the dock, where more than fifteen well-dressed men with pistols forced them to board the *Marie Cooper*. They sailed for seven days and eight nights, filled with angst and confusion, before its captain dropped them on a beach at Cape Gracias a Dios on the Honduran–Nicaraguan border – some 700 miles from Tampa. The captain had off-loaded them in the middle of the night with a few cans of corned beef, ham, and coffee to last a day. They lacked

---

[56] *La Federación*, August 24, 1901, 2–3.
[57] Ibid., "Suplemento a La Federación de Tampa, Fla.," September 10, 1901. See also: Long, "La Resistencia," 207–209; Mormino and Pozzetta, "Spanish Anarchism in Tampa," 190; Hewitt, *Southern Discomfort*, 128.

any change of clothing, much money, or even shoes. They did have a gun, though, purchased from one of the armed men aboard the ship. With these few provisions, they made their way to Trujillo, Honduras, where the shanghaied comrades telegraphed friends in Tampa to let them know they were safe, but authorities intercepted the telegram and did not deliver it. They also lacked enough money to pay for passage home. Their salvation? The US government, according to Barcia. "[T]he United States Consul loaned us some money," which they then paid back upon returning to Florida, adding some Havana cigars "rolled from free tobacco leaves that each cigar maker is allotted by the factory for personal use." So, essentially, Florida workers thanked the US government official in Honduras for helping their anarchist comrades to get home. Strange ironies indeed.

Some of the deported anarchists wondered what the future would hold for the workers in Tampa. Barcia, influenced by his long support of anarchist violence, thought armed struggle might be in that future. For those who believed that real change could come from peaceful strikes, maybe it was time to rethink that position. Future strikes were likely to be met with more violence. Thus, it was now necessary "to arm each and every striker with a rifle to fight force with force." The true lesson to draw here, Barcia concluded, was that "[i]f the strike had been more turbulent, it is likely that [the Citizens Committee] would have been less daring than they have been." In short, to prevent future abuses like those witnessed that August in 1901, workers and anarchists had to be prepared to use violence to assert their demands and protect themselves and their families.[58]

Tampa's elite would have none of this, nor would Anglo America in general. Barcia's calls to violence could not have been more poorly timed. While he wrote the letter on August 17, it was not published until September 10. Four days earlier, a lone, unaffiliated anarchist had assassinated US President William McKinley. Public perception, especially in Tampa, began to see all foreign workers as potential anarchists. The *Daily Tribune* even warned Tampans that the very anarchistic elements who killed McKinley were operating in their fair city.[59]

---

[58] All information from this account was derived from the letters reprinted in *La Federación*, "Suplemento a La Federación de Tampa, Fla.," September 10, 1901; and from "Autobiography of Luis Barcia," 41–55.

[59] Long, "La Resistencia," 213. Barcia only returned to Tampa many years later. Upon leaving Key West, he went to Guanabacoa, Cuba and then to St. Augustine, Florida, where he became a source of fundraising for the new anarchist weekly in Havana,

In New York, *El Despertar* urged readers to lend their aid to La Resistencia, but the paper soon received word that strikebreakers were arriving in Tampa.⁶⁰ Manufacturers successfully recruited tobacco workers from Key West, Havana, and elsewhere, taking advantage of strikes and unemployment in those cities. But the complicity of CMIU workers serving as strikebreakers was perhaps the most galling to the anarchists. Samuel Gompers and the AFL refused La Resistencia's request for aid because the anarchist-based union did not, in Gompers's eyes, conform to North American trade unionism. With strike funds running low and their jobs quickly being lost to AFL strikebreakers, La Resistencia threw in the towel. The strike ended in December 1901. The mortally wounded La Resistencia limped forward into the new year. However, in early 1902, Tampa's immigrant anarchist union and its newspaper folded.⁶¹

The fall of La Resistencia reverberated across the Straits to Cuba. With the Florida union crippled in late 1901, less money arrived in Havana and *El Nuevo Ideal* ceased publication. In a sense, US Anglo persecution against Luis Barcia in Florida in 1901 also brought down the newspaper that Barcia had helped to found in Havana in 1899. But beginning in late 1902, Tampa's anarchists found a new communication outlet when they linked themselves as strongly as ever with anarchists in Havana. In November, the Havana-based anarchist group ¡Tierra! began publishing its weekly newspaper. Until it folded in 1915, *¡Tierra!* collected money from Tampa and published regular columns from the city. The Havana newspaper became the voice of Florida's Spanish-speaking anarchist community, thus continuing the link between the Florida node of the Caribbean network and the emerging radical hub in Cuba.

¡Tierra!. Meanwhile, another deportee – Félix Menéndez – returned to Tampa only to be kidnapped again by the Citizens Committee. See: "Autobiography of Luis Barcia," 55–59; "Manifiesto a los Obreros y al Pueblo de Tampa en general," Tampa Microform Reel N53, University of South Florida Library.

[60] New York's *El Despertar* issued a manifesto that proclaimed the deportations as without equal: "We are going to narrate to you a story such as has not had an equal since the world's creation. It is so exceptional, that we fear not being believed." The paper portrayed the kidnappings as more infamous than even the Haymarket Square events. See *El Despertar*, September 10, 1901, 1.

[61] Long, "La Resistencia," 211–213. Anarchist agitation and activity in South Florida fell for years to come. Some anarchists aligned with the CMIU and published in the CMIU newspaper, *El Internacional*. Barcia claimed years later that this was "a big mistake," in part because black members of La Resistencia could not join the CMIU because it did not accept blacks. See "Autobiography of Luis Barcia," 60.

¡TIERRA!: THE REGIONAL ANARCHIST NEWSPAPER

¡Tierra! was launched in November 1902, and during its first five years Florida anarchists in Tampa, Key West, and St. Augustine became major financial backers (Figure 2.2). Florida money completely financed an issue in April 1903 and partially financed 66 of 135 issues (49 percent) from April 1903 to November 1907. Money went for donations, subscriptions, and to help write down the paper's debt. Most of the funds came from Tampa, with frequently large contributions coming from Key West and St. Augustine. Luis Barcia always collected and sent in the St. Augustine contributions. So, while Havana played the role of "anarchist hub" with its new waves of anarchists arriving from Spain and its publication of the weekly ¡Tierra!, it was the strong "node" of Florida that played a fundamental role in financing this hub during the newspaper's first years.[62]

While Florida was financially important for ¡Tierra!, the paper also became a tool for Tampa anarchists to frame the issues facing workers in or thinking of coming to Florida. For instance, the paper printed Florida correspondence, which became a guide for Cuban workers on what to expect when they arrived in Florida and to be prepared to confront an ongoing barrage of problems that anarchists and workers faced. One key problem that continuously threatened solidarity was ethnic rivalry. Despite repeated efforts, Florida's anarchists still regularly encountered Cuban workers who wanted to block Italians and Spaniards from the workforce. In mid-summer 1903, the mainstream Havana newspaper *La Discusión* fed this nationalist rant by publishing letters from Cubans living in Tampa who criticized Tampa's Italian community for taking jobs that Cubans should be doing. Florida-based Italian anarchists Vicente Antinori and Filippo Di Bona responded in ¡Tierra!, attacking the writer for undermining worker unity in Tampa. Italians had come to Tampa to learn a trade, and often their wives had to work either in the factories or at home – just like Cuban workers and their wives. Rather than portray this reality of workers' lives in a nationalistic context, the writers reminded readers of the principles of anarchist internationalism and that "as anarchists we protest against the kind of privilege that the writer exalts: that of propriety of an industry for Cubans." After all, continued Antinori and Di Bona, in the United States "Italians are no less

---

[62] These conclusions are based on the published finances of ¡Tierra! each week from 1903 to 1907. See Shaffer, "Havana Hub," 61–65.

FIGURE 2.2 *¡Tierra!* (1903, 1905, 1913): the longest-running anarchist newspaper in Cuba (1902–1915) and the key Caribbean regional information source with brief iterations in the 1920s and 1930s.
International Institute of Social History (Amsterdam)

foreign than Cubans or Spaniards, so based on what right does the letter writer want Cuban privilege?"[63]

¡Tierra! would play another solidarity role linking Cuba and Florida in the early 1900s. When anarchists in Havana were harassed or faced arrest, they could flee into the Cuban countryside. But it was just as possible to jump on board the *Mascotte* or the *Olivette* and cross the Straits. In mid-1903, Havana employers refused to hire Manuel Martínez Abello (with whom Luis Barcia lived in Cuba when he returned from Honduras and before heading to Jacksonville). So, Martínez Abello went to Tampa. *¡Tierra!* acted as a letter of introduction when the editors reminded Florida comrades who Martínez Abello was. "Tampa workers know how much work he dedicated to the Cuban cause [during the war]. Other persons who today are in high places of power know the money that he delivered to the Revolutionary Delegation." The anarchist was to be warmly welcomed by the workers as a comrade, not some Spaniard trying to steal a job.[64]

[63] *¡Tierra!*, July 25, 1903, 3–4.   [64] Ibid., August 29, 1903, 2.

For a brief time, Tampa's anarchists complemented *¡Tierra!* with their own paper. In 1906, they published *Antorcha*, the official organ of the Institución Homóloga dedicated to "raising the intellectual level of human beings to the point whereby they can liberate themselves from all economic, political, and religious tutelage." With sections on the arts, sociology, recreation, and economics, the periodical was less an ideological rag than it was a fountain of advice for people, or, as the paper put it "theorizing practice and practicing theory."[65] One of the editors was the shanghaied anarchist and regular contributor to *¡Tierra!*, J. Fueyo. One of the Institute's features was a regular *velada* (social gathering) on topics like remembering the Haymarket Martyrs. Pedro Esteve gave a "friendly Sunday chat" on labor organizing, and the Italian Luce Society held its meetings at a branch of the Institute where men and women spoke and sang in both Italian and Spanish. The long-time Havana-based anarchist Manuel Fuentes joined efforts in the Institute, where he hoped it would be a small place "to refresh oneself ... in the arid desert" of one's life and where one could "fortify the spirit." However dedicated were Fuentes and his comrades, the Institute apparently was short-lived owing – one can suspect – to low interest among the workers, as one writer complained about the sparsely attended twentieth-anniversary remembrance of the Haymarket Affair.[66]

If *¡Tierra!* was becoming Florida's anarchist newspaper, it of course was also the leading anarchist voice for Cuba. After 1898, US private investment poured onto the island as agribusiness firms resurrected sugar estates in the west and expanded to new lands in the central and eastern parts of the island. As noted earlier, anarchists followed this rural expansion. Between 1902 and 1913, nearly half of all newly created anarchist groups were launched beyond Havana Province. The majority of these arose in the sugar and mining zones of central and eastern Cuba.[67] Regularly, native reporters from throughout the island were themselves leading activists in those zones. As such, they wrote, organized local events, collected money, and sold copies of *¡Tierra!*. Frequently, when a column arrived from outside Havana, there was a corresponding financial contribution arriving from that same location dedicated to purchasing more copies of the newspaper, purchasing copies of Spanish and New York anarchist papers, and underwriting *¡Tierra!*'s expenses.[68] These

---

[65] *Antorcha*, November 17, 1906, 2–3.
[66] Ibid., November 17, 1906; November 24, 1906; November 8, 1906.
[67] Sánchez Cobos, *Sembrando Ideales*, 178.
[68] See, for instance, *¡Tierra!*, May 14, 1904, 4; June 12, 1907, 4; October 8, 1910, 3–4; January 18, 1913, 4; February 21, 1913, 4; May 7, 1914, 4.

native reporters wrote about work and pay conditions, strike activities, and the political chicaneries of local politicians.

José García was a long-time correspondent from the sugar zones of central Cuba. In 1903, García kept island readers abreast of the assassination of two labor leaders in Santa Clara, accusing the local police of the murders and cover-ups. García and the Havana-based editors used the events in central Cuba to frame an image of incompetence, deception, and brutality characterizing the Cuban government and the rural police.[69] When laborers in the small town of Ranchuelo protested the authorities' actions, police shut down the meeting and arrested four people, despite, as García described it, merely practicing their "freedom of thought that the Constitution grants all citizens." This was how the new government treated four veterans of the wars for independence.[70] For his efforts, García was arrested and sentenced to jail. Over the following year, until his release in July 1905, ¡Tierra! regularly published his prison letters that described conditions that ever-increasing numbers of workers faced in the new sugar estates, including underemployment, seasonal jobs, poor pay, and workers forced to sleep on the ground around the sugar mill machinery. García called the conditions worse than in the era of African chattel slavery – a condition that had ended only in the previous generation.[71] For workers in Cuban cities contemplating a move to the rural economy – or for migrants from Spain or Florida considering traveling to Cuba for work in the sugar mills – García's ¡Tierra! columns helped people understand the effects of industrialization on rural Cuba and what awaited them if they moved there to work.

From May through June 1907, the recently arrived Spanish anarchists Marcial Lores and Abelardo Saavedra traveled around Cuba on a propaganda tour with anarchists from across Cuba, including García. Their regular reports to ¡Tierra! described the large receptions in city and town alike, audiences curious to evaluate for themselves the government's description of anarchists as wild-eyed, crazy devil-worshippers, and the occasional hostility they met from mayors and priests who leaped on stage to decry the infidels and escort speakers to the town limits under armed guard. Reports from the tour stops included speeches by local comrades who analyzed local conditions from anarchist perspectives. At one stop in Cruces, 4000 people attended a four-hour-long meeting.[72]

---

[69] ¡Tierra!, August 15, 1903, 1; August 22, 1903, 1 and 3; August 29, 1903, 2–4; September 5, 1903, 1; September 12, 1903, 1 and 3.
[70] Ibid., September 12, 1903, 1; September 19, 1903, 1. [71] Ibid., October 29, 1904, 2.
[72] Ibid., April 30, 1907, 1; May 25, 1907, 2; June 1, 1907, 3–4; June 12, 1907, 2; June 22, 1907, 3; July 7, 1907, 3; August 10, 1907, 2.

In all, the propaganda tour united small groups in the island's interior with larger groups in Havana. If one purpose of the excursion was to raise the consciousness of workers throughout the island, just as importantly the tour aimed to invigorate Havana's radicals, who now saw the anarchist message rising in the island's interior, and with it new waves of support for the Havana-based movement. Coverage in ¡Tierra! facilitated this.

Besides these correspondent columns, rural areas and cities beyond Havana often played a vital role in sustaining the newspaper's finances. The newspaper finances and contributors' lists reveal that Cuban readers outside of Havana and its immediate suburbs regularly contributed as much or more money to the paper than did Havana-area readers.

Cuban contributions to ¡Tierra! *from beyond* Metro Havana *and from* Metro Havana, 1903–1914 *(average weekly percentages of the newspaper's income by year)*

	Beyond Metro Havana (percent)	Metro Havana (percent)
1903	35	38
1904	43	35
1905	35	43
1906	38	49
1907	48	37
1908	53	39
1909	48	39
1910	55	29
1911	58	30
1912	52	29
1913	56	19
1914	60	23

Source: ¡Tierra!, April 1903 to December 1914. All percentages are rounded to the nearest whole number. Percentages may not equal 100 percent due to contributions arriving from outside Cuba that are not reflected in these numbers.

Non-Havana money did not always arrive, nor arrive in large amounts to the newspaper's offices. However, it was significant. For instance, in 1903, Cuban anarchists outside of Havana contributed an average of 35 percent of ¡Tierra!'s weekly income throughout the year. Over the next eleven years, non-Havana money generally ticked upward so that their contributions averaged 60 percent of the newspaper's weekly income in 1914. Meanwhile, the percentage of Havana anarchists' contributions fell at comparable rates.

The shift reflects economic development of central and eastern Cuba during these years as more Cuban and Spanish laborers made their way from Havana to other port cities and to the emerging mostly US-owned sugar complexes across the island. While considerable amounts of money came from working-class cities like Cárdenas, Matanzas, Camagüey, Cienfuegos, and Santiago de Cuba – all cities lacking their own anarchist press – ¡Tierra! also reached into small towns around the island where anarchist sympathizers sent money from places like Firmeza, Guamo, and Niquero in southeastern Cuba, Macurijes in western Cuba, and Jatibonico and Remedios in central Cuba.[73] The paper could not have thrived as long and regularly as it did without large financial contributions coming from the factories, fields, mills, mines, and ports scattered beyond Havana – whether that money came from Florida or the rest of Cuba.

This growing islandwide and cross-Straits network fueled demand for copies of the newspaper, leading to increased circulation. In 1905, the editors regularly printed 2000 copies of ¡Tierra!. But as contributions from the network poured into Havana, circulation exploded. In 1910, 3500 weekly copies were printed. This rose to 4250 copies by early 1912 and peaked at 5500 weekly copies in mid-1913.[74] The growing demand for ¡Tierra!, coupled with the emergence of groups around the island, led to the creation of the Havana-based Federación Anarquista de Cuba (Anarchist Federation of Cuba) in 1914. While money continued to arrive for copies of the newspaper, now anarchists throughout Cuba were sending money to fund the Federation – the first islandwide attempt to coordinate anarchist activities via more than just a weekly paper.[75] However, in late 1914 the Cuban government grew increasingly wary of anarchist activities and the growth of the movement. Officials launched a wave of repressive actions against anarchists through deportations and arrests. As a result, anarchist money began drying up. The newspaper's weekly average income fell from 62.79 pesos in the first six months of 1914 to a weekly average of just 38.09 pesos in the second six months of

---

[73] These small towns and many others can be found in issue after issue. See, for instance, the following editions of ¡Tierra!. 1903: July 11, July 25, October 24; 1904: April 23, May 14, May 21, June 11; 1905: January 14, March 14, April 8, July 8; 1906: June 2, July 21; 1907: February 2, April 6, June 12; 1909: July 31; 1910: February 26, March 26, April 23, May 7, October 1, October 8; 1912: April 13, May 11, May 18, September 7, October 12, October 19, November 2.
[74] ¡Tierra!, April 8, 1905, 4; March 19, 1910, 4; February 17, 1912, 4; August 8, 1913, 4.
[75] Ibid., October 1, 1914, 4.

the year.[76] In January 1915, ¡Tierra! ceased publication due to governmental repression and financial ruin. The paper's demise was a severe loss to the network since it had been the leading regional networking tool for anarchists across the Continental Caribbean.

FELLOW TRAVELING WITH NON-ANARCHISTS IN "DEMOCRATIC" PUERTO RICO AND TAMPA

For Santiago Iglesias – the man who quickly rose to lead the Puerto Rican labor movement – the United States long had been a model of democratic progress. Having grown up in the monarchical tyranny of late-nineteenth-century Spain, lived through the first year of Cuba's war for independence, seen many of his Cuban anarchist friends deported and been victimized himself by Spanish officials both in Cuba and Puerto Rico, the image of North American freedoms of speech, press, and assembly had a powerful hold on Iglesias's political imagination. Plus, the Americans had freed him from a Spanish jail in Puerto Rico in 1898 and not given him to Spanish authorities who had demanded his return for supposed dangerous anarchist activities. With this in mind and with Puerto Rico increasingly linked to the United States via military occupation in late 1898, Iglesias and many of his labor comrades made a choice. They abandoned anarchism, accepted Washington's Americanization project for the island, and joined forces with the US labor movement.

Puerto Rico's Federación Regional de los Trabajadores (Regional Federation of Workers, or FRT) included leftists of all stripes, ranging from Iglesias, who was moving toward parliamentary socialism, to anarchists like Severo Sirino and Emiliano Ramos. But it was Iglesias's leadership that proved important in shaping the FRT's direction in the early years of US control. By late October 1898, he increasingly believed that Puerto Rican workers would find salvation by linking themselves to the United States. In the FRT's first meeting, several keynote speakers – including Iglesias – praised the fate of US workers and how this supposed progress would extend to workers in Puerto Rico.[77] Maybe, but if Puerto Ricans had been reading *El Esclavo* in Tampa in the 1890s, they might have drawn a different conclusion.

In 1899, the labor movement celebrated the island's first May Day. Published calls for unions to plan and participate in the events were

---

[76] Figures calculated from 42 extant copies of ¡Tierra! from 1914.
[77] *El Porvenir Social*, October 27, 1898, 1.

accompanied by an illustration of a woman holding the US flag.[78] The May Day festivities mixed pro-Americanism and socialism. The parade began at the FRT local in San Juan and was led by the flag of the United States. Local unions followed, carrying slogans praising the FRT and various defenders of the working class. A red banner with gold trim included the slogan "¡Gloria al trabajo!" with a picture of an eagle and the US flag. Next came the red flag of socialism, followed by a portrait of US President McKinley.[79]

A month earlier, Daniel de León, the Venezuelan–Curaçaoan–American leader of the Socialist Labor Party of the United States (SLP), had contacted Iglesias. He invited the FRT and its members to join the SLP and form a branch of the party in Puerto Rico. The FRT adopted the SLP platform: an eight-hour work day, a democratic public administration, a public education system, a health and sanitation system, maternity leave, a minimum wage, public kitchens for workers, an end to sales taxes, and so on.[80] The Federation leadership hoped that the United States would implement and protect the democratization of Puerto Rico that would benefit the island's workers.[81] Following a split between leftist and moderate members within the FRT in mid-1899, Iglesias and his allies founded the Federación Libre de Trabajadores (Free Federation of Workers, or FLT) and created the Puerto Rican branch of the SLP. By September, *El Porvenir Social* was the "Official Organ of the State Committee of Puerto Rico, of the Socialist Workers Party of the United States of America."[82]

While union leadership steered the FLT toward republican politics and a decidedly pro-American political stance, anarchists who belonged to the FLT's rank-and-file continued to agitate for their positions within the union, spoke at rallies, and wrote for the SLP paper. One of the first celebrations of anarchism in *El Porvenir Social* occurred when Iglesias wrote a brief but glowing piece about his old comrade Manuel María Miranda, who was returning to the Caribbean after his wartime imprisonment on Fernando

---

[78] Ibid., April 11, 1899, 2; Erick J. Pérez, "May Day 1899 in Puerto Rico," in *The Memory of May Day; An Iconographic History of the Origins and Implanting of a Workers' Holiday* (Venezia: Marsilio Editori, 1989), 679.
[79] *El Porvenir Social*, May 4, 1899, 1–2; May 6, 1899, 1; Pérez, "May Day 1899 in Puerto Rico," 683.
[80] Iglesias Pantín, *Luchas emancipadoras*, 96.
[81] Gervasio L. Gervasio and A. G. Quintero Rivera, *Desafío y solidaridad: breve historia del movimiento obrero puertorriqueño* (Río Piedras, PR: Ediciones Huracán, 1982), 33.
[82] *El Porvenir Social*, August 1, 1899, 1; August 5, 1899, 1; September 7, 1899, 1.

Póo. On February 5, Miranda boarded the *Larache*, the same steamer that had brought him to the island from Spain. The return trip took him to Puerto Rico, where he disembarked for a few hours, meeting his old comrade Iglesias for a quick catch-up, and then set sail for his Cuban home. In the tribute to his friend, Iglesias celebrated Miranda's anarchism by noting how Miranda was "a propagator of absolute freedom for the people."[83] And now Miranda was once again free himself.

Soon, though, Iglesias broke from the SLP, transitioned to supporting the North American trade unionism of the AFL, and began criticizing the island's anarchists. Tensions over ideology and the appropriate relationship with the United States often brought reformists and radicals in the FLT into conflict. The beginning of this conflict rested in Santiago Iglesias's 1900 trip to the United States and his inaugural meetings with AFL leader Samuel Gompers.[84] In August, Iglesias fled increased harassment from island authorities and by September arrived in New York City, where he worked as a cabinetmaker, listened to leading socialists and anarchists, and wrote for local radical newspapers. He grew to believe that Puerto Rican workers should no longer affiliate with the SLP and began to look elsewhere for US allies. For Iglesias, the AFL – the largest labor organization in the United States – offered Puerto Rican workers their best hope. To this end, Iglesias attended the AFL convention in Louisville, Kentucky in December – just as the AFL's CMIU union was being shamed in Tampa for its pro-business, antiworker letter.[85]

However, anarchist FLT members on the island complicated Iglesias's efforts. In March 1901, José Ferrer y Ferrer made light of Puerto Rican politicians' inability and lack of power to do anything about the abuses suffered by Puerto Rican workers. US leaders, he wrote, "desire that Puerto Rico become totally Americanized, and from there arises the paralysis of State and Municipal works, so that the people, shrouded in misery, emigrate to distant climes in search of Bread and Shelter, obtaining in exchange for that eternal struggle for existence, a miserable exile."[86] "Un Hambriento" described the emigration as nothing short of a

---

[83] Miranda, *Memorias de un deportado*, 55–58; *El Porvenir Social*, March 16, 1899, 1; Casanovas Codina, *Bread, or Bullets!*, 205–206, 227–228.

[84] For an introduction on the AFL in the Caribbean, see Joseph Bedford, "Samuel Gompers & the Caribbean: The AFL, Cuba & Puerto Rico, 1898–1906," *Labor's Heritage* 6, no. 4 (1995): 4–25

[85] Iglesias Pantín, *Luchas emancipadoras*, 199–202; García and Quintero Rivera, *Desafío y solidaridad*, 35–39.

[86] *La Miseria*, March 6, 1901.

US plot to Americanize Puerto Rico.[87] If the United States could depopulate workers by sending them to work in places like Hawai'i, there would be fewer Puerto Ricans to Americanize. Meanwhile, Ramón Romero Rosa issued a call for all unions around the island to maintain their anarchist spirit when he announced that "workers associations will be purely libertarian," and anarchists Venancio Cruz and Alfonso Torres coordinated workers to create a union in Caguas. On May Day 1901, the anarchist Severo Sirino was on the FLT program for the day's festivities, and the Grupo "Juventud Socialista" performed the play "Fin de fiesta" by Cuba's leading anarchist author Palmiro de Lidia.[88]

Iglesias soon challenged the island's anarchists. Ten days after the May Day celebrations, the FLT-affiliated *La Miseria* reprinted an article that Iglesias had published in the *New York Journal*. Now firmly allied with the AFL, Iglesias for the first time openly attacked anarchism. "And the sad truth is that anarchists squander their time so pathetically ... Anarchists," he concluded, "your time has passed. Your function is archaic ... For you there is nothing else to do." Iglesias's message seemed clear. Puerto Ricans should abandon anarchism. The island's working-class future lay with the AFL.[89] In September, the AFL recognized the FLT. In October, Gompers named Iglesias the AFL general organizer for Cuba and Puerto Rico, and Iglesias accompanied Gompers to the White House to meet President Roosevelt, who had assumed the presidency following the anarchist assassination of President McKinley the month before. In November, after having been gone from the island for over a year, Iglesias returned to Puerto Rico.[90]

Anarchists immediately questioned whether the US-based AFL truly cared about the island's workers. Anarchists continued to work within the FLT and freely challenged the AFL and FLT leadership from within the union. In 1905, in the central-eastern town of Caguas, a group of anarchists led by José Ferrer y Ferrer and Pablo Vega Santos dominated the FLT local. They first communicated with *¡Tierra!* and Cuban comrades in January.[91] Juan Vilar and other Caguas-based tobacco workers organized Grupo "Solidaridad" that spring. This early organization held meetings, wrote columns to their comrades in Cuba, founded an

---

[87] Ibid., April 9, 1901.
[88] Ibid., March 1, 1901; April 9, 1901; April 11, 1901; April 25, 1901.
[89] Ibid., May 11, 1901.   [90] Iglesias Pantín, *Luchas emancipadoras*, 216–218.
[91] *¡Tierra!*, January 14, 1905, 4.

educational center, and on May 22, 1905, began publishing their own short-lived newspaper *Voz Humana*.[92]

The epitome of this love–hate relationship between reformist AFL-linked organizations and Puerto Rico's revolutionary anarchists can be seen in a three-month span in mid-1909 that was reported to ¡*Tierra!*. In April, Iglesias called anarchists "rogues," prompting one Puerto Rican anarchist to call Iglesias a sell-out and a hypocrite: "you were one of them [an anarchist], with the difference that you lost your old work shoes while we, with dignity, kept ours." He charged Iglesias with having become part of the labor aristocracy suckling money and support "from [US President] Taft's teat."[93] While such animosity flourished between anarchists and the union leadership, anarchists still worked among the FLT rank-and-file. For instance, just months after the charges against Iglesias appeared, anarchists were working intimately with the FLT's "Cruzada del Ideal" – a 1909–1911 propaganda campaign to organize workers in which working-class intellectuals spoke at public meetings and demonstrations.[94] Then, in the FLT's 1910 conference, delegates voted to no longer support any political party – a stance bringing it firmly in line with the AFL's antipolitics position but also the longer history of anarchist denunciations of electoral participation.[95]

The FLT–AFL Americanization project also clashed with ideas about the United States that one also found among Florida and Cuban anarchists. Puerto Rico's status was always clouded by US refusal to outright annex or incorporate the island as a state. Because the governor was a US presidential appointee, anarchists naturally extended their antipolitics rhetoric into an anti-imperialist attack. Alfonso Torres in San Juan addressed this specifically: "Here in Puerto Rico, where we cannot count on our own government ... here where no power exists other than that of the North Americans, here where the governor and the executive council are the same rulers, what they order, oppresses the people, so that the struggles of the political parties are not really about power because power is in foreign hands."[96] For those politicians who claimed that the November

---

[92] Ibid., June 24, 1905, 3; *Cultura Obrera*, May 22, 1915.
[93] ¡*Tierra!*, April 14, 1909, 2.
[94] Luisa Capetillo, *Amor y anarquía: Los escritos de Luisa Capetillo*, ed. Julio Ramos (San Juan: Ediciones Huracán, 1992), 34–35, 75–78.
[95] *Procedimientos del sexto congreso obrero de la Federación Libre de los Trabajadores de Puerto Rico. Celebrado del 18 al 24 de marzo de 1910, en la ciudad de Juncos, Puerto Rico* (San Juan: Tipografía de M. Burillo & Co., 1910).
[96] ¡*Tierra!*, August 4, 1906, 2.

1906 elections would be a watershed event in Puerto Rican history, anarchists in Caguas sarcastically opined in their newspaper *Voz Humana*: "The country will be saved" by the elections.[97] Well, no, it wasn't.

Anarchists regularly expressed anti-American sentiment in their international correspondence columns to Havana. Juan Vilar documented police abuse of strikers, asking how such events could occur in a "democratic" land.[98] Paca Escabí echoed a theme that anarchists in Cuba were espousing at the same time. Since the US invasion, all that had really changed was that the North Americans, who led people to dream of a better life, had crushed people's hopes. "The American invasion of Puerto Rico only means division among workers, scandals in the administration, moral disorder, and hunger, exodus and grief for the people." She added that "the government is incompetent, and the people's political representatives have done nothing but foolishly approve laws acting against the interests of the Puerto Rican people and the working class in particular."[99]

Anarchists Alfonso Torres and Venancio Cruz cautioned readers that the US-imposed institutions of republican democracy were not the answer to Puerto Rican workers' plights. Like Vilar and Escabí, Torres charged that little was different from the Spanish era: "the laboring classes are as enslaved, as exploited, and as ignorant today as they were yesterday." He continued, "if [workers] have improved in anything it is not because of some governmental formula that is more or less democratic, but on the contrary due to their own efforts."[100] Cruz argued that the arrival of democratic institutions on the island provided a new means for elites to pass laws in their favor "with no further objective than the subjugation of the masses." One had to question the value of democracy in Puerto Rico, how it came about and who benefited: "Democracy, oh Democracy! Yesterday the people coveted it because it was offered to them by the bloodsuckers of capital and government. Democracy then today is a farce, constituting the ultimate refuge for political tyrants."[101]

Thus, the political struggle for votes was pointless for the working man. "We should forget political questions because they benefit only those who live for politics. Our place is not in the political camp, but

---

[97] *Voz Humana*, October 22, 1906, 1.   [98] *¡Tierra!*, September 2, 1905, 2.
[99] Ibid., October 7, 1905, 2.
[100] Alfonso Torres, *¡Solidaridad!* (San Juan: Unión Tipográfica, 1905), 8.
[101] Venancio Cruz, *Hacia el porvenir* (San Juan: La República Española, 1906), 11.

rather in the economic camp, the social camp," concluded Torres.[102] Rather than engaging in politics, Torres urged workers to make the unions their central focus for improving lives and conditions. In Puerto Rico, that meant that anarchists had to work with the AFL-linked unions. While not ideal, the FLT was about all they had, so anarchists maintained their anarchist principles and links to Havana while working within the FLT. Torres surmised that only the FLT "will be able to achieve that great benefit [improved living conditions] for this unhappy people."[103] Thus, despite the FLT's submission to the AFL, anarchists needed to operate within the FLT and try to shape the most significant union on the island away from politics and Americanization.

Meanwhile, in Tampa, anarchists faced very similar issues: small but dedicated numbers, no long-term newspaper, reliance on transnational communications with Havana, and a decision to join with AFL-linked unions. Because the CMIU remained the only union working for Tampa tobacco workers from 1903 to 1910, anarchists believed that they had to give it at least their tentative support. According to one anarchist, while the International was conservative, centrist, and did not always act in a way that seemed best for all workers, it was the only union around. "But between the factory owners and it [CMIU], I remain with the International, though we will have to make it respect us a bit more."[104] Many anarchists were uncomfortable with this broader working-class alliance, but few alternatives existed. As one anarchist put it, a new anarchist organization in a city like Tampa was impossible. So, he urged anarchists to organize within the International, concluding that the fate of Tampa's workers was simple: "either organized or unemployed."[105] Fellow traveling was an unfortunate necessity.

While anarchists joined the International, they continued to fund *¡Tierra!*. As the International grew to dominate the Tampa labor movement, anarchists sold *¡Tierra!* in the city and urged *lectores* to read it in the factories. Despite US government and postal official efforts to prevent the distribution of the newspaper, it nevertheless could be purchased at various shops in Tampa. Most workers' exposure to anarchist journalism remained on the shop floor where the *lectores* read aloud to cigar rollers. Workers paid the reader's salary. In theory, the reader was to read whatever the workers asked him or her to read. But in Tampa, problems

---

[102] Ibid., 20.   [103] Ibid., 14–16.   [104] *¡Tierra!*, February 26, 1910, 4.
[105] Ibid., April 2, 1904, 3. See similar half-hearted support for International membership in April 23, 1904, 4 and May 21, 1904, 4.

emerged. *Lectores* occasionally refused to read the paper. Apparently, some *lectores* feared losing their positions if they read *¡Tierra!*. Other *lectores* simply rejected anarchism and refused to be associated with it. According to one correspondent, *lectores* spent more time reading accounts like a dance at Havana's presidential palace for President Roosevelt's visiting daughter rather than labor actions or anarchist theory. However, if a worker did bring in a copy of *¡Tierra!* for the *lector*, only one or two articles were read before dropping it and changing to something else.[106] Ambrosio Martínez wrote how some workers in the Gato cigar rolling factory were preventing the *lector* from reading *¡Tierra!*. Anarchists suspected the real culprits trying to suppress *¡Tierra!* were elements within the International.[107]

But public reading of *¡Tierra!* was vital, not just as a method of communication, agitation, and consciousness raising, but also to raise money. For instance, in January 1909 Tampa cigar workers raised funds for "victims of social questions" in Spain and Cuba.[108] They launched the effort after hearing a *lector* read about arrests and deportations in the pages of *¡Tierra!*. Consequently, any effort to silence the reading of the newspaper was more than simply a free speech issue or an attempt to silence anarchism. To prevent the newspaper's reading was to restrict the communication transfer across the network that facilitated transnational efforts to raise money for anarchist causes.

Sometimes Florida anarchists used *¡Tierra!* to generate support for CMIU actions. In late July 1910, workers throughout Tampa's cigar factories walked off the job, protesting the replacement of local tobacco leaf selectors with selectors from Havana, as well as the refusal of the factories to recognize local CMIU unions. By late 1910, approximately 12,000 men and women had called a general strike to force factory owners to recognize the CMIU throughout the tobacco industry. Anglo authorities and vigilantes attacked. When Italian workers Angelo Albano and Castronse Figarretta were arrested for killing an Anglo bookkeeper, a mob lynched the Italians before they could go on trial. Police arrested strike leaders for inciting violence after arsonists attacked newspaper and factory buildings. Citizens patrols raided the newspaper office of the CMIU's *El Internacional*, destroyed presses, intimidated staff, and arrested the editor. When companies brought in strikebreakers, women

---

[106] Ibid., March 9, 1906, 3.   [107] Ibid., July 20, 1912, 3.
[108] Ibid., January 3, 1909, 3. For postal efforts to censor distribution, see August 22, 1913, 4.

jeered and insulted the strikebreakers, prompting the women's arrests. Citizens accosted workers too, either verbally or shooting at them with pistols.[109] In Havana, anarchists urged worker solidarity with the CMIU strikers in Tampa but went further in analyzing the virulent public reaction to workers' demands. As ¡Tierra!'s editors noted in October, Tampa's elite had to side with the owners; to do otherwise (or to allow workers to have their way) would result in factory owners abandoning Tampa. If that happened, the banks and businesses would be shuttered. There would be no reason for the gas, electric, and tram companies to continue operation. And the whole city would revert to what it once was: "a one-horse town surrounded by orange groves planted on the rubbish heap of a famous city raised on the efforts of an enslaved population that dedicated itself to the production of Havana cigars."[110]

For anarchists, the events in 1910 were troublesome reminders of abuses they suffered during the 1901 strike that saw the destruction of La Resistencia. ¡Tierra! and its Tampa-based correspondents cautioned workers on both sides of the Straits and beyond that the new strike was in danger of failing. They urged workers to consider one important point about being radical workers in a foreign land. Since the fall of La Resistencia, international workers had joined the ranks of the CMIU. The problem was that "for the bourgeoisie the International and Resistencia are the same thing." Both were labor unions made up mostly of foreign-born, non-English-speaking workers. Whenever citizens' groups in Yanquilandia looked at these workers, they saw the essence of un-Americanism in their faces and heard it in their voices. The memory of 1901 played heavily on people's minds. The editors recalled the 1901 debacles that saw La Resistencia leaders illegally deported to Honduras.[111] And, for anyone looking for a lesson, it was not hard to find: Belonging to a reformist "American" union was proving just as dangerous as belonging to a radical "international" one if you did not look or sound like the Anglo merchants and political leaders of the city.

What could one do? Luis Barcia told workers in 1901 to be more assertive and stand up more forcefully to their Anglo detractors. In 1910, ¡Tierra! urged Tampa workers to do the same. Workers had to respond differently than they did in 1901. After all, Anglo business elites "are few,

---

[109] Mormino and Pozzetta, "Spanish Anarchism in Tampa," 191; Joe Scaglione, "City in Turmoil: Tampa and the Strike of 1910," *Sunland Tribune*, November 18, 1992, 29–36; ¡Tierra!, October 29, 1910, 2; November 12, 1910, 3; November 19, 1910, 3.

[110] ¡Tierra!, October 1, 1910, 4.   [111] Ibid., October 8, 1910, 3; November 19, 1910, 2.

you are many; they are nothing and you are everything; they produce nothing, and you have created all, and he who creates also has the power and the right to destroy when he cannot participate in what he has created."[112] The situation grew tense. In October, for example, arsonists burned a factory. Anarchists pointed out that the same Mayor McKay who led the vigilantes in 1901 now directed the antistrike activities in 1910. They warned that vigilante violence was returning, but it would soon be matched, "because this city was bordering on armed conflict as the people – tired of suffering at the hands of the citizens – were preparing themselves to confront force with force." Whether rumor, hyperbole, fact, or some combination, ¡Tierra! reported on a plot by an Anglo mob to attack printing presses sympathetic to strikers. In response, workers planned to form their own units composed of forty armed workers to meet the citizens head-on and slow them down so that another group of 400 armed workers could attack the American mob. The threat of growing violence alarmed Florida Governor Albert Gilchrist. The governor intervened in the strike by investigating the causes and possible solutions for a peaceful resolution.[113]

In January 1911, the strike ended. Arrests of activists, depletion of union resources, vigilante violence, and the failure of the AFL to commit to substantial, long-term assistance of its affiliated union doomed the strike. The CMIU failed to gain recognition from the factory owners, and the native-born CMIU leadership came away from the strike harboring its own resentments about Tampa's foreign labor leaders and radicals. As historian Nancy Hewitt puts it, the union's Anglo leaders blamed migrants, "convinced that it was their Latin temperament and their lack of discipline rather than the overwhelming power of Anglo authorities and the lack of financial resources that led to defeat."[114] Such a stance further alienated Latin leftists in Tampa, causing them to renew their hesitations about working with reformist unions like the CMIU. Ultimately, fellow traveling with the International did not work out any better for anarchists than going it alone a decade earlier.

THE EMERGENCE OF THE IWW IN THE CARIBBEAN NETWORK

In 1908, as Tampa's anarchists split their energies between the CMIU and ¡Tierra!, the Industrial Workers of the World arrived in the city. The

---

[112] Ibid., December 3, 1910, 2–3.
[113] Ibid., December 24, 1910, 2–3; December 31, 1910, 2–3.
[114] Hewitt, *Southern Discomfort*, 213.

speaking appearances by the Wobbly Big Bill Haywood concerned CMIU leadership because the visit signaled that a more radical alternative route for workers lay in anarchist industrial unionism.[115] Three years later, in the wake of the failed CMIU strike and growing anarchist disappointment with the CMIU, Florida's Spanish-speaking anarchists launched the first IWW efforts. Several activists and columnists were at the ready to spearhead a new anarcho-syndicalist initiative. Issue after issue of *¡Tierra!* included columns from Tampa. The fact that there was no shortage of writers and activists in the Tampa area helps explain the sudden surge in newspapers. Florida anarchists launched five Spanish-language newspapers between 1911 and 1914.[116] In Key West, Manuel de J. Parrilla edited *Despertad!*, a newspaper sent around the Caribbean Basin, where it ended up being read as far away as Costa Rica.[117] In late November 1912, Jesús Iglesias and Luis Mouroa edited *¡Liberación!* in Tampa.[118] *¡Liberación!*'s writers included the Cuban Marcelo Salinas, the Spaniard Maximiliano Olay, and the Puerto Rican Ventura Mijón.[119]

¡Liberación! is instructive about continued tensions between the city's anarchists and the International, how the paper reflected the transnational dimensions of anarchism still at play in the city, and the emerging anarchist support for the IWW. AFL supporters wasted few chances to level disparaging remarks on *Liberación*'s anarchists. One of these came in late 1912, when the CMIU criticized Salinas for certain personal shortcomings. Salinas responded to these accusations: "*El Internacional* says that I am a pimp; that I play at the gaming tables; that in Cuba I helped strikebreakers, and that I stole funds that I collected in a shop where I worked." Well, he answered in blunt but humble words, yes, as a single man he did visit the red-light district on occasion, where he shamefully bought "my sisters" to satisfy natural urges. But he never had been involved in a scandal. Just because someone gambled a bit or went to a prostitute was not enough "to discredit a man active in the struggle." After all, men in the International gambled too. And to his actions in Cuba, let his comrades Barcia, Sola, Saavedra, Esteve, and others attest to his character and actions. He concluded this remarkably candid open letter by charging his accusers with

---

[115] Ibid., 205–206.
[116] The five were *Despertad*, *Risveglio*, *¡Liberación!*, *Conciencia Industrial*, and *El Obrero Industrial*.
[117] *Renovación*, February 5, 1912, front cover.   [118] *¡Tierra!*, November 12, 1912, 4.
[119] *¡Liberación!*, October 19, 1912, 4; *¡Tierra!*, February 1, 1914, 4. As we will see, Mijón became a founding member in 1920 of the Puerto Rican anarchist *El Comunista* and in 1934 of Puerto Rico's Communist Party.

doing anything to undermine the anarchist cause because they saw anarchism as "a threat to their livelihoods."[120]

The rise of ¡Liberación! coincided with the emergence of the IWW in Florida. The paper, while not an official IWW publication, nevertheless sympathized with the Wobblies. In one issue, the editors printed the preambles to both the AFL and the IWW constitutions. The editors preferred the IWW, referring to Gompers's union as the "insipid and authoritarian" AFL.[121] In 1911, anarchists began organizing two IWW Locals in Key West and Tampa. That year, Herminio González arrived in Key West and attempted to open one local, but his efforts came to naught. He soon returned to Havana.[122] However, by 1914, there was a Key West IWW Local 108 that published the newspaper *Conciencia Industrial*.[123] Between 1911 and 1915, anarchists in Tampa published the Wobbly *El Obrero Industrial* – the official organ of IWW Local 102, founded in part by Salinas. By 1914, González had returned to Florida from Havana to edit *El Obrero Industrial*.[124] Like its other Spanish-language IWW counterparts in the Americas, the paper printed translated columns originating out of IWW headquarters in Chicago, but also included columns and coverage of particular interest to Spanish and Latin American workers. As an example, one issue carried a front-page picture of the young Texas anarchist León Cárdenas Martínez, who was murdered by authorities in Waco. The photo and caption were surrounded by a column critical of the CMIU.[125]

During the IWW years, Tampa anarchists strengthened relations with New York City. In November 1911, Pedro Esteve's *Cultura Obrera* became the most influential, regularly published Spanish-language anarchist newspaper in the United States. Following May Day activities in 1913, the newspaper became an official publication of the IWW, and Esteve became secretary of his local Maritime Transport Workers (MTW) Union affiliated with the IWW.[126] On occasion, Tampa columns arrived in New York, and periodically Tampa anarchists sent money to the paper. The Puerto Rican anarchist Luisa Capetillo – recently arrived in Tampa

---

[120] ¡Liberación!, October 19, 1912, 1–3.   [121] Ibid., October 19, 1912, 3–4.
[122] ¡Tierra!, May 23, 1913, 1–2.   [123] Ibid., July 30, 1914, 4.
[124] The 1915 ending date is derived from a notice in *El Rebelde*, November 12, 1915, 1.
[125] *El Obrero Industrial*, May 30, 1914, 1.
[126] *Cultura Obrera*, May 13, 1913, 1; Bieito Alonso Fernández, "Spanish Anarchists and Maritime Workers in the IWW," in *Wobblies of the World: A Global History of the IWW*, eds. Peter Cole, David Struthers, and Kenyon Zimmer (Chicago: Pluto Press, 2017), 95.

from New York herself – wrote from Florida in July 1913. In August 1914, the paper carried a letter describing the continued acrimony between the International and the IWW. And, Luis Barcia – able to show his face in Tampa by 1913 – collected money for *Cultura Obrera*.[127]

From June 1912 to January 1914 – the height of IWW activity and *El Obrero Industrial* in Florida – anarchists also sent money to and purchased copies of Spanish anarchist Jaime Vidal's newspapers *Brazo y Cerebro* and *Fuerza y Consciente*. Highly illustrated and functioning more as propaganda organs than periodicals discussing news items, Vidal's papers were a hit in Tampa. Capetillo wrote from Tampa, and Marcelo Salinas sent poetry.[128] Luis Barcia, the Key West anarchists in Grupo ¡Despertad!, and the IWW Locals 102 and 108 even began sending more money regularly to Vidal's papers than to Esteve's by mid-1914. In late 1913 and early 1914, Tampa's Wobblies were responsible for one-eighth of *Fuerza Consciente*'s income.[129] By 1915, Tampa's Wobbly newspaper had ceased operations, but IWW 102 continued to function, holding weekly meetings every Friday through at least the summer 1916 while the anarchist group "Los Incognitos" raised money to support IWW newspapers elsewhere.[130] Meanwhile, US-based, Spanish-speaking anarcho-syndicalists were key to growing sea-based IWW unionization efforts along the US East Coast. For instance, in Philadelphia, MTW Local 8 included 500 Spanish sailors, many of whom had Caribbean connections, like its early leader Manuel Rey, who arrived from Cuba in 1910.[131] As Peter Cole illustrates, Spanish seamen left the AFL unions along the East Coast in droves in the early 1910s to join the IWW.[132] The fact that a Spanish-speaking, anarcho-syndicalist Wobbly organization operated in the northern node of the Caribbean network for four years

---

[127] *Cultura Obrera*, December 14, 1912, 4; July 5, 1913, 2; August 15, 1914, 4; October 6, 1917, 4.
[128] *Fuerza Consciente*, August 9, 1913, 6–7; November 15, 1913, 13.
[129] *¡Tierra!*, September 10, 1914, 4; July 30, 1914, 4. See finance pages in *Brazo y Cerebro*, October 22, 1912, 33; *Fuerza Consciente*, August 9, 1913, 33; December 15, 1913, no page number; January 15, 1914, no page number. For *¡Tierra!*, see editions from January 4, 1913 to December 31, 1914, when Florida anarchists sent money to the Havana paper only thirty-one times.
[130] *El Rebelde*, December 8, 1914, 4; August 5, 1916, 4.
[131] Alonso, "Spanish Anarchists," 95–96.
[132] See Peter Cole, *Wobblies on the Waterfront: Interracial Unionism in Progressive-Era Philadelphia* (Urbana: University of Illinois Press, 2007), 66–68; Bieto Alonso Fernández, "Migración y sindicalismo. Marineros y anarquistas españoles en Nueva York (1902–1930)," *Historia Social* 54 (2006): 113-135.

attests to the still strong and dedicated nucleus of anarchist-leaning activists there. While there was little IWW contact in the rest of the Caribbean network before the Great War, Tampa's Cuban, Puerto Rican, and Spanish Wobblies were able to link the Caribbean with the broader US network – something I explore further in Chapter 5.

THE NETWORK EXTENDS TO PANAMA: CANAL ANARCHISTS VERSUS NORTH AMERICAN OVERSEERS

Like Cuba and Puerto Rico, Panama's geopolitical fate seemed sealed in that five-year span between 1898 and 1903. Cuba was politically "free," but under the dictates of 1902's Platt Amendment. After the US Supreme Court's Insular Cases decision, Puerto Rico was a colony of the United States, but nobody officially called it that. And now Panama was geopolitically and constitutionally linked to the United States too. Colombia's most northern province, Panama, became the chosen site for Washington to construct a transisthmian canal, and to that end the Roosevelt Administration facilitated the province's liberation from Colombia in November 1903. Between 1904 and 1914, tens of thousands of laborers from around the world made their way to this slice of North American territory in the heart of the tropics. Anarchists from Italy, Spain, and the Americas were among these migrant laborers, and throughout the construction era they spread the cause of anarchist freedom, attacked the United States, and maintained links to Cuba and Spain.

Since the 1500s, the Panamanian isthmus has been a major global transit point. Imperial Spain crossed it overland to traverse between the Atlantic and Pacific realms of its empire. Following Colombia's independence, the New York-based Panama Railroad Company laid tracks across the province of Panama. The transisthmian railroad built from 1850 to 1855 served as a key transit point for people heading to California for the gold rush. The transportation industry witnessed the first strikes in the province when employees of the Pacific Mail Steamship Company on the Pacific island of Taboga struck in 1853 and 1855. The isthmus saw its first anarchists when Élisée Reclus arrived in Portobelo on his way to Sierra Nevada de Santa Marta in Colombia in August 1855 and Mikhail Bakunin rode the rails across Panama from Asia to Europe in 1861.[133]

---

[133] Soler, *Panamá*, 45; Ángel Cappelletti, *Hechos y figures del anarquismo hispanoamericano* (Madrid: Ediciones Madre Tierra, 1990), 41; Mark Leier, *Bakunin: The Creative Passion* (New York: Seven Stories Press, 2009), 178.

In the 1880s, the French attempted to build a canal through the isthmus. Over 50,000 workers, especially from the Caribbean, migrated to the construction project, whose chief engineer was Ferdinand de Lesseps – the architect of the Suez Canal. From the beginning, workers faced abysmal conditions due to poor planning and insufficient engineering. The canal's first strike erupted in 1881, but to little avail for workers. After at least 20,000 deaths, engineering fiascos, financial improprieties, and disease, the French abandoned their project in 1889.[134] It is likely that some anarchist presence emerged during the failed French attempt. However, the French anarchist press – focused primarily on issues relevant to workers in France – paid little attention to the project other than to decry, for instance, how workers in Panama were doing all of the work, but served in veritable "bondage" and "misery" to those overseeing the canal project, who were set to profit like "parasites" off the work of 30,000 laborers.[135] Any actual anarchist presence must have been very small and met with little success. European workers were a distinct minority in Panama because most workers came from the French West Indies, where there was no history of anarchist organizing. We know that workers sympathetic to syndicalism did work for a time on the French project, but seemingly with no impact.[136] Thus, in the 1880s and 1890s, anarchists overall focused little on the isthmus. While there were small labor organizations, artisan-based actions and mutual-aid societies in other parts of nineteenth-century Colombia, little emerged in the Panamanian province.[137]

Ultimately, it was American imperial expansion that brought thousands of Spanish-speaking workers to build the canal, and anarchists came with them. Obviously this was never the intention of either the Panamanian or US governments. Both feared any anarchist presence. For the new government of the Republic of Panama, the last thing they needed was a group of foreign agitators spreading ideas of social revolution just as a new government was organizing Panama for the interests of the middle and upper classes. One only had to look to the new country of

---

[134] Soler, *Panamá*, 45–46; Conniff, *Black Labor on a White Canal*, 17–21; Greene, *The Canal Builders*, 2–3, 20–21.
[135] *L'Idée Ouvriere*, September 10–17, 1887, 2–3.
[136] Personal conversation with the late historian Bert Altena on Dutch syndicalism, April 2012.
[137] See, for instance, David Sowell, *The Early Colombian Labor Movement: Artisans and Politics in Bogotá, 1832–1919* (Philadelphia: Temple University Press, 1992); Charles Bergquist, *Labor in Latin America: Comparative Essays on Chile, Argentina, Venezuela and Colombia* (Palo Alto: Stanford University Press, 1986).

Cuba to see how anarchists could cause problems for a new government. Meanwhile, the Roosevelt government wanted nothing standing in its way to prevent or slow down a project envisioned as key to expanding US power.

As a result, both governments tried to prohibit anarchist migration to the isthmus. On May 9, 1904, President Roosevelt issued an Executive Order authorizing the Isthmian Canal Commission (ICC) to restrict immigration. To gauge how the US administration viewed anarchism, one has merely to see how anarchists were placed in a category with other undesirables also banned from the isthmus. The order prohibited

> idiots, the insane, epileptics, paupers, criminals, professional beggars, persons afflicted with loathsome or dangerous contagious diseases; those who have been convicted of felony, anarchists; those whose purpose is to incite insurrection and others whose presence it is believed by the Commission would tend to create public disorder, endanger the public health, or in any manner impede the prosecution of the work of opening the canal.

The ICC granted the canal governor, George Davis, the power to enforce this prohibition as he saw fit.[138] While Davis left in 1905, it would be Davis's successor who benefited from the clarity of this prohibition when General Charles Magoon became the new governor of the canal. For a year, Magoon oversaw the canal and its prohibitions against anarchist immigration, creating a relatively peaceful era that he would have longed to take with him when, in 1906, he was reassigned as provisional military governor of Cuba during the second US occupation, which lasted from 1906 to 1909, and when that island's anarchist movement began to blossom anew.[139]

The Panamanian government took its cue from the Roosevelt Administration. On June 11, Panama passed Law 72, Article 5 on immigration. It banned anarchists from the Republic of Panama, lumping anarchists into the same diseased and criminal populations as the Roosevelt Administration had done. Excluded from the country were "idiots, professional beggars, anarchists, criminals, individuals of known bad conduct, sufferers of tuberculosis, lepers, epileptics, and in general all foreigners suffering from repugnant and contagious illnesses."[140]

---

[138] *Proceedings of the First Canal Commission: March 22, 1904 to March 29, 1905* (Washington: ICC, 1905), 372–373; Davíd Viñas, *Anarquistas en América Latina* (Mexico City: Editorial Katun, 1983), 99.
[139] For treatment of Magoon and the Cuban anarchists, see Shaffer, *Anarchism and Countercultural Politics*, 50–51, 109–110, 172, 196.
[140] *Gaceta Oficial, Segunda Época*, June 23, 1904, 1, no. 31, 2.

Feeling secure that the scum of the Earth would never arrive to threaten this glorious enterprise, the United States began the onerous task of bringing laborers to the site. Canal administrators embarked on a global recruitment effort that initially brought construction workers on contract. From 1906 to 1908, over 8000 workers arrived from Spain. Additionally, thousands of contracted and non-contracted workers came from Greece, Italy, Cuba, and the West Indies.[141] Despite lacking guaranteed repatriation, many Spaniards saw work in Panama as a salvation to their destitution. As a result, groups of contracted and non-contracted laborers – sometimes accompanied by wives and children – began to arrive from the same Spanish town, with the largest numbers from the towns and villages of northwestern Spain. Meanwhile, the ICC chairman, Theodore Shonts, began to acquire Spaniards working on Cuban sugar plantations and building roads and railroads in Cuba. It is likely that Shonts could have attracted more of such workers had the Cuban planters and their allies in the Cuban government not protested the pilfering of "their" laborers.[142]

Upon arriving in the Canal Zone, workers found a never-ending array of poor living and working conditions. Good food was scarce. Many families resorted to living in tenements, shacks, or even abandoned boxcars.[143] Vice – that ever-present destroyer of virtue in the minds of both authorities and anarchists – ran rampant. While US officials in the Canal Zone banned gambling and prostitution, these activities were legal next door in Panama. American observer Arthur Bullard described Panama City and Colón as having "sections nearest to the American territory—which are given over to debauchery." It was easy for workers to simply cross "the border to the jurisdiction where the Ten Commandments are not so effectively backed up by the police."[144]

---

[141] Luis Navas, *El movimiento obrero en Panamá (1880–1914)* (San José, Costa Rica: Editorial Universitaria Centroamericana, 1979), 120–125; Julie Greene, "Spaniards on the Silver Roll: Labor Troubles and Liminality in the Panama Canal Zone, 1904–1914," *International Labor and Working-Class History* 66 (2004): 82; Yolanda Marco Serra, *Los obreros españoles en la construcción del canal de Panamá: La emigración española hacia Panamá vista a través de la prensa Española* (Panama City: Editorial Portobelo, 1997), 14.

[142] Harry A. Franck, *Zone Policeman 88: A Close Range Study of the Panama Canal and Its Workers* (New York: The Century Company, 1913), 105, 120; Greene, *The Canal Builders*, 50, 161.

[143] Franck, *Zone Policeman*, 105; Greene, *The Canal Builders*, 163.

[144] Arthur Bullard, *Panama: The Canal, the Country, and the People*, revised edition (New York: Macmillan Company, 1914), 61–62.

For those fearful of vice's influence, cities and towns along the frontier posed threats to individual virtue, one's savings, and the development of working-class consciousness. For those concerned with the state of womanhood, these conditions bred a spirit of promiscuity. By 1912, nearly 54,000 men worked in the Canal Zone. Nearly 18,000 women accompanied them. Some of these women were traditional homemakers. Others were independent or supplemented their husbands' income by serving as cooks, vendors, laundresses, hotel staff, and prostitutes. Historians and contemporaries alike described how the promiscuous, vice-filled frontier helped to "disintegrate the nuclear family: the feminine image (woman–wife–mother) fell vulnerable" to the prevalence of vice, crime, and violence.[145]

Probably the biggest shock for Spanish and Cuban workers was the realization that US Canal Zone authorities did not consider them to be "white." The situation was truly odd. After all, one of the reasons that employers initially sought Spanish workers was the belief that they worked harder than black West Indians. But in the Canal Zone, Spaniards officially became "semi-white." More important than any psychological torment that this might have brought on was the fact that being listed as "semi-white" meant that one was relegated to the "silver roll" – a euphemism really in which non-white and semi-white workers received lower pay than white North Americans while doing the most dangerous work.

These were the conditions that anarchists found when they managed to avoid the antianarchist laws and arrived in the Canal Zone – illustrating again the porousness of the empire. In July 1905, Panama-based anarchists initiated the first network links between Cuba and the Canal Zone. The migrant anarchist Luis Prats sent Havana's ¡Tierra! $1.30 in US currency. Prats was no stranger to Cuban anarchism. He was active with the city's anarchist group publishing ¡Tierra! in May 1903, but he left the city with his colleague Florencio Basora and headed to the United States. While Basora went to Vermont, Prats went to Washington from where he sent money to ¡Tierra! that November and in February 1904.[146] In June, he met up with Basora in St. Louis – a city that was

---

[145] Eyra Marcela Reyes Rivas, *El trabajo de las mujeres en la historia de la Construcción del Canal de Panamá, 1881–1914* (Panama City: Universidad de Panamá's Instituto de la Mujer, 2000), 26–33. See also, Greene, *The Canal Builders*, 226–266.

[146] *¡Tierra!*, May 23, 1903, 4; November 28, 1903, 4; August 22, 1903, 4; June 25, 1904; July 2, 1904, 4; August 20, 1904, 4.

attracting radicals, including the anti-Porfirio Díaz and soon-to-be notable anarchist Flores Magón brothers who had fled Mexico and then Texas before arriving in St. Louis in early 1905.[147] Prats soon left St. Louis, headed to Chicago, and by January 1905 was living in Hoboken, New Jersey. From there he went to Panama, and by July was communicating with his old comrade Domingo Mir in Havana, when he sent the first Panama-based contributions to ¡Tierra!. For a few more months he continued to sustain the Panama–Cuba link, but soon Serafín González replaced Prats in this transnational role. González was born in Lugo, Spain. At the age of thirty-two he went to Panama and began work in the Canal Zone in July 1905 as a foreman in the engineering department. However, he was constantly demoted until he was discharged in July 1906 for "incompetency."[148] Was it incompetency or were officials worried that González was an anarchist? Nevertheless, González lingered and agitated for anarchism in the Canal Zone, sustaining relations between Panama and Cuba, and inviting José María Blázquez de Pedro to Panama in 1914.[149]

More anarchists arrived in Panama, and they spread throughout the isthmus.[150] Anarchists became visible and numerous enough to attract the attention of US officials, especially in November 1906, when President Roosevelt arrived to inspect the construction project. The trip was the first time that a sitting US president had set foot on soil beyond US borders. On the afternoon of November 14, Roosevelt steamed into the Caribbean port of Colón on the battleship *Louisiana*. The trip posed significant security concerns for the Secret Service and canal authorities, who rounded up and detained anarchists before Roosevelt's arrival. They were held in custody until the president left.[151] During his visit, Roosevelt warned Panamanians to be vigilant against revolutions, praised the work of the canal police for maintaining order, and promised workers better

---

[147] On St. Louis as a destination for radicals, see Salvador Hernández Padilla, *El magonismo: historia de una pasión libertaria, 1900–1922*, 2nd edition (Mexico City: Ediciones Era, 1988), 24.

[148] "United States, Panama Canal Zone, Employment Records and Sailing lists, 1905–1937," database with images, *FamilySearch* (https://familysearch.org/ark:/61903/1:1:QVSH-714R, March 5, 2015), Serafin Gonzales, July 1, 1905; citing piece/folio, Service Record Cards,1904–1920, 7226556, Record Group 185, National Personnel Records Center, United States National Archives, St. Louis, Missouri.

[149] *¡Tierra!*, January 14, 1905, 4; July 8, 1905, 4. For González, see *¡Tierra!*, January 13, 1906, 4; April 9, 1914, 4.

[150] Greene, "Spaniards on the Silver Roll," 92.

[151] *New York Times*, November 15, 1906, 1.

living conditions.[152] Following the visit, authorities released anarchists from their illegal preventive detention without *habeas corpus*. They set out to agitate like never before in the Canal Zone, launching a multi-year effort attacking US rulers of the canal.

Anarchists continued to engage the international anarchist community. From 1907 onward, they strengthened relations with comrades in Cuba and Spain. In the wake of strikes in early 1907, Canal Zone-based anarchists such as A. Córdoba, A. Sans, R. Fernández, and others collected money and sent it to Havana to buy copies of *¡Tierra!* to distribute among their fellow workers. With the monetary donations came letters outlining labor issues in Panama. The first of these letters, published in September 1907, described a recent meeting urging workers to demand the eight-hour, ten-dollar day, with sixteen dollars for work on holidays. The writer also denounced US control and working conditions. As he put it, canal employment recruiters deliberately lied to workers by painting scenarios of excellent working conditions to lure cheap labor, and once there they faced routine police harassment. To add insult to injury, some US foremen even expelled workers from the job for doing nothing more than smoking a cigar while working. Signed by thirty-seven men, the letter urged *¡Tierra!*'s editors to send this notice to Spanish anarchist papers in order to spread the word to those "still in Spain with illusions of coming" to Panama that if they still wanted to come, then they had better expect poor conditions and abuse from police and foremen. That was, if you could avoid disasters like the one producing the single largest death toll, which occurred on December 12, 1908 in the Bas Obispo section of the construction project. For months, miners were blasting through solid rock. On December 12, over fifty drilled holes had been packed with over twenty tons of dynamite. Unexpectedly, the dynamite exploded, killing as many as 230 and injuring 50. The anarchist Ángel Talía decried American administrators for trying to censor news of the explosion and death toll.[153] Thus, like their comrades in Florida and Cuba, Canal Zone anarchists used *¡Tierra!* to warn potential migrants.

In the first half of 1907, attention turned to the canal's West Indian workforce, which US officials were increasingly using to replace

---

[152] Ibid., November 16, 1906, 1; November 17, 1906, 1; November 18, 1906, 1; November 20, 1906, 1.
[153] *¡Tierra!*, September 7, 1907, 3; January 16, 1909, 2; *Tierra y Libertad*, January 31, 1907, 2. Casualty figures for the explosion vary. For early low estimates, see *Los Angeles Herald*, December 14, 1908, which claimed there were fourteen deaths and fifty injuries.

Spaniards – that is, fellow silver-roll workers. Spanish workers challenged the West Indian laborforce, accusing it of undermining labor militancy and driving down wage rates.[154] While anarchists have been accused of essentially being racist toward black workers and joining in the denunciations, one should be cautious in making such an assessment.[155] Spanish-speaking militants were hostile not only to black workers, and not because they were black! British West Indians tended to stay within their communities. Language differences obviously played a role in this, but as historians have noted, these Antillean workers also tended to be more religious and conservative than their Spanish, and particularly anarchist, counterparts.[156]

Anarchists saw several interrelated issues here. First, they viewed the ever-increasing numbers of Antillean laborers as a plot by US canal managers to undermine working-class unity and drive down wages. Second, anarchists, who despised the influence of all organized religion, saw the Anglican, Episcopalian, Baptist, and Catholic Churches – all encouraged by the ICC and widely attended by Antillean workers – as corrupting influences that deradicalized those workers. This was not a "racist" assault on West Indians. Anarchists criticized all workers regardless of color for attending church services. This was standard anarchist practice everywhere. Third, while anarchists in the Canal Zone have been contrasted with their Cuban counterparts for not developing an antiracism stance in the canal, the reality is that anarchists in Cuba never did either. Race was not an issue of concern other than when governments used it as a wedge to divide workers or when cultural conservatism (like religious practices) distracted workers from working-class consciousness and labor militancy – both in Cuba and in Panama.[157] Fourth, as anarchist M. D. Rodríguez argued, all foreign workers suffered from the policies of Uncle Sam, especially Antilleans, who were the poorest paid and lived in the worst conditions. And how did so many distraught and condemned workers solve their problems, he asked. They throw "themselves in front of a passing locomotive."

---

[154] Greene, "Spaniards on the Silver Roll," 86.
[155] Ibid., 92; J. A. Zumoff, "Black Caribbean Labor Radicalism in Panama, 1914–1921," *Journal of Social History* 47, no. 2 (2013): 435.
[156] Navas, *El movimiento obrero en Panamá*, 146–147; Conniff, *Black Labor on a White Canal*, 38.
[157] Shaffer, *Anarchism and Countercultural Politics*, 90–104; Greene, *The Canal Builders*, 174–175.

Working for anarchy was a better option.[158] Thus, labor organizations in the canal were undermined less by anarchist antiblack policies and more by language divisions, religious conservatism, the elitism of North American workers who enjoyed better pay and conditions on the "gold roll," and ICC policies.

EL ÚNICO AND INTENSIFICATION OF ANARCHIST ANTI-AMERICANISM ON THE CANAL

The arrival of M. D. Rodríguez in 1910 energized anarchist organizing in the Canal Zone.[159] Hailing from northwest Spain, Rodríguez epitomized the migrating anarchist. After leaving Spain, he worked for anarchist causes in Rosario, Argentina in 1907.[160] In November 1907, authorities deported him from Argentina and he moved to Havana, working in the growing Cuban anarchist movement by 1908. In early 1910, Rodríguez traveled to the Canal Zone where he immediately began writing to Barcelona. Month after month, Rodríguez leveled scorn upon the United States: US administration of the canal, the separate hospital wards for Americans, the higher pay for Americans, the severe exploitation of black workers, and the practice of officials illegally opening mail and destroying radical newspapers.[161]

During 1910 and early 1911, Rodríguez, Salvatore Olivé, and Juan Chacón Uceda nurtured links with Havana. Rodríguez (going by B. Pérez) sent money to *¡Tierra!*. He and Chacón Uceda bought bundles of revolutionary pamphlets to distribute in the Canal Zone. Olivé and many of his comrades consistently sent money to the Liga Internacional Racionalista Sección de Cuba (International Rationalist League of Cuba) to help finance Havana's emerging anarchist schools.[162] In July 1911, worker insubordination spread throughout the Canal Zone as laborers protested

---

[158] *Tierra y Libertad*, May 19, 1910, 3; June 8, 1910, 4. Quote from June 8.
[159] Rodríguez went by several names in the Canal Zone, including Bernardo Pérez and Intransigente. The ICC referred to him as "Bernardo Pérez," but he was most widely referred to as Rodríguez in the international anarchist press, especially by the Argentineans, Cubans, and Spaniards who knew him best.
[160] For some of his correspondence from Argentina to Spain, see *Tierra y Libertad* from June through July 1907. See *Acción Libertaria*, March 31, 1911, 4 for his take on his deportation.
[161] For an overview of these critiques, see his monthly and sometimes weekly columns in *Tierra y Libertad* throughout the second half of 1910 and into 1911.
[162] *¡Tierra!*, April 9, 1910, 4; April 16, 1910, 4; July 16, 1910, 4; April 22, 1911, 4; May 20, 1911, 4.

conditions, their American overseers, and again the perceived replacement of Spanish workers with West Indians. Sympathy strikes arose throughout the Canal Zone, especially among Spanish workers who anarchists increasingly targeted with propaganda. Anarchist initiatives spread throughout the Canal Zone as Rodríguez became the driving force to build a series of anarchist groups across the isthmus in Gatún, Balboa, Culebra, Las Cascadas, Gorgona, Tabernilla, Colón, and Emperador and coordinate their activities into the Federación Anarquista de Panamá (Anarchist Federation of Panama).

In September 1911, Rodríguez and his comrades launched Panama's first anarchist publication, *El Único*.[163] Ideologically, the magazine reflected "individualist anarchism" and proclaimed itself the publication of the Federación Individualista Internacional (International Individualist Federation, or FII) – a federation with associated groups in Spain, Panama, and Vancouver. By February 1912, the federation claimed to represent fifteen separate anarchist groups throughout the Canal Zone.[164] While individualist anarchism was not a particularly strong variant in Latin America generally or the Caribbean specifically, it did have a strong following in northwestern Spain, from where large numbers of Spanish laborers on the canal originated, including many of the writers for *El Único*. As individualists, Rodríguez and his comrades followed the writings of Max Stirner. Even the magazine's name – *El Único* – was taken from Stirner's most famous book *The Ego and His Own*, which had been translated into Spanish as *El Único y su propiedad*.[165] The nineteenth-century Stirner condemned governments and all forms of religion. He also rejected communism and syndicalism. He believed that communism (of any type) crushed the individual. While anarcho-communists stressed that the individual could be truly free only if society were free from coercive and authoritarian institutions, individualists put the equation the other way around: Society could only be free if the individual were first free. For anarcho-syndicalists, the workplace was where men and women could best organize to create an anarchist future of decentralized, grass roots democracy that would federate horizontally. Individualists countered, fearing that the union

---

[163] There is a reference to a newspaper from the zone titled *La Ráfaga* from December 1908. If it did exist, no copies seem to have survived. See *¡Tierra!*, December 26, 1908, 4. The federation even had a telephone, making them possibly the first anarchists in the Caribbean to have one. *El Único*, February 12, 1912, 81.
[164] *El Único*, February 12, 1912, back cover.   [165] Ibid., March 12, 1912, 91.

itself was an example of excessive centralizing powers in the hands of a few union leaders who would never relinquish authority to individual men and women, and who would crush individual dissent. Rodríguez adapted Stirner's ideas into his own individualist program for the FII and the magazine.

From October 1911 to April 1912, the staff printed 2500 copies of *El Único* each month, except for January 1912 when 4250 copies were printed and distributed in the Canal Zone, Spain, Cuba, and Vancouver. Money arrived from Spain, Argentina, Brazil, Cuba, Portugal, Italy, France, Panama, and Uruguay for the FII's Comité Pro-Presos Internacional (International Prisoners Support Committee) and to purchase a printing press.[166] To facilitate fundraising, the editors resorted to a bit of coercion as well as consciousness raising. The editors demanded that all restaurants, saloons, barber shops, and anywhere else patronized by Spanish workers have copies of *El Único* available and displayed prominently. Otherwise, those places would be boycotted.[167]

Through the pages of *El Único* and at regular public meetings, Rodríguez and his associates joined earlier anarchist complaints about canal conditions with blatant political challenges to the ICC. For instance, workers struck by disease and injuries filled Canal Zone hospitals. The chief medical officer, William Gorgas, who in Cuba had worked with Dr. Carlos Finlay to drastically reduce mosquito-borne diseases on the island – an eradication campaign the United States then exported to the Canal Zone – reported how Spanish patients in the canal's hospitals always had anarchist reading materials from Spain and Cuba.[168] When the ICC banned the anarchist press in the hospital at Ancón, *El Único* asked "Where is freedom of opinion so often mentioned by the North Americans?"[169]

Anarchists also took aim at representatives of other countries who they charged with American collusion. One target was abusive foremen who supervised labor gangs for the ICC. *El Único* established a system for workers to identify and complain about foremen and bosses. Such complaints could wind up in the magazine's pages and be read throughout the Canal Zone.[170] For instance, *El Único* attacked Greek foremen for

---

[166] See the inside front and back covers for this information.
[167] Report on Meeting of European Laborers at Mireaflores [sic], September 17, 1911, to the Ancón Chief of Police, Record Group 185 General Files of the Panama Canal 1905–1914 (hereafter referred to as RG 185 ICC 1905–1914), 2-P-59, United States National Archives, College Park, MD.
[168] Greene, *The Canal Builders*, 175.   [169] *El Único*, January 12, 1912, 61–62.
[170] Ibid., October 12, 1911 (inside back cover).

abusing Spanish workers. "Instead of using their positions to repudiate the exploiters of labor, they do the opposite. Why do these Athenians work so despotically? It is because they are Americanized."[171]

The magazine was true to anarchism's anticlerical roots as well. Anarchists regularly complained about the presence of churches in the Canal Zone – a presence urged by the ICC as a way to undermine radicalization of the labor force.[172] Such sentiments occurred in the first issue when Rodríguez published a column entitled "Flee Monk" by the Spanish-born anarchist educator Juan Moncaleano, who was then leading rationalist schools in Cuba after fleeing Colombia. The column, along with the magazine's anti-state writings, was reinforced under the magazine's mast head, which read, "READING PROHIBITED BY CLERGY, POLITICIANS, EXPLOITERS, AND GOVERNMENT OFFICALS." Following in the spirit of antireligious appeals, Rodríguez recognized those workers who refused to succumb to religious temptations. For instance, he praised an unnamed anarchist worker in Las Cascadas when he and his wife refused to baptize their child.[173] Anarchist complaints of US-provided living conditions could merge with their assaults on religion and authoritarianism in general. For instance, Rodríguez complained that any ICC talk of improving worker housing was a chimera if it did not include, among other things, the "demolition of all churches, convents, jails, army barracks, forts, police stations, arsenals, and factories that are exterminators of men. Then these materials will be used in the construction of modern residences."[174]

In response, Catholic priests complained to US officials. Father D. Quijano could not believe that the ICC allowed anarchists to hold meetings in the Canal Zone, where they could freely proselytize to "some innocent boys ... Of course, the few good men that there are among the laborers are intimidated and obliged to join the anarchists." In October 1911, anarchists planned a rally commemorating the 1909 execution of radical education practitioner Francisco Ferrer y Guardia in Spain. In the planning, Rodríguez announced that the meal at the rally would consist of, among other items, "Fried Priest Heart" and "Iced Jesuit's Blood." Father Henry Collins expressed outrage to ICC chairman George Goethals, claiming that *El Único* and the anarchists in the Canal Zone were part of an international conspiracy ultimately aimed at revolution:

---

[171] Ibid., May 18, 1912, 126.   [172] Conniff, *Black Labor on a White Canal*, 38.
[173] *El Único*, September 12, 1911, supplemental, 14; October 12, 1911, 7.
[174] Ibid., December 12, 1911, 33.

"the government of Panama would be just what they could possibly wish for!"[175] The charge – somewhat preposterous – implied that anarchists in the Canal Zone desired to overthrow the Panamanian government. No anarchist in the Canal Zone advocated this – at least not publicly.

Yet, while anarchist-led labor organizing frustrated the ICC, its foremen, and its religious associates, US officials in the Canal Zone by 1912 began to believe that anarchists were not a violent threat to either the canal or public order, leading to the end of ICC surveillance of anarchist groups by March 1912.[176] Still, anarchist activity in the Canal Zone continued at relatively high rates until early 1914, when construction drew to a close. In 1912, some 4000 Spaniards remained in the Panama Canal Zone. From 1912 to 1914, anarchist activities centered around associations like Grupo "Los Nada" in Pedro Miguel and Grupo "Libre Pensamiento" in Gatún, while smaller groups operated in Miraflores (Grupo "Los Libertarios"), Culebra (Grupo "Germinal"), and Toro Point (Grupo "Solidaridad"). They sent money to and bought subscriptions of ¡Tierra!, as well as helped to fund international campaigns to free political prisoners in Cuba and the United States. Increasingly, they sent money to buy copies of the two New York City-based newspapers *Cultura Obrera* and *Fuerza Consciente*.[177]

By late 1912, as most people knew that their futures either meant leaving the isthmus or finding work in Panama, canal-based anarchists began turning their attention to political and social issues in the Panamanian Republic. In 1912, Liberal politician Belisario Porras won the presidency. Porras embarked on several social reforms – including a much-vaunted eight-hour workday in 1914.[178] Anarchists were unimpressed with both Porras's pro-labor rhetoric and the US-designed political system. "Sin Dios" lamented how Panamanians had blindly gone to the polls to elect "a tyrant, the same who perhaps tomorrow will order his knaves to shoot and jail those who have gone to the polls to vote for his

---

[175] See letters from Quijano and Collins from August to October 1911 in ICC 1905–1914, 2-P-59.

[176] Memoranda from Paul Wilson to ICC Secretary Joseph Bishop, August 31, 1911 and September 2, 1911, RG 185 ICC 1905–1914, 2-P-59; Greene, *The Canal Builders*, 177; Franck, *Zone Policeman*, 63–64, 256–257.

[177] For examples, see ¡Tierra!, October 19, 1912, 4; November 23, 1912, 4; January 18, 1913, 4; May 30, 1913, 4; October 17, 1913, 1; and, May 7, 1914, 4; *Cultura Obrera*, December 1912, 4; *Fuerza Consciente*, various issues between August 1913 and January 1914.

[178] Jorge Turner, *Raíz, historia y perspectivas del movimiento obrero panameño* (Mexico City: Editorial Signos, 1982), 29–30.

elevation to power."[179] From Pedro Miguel, Braulio Hurtado wrote a series of columns to ¡Tierra! from September 1912 to May 1913, declaring all politicians (no matter how many poor people voted for them or the pro-labor initiatives they led) to be deceivers, only seeking power. Just before Porras's inauguration in October 1912, Hurtado asked why Panamanian workers should get excited about a new president. Yet, many did get excited by Porras's populist agenda. Hurtado described how Panamanians – some barefoot and living on a diet of coffee, bread, water, and canned sardines – had voted for their new "caciques" (chiefs). At least, he concluded, "we *foreigners* won't be participants in such cultural and moral stooping."[180]

The Colombia-born Biófilo Panclasta traveled to Panama in mid-1913 and was not impressed with the neocolonial institutions or mindsets created under US influence either. In his characteristic hyperbole, he wrote that Washington had turned Panama into a slave prison. Here, he said, they exploit blacks as they did in the United States. Average Panamanians were to blame for this condition: "Panamanians, the majority of whom are like monkeys, love their executioners, kiss their chains." But they are oh so proud of their independence: "their martyrs fill them with pride. 'Here you have our homes, our women, our riches,' says a police chief to the Americans.' What horror!"[181] Ultimately, Panclasta's bitter remarks toward Panamanian nationalism sounded very close to those anarchists in Cuba who at that same moment were lamenting working-class Cubans who praised *Cuba libre* and thus thought nothing more needed to be done.

Amid these political critiques, the Argentina-born, Panama-based Julio Carrasco urged anarchists to reinvigorate the movement by organizing workers centers – something anarchists had wanted to create in the Canal Zone since early 1910, when Jorgonis Uceda called for such a center to not only unify "centers of resistance, our libraries, our anarchist newspapers," but also as a sign of strength and a show of force: "the North Americans will respect us as men" as "we will have at hand a means by which to launch a general strike in the zone."[182] Carrasco declared that it was time to launch "a Workers Center, that is, a resistance society, that with a little sacrifice and will" workers can pursue education, culture, and science "that guides man to be free and to have good health to combat the

---

[179] *El Libertario*, September 28, 1912, 4.
[180] *¡Tierra!*, September 7, 1912, 4. Italics in original; Greene, *The Canal Builders*, 161.
[181] *Acción Libertaria*, July 11, 1913, 3.   [182] *¡Tierra!*, April 23, 1910, 2.

many evils that continually threaten their existence."[183] The center could also be a symbolic anti-imperialist challenge to "those barbaric misters of the North," showing them that workers in the Canal Zone had the force of will and understanding to stand up to North American despotism. In November 1912, workers in Gatún opened a new Workers Center. From there, Canal Zone anarchists continued to agitate while also sending money to Cuba, ordering newspapers out of Havana, and mailing funds for anarchist causes in Cuba, Spain, and the United States.[184]

As canal construction wound down before 1914's opening, anarchists continued to fight against US rule and abuse. For instance, the ICC boasted that the death rate in the canal was lower than in some US states. José Novo had been one of the witnesses to the premature explosion at Bas Obispo in 1908 that killed hundreds of workers. Other explosions and landslides brought quick death or lingering misery. And what was the United States's response to these disasters over the years now that the canal project was ending, asked Novo? "What did the Yanqui government pay the families ...? Absolutely nothing." As a superintendent for the Emperador division supposedly said, Spain, Italy, England, and other countries had an abundance of workers who would take the risk. So why should the United States pay death compensations?[185] Such a position represented the lack of justice one found in a land controlled by the "great North American republic," charged another anarchist. Anarchists suspected that this behavior reflected the real United States beyond its superficial progressive rhetoric. "If all the Yanquis are like this, undoubtedly it would be better to be a subject of the emperor of Japan than a citizen of North America. At least there, no one talks pompously, like in Yanquilandia, of Equality, Freedom, and Fraternity."[186]

At its core, this was a political attack on US republicanism and expansionism. The quintessential republic – the United States – was at the root of the problem. If it was the model, then wouldn't all countries who called themselves republics and implemented US-style political systems also behave as the United States did – or worse? Like anarchists in Cuba, Florida, and Puerto Rico, to attack republicanism was to attack US expansionism. Those thoughts found international expression in 1912 when W. C. Owen, working with the anarchist *magonistas* in Los Angeles, California, weighed in on the pages of the Partido Liberal

---

[183] Ibid., October 19, 1912, 4.   [184] Ibid., November 23, 1912, 3.
[185] Greene, *The Canal Builders*, 132; *Tierra y Libertad*, July 13, 1912, 2.
[186] *El Libertario*, January 25, 1913, 4.

Mexicano's (Mexican Liberal Party, or PLM) *Regeneración*. Owen noted that Panama had become a virtual extension of the United States – a US-controlled and -guarded transshipment point for the benefit primarily of the North American capitalist class, and a surrounding country that on the surface appeared to be a free, independent republican nation. However, "[the United States owns] the Panama Canal and Panama, as we own the Philippines, Hawaii, Porto Rico, Cuba. [The United States] shall fortify the canal and transform what might have been the world's greatest instrument for peace into a constant threat of war" and will make the canal "a national possession, and thereby once more block the road to that world brotherhood of which steam and electricity were harbingers."[187]

While throughout 1913 Braulio Hurtado still raised money to send to Havana to help *¡Tierra!* buy its own printing press, sixty people signed a statement and sent money to purchase Spanish and Cuban anarchist periodicals, and the anarchist Marcelino Díaz wrote from his "Harmony Colony" somewhere in Panama that times were changing and people were leaving the Canal Zone due to its near completion.[188] In September 1913, the Miraflores-based group "Los Iguales" folded. In October, the FII moved to Panama City. They tried to put on a good face, claiming it was done to be closer to the sites of corruption and nearer to the most exploited.[189] Only small amounts of money arrived at *¡Tierra!*'s offices from this time through 1914, when in May and June two different groups announced their closure.[190] Likewise, FII money to Spain and *Acción Libertaria* dried up and the paper was not published in 1914. It only returned in January 1915 from Gijón, and with no records of money arriving from the Canal Zone.[191] Smaller anarchist groups continued to operate in Ancón, Cristóbal, Pedro Miguel, Culebra, and Balboa throughout 1914. Lacking their own newspaper, they continued to send small sums of money for subscriptions to *¡Tierra!*, but no Panamanian correspondence was published.

Still, anarchism did not completely evaporate. On August 15, 1914, navigation on the Panama Canal formally commenced. In May, just three months before this historic date, anarchists welcomed the arrival of the

---

[187] *Regeneración*, August 3, 1912, 4, reprinted in Spanish, August 24, 1912, 1.
[188] *¡Tierra!*, May 30, 1913, 4; July 4, 1913, 4; August 8, 1913, 4.
[189] *Acción Libertaria*, September 26, 1913, 4; October 17, 1913, 3–4.
[190] *¡Tierra!*, April 23, 1914, 4; June 11, 1914, 4.
[191] See *Acción Libertaria*, January 8, 1915 and beyond.

thirty-nine-year-old, internationally known anarchist José María Blázquez de Pedro from Spain. An anarchist author and agitator since the turn of the century, one remembers that this was not his first trip to the Caribbean because two decades earlier he had been a young Spanish soldier sent to Cuba to put down the Cuban rebellion. Blázquez de Pedro arrived in Panama at the invitation of the long-time isthmian anarchist Serafín G. González, who, like Blázquez de Pedro, was a Spanish veteran of the Cuban War.[192]

Upon disembarking in Colón, Blázquez de Pedro began a regular writing schedule.[193] He was no stranger to Havana's anarchists. From 1907 to 1912, Cuban anarchists had advertised his works like *La agonía del repatriado* (The Agony of the Repatriated) and *Rebeldías cantadas* (Rebellion Songs) in the pages of ¡*Tierra!*. Even before then, he was in communication with José Guardiola, an early anarchist presence in Havana who ran a bookstore that catered especially to workers.[194] Blázquez de Pedro's first columns from Colón to Havana discussed his book of poetry, *Pensares*, and Panamanian politics. Like Hurtado and Carrasco, Blázquez de Pedro attacked Panamanian politicians and the very imported political system itself. "Without the patriotic, the religious, the governmental and the providers of alcohol, how few ballots would be cast into the ballot boxes in every country!"[195] That column to ¡*Tierra!* sowed the seeds for his later years of Panamanian activism. With the collapse of ¡*Tierra!* in early 1915, Blázquez de Pedro continued to write to the Barcelona newspaper *Tierra y Libertad*. Throughout the year, he sent almost weekly columns to Spain. They were devoted to theoretical issues mainly, like fanaticism and the origins of the Great War. These columns kept the anarchists in Panama linked to the outside world. Money often accompanied these columns, most of it collected by Blázquez de Pedro and González. The anarchist presence – hardly a movement by now – was hanging by a thread. In April 1916, the last two groups in the Canal Zone – "Los Autónomos" and "Los Sedientos" – merged and promptly

---

[192] ¡*Tierra!*, January 13, 1906, 4; November 8, 1913, 4; April 9, 1914, 4; *Tierra y Libertad*, February 4, 1907, 4. González was a mason by trade, whose Cuban-born *compañera* Amalia was the daughter of a Spanish typesetter. They had four daughters, two with the anarchist-friendly names Armonia and Libertaria. See Soriano Jiménez and Íñiguez, *José María Blázquez de Pedro*, 227–232.

[193] Franco Múñoz, *Blázquez de Pedro*, 173.

[194] ¡*Tierra!*, November 13, 1906, 4; June 12, 1907, 4; December 30, 1911, 4; March 30, 1911, 4.

[195] Ibid., July 16, 1914, 2; July 23, 1914, 2 (quote from the latter).

left the Canal Zone, establishing a base in Panama City, where Blázquez de Pedro had also relocated with his two brothers and sister.[196]

CONCLUSION

The birth of the newspaper ¡Tierra! in late 1902 solidified Havana as the hub of the emerging anarchist network. For twelve years, anarchists across Cuba, Florida, Puerto Rico, and the Panamanian isthmus made ¡Tierra! their own. The paper could not have been successful or crucial to anarchist mobilization without transnational support. Through sharing money and news, regional anarchists began to create a Caribbean anarchist community. They shared similar experiences attacking a rapacious capitalist system, democratic political systems that seemed to merely reinforce wealth divides and exploitation of peasants and workers, and an American oversight that often saw US military and political personnel being transferred to different posts around the region. Anarchists throughout the network shared their anti-American experiences in the pages of the newspaper, which was then mailed across the network. In this way, anarchists and their readers could see that their struggles were not isolated.

As a regional paper, ¡Tierra! reported on news from throughout the region and exposed anarchists to new groups emerging around the Caribbean Basin from places like Nicaragua or Colombia. Though on the fringe of the network, there was a vibrant movement in Costa Rica, where, in January 1911, José María Zeledón – a long-time anarchist in San José – helped to launch the first anarchist periodical in the country: *Renovación*.[197] As the Costa Rican anarchists grew, they reached out to ¡Tierra!. Cuban anarchists became regular consumers of the San José journal, praising each new issue. *Renovación* also published writers mostly unknown to readers in the network, including the works of Salvadoran sociologist Alberto Masferrer, Colombian poet Guillermo Valencia, and

---

[196] *Tierra y Libertad*, December 29, 1915, 4; May 3, 1916, 4; ¡Tierra!, December 10, 1910, 4. Perhaps it was no coincidence that in 1910 Blázquez de Pedro also had founded a group called "Los Autónomos" in his city of Béjar, Spain.

[197] For instance, see ¡Tierra!, January 13, 1912, 4; December 25, 1913, 4. *Renovación*, January 15, 1911, 1 and 3; David Díaz-Arias, "From Radicals to Heroes of the Republic: Anarchism and National Identity in Costa Rica, 1900–1977" in *In Defiance of Boundaries: Anarchism in Latin American History*, eds. Geoffroy de Laforcade and Kirwin Shaffer (Gainesville: University Press of Florida, 2015), 232.

Nicaraguan writer Leonardo Mantalbán.[198] Thus, the paper's distribution also brought the writings of Central American and Colombian writers to audiences in Cuba, facilitating a new dimension in transnational transfers of information and ideas. Of course, the transfer went both ways as Costa Rican readers could read the perspectives and issues facing anarchists around the region in ¡Tierra! when it arrived in San José.[199]

In the years following the Cuban War, anarchists across the Florida Straits continued their relationships as men, money, and newspapers traveled back and forth between Florida and Havana. This embryonic network then grew – not the least because US military, political, and economic interests began expanding across the Caribbean and anarchists went with them. By the mid-1910s, anarchists in Florida, Cuba, Puerto Rico, and the Panama Canal Zone had established numerous groups agitating for anarchist causes and improved conditions for workers. Anarchists attacked US rule, oversight, and US-inspired political activities. In Cuba, anarchists challenged the limits set on Malatesta's visit in 1900, the Platt Amendment to the Cuban Constitution in 1902, repeated efforts to impose a US-designed electoral system on the island, and a Cuban political elite who repressed or deported anarchists when radicalism threatened to cause the United States to invade. Puerto Rico-based anarchists fought against some of these as well. Their critiques of electoral systems mirrored those of their Cuban comrades. The Panama Canal Zone offered a different scenario. While anarchists had to fight against US control, abusive foremen, and overzealous canal police, there was no electoral system in the Canal Zone itself. But by the 1910s, anarchists turned their sights upon the Republic of Panama's US-imported political system too. Unlike Cuba or Puerto Rico, there were no native, that is Panamanian, anarchists in the isthmus. This was entirely a migrant movement that could not fall back on the defense of being citizens of the place where they agitated or as heroes of independence wars. In addition, anarchists in the Canal Zone and the republic were clearly there in violation of US and Panamanian laws that explicitly excluded them. To agitate openly – as they did and would continue to do – placed these

---

[198] See, for instance, ¡Tierra!, November 4, 1911, 4; April 20, 1912, 4; May 18, 1912, 4; June 18, 1912, 4; July 11, 1913, 4; Renovación, March 5, 1911, 69; March 30, 1911, 125–126; May 15, 1911, inside front cover; October 1911, 306; November 1911, 306.
[199] Renovación, February 5, 1912; September 10, 1912; October 10, 1912 (all inside the front covers). Other anarchist papers took part in this sharing with Renovación: El Único (Panama), Nuevos Horizontes (Puerto Rico), ¡Despertad! (Key West), and La Razón (El Salvador).

international anarchists in constant danger of deportation from the Canal Zone and Panama if the authorities chose to enforce the law. Florida anarchists had still different dilemmas as often unwelcome foreign agitators in the United States – especially in the wake of antianarchist laws and the anarchist assassination of President McKinley. It wasn't just federal officials and laws though. Perhaps the biggest threats to Florida anarchists came from Anglos – both those who led the AFL-linked unions and distrusted foreign radical workers as well as the Florida business and political elite who stooped to kidnapping and illegal deportation to thwart the anarchist tide in Tampa.

So, then, what was the meaning of democracy in the American Mediterranean? Anarchists had no love for democratic politics, as we know. After all, "anarchy" meant "without rulers." But for peoples coming out of years of harsh colonial tyranny, like in Cuba or Puerto Rico, the allure of a form of government based on, by, and for the people nevertheless had to look attractive. That attraction quickly faded when a republican government attacked workers who challenged the bourgeois rulers or the foreign corporations with which they colluded. Anarchist experiences with the democratic United States in the 1890s continued into the twentieth century as anarchists experienced the same political intrigues and government–capitalist collusion in Panama, Puerto Rico, Cuba, and of course Tampa. To anarchists, tyrannous neocolonialism thrived – this time under the guise of American republican enlightenment. Was the US democratic era really any better for the masses than despotic Spanish or Colombian rule that preceded it?

The revolutionary struggle against neocolonialism soon became intertwined with the violence of the Mexican Revolution. In fact, the Mexican Revolution would take center stage in the anarchist platform by 1911 as radicals across the network adopted the anarchist PLM's cause as their own. Armed anarchists had failed to create the Social Revolution in Cuba. Calls to arms against Anglo vigilantes in Florida went nowhere. But in the borderlands between Mexico and the United States, anarchists in Cuba, Puerto Rico, Florida, and Panama saw the potential for a revolutionary new dawn achieved by armed insurrection. Unfortunately for the cause, not everyone saw the Mexican Revolution in the same way. The revolution would cause the first great ideological disruption in the Caribbean anarchist network – a disruption just as profound as shanghaiing vigilantes, abusive foremen, and pro-American trade unions.

3

¡Tierra y Libertad!

Caribbean Anarchists and the Mexican Revolution, 1905–1930

> I see my dreams of happiness being realized there, in the wretched people of Mexico ... My friends, I would love to hear the bomb blasts destroying the damned factories and workshops. And I would look forward to seeing this stupid society blown to a thousand bits ... dying and the cowards suffocating from the smell of dynamite.
>
> Ángel María Dieppa, Puerto Rico, 1912

The historian of French anarchism, Richard Sonn, once wrote that anarchists – with all of their projects like schools, healthcare, performances, naturism, and the like – tended to be more concerned with "living the revolution" than with going to the barricades and "making revolution."[1] Few actually had much of a choice in the matter. In the history of global anarchism, opportunities to launch or join an armed insurrection were few and far between. The Caribbean Basin, though, offered anarchists two distinct chances to pick up arms and struggle to free humanity: the Cuban War for Independence in the 1890s and the Mexican Revolution in the 1910s. If one were of the right age, born in, say, the 1870s to early 1880s and living in, say, Havana, then one experienced these two revolutionary upheavals and the anarchist efforts to violently overthrow authoritarianism in all its guises. Just as anarchists had joined their struggle to the Cuban War in the 1890s, they linked their identity and future to Mexico in 1910.

This chapter first briefly examines the pre-revolution contacts between anarchists in Mexico and Cuba as the network built on a history of

---

[1] Richard Sonn, *Anarchism* (New York: Twayne Publishers, 1992), 52.

pro-Cuban independence insurgents who moved to Mexico in the 1890s. We then see how Caribbean anarchists made the Mexican Revolution their own cause, with Havana serving as a key source of regional fundraising for and information about the Partido Liberal Mexicano (Mexican Liberal Party, or PLM). Meanwhile, some anarchists moved to the revolutionary zone. Caribbean anarchists also condemned the Mexican revolutionary Francisco Madero and the United States when anarchists saw them colluding to stop PLM and Industrial Workers of the World (IWW) activists in Mexico. As a sign of how anarchists saw the Mexican Revolution as their own struggle, we explore examples of anarchist literature produced in the Caribbean about the revolution. Finally, the revolution created controversy and division in the network, sparking anarchists across the Caribbean to rise and defend revolutionary heroes like Ricardo Florés Magón. Revolution was a dangerous business, especially when your own loyalties found you crossing numerous political borders and thus confronting numerous governments out to stop you. But danger also could come from within. One had to trust comrades to do what was right and confront those perceived to be doing wrong. When questions of loyalty to the cause and the *magonistas* emerged, anarchists across the network unleashed their own policing function to expose possible frauds, turncoats, and spies whose actions undermined the anarchist dimensions of the Mexican Revolution.

HAVANA AND THE YUCATÁN

During the Cuban independence struggles of the nineteenth century, independence supporters often left Cuba for New York City, Key West, and Tampa. However, because of Mexico's proximity to Cuba, many also made their way across the Gulf of Mexico to the Yucatán Peninsula, especially to cities like Mérida, which was less than 500 miles (800 km) from Havana.[2] One recalls that Manuel Miranda had planned to do just that before being ensnared in a trap and deported to Fernando Póo instead. These 1890s linkages did not disappear as the new century unfolded. Years before Francisco Madero or the Flores Magón brothers called for revolution, Havana's anarchists engaged fellow radicals in the Yucatán. In April 1903, Mérida-based anarchists began buying *¡Tierra!* and communicating with Havana's anarchists, making it the "first foreign anarchist newspaper to establish contacts on Mexican soil," in the words

[2] Muller, *Cuban Émigrés*, 63–74.

of Jacinto Barrera Bassols.[3] In mid-1903, Francisco Ros Planas left Cuba and moved to Mérida to organize radicals in the city. Ros Planas was not alone. Mexican authorities grew increasingly alarmed at the number of Spanish, Cuban, and Italian radicals arriving to organize with Yucatecan labor leaders. In 1905, Ros Planas, Antonio J. Duch, and Tomás Pérez Ponce – the latter of whom would open a Libertarian Circle – regularly communicated with Havana. For the next several years, anarchists in Mérida consistently purchased copies of ¡Tierra!, supported jailed Cuban radicals, and forwarded money via Havana to Russian revolutionaries. Yucatecan purchases of ¡Tierra! were at times rather significant. In fact, Mérida's anarchists completely financed the March 26, 1904 issue of the Cuban paper.[4]

In late 1907, the Mexican government grew alarmed about these transnational anarchist connections and arrested Ros Planas and Duch. While ¡Tierra!'s Mexican correspondents awaited trial, Mexico persuaded authorities in Havana to act against the newspaper's editor, Abelardo Saavedra. In January 1908, Cuban police arrested Saavedra and charged him with defaming the Mexican dictator Porfirio Díaz. While Saavedra was acquitted in Havana – thanks to the efforts of his defense lawyer, the former Tampa-based Italian anarchist Orestes Ferrara – Mexican authorities sentenced Duch to seventeen months in a Mérida prison. Upon release from jail, authorities deported him to Spain. Mexico asked US authorities then occupying Cuba not to allow Ros Planas to disembark in Havana. US Supervisor Enoch Crowder – after initially refusing because he found nothing in Cuban immigration law that banned anarchists from entering the island – ultimately reversed himself: "The wishes of the Mexican Government will be respected and orders have been issued to prevent the landing on Cuban soil of Anarchist Francisco Ros Planas."[5] This would not be the last time the Mexican and US governments cooperated against anarchists. For several years after that, communications were

---

[3] ¡Tierra!, April 25, 1903; May 16, 1903; Jacinto Barrera Bassols, Los rebeldes de la bandera roja: Textos del periódico anarquista ¡Tierra!, de la Habana, sobre la revolución Mexicana (Mexico City: Instituto Nacional de Antropología e Historia, 2011), 14.

[4] For examples, see ¡Tierra!, May 16, 1903; January 2, 1904; March 26, 1904; April 22, 1905; May 20, 1905; December 9, 1905; and April 14, 1907; all information can be found on page four of each issue. See also, Alan Wells and Gilbert Joseph, Summer of Discontent, Season of Upheaval: Elite Politics and Rural Insurgency in Yucatán, 1876–1915 (Palo Alto: Stanford University Press, 1996), 71–73.

[5] Barrera Bassols, Los rebeldes, 23–26; Memo for Provisional Governor Magoon, 1/13/08. RG 199 Records of the Provisional Government [in Cuba]: "Confidential" Correspondence, 1906–1909, Box 9, File 214/3. United States National Archives.

sporadic at best between the Yucatán and Cuba, but Ros Planas eventually returned from Spain to Mérida, where as late as June 1913 he again was sending money to Havana to keep the link alive.[6]

CARIBBEAN SUPPORT FOR MEXICAN REVOLUTIONARIES

The first contacts between the PLM and Havana's anarchists emerged in 1905 when *magonistas* communicated from St. Louis, where they had moved after leaving their first exile stop in Texas. Key to this connection was Spanish anarchist Florencio Basora, who had worked with *¡Tierra!* in mid-1903, before traveling to Vermont and then St. Louis by early 1904, where he would soon link up with the PLM exiles.[7] When the PLM leaders moved to Los Angeles in 1907, the Havana link went with them. For the first time, communications connected Los Angeles with Havana mainly, but also Puerto Rico, South Florida, and Panama, thus forging a new network linkage between the Caribbean and the United States–Mexico borderlands.

While the PLM was challenging President Díaz years before the official beginning of the revolution, it was the 1910 call to revolution by Francisco Madero that ushered in a nationwide uprising. In January 1911, anarchists invaded the Mexican state of Baja California to establish an autonomous anarchist region. Caribbean anarchists came to see this as their struggle. The opportunity had arrived to destroy authoritarianism, redistribute land, and give rise to a new era of freedom, autonomy, and egalitarianism. As Marcelo Salinas noted from Tampa in March 1911, anarchists were paying with their lives to bring forth a new dawn of freedom while others raised the red flag over the city of Mexicali as PLM and IWW supporters poured into the Baja.[8] *¡Tierra!* published its first article by Ricardo Flores Magón in February 1911 – an article sent by a PLM supporter in Bridgeport, Texas in the immediate aftermath of PLM writer and military leader Práxedis Guerrero's death.[9] Guerrero had led an armed group into the Mexican state of Chihuahua from the United States, but was killed in battle in late

---

[6] *¡Tierra!*, June 6, 1913, 4.
[7] Ibid., May 23, 1903; February 27, 1904; January 14, 1905; Barrera Bassols, *Los rebeldes*, 16–19. On St. Louis as a radical destination, see Hernández Padilla, *El magonismo*, 24.
[8] *¡Tierra!*, March 18, 1911, 3.
[9] Ibid., February 18, 1911, 1. See also Ward Albro, *To Die on Your Feet: The Life, Times, and Writings of Práxedis G. Guerrero* (Fort Worth: Texas Christian University Press, 1996).

December 1910. Caribbean anarchists like Francisca Barrios in Bayamón, Puerto Rico eulogized Guerrero and equated his sacrifice with the Haymarket Martyrs.[10]

By June, Díaz had resigned, an interim government was in place, and Madero was the strongest political force in Mexico. While ¡Tierra! continued its support for the PLM, the Cuban anarchists began to bitterly condemn Madero even before Díaz's resignation or the election of Madero at the end of the year. In April 1911, ¡Tierra! published the Program of the PLM on page one, praised the PLM's newspaper *Regeneración*, and condemned Madero as no better than Díaz. According to the paper, both Díaz and Madero worked with US President Taft against "the true revolutionaries [who] declared war on all powers that squeeze and impoverish the longsuffering and unwitting Mexican people."[11] In late April 1911, ¡Tierra! held its first fundraising meeting for the PLM. Attendees condemned Madero for being a "millionaire." Later columns called Madero a "tyrant," "bandit," "judas," and "imbecile."[12] Meanwhile, the paper extensively covered Mexican news and the writings of Ricardo Flores Magón. Even Peter Kropotkin praised ¡Tierra! for its coverage of the revolution and the PLM.[13]

The US government's attitudes to the revolution in general and the PLM specifically riled Caribbean anarchists. One main anarchist concern centered on US military intervention and Washington's collusion against the Baja anarchists. Madero had begun to attack the PLM and called on the anarchists to lay down their arms. The Cuban press aimed its vitriol at Madero, portraying him as colluding with Washington to crush the Baja radicals. José Pujal in Havana dreamed that "it would be a great work for all maritime workers to declare a boycott or to sabotage all American goods in response to the United States government having allowed Mexican troops to pass through US soil to fight our brothers."[14] Anger against Washington further focused on US federal cases filed against the PLM. In June 1911, Luis Barcia wrote to his Havana comrades from Tampa that the Flores Magón brothers, Ricardo and Enrique, had been arrested for violating US neutrality laws. ¡Tierra! urged readers to donate money to support the PLM legal defense, condemned the hypocrisy of US actions, and asked how residents of the United States (the Flores Magón brothers)

---

[10] *Labor Culture*, May 25, 1912, 3.   [11] Ibid., April 8, 1911, 1.
[12] These terms can be found throughout 1911 editions. The April meeting and first "millionaire" reference is from ¡Tierra!, April 29, 1911, 1.
[13] ¡Tierra!, January 20, 1912, 1.   [14] Ibid., August 19, 1911, 3.

could be charged for violating neutrality into Mexican affairs when the US government was doing the same thing?[15]

Caribbean anarchists offered more reasons to support the Mexican Revolution. While the Cuban War for Independence failed to bring forth a social revolution, that goal seemed within reach in Mexico. If anarchists could fulfill the goals of Land and Freedom in Mexico, this would be a symbol for anarchists elsewhere. As Barrera Bassols notes, anarchists in Cuba came to see the Mexican Revolution as a step to worldwide revolution, and thus worthy of all anarchists' support.[16] But a free Mexico also could have less idealistic benefits. As José Pujal put it, this "redeemed Mexican soil" could become a place of refuge for anarchists. As anarchists were abused wherever they agitated, a free libertarian Mexico could be a zone for asylum and autonomy.[17] In fact, this would become the case in the 1920s, when Cuban radicals fled to Mexico City to escape the fascistic repression unleashed by a new Cuban regime.

While it was one thing to write and speak in support of the *magonistas*, Caribbean radicals went beyond lip service. Some joined the struggle in Mexico while hundreds more dug deep in their pockets to finance the PLM. Among those who traveled the network to fight in one way or another were people like Juan Moncaleano, who left Cuba to organize rationalist schools and anarchist organizations in Mexico and then Los Angeles. Some went to Mexico to fight. Take the case of Rafael de Nogales Méndez from Venezuela. In 1911, this ex-soldier-turned-gunrunner, who had fought for Spain against the United States in 1898, found himself in northern Mexico, where he joined the PLM's anarchist insurrection and commanded a column of one hundred men in Chihuahua, Durango, and Sonora.[18]

In April 1911, *El Internacional* in Tampa – still publishing despite the CMIU's strike defeat several months earlier – printed a manifesto praising the Mexican Revolution. The manifesto came not from the PLM in Los Angeles but from the anarchist Rafael Romero Palacios in Milwaukee,

---

[15] Ibid., June 17, 1911, 1–2; June 24, 1911, 1; July 1, 1911, 1. Over time, Caribbean anarchists continued to link their anti-American rhetoric with the PLM. For instance, the Puerto Rican Juan José López's column "Crimes of the Yankee Empire" appeared as the lead article in *Regeneración*, September 20, 1913, 1.

[16] Barrera Bassols, *Los rebeldes*, 30.   [17] *¡Tierra!*, August 19, 1911, 3.

[18] Nogales Méndez would return to Venezuela, head to Turkey during the Great War and eventually return to the Americas, where he fought with Sandino in Nicaragua. See Rodolfo Montes de Oca, *Contracorriente: Historia del movimiento anarquista en Venezuela (1811–1998)* (Caracas: El Libertario, 2016), 82–86.

Wisconsin – a man soon to be embroiled in PLM intrigue. The manifesto outlined the anarchist dimensions of the PLM as a "party that is going to employ 'direct action'" to free the proletariat from the millionaire revolutionary Francisco Madero. While the US bourgeoisie was determined to fight against the revolution, working men and women had to stand up to support the struggle.

> Through lack of solidarity, the social revolution has been delayed. What have we, the disinherited of all the world, done for our brothers in Chicago? ... Did we respond with insurrection to the Paris Commune? And with the General Strike to the renounced effort of our brothers, the strikers of Barcelona, of Paris, of Tampa, and of a hundred other places?

Romero Palacios placed Tampa's recent failed strike squarely in the realm of the international struggle. The strike failed because workers did not rise to the occasion as in so many other times. To avoid something similar happening to the PLM, now was the time for workers in Tampa to respond to the *magonista* revolt and the cry of "Land and Freedom."[19]

Efforts to link Tampa with the Mexican anarchist revolution continued, thanks to Pedro Esteve. In mid-1911, Esteve left New York City and went to Tampa.[20] In July he served as secretary of the group "Pro-Revolución Mexicana," raising money among Tampa's workers and sending it to Los Angeles to support PLM propaganda and armed efforts in Mexico, as well as to purchase copies of *Regeneración* to sell in Tampa.[21] During his recruiting and organizing efforts in the Tampa region, Esteve came under growing suspicion and surveillance by the city's Anglo citizens. Fearing vigilantes were out to hang him, Esteve hid in a friend's house, shaved off his beard, and returned to New York City, where he soon launched *Cultura Obrera*.[22]

Often Caribbean anarchists sent money to *¡Tierra!*, which pooled the funds from the region and sent them to Los Angeles. Money came from 15 different towns and cities across Cuba. The first money from Puerto Rico to *¡Tierra!* arrived in August 1911. In September, Panama Canal Zone-based anarchists made their first contributions. Because of *¡Tierra!*'s broad geographical distribution and importance in the Spanish-speaking anarchist communities in the United States, occasionally anarchists there

---

[19] *El Internacional*, April 14, 1911, 6.
[20] Paul Avrich, *Anarchist Voices: An Oral History of Anarchism in America* (Chico, CA: AK Press, 2005), 391.
[21] *¡Tierra!*, July 29, 1911, 2.   [22] Avrich, *Anarchist Voices*, 391.

sent money to Havana for distribution in California, as occurred in July 1911 when anarchists in Hartford, Connecticut sent a small sum.[23]

Anarchist financial support for the Mexican Revolution must be considered in the larger context of both Mexican affairs and what was going on in Cuba during these years. By late 1911, Cuban anarchists were raising money for a plethora of causes: families of deported anarchists, tickets so that deported anarchists could return from Spain, ¡Tierra!'s operating expenses and deficit reduction, special issues to commemorate the execution of Francisco Ferrer y Guardia, a printing press, and aid for the family of Juan Moncaleano, which he had left behind in Cuba when he went to Mexico. The revolutionary fundraising also came during efforts to expand rationalist schools in Havana. This was an important, long-term effort in the Cuban capital as anarchists devoted several years to operating schools for their children. In mid-1911, just as Havana's anarchists sought money to support the Baja operations and to fund the *magonista* legal defense, anarchists on the island struggled to raise money for their schools. From 1911 to 1914, efforts to raise money for Mexico usually outpaced any single Cuban-based issue. This was especially true regarding schools.[24]

Poor workers with shallow pockets could only stretch their funds so far. This financial reality countered those who claimed workers were not doing enough to support the revolution. In fact, one could argue that so much Cuban money left the island for Los Angeles that it imperiled the island's anarchist education initiatives. It is true that the Mexican Revolution was that rare opportunity that galvanized anarchist support. It was a living, breathing symbol of revolt that had to be supported. However, there is no doubt that transnational financial support for the revolution

---

[23] ¡Tierra!, April 29, 1911, 4; May 13, 1911, 1; July 22, 1911, 4; August 19, 1911, 4; September 30, 1911, 4. The first PLM funds to Havana arrived in August 1911 and were sent by María Brousse, Ricardo Flores Magón's *compañera*. Anarchists from around the Caribbean also sent money directly to *Regeneración*, such as in 1912 when supporters in the anarchist strongholds of Bayamón and San Juan, Puerto Rico sent funds to Los Angeles. In 1913, cigar makers in San Juan – led by the anarchist writer Juan José López – did the same. Then, in January 1914, the Puerto Rican-based "Grupo Pro-Regeneración" sent money and columns from anarchists like López and Ángel María Dieppa. See ¡Tierra!, August 19, 1911, 4. Regeneración, April 27, 1912, 3; June 8, 1912, 3; March 22, 1913, 3; January 23, 1914, 1; January 31, 1914, 3.

[24] ¡Tierra!, July 8, 1911, 4; January 27, 1912, 4; June 6, 1913, 4. For instance, in July 1911, January 1912, and June 1913 (representative examples across the years), money collected for the Mexican Revolution surpassed education donations: $11 versus $8.42, $5.18 versus $2.65, and $3.40 versus $.85 respectively.

drained away funds needed for anarchist schools in Cuba. With that said, it is hard not to be impressed by anarchists' long-term dedication to the PLM. For three-and-a-half years from April 1911 to August 1914, they regularly raised money for the struggle in what was the longest-running, single-issue fundraising campaign in the history of Caribbean anarchism.

THE MEXICAN REVOLUTION IN ANARCHIST CULTURAL POLITICS

While letters and columns helped raise consciousness, revolutionary culture generated an image of revolution and a future world that showcased what fellow anarchists were doing at the time while providing guidance for future actions. The Mexican Revolution served as a "revolutionary muse" in Puerto Rico, Florida, and Cuba as prominent anarchists throughout the network wrote poems, dream reflections, and a short novel inspired by the struggles of Mexico's revolutionaries.

In Puerto Rico, anarchists Juan José López and Ángel María Dieppa looked at Mexico and imagined what Puerto Rico could be like if islanders turned toward revolutionary struggle. In his 1910 *Voces Libertarias* (Libertarian Voices), López published works critical of politics and patriotic nationalism. In "Subamos" (Let's Rise Up), he critiqued how recent Puerto Rican agricultural strikes had been repressed and strike leaders persecuted, how Washington failed to do anything to help the laborers' plight, and how all of this was little more than a cruel joke waged by "the grand republic" of the United States and its island lackeys to keep the masses down. Criminally, he argued, the same thing had been happening elsewhere with US complicity: the trials and state executions of Chicago's Haymarket anarchists in the nineteenth century, a recent lynching of tobacco workers in Tampa, and harassment of the Flores Magón brothers by US authorities. Inspired by news of the Mexican Revolution, López urged workers in "Subamos" to ignore patriotism and the flag and "come with us, the anarchists ... Let's rise up!"[25] Such a call to arms ended a book that began with López's poem "Lucha Roja" (Red Struggle), in which he argued that rational beings could not defend a national flag, should ignore parliamentary socialism, choose anarchism, and unite in an armed uprising. In the final stanza, López writes: "Decent people should unite around her [anarchy] / Together with all that is good and benevolent / To fall in with the so-called RED STRUGGLE / She invites you to the

---

[25] Juan José López, *Voces Libertarias* (San Juan: Tipografía La Bomba, 1910), 32.

triumph of love / She incites you to kill the rulers / We will ignite the bonfire in her name."[26]

López's comrade Ángel María Dieppa agitated and wrote from throughout network cities like San Juan, Tampa, and New York. His columns appeared in anarchist newspapers in all three cities and Havana. The year 1912 marked a major transnational moment for Dieppa. At one point, he worked in Tampa with his Puerto Rican comrade Ventura Mijón and Cuban Marcelo Salinas to help found IWW Local 102.[27] At other times, he worked in San Juan, but his columns could be found far and wide, including his pro-Mexican Revolution piece that appeared in New York's *Cultura Obrera* in February. Titled "Sueños de Rebelde" (Rebel Dreams) and dedicated to the Flores Magón brothers, the column begins with him recounting a dream he had one night about the social revolution. As tyranny falls, people sing the "La Marseillaise," red flags rise, and justice appears throughout the land. Then he wakes to his Puerto Rican reality and becomes disheartened. However, his mood soon changes when he looks across the Caribbean toward Mexico. "I see my dreams of happiness being realized there, in the wretched people of Mexico ... My friends, I would love to hear the bomb blasts destroying the damned factories and workshops. And I would look forward to seeing this stupid society blown to a thousand bits ... dying and the cowards suffocating from the smell of dynamite."[28] The Mexican Revolution offered Dieppa a new dream for his beloved island. Armed revolt was the future.[29]

Dieppa's revolutionary activism in Tampa in 1912 led him to work with anarchist comrades from Cuba and Spain, including Salinas, Manuel Pardiñas, and Maximiliano Olay. In late 1912, Pardiñas left Tampa, traveled to Madrid, and assassinated Spanish Prime Minister José Canalejas. Before he could be arrested, Pardiñas turned the gun on himself and took his own life. The anarchist practice of propaganda by the deed, which in Spain frequently meant assassination attempts on government officials, touched off international investigations. US authorities soon realized that Pardiñas had been working in Tampa just before his return to Spain. While in Tampa, he purchased a pistol and every day went to the city's outskirts for target practice. Soon, US authorities discovered that Salinas and Olay were his roommates.[30]

---

[26] Ibid., 7.   [27] Shaffer, *Black Flag Boricuas*, 172.
[28] *Cultura Obrera*, February 24, 1912, 2.   [29] Ibid., February 24, 1912, 2.
[30] Maximiliano Olay, *Mirando al Mundo* (Buenos Aires: Impresos Americalee, 1941), 16.

Salinas was born to a poor family outside of Havana in 1889. He was a young boy when war erupted in 1895. He taught himself to read, became a devoted follower of anarchist ideas, and then moved to Tampa, where from 1910 to 1913 he worked as a cigar maker. Like many Spanish-speaking anarchists in the United States, he learned Italian and worked within Cuban, Spanish, and Italian anarchist circles.[31] Salinas wrote Pardiñas's obituary with Pedro Esteve for *Cultura Obrera*. In it he praised Pardiñas as a committed anarchist who had planned to earn enough money to go to Mexico and fight with the PLM. Instead, he decided to return to Spain and kill the prime minister.[32] Born in the small Asturian town of Colloto, Spain on the eve of the Cuban War for Independence, Maximiliano Olay arrived in Havana in 1908 as a fifteen-year-old working with his uncle, who then sent him to Tampa where he learned to roll cigars, became involved in union organizing, and gravitated toward the city's anarchists. As the PLM launched its war on Díaz and then Madero, Olay regularly collected money for the *magonistas*.

In January 1913 – two months after the Canalejas assassination – the Mexican consul at Mobile, Alabama contacted the US Bureau of Investigation about a global anarchist plot to kill world leaders. While Pardiñas had assassinated the Spanish prime minister, the consul warned that Pardiñas's two Tampa roommates (Olay and Salinas) were plotting to kill President Francisco Madero. On January 19, US officials arrested Olay and Salinas at their Tampa residence, confiscated books and literature, and jailed the two anarchists on flimsy charges of vagrancy (Figure 3.1). Association with Pardiñas, the Mexican warning, and Salinas's confession that he was an anarchist convinced US officials to deport Salinas to Havana following a February 6 conviction.[33] When authorities discovered that Olay had two dollars in the bank, they dropped the vagrancy charge and released him. He soon returned to Spain via New Orleans and was under constant surveillance from the moment his ship landed in Cádiz.[34] In the end, no global anarchist conspiracy existed.

---

[31] Justo Muriel, "Este hombre generoso que no sabía odiar," *Guángara Libertaria* (1986): 20–21.

[32] *Cultura Obrera*, November 30, 1912, 1.

[33] Federal Bureau of Investigation. #5606, Record Group 65. Investigative Case Files of the Bureau, 1908–1922 (hereafter referred to as RG65); *Cultura Obrera*, February 1, 1913, 1; Avrich, *Anarchist Voices*, 397–398; Mormino and Pozzetta, "Spanish Anarchism in Tampa," 192–193; *Cultura Obrera*, November 30, 1912, 1.

[34] Olay, *Mirando al Mundo*, 12–22. Olay returned to Havana later in 1913, where he worked with the group "Voluntad." In 1914, US authorities prevented him from entering

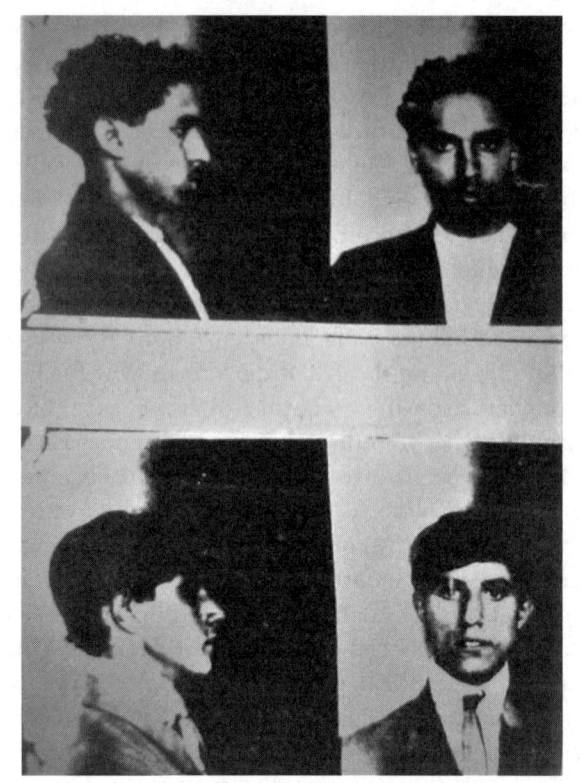

FIGURE 3.1 Mug shots of Marcelo Salinas and Maximiliano Olay in Tampa after being arrested for "conspiring" to assassinate President Madero of Mexico in January 1913.
United States National Archives (College Park, Maryland)

Neither Olay nor Salinas had plans to kill Madero, though undoubtedly they would not have minded seeing him pay for his violence against the PLM. Nevertheless, on February 22, sixteen days after Salinas's conviction, President Madero was assassinated – by his own rebellious military and political rivals, not by an anarchist.

Part of the "evidence" against Salinas had come from his IWW work and his writings on Mexico. For instance, in May 1912, Salinas offered

> the United States. Upon his return journey to Havana, he changed his name to "Juan Escoto," was outed by a reporter as "the dangerous anarchist Maximiliano Olay," and forced to flee to interior Cuba to escape arrest by Cuban authorities. By 1916, Olay was living in New York City, where he worked with anarchists in New York and Chicago for decades until his death in Chicago in April 1941.

his fervent support for the Mexican Revolution. He wrote a poem that was one of his first published works in a long and illustrious writing career. The poem, written in Tampa and published in ¡Tierra!, was titled "¡Tierra y Libertad: a los rebeldes mexicanos" (Land and Freedom: To the Mexican Rebels). In five stanzas, Salinas praises the revolutionaries who lead by example: "¡Cheers comrades! Brave champions / the proletariat world with open admiration / contemplates your effort to carry to the limits / of the rugged jungle your cry of redemption!" Salinas assured readers that this was not some isolated event, but stretched to the cities and countryside: "Your thundering bugle rings in the ramparts / rings in the cities of luxury and ambition / the humble peasants, transformed into soldiers / feverishly loving the great revolution." The revolution was also global, inspiring those wherever misery and injustice ruled: "Therefore wherever the exploited live / and in their noble chests there is longing for a better future / you will have a brother, you will have an ally / who shares with you the glories and the suffering."[35] The revolutionary consciousness evoked in the poem is the same consciousness that found Salinas working for the revolution in the coming months and which likewise found him victimized by transnational intelligence agencies, leading to his deportation for being an anarchist who might have wanted to kill Madero.

Salinas's soon-to-be anarchist literary partner Adrián del Valle also looked to Mexico for inspiration. For nearly half a century, Adrián del Valle published newspapers, wrote regular columns in Cuban newspapers and magazines, served as the leading librarian in Havana's Sociedad Económica de Amigos del País, and wrote more anarchist books, plays, and short novels than any other Caribbean anarchist. He seems not to have written about the Mexican Revolution during the most violent times of the struggle in the 1910s. Nevertheless, during the height of the violence following the assassination of Mexican President Madero in early 1913, del Valle was active in Havana's free-thought movement, serving as secretary of the Society of Free Thinkers. He also published in the society's magazine, El Audaz. The magazine regularly printed articles about and was supportive of the two anarchist fronts in Mexico: Emiliano Zapata in the south and the PLM in the north.[36]

By the 1920s, the internecine violence of the Mexican Revolution had settled into an attempt to build a revolutionary society – despite

---

[35] ¡Tierra!, May 18, 1912, 3. [36] See, for instance, El Audaz, January 30, 1913, 12.

FIGURE 3.2 Adrián del Valle's *De maestro a guerrillero* and his ode to revolutionary violence for anarchist justice during the Mexican Revolution, though written in the late 1920s when Cuba was ruled by the dictator Machado – perhaps a larger call to anarchists to resist the dictatorship.
International Institute of Social History (Amsterdam)

occasional flare-ups such as the Cristero movement of Catholics who resisted the revolution's secularization efforts. At decade's end, del Valle penned a tragic tale of revolutionary action by drawing on the early years of violent struggle in the Mexican Revolution. This was the context for his ode to anarchist revolutionary violence and radical land reform in *De maestro a guerrillero* (From Teacher to Guerrilla Fighter) (Figure 3.2). Sancho Canales is a teacher sent to a small Indian community in Baja California by the Madero government. He teaches people how to read and write, and instructs on hygiene, the history and cruelty of the Spanish conquest, and how political independence had little to no impact on improving Indians' lives. Sancho falls in love with a twenty-year-old indigenous girl, who constantly fights off the advances of the son of Don Romero, a large landowner. Following Madero's assassination in 1913, Don Romero closes the public school. Then, Don Romero's son and his friends kidnap and gang-rape the girl. When Sancho bursts in on the rapists they flee, but not before shooting the girl to death. The outrage triggers a violent response in Sancho. "Now is not the time for teaching, but for fighting." He takes to the hills to war against the landowners, going from being a simple teacher to a guerrilla fighter. Inspired by land redistribution efforts in southern Mexico by Emiliano Zapata, Sancho liberates Don Romero's lands and home, redistributing plots to people and turning the house into a school and recreation center. But still Sancho is not satisfied. In the end, he proclaims that for the indigenous masses to truly benefit, there must be complete communalization of lands, and thus he continues his violent campaign to achieve that goal.[37]

Literature was a staple of anarchist movements. Poems, stories, and plays targeted people's imaginations in ways that strike manifestos, letter-writing campaigns, fundraisers, or newspaper columns could not. Anarchist culture was always a culture of resistance, but it was also a culture of conscience. It was one thing to resist authoritarianism in all its guises and to raise people's awareness of injustice. But any resistance had to fight not just "against" something but "for" something. As such, anarchist literature like Caribbean examples about the Mexican Revolution sought to empower people to pursue what was right – in short, to seek anarchist justice – and, when necessary, not to shy away from picking up arms, dynamite, whatever to pursue that justice. The violence called for in these examples is not allegorical; it was a growing recognition around the network that violent struggle might be the only answer to fight authoritarian injustice and create a new world built on the bonfire's ashes.

THE MEXICAN REVOLUTION AND ANARCHIST TRANSNATIONAL SELF-POLICING

While the Mexican Revolution inspired Caribbean anarchists, it also brought controversy to the network. Between 1911 and 1913, anarchists in Los Angeles, Havana, Tampa, and the Panama Canal Zone fought bitter internecine feuds centering on the PLM. Both the disputes' origins and responses were transnational. The networks unleashed a "policing" function as anarchists communicated with one another to monitor suspected infidels and troublemakers who some suspected of undermining not just the Mexican Revolution, but also the greater anarchist cause.

---

[37] Adrián del Valle, *De maestro a guerrillero* (Barcelona: La Revista Blanca, n.d.), quote from p. 25.

M. D. Rodríguez: Schism and Betrayal in the Canal Zone

Soon after launching *El Único* in mid-1911, M. D. Rodríguez began to attack fellow anarchists in Panama with whom he disagreed. This local bickering, though, quickly grew to international dimensions when he also turned his anger on bigger foes, especially anarcho-communists in Cuba and Ricardo Flores Magón and the PLM. Rodríguez set out to raise funds in Panama to create a print shop in Spain dedicated to publishing only anarchist newspapers and other propaganda.[38] Fundraising would be coordinated through three publications – one in Spain, one in Cuba, and *El Único* in Panama. The Cuban link would not be through *¡Tierra!*, but through a new publication: *Vía Libre*. Rodríguez's shutting out the most important and widely disseminated anarchist publication in the Caribbean reflected a growing schism emerging among anarchists in the region. In Cuba, the movement had begun to diversify and even fracture as anarchists in Havana alone began publishing three newspapers. Part of this fracturing rested on a series of personality and ideological disputes that came to pit groups linked to either *¡Tierra!* or *La Voz del Dependiente*, the anarcho-syndicalist newspaper of the restaurant and café workers in Havana. By 1911, Aquilino López was one of the editors for *La Voz del Dependiente*. In June 1911, the paper folded. The editorial board told readers why: One of the editors – Carlos Vega – had been a police informant, passing unknown numbers and amounts of names and information to authorities. The board shut down the paper and created a new one: *El Dependiente*. The new paper, launched on June 26, effectively shut out Vega, who retaliated by trying to get the authorities to arrest López.[39] Amid the turmoil, López left Cuba, headed to the Panamanian isthmus, and joined Rodríguez.[40] While *¡Tierra!* and the anarchist groups who published it had been early recipients of Panamanian money and correspondence, López and Rodríguez became the leading militants in Panama who now collected money to support *Vía Libre*. In fact, Panamanian-based anarchists became crucial financial backers of *Vía Libre* in its early issues. For instance, in August 1911, Cubans in Havana and Manzanillo contributed 7.54 pesos for *Vía Libre*, while groups and individuals in Panama contributed nearly 27 pesos. López's position as a transnational intermediary in this network helps to explain this strong linkage.[41]

---

[38] *Acción Libertaria*, June 30, 1911, 4. [39] *El Dependiente*, June 26, 1911, 4.
[40] Greene, "Spaniards on the Silver Roll," 90–92; *The Canal Builders*, 172.
[41] *Vía Libre*, August 5, 1911, 1 and 4.

By late summer 1911, ¡Tierra! reemerged as an important voice of the Caribbean network.[42] Some canal-based anarchists resumed their relations with ¡Tierra!, but a closer look reveals something disastrous at work in the isthmus. While Panamanian money and correspondence began to appear again in ¡Tierra!, those connections were not linked to Rodríguez's Federación Anarquista de Panamá. Rather, a schism in the anarchist movement in the Canal Zone was about to tear the isthmian efforts apart.

In the Canal Zone, a rivalry was developing between two different anarchist camps. One camp was represented by anarcho-communists who had been in the zone for many years and initiated, then continued, correspondence with ¡Tierra!. People like Braulio Hurtado, José Novo, Antonio Sanz, and Serafín G. González resisted the sway of Rodríguez and continued their relations with ¡Tierra!. Meanwhile, Rodríguez urged readers to boycott ¡Tierra! and only give money and readership to Havana's Vía Libre. Because ¡Tierra! and those who supported it were primarily anarcho-communists, Rodríguez saw them as "authoritarians" and not true anarchists. Then, Rodríguez amped up his holy war. In late 1911, soon after El Único emerged, internal disputes severed the editorial board as Rodríguez targeted his inquisitorial campaign against fellow El Único anarchists. Over the next six months, the magazine became Rodríguez's monthly tool to condemn anarchists who strayed from his individualist orthodoxy. In the campaign that followed, Rodríguez, the anticlerical zealot, used his pulpit to "excommunicate" anarchists from the Federation, urged anarchist readers abroad to deny their support and "tithes" (monetary contributions) to anarchists with whom he disagreed, and said former El Único collaborators were ex-policemen.

One of his targets was Italian anarchist Salvatore "Sem" Campo. Campo had arrived in Panama from Los Angeles, where the PLM was headquartered, in December 1910. He was hired as a foreman in the engineering department, and then stationed in Gatún. Radicalized while in Los Angeles, Campo began writing for El Único in October and November 1911. But soon Rodríguez turned on him, charging Campo with being a work gang foreman who forced those under him to contribute twenty-five cents gold coin to sustain a small chapel where mass was pronounced in English and Spanish. In a rather bizarre move for any anarchist, Campo took Rodríguez to court, charging him and the

---

[42] For the overall history of these Cuban divisions and the end of the divide, see Shaffer, *Anarchism and Countercultural Politics*, 178–183.

magazine with libel in the US Superior Court in the Canal Zone city of Cristóbal. If Campo was the focus of Rodríguez's ire before, now he truly scorned the Italian. After all, what anarchist goes to court? In the end, despite the efforts of his English-speaking lawyer, C. P. Fairman, the court convicted Rodríguez of libel, fined him fifteen dollars, and made him pay court costs. Campo would weather further attacks on his character, but soon resigned from his job and left the canal.[43] At the same time, Rodríguez turned his attention on another former *El Único* colleague when he attacked Aquilino López, charging him with not only being a bad anarchist but also a freeloader who refused to pay back Rodríguez and others who had loaned López money and clothes upon arriving in Panama from Cuba in mid-1911. Ultimately, in his increasingly paranoid worldview, Rodríguez saw López as a troublemaker and probably a spy sent by Rodríguez's enemies in Cuba.[44] This whole sordid internal and Cuban affair drew the Mexican Revolution into the mess as global controversy erupted over whether the Mexican revolutionaries in Los Angeles deserved anarchist support.[45]

In 1911, some anarchists around the world questioned whether anarchists should ally with and aid the PLM. Pedro Esteve – who raised money for the PLM early on – had some doubts about anarchists joining the Mexican Revolution, fearing those who joined to fight would suffer the same physical and ideological wounds as those anarchists who fought for Cuban independence.[46] But other anarchists questioned the very nature of the PLM. The US-based Italian-language *Cronaca Sovversiva* and the France-based *Les Temps Nouveaux* began to challenge the validity of the Mexican Revolution generally and the anarchism of the PLM specifically. They asked how a universal anarchist revolution could be led

---

[43] The magazine referred to him as "Sem," but other sources say "Sam." *El Único*, November 12, 1911, inside front and back covers; January 12, 1912, 61–62 and 64–65; January 20, 1912, Suplemento, 2; March 12, 1912, 95; May 10, 1912, 124; "United States, Panama Canal Zone, Employment Records and Sailing lists, 1905–1937," database with images, FamilySearch (https://familysearch.org/ark:/61903/1:1:QVSH-7PK6, 5 March 2015), Sam Campo, December 1, 1910; citing piece/folio, Service Record Cards,1904–1920, 7226556, NARA record group 185, National Personnel Records Center, St. Louis, Missouri.

[44] *El Único*, March 12, 1912, 94.

[45] We can reflect on something else here: What did US authorities make of the brewing anarchist civil war during the canal construction? Well, nothing apparently. There is no mention of this conflict in the ICC records. Ultimately, one must wonder how effective ICC surveillance and intelligence efforts were since nobody in the ICC reported on the transnational anarchist civil war occurring under their noses.

[46] Zimmer, *Immigrants against the State*, 128–130.

¡Tierra y Libertad! 143

by a "national" political party, that is a party that had the name of one country (Mexico) in its title, and how the same "party" could be "liberal"? Anarchism was not national, not a political party, not liberal but global, antipolitical, and radical, they argued.[47]

Rodríguez and *El Único* joined this criticism. On a monthly basis, he lampooned the *magonistas* and their newspaper *Regeneración*, referring to it as "Degeneración" (Degeneration).[48] The Rodríguez–PLM controversy began just as *El Único* appeared in September 1911 when Rodríguez's early ally – Aquilino López – spoke out against the PLM at a meeting in Ancón.[49] That same month, Ricardo Flores Magón warned international readers (especially subscribers to *Regeneración* in the Canal Zone) about Rodríguez. He suggested that Rodríguez was "nothing more than an 'organizer'" who preferred to live the good life off the backs of the workers. Equally bad, while just as the PLM was actively taking up arms to do something concrete for the anarchist ideal, along came Rodríguez to say take it slow. Just when funds were being collected to help the Mexican anarchists in their revolutionary struggle, Rodríguez cast a chill by urging people not to send money.[50]

In November, Rodríguez responded by condemning the PLM for promising Mexicans a better future if the PLM won the revolution, but what about everyone else, Rodríguez asked? "We know that the foreman of Magón Company aspires to conquer ... the lands for Mexicans while foreigners and natives who violate the [PLM] slogan 'Tierra y Libertad' get the gallows."[51] Rodríguez clarified why it was wrong to send money to the PLM: "While modern schools are closing, advanced newspapers disappear, prisoners are deprived of needed solidarity and the free diffusion of newspapers and pamphlets is forgotten, anarchists invest their few cents to sustain a battle denying Anarchy, which is the liberal Mexican *revolution*."[52] As noted earlier, Cuban donations to the PLM did, in fact, take money away from the island's schools. So, Rodrigúez was right on that score.

In late 1911, Spanish and Cuban anarchists joined the attack against Rodríguez. According to Enrique T. Chas from Spain, Rodríguez's infamy emerged during a general strike in Rosario, Argentina in 1906 and 1907.

---

[47] Barrera Bassols, *Los rebeldes*, 33.   [48] *El Único*, March 12, 1912, 88.
[49] Police report to Isthmian Canal Commission Secretary Bishop, September 25, 1911 in RG185 ICC 1905–1914, 2-P-59, United States National Archives.
[50] *Regeneración*, September 30, 1911, 3.   [51] *El Único*, November 12, 1911, 28.
[52] Ibid., January 12, 1912, 58–59. Italics in original.

Rather than aid the strike, Rodríguez wrote a column for a bourgeois newspaper, claiming strikers had amassed 300 rifles, and they intended to burn down the piers at the Port of Rosario. The resulting police crackdown led to a mass jailing and the death of at least one comrade. Knowing that the strikers would want revenge upon him, Rodríguez organized his own deportation from Argentina to Cuba before heading to Panama.[53]

In a January 1912 letter to the Anarchist Federation in the Canal Zone, ¡Tierra! outlined Rodríguez's nefarious deeds in Cuba between 1908 and 1910, accusing him of giving information to the secret police that led to the deportation of anarchist newspaper publisher Abelardo Saavedra, helping to break a construction workers' strike, selling religious trinkets to make money, and more. Rodríguez, "in the end, had to leave Cuba, despised by all dignified men who feared coming in contact with his filthy slobber." The editors hoped that this trans-Caribbean information sharing would help reconnect most anarchists in Cuba with those in the Canal Zone.[54]

Rodríguez struck back, quoting Argentinean colleagues who praised his actions in Rosario.[55] Then, he leveled fourteen charges against ¡Tierra!, including turning the Havana paper into a liberal rag, defamation of Rodríguez, taking money without spending it on its intended purpose, boycotting and defaming Vía Libre, withholding information to Panamanian groups when requested, siding with El Único's Canal Zone rivals, and "selling buttons of the liberal communist virgin who in Los Angeles, California is very devoted to the Liberal Party, whose chief, Flores Magón, the illustrious Ricardo, so sweetly devours the centavos that anarchists send to his children, believing the money is being used for Anarchy."[56]

Throughout the first months of 1912, accusations flew back and forth. The female anarchist Teófila Rebolledo attacked Rodríguez and his allies – "these people with their fanaticism" – and declared Rodríguez "the persecutor of all anarchists in Panama." In mid-February, López wrote to Cuban and Panamanian anarchists, saying Rodríguez was as big an egomaniacal phony as others had described – even seeing himself as "a new Christ." López recalled the spirit of solidarity throughout the Canal Zone in mid-1911, when the Anarchist Federation set out to launch

---

[53] Regeneración, November 25, 1911, 1.
[54] ¡Tierra!, December 2, 1911, 3; ¡Tierra!, January 20, 1912, 2.
[55] El Único, March 12, 1912, 95–96; April 12, 1912, 109.
[56] Ibid., February 12, 1912, 77.

its own publication to raise consciousness and a movement in the zone while generating money for a printing press in Spain to publish an anarchist daily newspaper. But *El Único* quickly fell into debt and, even worse, the Federation spent a large amount of money to publish *El Único*, "which only served to fight against the purest initiatives and to defame *compañeros* domestically and internationally" while making Panamanian anarchists look like a joke to their comrades around the world. Instead, no daily newspaper existed, the movement in Panama was divided and in turmoil, and countless potential followers had been lost. In response, all Rodríguez could do was decry the charges and condemn López as "an agent provocateur."[57]

Ultimately, Rodríguez lost and by mid-1912 *El Único* folded. He arranged with anarchists in Spain to create *El Libertario* to carry on the campaign to raise money for a printing press. He balanced *El Único*'s books and was in possession of over 800 gold pesetas for the new newspaper and campaign.[58] A year later in May 1913, Madrid's *Acción Libertaria* recorded that since October 1912 the campaign had raised nearly 2200 pesetas, almost all of it from the Anarchist Federation of Panama.[59] But a nagging question remained. Where was Rodríguez and the money he was holding? "Several months have passed without any notice regarding our revered *compañero*, notwithstanding the efforts we have made to find out," noted one comrade. Giving him the benefit of the doubt, *Acción Libertaria*'s editors feared he might have become a victim of "some disgrace or illness." Ultimately, they asked if anyone in the network knew where Rodríguez was.[60]

The last word came from one of Rodríguez's strongest former allies in the Panamanian federation, Jesús Louzara. In August, he seemed to confirm the worst. Just as Rodríguez had never expressed qualms about "exposing" supposed anarchists and "ex-communicating" them from the Federation, now Louzara was forced to do the same:

We earnestly beg *compañero* M.D. Rodríguez, *Intransigente*, to get in touch with us upon reading this notice. By not doing so, and since his silence toward this [Anarchist Federation] can only increase our doubts, we advise him to be aware of the consequences that we will have to adopt against him. If *Intransigente* wants to continue to merit the title of *compañero*, we hope that this notice will be enough for him to tell us where he currently resides.[61]

---

[57] *¡Tierra!*, February 17, 1912, 3–4; February 24, 1912, 3; April 27, 1912, 4.
[58] *El Libertario*, August 10, 1912, 4.   [59] *Acción Libertaria*, May 23, 1913, 4.
[60] Ibid., June 27, 1913, 4.   [61] Ibid., August 15, 1913, 4.

Rodríguez did not respond. In one of his last writings for the magazine, he had urged people to start a "Libertarian Colony" in the isthmus, where people could live a true anarchist life.[62] Maybe he disappeared to try to start such an enterprise with the money that he held, but there is no evidence to support the idea. Rodríguez had been at the forefront of forging a consolidated anarchist presence in the zone against the ICC and developing transnational ties between anarchists across the Caribbean and Atlantic. But soon he challenged the ideological purity of anarchists in the Canal Zone and – even worse – attacked the PLM and the Flores Magóns. In the end, it was not US or Panamanian authorities who brought down Rodríguez, but his self-generated controversies. These were too much for the international community, which responded in a coordinated transnational self-policing exercise to silence the renegade Rodríguez. If he had just targeted anarchists in the isthmus, maybe the network would not have done much, but when he began targeting the anarchist *cause cèlébre* of the moment – the *magonista* wing of the Mexican Revolution – he had crossed the line.

Rafael Romero Palacios and the PLM

In 1911, Rafael Romero Palacios lived in and agitated for the anarchist cause in Milwaukee, Wisconsin. There, he collected money to be sent to the PLM in Los Angeles.[63] However, he wanted to be more involved. With the PLM leadership in jail in mid-1911, Romero Palacios set out for Los Angeles, arriving in July to help run *Regeneración*.[64] For two years, he worked with the PLM and ran the newspaper. By mid-1913, a major schism rocked the PLM community in Los Angeles. PLM members led by Antonio P. de Araujo accused him and others of stealing money from the newspaper. After being forced out of *Regeneración*, Romero Palacios published and distributed a circular that condemned the new PLM leadership. Readers condemned the circular.[65] Soon, he left Los Angeles and headed to Florida, where he and his partner Francisca J. Mendoza began publishing columns in the bilingual anarchist newspaper *Risveglio*. By all accounts, they retained their anarchist ideals, with him writing about why workers should avoid sporting events like boxing and baseball and instead work to develop their intellect. She praised Francisco Ferrer y Guardia and continued to promote rationalist education.[66]

---

[62] *El Único*, May 10, 1912, 4.   [63] *Regeneración*, March 18, 1911, 3.
[64] Ibid., July 8, 1911, 3.   [65] Ibid., September 20, 1913, 3.
[66] *Risveglio*, June 1913, 2.

However, the policing function of the anarchist press reemerged in 1914. In February, Ricardo Flores Magón personally warned readers about Romero Palacios, such as about how he had stolen money from *Regeneración* in order to buy fancy dresses and other items for his lover, Mendoza. Flores Magón warned Florida anarchists that these two did not love the revolution or the workers or the PLM, but instead hated them as much as "the Mexican bourgeoisie and the Wall Street pirates" hated them. Over the coming weeks in 1914, *Regeneración* printed letters and testimonies from people who had known Romero Palacios in an effort to portray him as abusive, exploitative, seeking only riches and fame, and who visited the Mexican Consulate in Los Angeles to turn over private PLM documents and denounce his PLM comrades. He concluded his exposé of Mendoza and Romero Palacios by exposing their luxurious cross-country travel with money stolen from *Regeneración*. Anarchists in Florida had been warned, but the warnings seem to have been ignored by other anarchists because in 1916 Pedro Esteve and the Paterson, New Jersey anarchists hosted an Italian anarchist picnic that feted Romero Palacios.[67]

Juan Francisco Moncaleano: Revolutionary Educator? Hero? Traitor? Child Molester?

From 1911 to 1913, the name "Moncaleano" was a rallying cry for Caribbean anarchists. Juan Moncaleano (Figure 3.3) had been a colonel in Colombia's Liberal Party from 1895 to 1899 during that country's infamous civil wars. He abandoned military life and moved toward radicalism. Within a decade, he and his wife Blanca taught in rationalist schools in Bogota. There, in June 1910, Juan founded the anticlerical newspaper *Ravachol* that promoted Ferrer y Guardia's rationalist education. The Catholic Church promptly excommunicated him – a rather fine anarchist badge of honor. The Moncaleanos and their children left Colombia and arrived in Havana.[68] In October 1911, Juan joined Antonio Juan Torres as a teacher in the new rationalist school in

---

[67] *Regeneración*, February 21, 1914, 3; February 28, 1914, 3; Zimmer, *Immigrants against the State*, 56.
[68] Mauricio Flórez Pinzón, "Anarquismo y anarcosindicalismo en Colombia antes de 1924," in *Pasado y presente del anarquismo y del anarcosindicalismo en Colombia*, ed. CILEP (Bogota: CILEP, 2011), 43; Orlando Villanueva Martínez, ed., *Biófila Panclasta: El eterno prisionero* (Bogota: Editorial CODICE LTDA., 1992), 64–72.

FIGURE 3.3 Juan Francisco Moncaleano, a stalwart example of anarchist transnationalism, with activism in Colombia, Cuba, Mexico, and the United States, until the transnational network outed him as a potential child molester. Author's personal collection

Havana's Cerro suburb. They were soon educating forty boys and girls, three of whom were Moncaleano's own children.[69] When Juan left for Mexico, Blanca continued to operate the school, but despite her efforts the Cerro school withered away until it closed in summer 1912.[70] With the school's closing, Blanca soon packed up the children to join Juan in Mexico City, where he was publishing *Luz* with other Mexican anarchists. However, before she arrived, the Madero government closed the paper and deported Juan to Spain. Blanca and the children found themselves alone and with no funds.

Now a single mother with three children stranded in Mexico, Blanca maintained her revolutionary intensity and took up her pen. In December 1912, she described the Mexican Revolution as she saw it for ¡*Tierra!* and its Caribbean readership. In what proved to be the final months of Madero's presidency, she attacked Madero for attacking anarchists. She also damned Madero for trying to force the Mexican people to abandon their weapons so that they could become servants of the American

---

[69] ¡*Tierra!*, October 21, 1911, 2.   [70] Ibid., June 8, 1912, 3; January 14, 1913, 2.

bourgeoisie. Meanwhile, Emiliano Zapata ("the Mexican Spartacus") was leading his *campesinos* in the "beautiful eruption of libertarian lions" against "property, pulverizing temples, and defeating governments." She told her readers to do everything possible to sustain *Regeneración*, "the mouthpiece of the revolution." Besides money, she urged readers to consider "going to the United States and from there invading Sonora [Mexico]. The revolution needs conscientious men to go into the encampments as role models, men who are not afraid to fight on the side of those indomitable titans who shout *Tierra y Libertad*, breaking the chains of slavery while singing in tune the triumphant 'La Marseillaise.'" And "women! On your feet because the theocratic viper wraps itself around your children's necks. Stand up in order to put an end once and for all to this intolerable absolutism!"[71]

Cuban anarchists did not abandon their sister in Mexico. They launched a fundraising campaign for Blanca, raising some $60 to help her and the children move to Los Angeles in January 1913.[72] Anarchists from Havana to Los Angeles used Juan's deportation and the story of a destitute comrade mother to denounce the Madero government. *¡Tierra!* published columns from Cuba, Mexico, and Los Angeles praising Juan for his "crime of opening workers' eyes," and denouncing his deportation. Juan Moncaleano contributed to his image as a persecuted revolutionary in a letter from La Coruña, Spain dated September 30, 1912 and published in *¡Tierra!*, describing how the Madero government arrested him and five other male and female comrades, executed four of them, and deported him for being a foreign anarchist.[73]

The family reunited in Los Angeles in early 1913, immediately joined forces with the *magonistas* to help run *Regeneración*, and opened a rationalist school in the city's Casa del Obrero Internacional.[74] But resumption of their anarchist activities on the US West Coast sparked controversy. Accusations began to circulate in the Caribbean network that Juan Moncaleano might not be who he said he was. M. D. Rodríguez in the Canal Zone had charged that Moncaleano was less an anarchist than a "spiritist."[75] Just as Juan arrived in the United States, his Havana-based friend Juan Tur had to come to his defense. Tur refuted accusations

[71] Ibid., December 21, 1912, 1–2.
[72] Ibid., see p. 4 for financial records from June 29, 1912 to January 11, 1913. *Regeneración* also raised funds beginning in October 1912. See *Regeneración*, October 5, 1912, 1.
[73] *¡Tierra!*, September 21, 1912, 3–4; October 12, 1912, 4; October 19, 1912, 3–4.
[74] *Regeneración*, February 15, 1913, 1.   [75] *El Único*, April 12, 1912, 111.

that Moncaleano had lived under a different name in Colombia, that he abused the wife of the Peruvian ambassador to Colombia, and that this latter incident led to his deportation from Colombia. Rather, said Tur, he had to leave because he was publishing *Ravachol*.[76] For the time being, a potential firestorm was averted.

But Juan Moncaleano proved a divisive figure. Beginning in May 1913, *Regeneración*'s editors, led by P. de Araujo, accused the Moncaleanos and others of trying to take over the paper and make it the official publication of the Casa del Obrero Internacional, not the PLM. When confronted, Moncaleano supposedly replied that he would create a new paper on the ashes of *Regeneración*. Enrique Flores Magón wrote from jail on McNeil Island that Moncaleano and his conspirators should be excluded from any further PLM activity. Then, P. de Araujo accused Moncaleano, Romero Palacios, and others of embezzling money sent from European comrades that was intended for PLM activities.[77]

Soon, the network went into a new round of self-policing. In July, *¡Tierra!* criticized *Regeneración*'s editors for resorting to personal attacks that sullied the anarchist cause. Tur suspended *¡Tierra!*'s activities collecting money for *Regeneración*. The Los Angeles paper reassured anarchists in Cuba that they could still send money to Los Angeles by giving it to José Pujal and the Grupo Internacional Regeneración Humana in Havana. Then, in August, *Regeneración* published letters from Cuban anarchists associated with the rationalist school movement on the island. Santiago Sánchez wrote that "I was studying and became convinced that [Moncaleano] had no love for the Ideal." Worse, said Sánchez, was that Moncaleano favored certain children with gifts, violating the spirit of egalitarianism. Still worse yet, he accused Moncaleano of abusing students, even locking one student in a toilet.[78] Juan Tenorio Aguilera, secretary of the Centro de Estudios Sociales (Social Studies Center, or CES) in Cerro where the Moncaleanos had been teachers, reported that the CES board had decided Juan was responsible for the school's declining enrollment. After the committee proclaimed that "he never was a rationalist professor," they removed him from his teaching duties. The Moncaleanos responded by denouncing the PLM. They accused

---

[76] *¡Tierra!*, December 21, 1912, 1.
[77] *Regeneración*, May 10, 1913, 3; June 7, 1913, 3; June 21, 1913, 3.
[78] Ibid., August 9, 1913, 2.

magonistas of not doing enough to lead workers to liberty and squandering $500,000 in international donations destined for the PLM.[79]

Such claims did not sit well, especially considering the picture that anarchists from Havana to Los Angeles were painting of Juan. But perhaps the death knell against him was not his supposed embezzlement of funds or that he was not the rationalist teacher that he portrayed himself to be. Rather, what most condemned him in the eyes of anarchists were charges of child abuse. Sánchez first raised eyebrows when he recalled how Moncaleano punished children by locking them in the bathroom. Tenorio Aguilera then charged sexual impropriety against Moncaleano, who he accused of "treating girls who attended the school" in a certain way. Then, in September, the charges intensified when P. de Araujo reported that Moncaleano had raped a comrade's wife in Los Angeles – an act that could only be overshadowed by Moncaleano's "extremely pornographic acts" with underage girls at the Casa.[80]

Juan's political troubles ended in January 1916 when he died from complications arising after stomach ulcer surgery. Blanca eventually changed her name to Blanche Lawson and lived out her days (apparently radicalism-free) in Los Angeles.[81] The Moncaleanos' educational enterprises in Colombia, Cuba, Mexico, and Los Angeles were undermined by fellow anarchists and hated governments alike – and maybe even by Juan himself if his detractors' claims were true. It would be easy to say that the Moncaleano Affair was a case of sectarian divisions and personality conflicts that arose in both Havana and Los Angeles. There is no doubt that some of this was the case. But what the episode clearly illustrates is how the Caribbean network went into effect during the Mexican Revolution to hunt down and destroy a man who at one time – like M. D. Rodríguez and Rafael Romero Palacios – had been considered an ally and hero fighting for the anarchist cause. Such men could no longer be trusted.

---

[79] James Sandos, *Rebellion in the Borderlands: Anarchism and the Plan de San Diego* (Norman: University of Oklahoma Press, 1992), 135–137.
[80] *Regeneración*, August 16, 1913, 3; September 13, 1913, 3. In 1913, Blanca began editing *Pluma Roja* in Los Angeles. Juan used the propaganda paper to communicate with former comrades in Cuba, praising them and their continued fight against the Menocal government, thus showing that – for him anyway – the California–Cuba linkage remained vital and important. See, for instance, *Pluma Roja*, December 14, 1913, 3.
[81] Nicolás Kanello, *Hispanic Immigrant Literature: El Sueño del Retorno* (Austin: University of Texas Press, 2011), 176 (en3).

CONCLUSION

The Mexican Revolution long has been understood as a transnational process that involved Mexican, Latino, and Anglo radicals, as well as the Mexican and US federal governments.[82] But the revolution's transnational impact stretched beyond the United States–Mexico borderlands. It was one thing to run schools, give talks, and stage inspirational plays to lay the groundwork for a revolution. But increasingly it was the violent uprisings in 1911 – especially the Baja invasion and its resulting suppression – as well as the transnational legal assault against the PLM leadership that inspired and riled Caribbean anarchists. Here next to them, anarchists were picking up arms to overthrow all vestiges of authoritarianism. Caribbean anarchists joined the fray. Writers regularly praised the Revolution in the pages of *¡Tierra!* and urged people to send what little money they could afford to create a liberated space in the Americas – a refuge for freedom. Anarchists created fiction and poetry as educational tools to raise awareness and celebrate the achievements of the Mexican anarchists. For anarchists in Florida and Cuba, the Mexican uprisings came just fifteen years after Cuba's War for Independence from Spain began. During that time, Cubans, Spaniards, Italians, and others on both sides of the Florida Straits raised money to fund the cause, bombed Spanish government buildings, conducted sabotage against the empire, and picked up guns to fight the Spanish monarchy in the name of freedom. Many of those same revolutionaries were still alive when the Mexican Revolution began. This time they dedicated themselves to trying to make sure the social revolution succeeded rather than be trampled by Mexican politicians in the same way that Cuba's postcolonial leaders abandoned the goals of social revolution after 1898.

However, this transnational inspiration frequently encountered transnational contention. Who was the "true" anarchist? Several times

---

[82] Recently, Devra Weber has illustrated how transnationalism operated at the grass roots level with Mexican *magonistas* support of the Wobblies directly linked to their on-the-ground lived experiences – in short, the node shaping the linkage, the dot shaping the line. Sonia Hernández brings an anarcho-feminist perspective to this borderlands history. See Devra Weber, "Wobblies of the Partido Liberal Mexicano: Reenvisioning Internationalist and Transnationalist Movements through Mexican Lenses," *Pacific Historical Review* 85, no. 2 (2016): 188–226; Sonia Hernández, "Chicanas in the Borderlands: Trans-Border Conversations of Feminism and Anarchism, 1905–1938," in *A Promising Problem: The New Chicana/o History of the Twenty-First Century*, ed. Carlos K. Blanton (Austin: University of Texas Press, 2016), 135–160.

between 1911 and 1913, conflicts emerged in Los Angeles and in the Caribbean network over certain high-profile anarchist personalities like M. D. Rodríguez, Rafael Romero Palacios, and Juan Moncaleano. In all three cases, the anarchist network stretched across the hemisphere between the Caribbean and Los Angeles in order to reveal suspected villains in their midst, and thus to protect one version of the true anarchist revolution.

By the mid-to-late 1910s, anarchists found other internal and global issues to confront, including the Russian Revolution and the Great War in Europe. They largely turned their attention away from Mexico. But when leftists did return their gaze to Mexico, often it was toward the Yucatán, where anarchists had originally been interested. In 1919, Socialist Felipe Carrillo Puerto was governor of the state of Yucatán. Leftists found much to like. Here was a governor whose party had created a baseball league with team names like "Máximo Gorki," "Emiliano Zapata," and "The Chicago Martyrs." The IWW's *La Nueva Solidaridad* – the largest-circulation Spanish-language Wobbly newspaper in the United States – approved of the governor's efforts to bring forth "industrial communism" in the Yucatán. They especially praised the governor's education initiatives that, according to the paper, had created 600 schools with 2500 teachers and 40,000 students.[83]

The Cuban Socialist Carlos Loveira, who had a long love–hate relationship with Havana's anarchists but nevertheless was friendly with his fellow author Adrián del Valle, published his book *El socialismo en Yucatán* in 1923 – the year before rebellious army officers killed Carrillo Puerto. Loveira had been a migrant worker in the Panama Canal, Costa Rica, and Ecuador. Then, while a member of the Socialist Party in Cuba, he traveled to Yucatán.[84] In his book, Loveira praised the Yucatecan educational system for its "lay, rationalist" foundations, the development of libraries, and efforts to print "the works of Yucatecan authors and others that the socialist government believed adequate." In short, his overall assessment of Carrillo Puerto's government was rather myopic but one that perhaps most leftists – even anarchists – could support. After all, as we will see, many (perhaps most) anarchists across the region at that moment supported the Bolshevik Revolution, and thus were increasingly willing to offer support to radical governments. "[T]he Mexican Revolution," Loveira wrote, "was the first crystallization of universal

---

[83] *La Nueva Solidaridad*, April 28, 1919, 3.   [84] Carr, "'Across Seas and Borders,'" 224.

socialist propaganda ... Mexico," he concluded, "was Bolshevik before Bolshevism."[85] Some anarcho-syndicalists joined with Loveira in celebrating many of the Mexican Revolution's lasting impacts, but most Caribbean anarchists quickly refocused attention on events in Russia. Just as the Mexican Revolution caused both celebration and discord among Caribbean anarchists, the Bolshevik Revolution would also advance – and help destroy – so much anarchism in the Caribbean.

[85] Carlos Loveira, *El socialismo en Yucatán* (Havana: El Siglo XX, 1923), 43 and 46.

4

The Caribbean *Red* during the Red Scare

Anarchists and the Bolshevik Revolution, 1917–1924

> If we destroy, or let others destroy the Soviet Republic of Russia, we will find ourselves further from Anarchy rather than closer to her ... [T]he Soviet Republic of Russia constitutes a beacon, less luminous than we would have imagined and continue to imagine possible, but an unquestionable beacon, nonetheless.
>
> José María Blázquez de Pedro, Panama City, 1921

When news of the Russian Revolution reached the Caribbean in 1917, anarchists – like most of their global comrades – wasted little time linking themselves to the rise of Bolshevik power coming on the heels of armed insurrection. The world's anarchists early on were drawn to the revolutionaries in Moscow. They saw the Bolsheviks as far more radical than the old Socialist International; the original soviets appeared democratic and decentralized, and Moscow "raised slogans that seemed quite libertarian," as Michael Schmidt and Lucien van der Walt note. The Bolsheviks even unveiled a bust of Kropotkin in 1918. Around the Americas, anarchists founded or joined movements that publicly proclaimed themselves to be "Communist" with a capital C, but which followed libertarian anti-state principles. In places like Buenos Aires, news of the revolution increased an already radical fervency among anarchist port workers. Peruvian anarchists first heard about the revolution from anarchist newspapers shipped into Peru and quickly surmised that if the Bolsheviks scared the bourgeoisie, then the revolution in Russia must be good.[1]

---

[1] Michael Schmidt and Lucien van der Walt, *Black Flame: The Revolutionary Class Politics of Anarchism and Syndicalism* (Oakland: AK Press, 2009), 101–102; Geoffroy de

In the first part of this chapter, we explore how Caribbean anarchists joined this early wave of support, often working with Marxists in their midst. In the second part, we look at how some Caribbean anarchists remained defenders of the revolution deep into the 1920s – even after news of Bolshevik betrayals against rebels at Kronstadt and anarchists in Ukraine – but increasingly others rejected not only the Bolshevik Revolution but also the Marxists with whom they had associated. Then, the chapter transitions to explore the Red Scare campaigns against anarchists. While Washington had targeted anarchists since the late 1800s – and especially after the assassination of President McKinley – the new Red Scare was more intense and fervent than before. Like anarchism, the repression was regional as Washington took this campaign to its Caribbean outposts. As a result, intelligence agencies across the region waged a transnational campaign that targeted anarchists as "Communists" and "Bolshevikis."[2]

THE RUSSIAN REVOLUTION IN PANAMA

Throughout 1917, Panamanian radicals joined forces in the pages of the newspaper *Verbo Rojo* – a biweekly periodical with the masthead reading "To fight is to live; to live fighting is to triumph." This self-described "organ of the working class" challenged workers to fight for a socialist future. As one of the paper's editors, José Napoleón, wrote in the first issue, "anarchism is the most beautiful ideal ever conceived for humanity" while governments and the church are not only authoritarian but also "vicious institutions" that deny freedom.[3] As the Russian Revolution continued to rage halfway around the world, Napoleón and Blázquez de Pedro offered ever-more radical working-class critiques of Panamanian society, such as condemning growing capitalist penetration in agriculture

---

Laforcade, "Argentine Organized Labor: Culture, Representations, and Ideological Alignments in the Wake of the Bolshevik Revolution" and Steven Hirsch, "Ripple Effects: The Bolshevik Revolution and the Decline of Peruvian Anarchism, 1917–1930," papers presented at the LASA conference, Lima, April 2017.

[2] Newer scholarship on transnational counterradicalism can be found in Jensen's *The Battle against Anarchist Terrorism* (New York: Cambridge University Press, 2014) as well as a more Latin America-focused study in Martín Albornoz and Diego Galeano, "Anarquistas y policías en el atlántico sudamericano: una red transnacional, 1890–1910," *Boletín del Instituto de Historia Argentina y Americana "Dr. Emilio Ravignani"* 47 (2017): 101–134.

[3] *Verbo Rojo*, April 12, 1917, 1–2. See also, César Del Vasto, "'Verbo Rojo': Primer periódico liberal-socializante panameño," *Revista Panameño de Ciencias Sociales* 1 (2003): 37–40.

where people no longer worked their own land but had become wage slaves to large landowners; highlighting the hypocrisy of populist governments that said they worked for the people but mainly ruled to support private property; exposing "pro-labor" legislation that radicals called a guise "to prepare the re-election of certain congressmen" who like to use words like "proletariat" and "working people" to get votes; and criticizing conservatives for rallying people around some absurd form of patriotism.[4]

Verbo Rojo urged readers to rise out of their lamentable idleness and form new associations to create a new era. "The Russian Revolution teaches us that a people who truly wants to be free, eventually will be free," wrote Blázquez de Pedro.[5] He reminded workers of the meaning of May Day as a day of propaganda and reinvigoration of one's commitment to the struggle.[6] To galvanize working-class consciousness after May Day 1917, Napoleón published a series of articles on socialism.[7] In August and September 1917, *Verbo Rojo* called on Panamanian workers to seek a stateless society "without laws that restrict your actions, without gods that chain your consciences, and without fatherlands that limit your love." Yet, the paper argued that because egoism had yet to be destroyed, then one still needed a government "to unite, tutor, organize, distribute, and educate people" while holding property in the commons as a "transition period" to a time when egoism is destroyed, and the state is no longer necessary.[8] In some ways, Panama's anarchists were already promoting a Bolshevik agenda for the isthmus before the Bolsheviks came to power.

By mid-1919, the Bolsheviks had ruled Russia for a year and a half. That year, the 36-year-old Argentinean anarchist educator Julio Barcos arrived in Panama and helped to launch *Cuasimodo: Magazine Interamericano*, which critically approved of the Bolsheviks. In the inaugural issue, Barcos published Eusebio A. Morales's column that claimed the Bolshevik government merely had replaced one tyranny with another. Barcos countered that while he respected Morales's opinion, "we do not share all of his ideas and impressions concerning the scope and potential [of the tyrannous aspects] of the great Russian revolution."[9] This was

---

[4] *Verbo Rojo*, April 12, 1917, 5; April 26, 1917, 1; September 17, 1917, 2–3; August 9, 1917, 1; September 18, 1917, 1–3.
[5] Blázquez de Pedro, *Observaciones*, 86.   [6] *Verbo Rojo*, May 12, 1917, 1.
[7] Ibid., May 12, 1917, 4–5; May 24, 1917, 1.   [8] Ibid., August 9, 1917, 1.
[9] *Cuasimodo*, June 1919, 68. For overviews of the magazine, see Táctica [Ricaurte Soler], "*Cuasimodo*: alba de la utopía," *Tareas* 94 (1996): 9–38; Luis Navas, "Tareas sobre la marcha: *Cuasimodo* y el movimiento obrero." *Tareas* 97 (1997): 133–144.

evident when *Cuasimodo* published columns supportive of the Bolshevik Revolution by the Puerto Rican Luis Muñoz Marín and the Venezuelan Humberto Tejera. Barcos was fond of the young Socialist Muñoz Marín – who would in the future be the first popularly elected governor of the island. The two had met in San Juan in 1918 after Barcos left Buenos Aires. He described the Puerto Rican as dressing like some bohemian artist, hanging out with other writers and "revolutionary propagandists." "That boy was already a fugitive from the bourgeoisie who spontaneously passed into the ranks of socialism," noted Barcos. In his column on the Russian Revolution, Muñoz Marín criticized the West's support of counterrevolutionary measures in Russia, and said that the West's leaders were gutless "men who call themselves democrats" but refused to go to their own peoples to call for a real war if that was what they truly believed was necessary. Tejera celebrated the revolution's desire to end poverty and create a "socialism compatible with individual freedom."[10] To him, the revolution "inspired great humanitarian goals," and even if violence was being waged by the government against its dissenters, such violent reaction "was surely determined by the harshness and cruelty of the previous regime."[11] Puerto Rican and Venezuelan praise, published in a Panamanian magazine edited by an Argentinean anarchist illustrated – as the magazine's name implied – that there was broad, left-wing inter-American support for the Bolsheviks in what many hoped was a revolution to end misery, create equality, and unleash individual liberty.

Nevertheless, by the early 1920s, Panama's anarchists began debating whether to continue supporting the Bolsheviks as news of mounting Soviet repression emerged. Blázquez de Pedro was emphatic in early 1921: Yes, anarchists still needed to support the revolution. While Bolshevik policies might not represent his ideal, what choice did anarchists have? "If we destroy, or let others destroy the Soviet Republic of Russia, we will find ourselves further from Anarchy rather than closer to her." Despite the problems, "the Soviet Republic of Russia constitutes a beacon, less luminous than we would have imagined and continue to imagine possible, but an unquestionable beacon nonetheless."[12]

In July 1921, anarchists and Marxists united to form the Grupo Comunista. Weekly, the group met in Blázquez de Pedro's Panama City home. Each of the city's twelve labor organizations sent representatives to

[10] *Cuasimodo*, July 1920, 56–59 (quotes on page 57); December 1919, 5.
[11] Ibid., November 1919, 80–81.   [12] *El Obrero*, January 13, 1921, 3.

the meetings.[13] The group worked for material and moral improvement of all workers in Panama, regardless of national origins. Further, they argued that class struggle (not some populist state–capital–worker national harmony) was central to the Panamanian working-class's future. While this was a broad leftist coalition, the Grupo Comunista followed anarchist sentiments by opposing all politics and capitalism, declared themselves followers of communism (with a small 'c'), and viewed the Bolshevik government as the best and most practical contemporary expression of their own ideals.[14]

Between 1922 and 1924, Grupo Comunista anarchists maintained links with the international community by sending money to the New York-based *Aurora*, now edited by former canal worker Jorge de Borrán, while Blázquez de Pedro continued the links between Panamanian and Cuban-based anarchists by sending regular columns to Havana's *Nueva Luz*. In December 1922, Blázquez de Pedro illustrated the group's position on "communism" with the essay "Acción Directa y Comunismo." If his readers thought that a revolutionary government was his goal, he assured them this was not the case. "After having conquered private property and capitalism, the Ideal would still remain incomplete if there is no movement toward establishing full Communism [which] has to be anarchist or it will be neither true nor long-lasting." No government, no matter how "communist" and how tiny, could be allowed to continue because "that small authoritarian portion" would never disappear.[15] Thus, Blázquez de Pedro continued to openly call himself "communist" and support the Bolshevik cause, but he also reiterated his anarchist beliefs that a Communist government could not be the end goal.

CUBA'S ANARCHISTS AND THE BOLSHEVIKS

News of the revolution arrived in Cuba during a period of intensifying unionization efforts. Despite a wave of governmental repression and deportations of anarchists in early 1915 that led to the closing of *¡Tierra!*, anarchists continued to organize in the cities, the countryside, and the transport sector that united them. For instance, in 1916, they organized

---

[13] Memorandum for the Governor from Inspector George Vraff, November 17, 1921. RG185 General Files of the Panama Canal, 1914–1934 (hereafter referred to as RG185 ICC 1914–1934), 2-P-8.
[14] Gandásequi, *Las luchas obreras en Panamá*, 35, 52, 58–59; Soler, *Panamá*, 50–51; Franco Muñoz, *Blázquez de Pedro*, 176.
[15] *Aurora*, November 1, 1923, 17; *Nueva Luz*, December 7, 1922, 2.

the Grupo Acción Libertaria in the central Cuban city of Camagüey.[16] In 1917, revolutionary syndicalist organizations emerged across the island and the new periodical *Voz Rebelde* appeared with Antonio Penichet as one of its editors. In 1918, Penichet published his book *Del ambiente proletario*, calling in part for Cubans to create a Workers Center where the proletariat could come together for camaraderie and educate their children in a spirit of *"compañerismo."*[17]

From the beginning, anarchists mostly applauded the Bolsheviks. Anarcho-syndicalists like Alfredo López, Marcelo Salinas, and Penichet became some of the Revolution's most fervent early supporters. They praised Russia as proof that a union of working people and the military could launch a social revolution. The Federación de los Grupos Anarquistas (Federation of Anarchist Groups) organized campaigns to support the Russian Revolution. At the 1919 May Day celebration in Havana, anarchists joined with other leftists to commemorate the uprising of Russian workers, which one speaker called fundamentally libertarian. Meanwhile, Salinas and Penichet formed a "Sección Comunista de Cuba" (Cuban Communist Section). In the weeks following the 1919 May Day celebration, government surveillance and repression of anarchists increased. A government decree on May 23 led to the immediate deportations of twenty-one Spaniards and a US worker. That afternoon and the following day, police detained working-class leaders throughout Havana. Workers responded by going on strike and the government responded on May 30 by charging thirty-four workers with seeking to establish a Soviet republic in Cuba. Authorities arrested Penichet and Salinas, while their Spanish anarcho-syndicalist comrade José Rubio fled to Veracruz, Mexico, where he helped to create the group "Antorcha Libertario." But the arrests did not stifle the radical impulse. For instance, on August 18, an audience filled Havana's Teatro Alhambra to watch the play "Cubano vino Mefistófeles." During one scene, a character in the play denounced Bolshevism. Whether it was just by chance that radicals were attending the play, or they were there as part of an orchestrated effort, upon hearing the anti-Bolshevik speech an audience member shouted, "Long live anarchy; up with Bolshevism." The theater erupted in turmoil.[18]

---

[16] *Voluntad*, February 21, 1916, 4.
[17] Antonio Penichet, *Del ambiente proletario* (Havana: Avisador Comercial, 1918), 10–11.
[18] By mid-1921, Rubio had returned to Cuba and was editing *El Progreso* after being denied entry into the United States. His time in Veracruz would be important for the Mexican

Meanwhile, transnational radicalism stretched from the United States into Cuba. In 1918 and 1919, US-based Spanish-speaking Wobblies Genaro Pazos and Dalio Daniel (aka David Díaz) spearheaded new Industrial Workers of the World (IWW) efforts on the island. In letters to Cuban labor leaders Juan Arevalo, Aquilino López, and Hilario Alonso in Havana, Pazos claimed that the IWW was making progress and urged Cuban unions to unite into one big union. When Cuban authorities arrested Alonso and López, they seized IWW literature. When Díaz heard about the arrests, he decided to go to Cuba himself to organize IWW Locals. Arriving in November 1918, Cuban authorities – tipped off at his planned journey thanks to intercepting a letter he had written to Adrián del Valle – immediately arrested Díaz and deported him to Spain in December as a "pernicious foreigner." The level of IWW success in Cuba was questionable. Cuban intelligence said that Cuban workers did not understand what the IWW was.[19] But IWW organizers in the sugar belt around Matanzas successfully launched a general strike in March 1919, generated worker interest, and received requests for more IWW literature in Spanish.[20]

The Cuban government and mainstream liberal leaders in Cuba were aghast at the Bolshevik Revolution and the radicalism it was unleashing. Socialist Party member and University of Havana professor Francisco Carrera Jústiz and Orestes Ferrara – the one-time Italian anarchist who turned Cuban lawyer and politician – were repulsed by the Bolsheviks.[21] The writer and soon-to-be-editor of the magazine *Cuba Contemporanea*, Mario Guiral Moreno, condemned the Russian Revolution and the anarchists in Cuba who were trying to emulate it. Look around, he wrote, all recent uprisings were due to "more or less direct contact with foreign

---

anarchist José C. Valadés, as we'll see in Chapter 7. See also Sánchez Cobos, *Sembrando Ideales*, 310–315; *Crónica Cubana, 1919–1922*, ed. León Primelles (Havana: Editorial Lex, 1957), 91–95; Olga Cabrera, *Los que viven por sus manos* (Havana: Editorial de Ciencias Sociales, 1985), 203; "General Intelligence Bulletin," San Antonio, Texas Office, July 5, 1921. BS 202600-45, United States National Archives.

[19] Report to Special Agent Treadway, Department of Justice, Jacksonville, Fla. From Angel Corugedo, Havana, May 16, 1919. 364523 RG65, 65.2.2 Investigative Records, Old German Files, United States National Archives (hereafter cited as RG65 OGF USNA).

[20] "Spanish Anarchists." Coded report from interview with Francisco Patino in New York City, November 12, 1919. 237016 RG65 OGF USNA. If nothing else, they planted the Wobbly seed on the island. When workers arrived in Philadelphia from Cuba, the IWW's MTW 500 union always had Wobbly literature in Spanish ready for them. See "I.W.W. Matters: Special Weekly Report," June 20, 1921. BS 186701-232, United States National Archives.

[21] Sánchez Cobos, *Sembrando Ideales*, 307.

anarchist organizations who at every opportunity try to shatter the legal order of the Republic, greatly compromising its prosperity and riches." However, deporting foreign agitators was not enough. Guiral Moreno then quoted President Menocal's address to the Congress seeking the suspension of constitutional rights in order to suppress all radicals. "There are more than a few [Cuban] nationals participating with the same ideas ... [In order to] destroy at once these dangerous centers where their newspapers forge plots against public order, I need extraordinary powers that the Constitution has provided." Guiral Moreno approved of repression against the anarchists, claiming that it was bringing "tranquility to the country and re-establishing normality in all previously immobilized businesses and industries."[22]

The repression, though, was not working. US-based radicals – probably Wobblies – continued to send literature to Cuba advocating strikes and sabotage on sugar estates around Cruces.[23] In April 1920, with anarchist organizing now at its highest level in over five years, Havana's cigar rollers launched the Congreso Nacional Obrero, led in part by López and Salinas. Delegates supported a resolution of revolutionary solidarity with Russia, saluting "the first government by and for the workers. This commission considers Red Russia as a beacon of light ... and we send our revolutionary solidarity to our Russian brothers."[24] A year of new violence followed the April congress. Between mid-1920 and mid-1921, authorities blamed anarchists for an explosion at San Felipe Church and a wave of bombings against tram lines during a transit workers strike. Dozens were arrested and jailed, including the usual suspects: Penichet (Figure 4.1) and Salinas. In protest, someone detonated a bomb in the National Theater while international opera singer Enrico Caruso performed *Aida* in May 1920. Following their release, the Cuban secret police tracked Penichet's and Salinas's every move. In July 1921, police again arrested Salinas for possessing and disseminating pro-Bolshevik literature.[25] Yet, as their colleagues repeatedly went to jail,

---

[22] Mario Guiral Moreno, *La dictadura proletariado* (Havana: El Siglo XX, 1919), 8–18, 19–21.
[23] "Dispatch 59 from American Consul in Cienfuegos," 364523, January 10, 1920. RG65 OGF USNA.
[24] Evelio Tellería, *Los congreso obreros en Cuba* (Havana: Editorial de Ciencias Sociales, 1973), 99–107; *El movimiento obrero cubano*, 336.
[25] *Crónica Cubana*, 259–260, 412–415; Lazar S. Jeifets, Victor L. Jeifets, and Peter Huber, eds., *La Internacional Comunista y América Latina, 1919–1943: Diccionario Biográfico* (Moscow: Instituto de Latinoamérica de la Academia de las Ciencias, 2004), 255, 291,

FIGURE 4.1 Antonio Penichet, anarcho-syndicalist author, labor leader, pro-Bolshevik, and all-around bad-ass.
Author's personal collection

not all workers jumped to support radical change in Cuba. Sitting in a prison cell in August 1922, R. R. Espina marveled at how Cubans, who had risen up in the past to fight for freedom and "plot the course of progress and democracy to which the immortal Kropotkin devoted himself," were now willing to sit back and live in the past. Meanwhile, people in the "indomitable Russia" were creating a socialist society of freedom.[26]

Gradually, information about the centralizing and anti-libertarian sentiments of the Bolsheviks reached Cuban shores. In 1921, as many Cuban anarcho-syndicalists solidified their support for the Russian Revolution, some Cuban anarchists had second thoughts.[27] In July, the newly formed anarchist periodical *Los Tiempos Nuevos* printed several columns critical of Russia. In one front-page column, "Le Vieux" urged anarchists to

---

295–296; "Weekly Situation Survey for Week Ending May 12, 1920. 8000-377098 Military Intelligence Division, General Staff, Section M.I.4." 65.2.2 Investigative Records, RG65 OGF USNA and "Letter from Matthew C. Smith, Colonel, General Staff, War Department, Washington, DC to L.J. Baley, Chief, Bureau of Investigation, Department of Justice, Washington, DC," July 5, 1921. 202600-2233 RG65, 65.2.2 Investigative Records, Bureau Section Files, 1909–1921.

[26] R. R. Espina, "Rebeldía," in *Album X rari nantis in gurgite vasto*, ed. Francisco Alonso (unpublished manuscript, Presidio August 1922–January 1923), 42–43.

[27] Cabrera, *Los que viven por sus manos*, 207.

rethink their earlier, unquestioning advocacy for Bolshevism. The author called Lenin's regime "a government more tyrannical than any other in Europe, and more dangerous because it was more hypocritical."[28] The editors of *Acción Consciente* in late 1922 applauded early attempts to fulfill the Russian people's aspirations for freedom and satisfaction of economic needs. However, it was becoming clear, noted the editors, that the Russian people were being molded to fit a predetermined plan in accordance with the dictates of an all-powerful, centralized state. The newspaper concluded that the real Russian Revolution was continuing, but only in books, pamphlets, and the clandestine press, as well as in underground meetings directed against the new tyranny.[29]

On the other hand, *Nueva Luz*, soon to be the most widely read and longest-lived Caribbean anarchist paper of the 1920s, joined forces with the island's Marxists like Alejandro Barreiro, José Peña Vilaboa, and Carlos Baliño. The newspaper threw its support firmly behind the Bolsheviks while allowing anarchist dissidents to make their case in its pages. One writer – possibly Penichet – acknowledged that a state apparatus and anarchism were incompatible. However, "don't let that undermine the significance of that proletarian conquest, that up to now is the most extraordinary that has been seen in the annals of revolutionary history." Echoing sentiments expressed by José María Blázquez de Pedro in Panama at the same time, he concluded that it would be a mistake to stop supporting the revolutionary process which still had the possibility – or so he thought – of achieving anarchism.[30] So, from *Nueva Luz*'s point of view, yes, the Bolsheviks as a government were doing things that antigovernment anarchists might have opposed, but one still had to respect what the Bolsheviks and their working-class supporters had achieved and not attack anything that would undermine the masses' enthusiasm for revolutionary action.

With the creation of the USSR in 1922, some Cuban anarchists launched a new round of criticisms. "Florentino" suggested that the real lesson from the Russian Revolution was the danger of a top-down social transformation that left the revolution firmly in state control rather than in the decentralized hands of the people.[31] Adrián del Valle echoed this sentiment, charging that a true revolution could only be carried out if the

---

[28] *Los Tiempos Nuevos*, July 22, 1921, 1–2.
[29] *Acción Consciente*, December 25, 1922, 1.
[30] *Nueva Luz*, September 7, 1922, 1–2; Sánchez Cobos, *Sembrando Ideales*, 317–318.
[31] *Nueva Luz*, August 2, 1923, 4.

people had been prepared, which they were not in Russia. That lack of preparation exposed people to an array of Bolshevik abuses, not the least of which was Lenin's dictatorship. Yet, while condemning the Soviet state, del Valle suggested that the new social setting in the USSR was better than in a bourgeois democracy.[32] The USSR, while not anarchist, was better than the United States – or Cuba.

Through late 1924, Penichet and *Nueva Luz* continued to appeal for unity on the Cuban left. For Penichet, everyone had to compromise principles and focus on the common enemy, a position he had emphasized in his 1922 pamphlet *Tácticas en uso y tácticas a seguir*. Published by the anarchist group "Cultura y Emancipación" led by Penichet, Vicente Canoura, and Antonio Moyano, the book outlined how ideological and working-class groups should pool their resources and energies in a united front against the government and capitalists, use the full range of sabotage and boycotts available, and appeal to white-collar clerical workers who were just as exploited in offices as workers were in factories.[33] But the key was unity – a theme emphasized by Carlos Baliño, the Socialist Party leader and union official who worked with Penichet to open rationalist schools. Baliño wrote the book's prologue, where he described Penichet as his friend.[34] In chapter 1, as though to set the tone for the larger message of leftist unity, Penichet urged comrades to avoid sectarian conflict. The real divisions in the struggle should not concern ideological splits, but rather honor: "the only thing that ought to preoccupy us is whether they [other radicals] are honorable people."[35] One could align with Socialists and Communists, as long as those people were honorable and not acting treacherously against their fellow leftists.

But a new era of the newspaper ¡*Tierra!* slammed a united strategy, noting that the Bolsheviks were doing exactly what Penichet rejected: being treacherous against fellow leftists. "Principles are our base for launching and waging the struggle ... If we are libertarians, anarchists, everything that stands in opposition to freedom and independence of individuals, groups, and collectives is our enemy, our only enemy," proclaimed the newspaper. Marcelo Salinas, who had helped push the friendship-with-the-Bolsheviks resolution in the 1920 labor congress, by now had abandoned his long-time friend Penichet on this point. He too

---

[32] Ibid., May 10, 1923, 2.
[33] Antonio Penichet, *Tácticas en uso y tácticas a seguir* (Havana: El Ideal, 1922), 23–27.
[34] Ibid., 3.   [35] Ibid., 13.

wrote in *¡Tierra!*, opposing working with Marxists.[36] The newspaper published Penichet's response, claiming that a united front was not his real goal. Instead, he simply hoped that leftists would stop stabbing each other in the back and begin down the road of "cordial cooperation of all" against the current Cuban government. Besides, he noted, in the past, even the Federation of Anarchist Groups – of which *¡Tierra!* was the official organ – had invited spiritists and masons to protests.[37] If such cooperation were possible with mystics and the like, then surely socialists of varying stripes could – if not work together – then at least not belittle and attack one another about the Bolsheviks.

In the background to these arguments, Vladimir Lenin died in January 1924. Cuba's relationship with the USSR then took an unusual turn. The port city of Regla long had been a site of radicalism. The first anarchist-oriented schools were created in the city in 1906. In 1908, Miguel Martínez arrived in Regla from Spain, personally appointed by Francisco Ferrer y Guardia to open a rationalist school in the city. Abelardo Saavedra published *Rebelión!* in the city in 1908. Regla is reported to have been the first place in Cuba where the "Internationale" was sung.[38] By 1924, the city had elected Antonio Bosch as mayor. Bosch walked a line between progressive liberalism and parliamentary socialism. Following Lenin's death, Bosch oversaw the creation of a site dedicated to Lenin and situated on a hill above the city. The public memorial was the first in the Western Hemisphere dedicated to the fallen Communist leader.[39]

¡Tierra!'s anarchists hated the memorial for its religious and political symbolism. For some, the elevated reverence for Lenin amounted to little more than his canonization – and thus something against which to fight. On May Day 1924, Mayor Bosch ordered the planting of olive trees at the Lenin memorial. *¡Tierra!* condemned the planting and the overall reverence that "Cuban Bolsheviks" had for the fallen leader. For those who still believed the dictatorship of the proletariat was some form of bottom-up government representing the people, the editors noted that the true nature of "Saint Lenin's" regime was perfectly reflected by where the memorial was created: on top of a hill ... looking down on the people.[40]

---

[36] *¡Tierra!*, October 16, 1924, 2.   [37] Ibid., October 19, 1924, 2.
[38] Shaffer, *Anarchism and Countercultural Politics*, 178–179.
[39] Eduardo Gómez Luaces, "Monografía histórica del movimiento obrero en Regla (1833–1958)," unpublished manuscript, n.d.
[40] *¡Tierra!*, October 30, 1924, 2–3.

All one had to do, the newspaper noted months later, was read the correspondence from anarchist groups in the USSR who now had to live underground. With this knowledge, how could anarchists lionize a leader who killed their libertarian comrades?[41]

While it was one thing to criticize the increasingly dictatorial, freedom-crushing actions of the USSR thousands of miles away, it was another thing to deal with Marxists in your own neighborhood, workplace, and meeting halls – people you knew, and maybe whose kids played with yours. In fact, the early anarchist support for the Russian Revolution helped to bridge a larger pan-leftist alliance in Cuba. This alliance led to the creation of the Federación Obrera de la Habana (Havana Workers Federation, or FOH) in 1921, a series of rationalist schools across the country supported by Marxists and anarchists alike in the early 1920s, and the first truly islandwide labor organization in Cuba – the Confederación Nacional de Obreros Cubanos (National Confederation of Cuban Workers, or CNOC) founded in 1925.

Yet, some anarchists feared these new initiatives, and writers working with the influential anarcho-syndicalist newspaper of the factory workers – *El Progreso* – joined *¡Tierra!*'s attacks. *El Progreso* challenged the central committee of the FOH and one of its leaders, Alfredo López. López was an anarcho-syndicalist printer who worked closely with Penichet and Marxists to create the FOH and its rationalist school initiatives, even sending his two children to the first school opened by the FOH in 1922. By 1923, López began to work closely with leftist University of Havana students like Julio Antonio Mella, soon to be a founder of the Cuban Communist Party.[42] Paulino Díez led the challenge against López in late 1924. Just as critics of the Russian Revolution focused on strong, centralized government in the USSR, Díez and his supporters resented what they saw as the increasing centralization taking place within Cuba's labor movement. To them, calls for leftist unity and a united front were means to acquire more power for the FOH central committee. They further claimed that the FOH suppressed worker-led direct action, especially if such labor actions did not first have official endorsement from FOH leaders. Delegates from the Sindicato Fabril – the union publishing *El Progreso* – spoke out against the FOH's "odious centralization" that prevented grass roots initiatives. If the FOH were a true federation, *El Progreso*

---

[41] Ibid., January 22, 1925, 4.   [42] Cabrera, *Los que viven por sus manos*, 247, 333.

insisted, then local unions should be free to create their own initiatives or not follow FOH directives that a union local opposed. If the FOH refused this, then it was a federation in name only and an authoritarian structure in actuality.[43]

In mid-1925, all hell broke loose. Cubans elected Gerardo Machado to be the next president. Machado had pledged to rein-in growing militancy. He assured voters that by repressing the radical left, the United States would not invoke the Platt Amendment and invade to put down labor radicalism. Thus, with this pledge, he sealed his "nationalist" credentials and unleased a wave of repression against all leftists. As both Marxists and anarchists fell victim to the tyranny, Adrián del Valle offered one of the last anarchist words on the Bolsheviks. That year he published his biography, *Kropotkin, Vida y obras* (Kropotkin, Life and Works). Del Valle wrote how so many anarchists had accepted the Bolshevik experiment because the Bolsheviks initially welcomed different revolutionary elements. Even Kropotkin "maintained a benevolent attitude toward the Bolshevik State, considering it – despite its authoritarian defects – as a great step in the advancement toward complete societal liberation."[44] Over time, though, Bolshevik tyranny proved Kropotkin's quarter of a century warnings about "the incompatibility between a revolution strictly speaking and so-called revolutionary governments." In this sense, a true revolution "has to be produced by the free initiative of the people."[45] Why hadn't Kropotkin been more vocal about Bolshevik shortcomings before his death in Russia in 1921? What was the point, del Valle asked. "Protesting against the Russian government was a waste of time since its only preoccupation consisted in maintaining power without stopping to think about such 'insignificant' things as lives and human rights."[46] Del Valle's portrayal of Kropotkin reflected so much of the Cuban response to events in Russia: initial critical support and then a recognition of the Bolsheviks' shortcomings. But in 1925, when he published the biography, none of this much mattered in Cuba. Anarchists had new worries as the capitalist state – not Bolsheviks – turned its full murderous weight upon radicals, which we will see in Chapter 7.

---

[43] *El Progreso*, October 11, 1924, 4; October 25, 1924, 2; December 20, 1924, 1 and 4–5; Cabrera, *Los que vivan por sus manos*, 349.
[44] Adrián del Valle, *Kropotkin, Vida y obras* (Buenos Aires: Agrupación C. Cafiero, 1925), 15.
[45] Ibid., 37–38.   [46] Ibid., 39.

EL COMUNISTA AND PUERTO RICAN ANARCHIST SUPPORT FOR THE BOLSHEVIKS

Throughout the 1910s, anarchists refused to be silenced on the Puerto Rican left. They maintained positions within the Federación Libre de Trabajadores (Free Federation of Workers, or FLT) and published books, plays, and pamphlets to keep the message alive. The creation of the Socialist Party in 1915 had numerous effects. Some anarchists joined the party, forsaking direct action for parliamentary politics. Others joined the party and combined electoral campaigning with continued direct action – sort of like joining the FLT but remaining linked to *¡Tierra!*. Meanwhile, some leftists who joined the party reached out to their anarchist comrades. These socialists on the left wing of the party continued to identify with the larger social goals of anarchism and fondly remembered their associations in unions and educational efforts earlier in the decade. Nevertheless, the most dedicated anarchists refused to give up their antipolitics position, rejected the Socialists, and remained a thorn of consciousness and critique on the left until the end of the decade.

Between 1916 and 1917, a small but growing group of anarchists centered in the cigar-rolling city of Bayamón became the vanguard for Puerto Rican anarchism. Lacking a newspaper of their own, they turned to Esteve's *Cultura Obrera*. The growing importance of the New York paper for Puerto Rican anarchists went beyond being just a vehicle for rabble-rousing columns. Increasingly, Bayamón's anarchists became regular financial backers of the paper.[47] In April 1918, they formed "Grupo Souvarine" and created a new Centro de Estudios Sociales (Social Studies Center, or CES) with contacts in every part of the island.[48] Some contacts in Puerta de Tierra and Bayamón functioned as the Central Committee of a January 1919 strike against the Tobacco Trust.[49] US-based Wobblies were working with some of the Bayamón anarchists. Spanish anarchist José Martínez Gil, a tailor by training, migrated to Cuba and then the

---

[47] Between August 1916 and March 1917, for instance, Bayamón contributions accounted for between 3 and 5 percent of the paper's weekly. See, for instance, *Cultura Obrera*, August 5, 1916, 4; September 30, 1916, 4; October 14, 1916, 4; March 31, 1917, 4.

[48] *Yo Acuso*, April 20, 1918, 4.

[49] Ibid., April 20, 1918, 4; "La Huelga del Trust del Tobaco; Manifiesto de Información," January 22, 1919. In *Movimiento Obrero Puertorriqueño hojas sueltas 1898–1937*, Microfilm Periódicos Obreros Puertorriqueños. Colección Puertorriqueña, Universidad de Puerto Rico – Río Piedras (hereafter cited as MPOP).

United States in 1901, where he worked as a cigar maker. By 1919, Gil was a Wobbly who sought to create "one big union out of the three smaller cigar maker's unions" in the Tampa region. According to authorities, he worked with Puerto Rican anarchists Ramón Barrios and Alfredo Negrín from Bayamón. The two Puerto Rican radicals had recently traveled to Cuba to help organize workers and strengthen relations between anarchists on both islands. However, Cuban authorities quickly arrested them in Havana and found anarchist and strike propaganda as well as letters to Gil in their possession. Officials believed that Barrios and Negrín were working with Cuban and Florida anarchist cigar makers to launch a simultaneous general strike in all three locations before Cuban authorities stumbled upon them. They were deported to Puerto Rico – that is Cubans deported anarchists to the United States. Meanwhile, another Puerto Rican red – Enrique Plaza – remained in Cuba, editing *El Productor Panadero* and *Germinal*.[50]

By November 1919, Antonio Palau, Juan M. Alicea, and Emiliano Ramos – the latter an anarchist who had been active on the island since the 1890s – renamed the Bayamón group "El Grupo Soviet de Bayamón." In the heady days of global revolution – now two years into the Bolshevik regime in Moscow and anarcho-Bolshevik activism in Havana – the Bayamón anarchists called for more labor militancy and adopted the "soviet" image as part of their identity. In a manifesto, the group offered their support to a transport workers' strike in the United States, urging island workers to side with their mainland allies in a show of strength. The anarchist manifesto showed that there was another voice on the island speaking for the working class besides just the FLT and the Socialists.[51]

By 1919, the island's anarchists had also established a consistent presence in New York, where they engaged other Puerto Ricans, worked with other Spanish-speaking radicals, and cooperated with organizations like the IWW and the American Communist Party (ACP). But they also maintained close relations with comrades still in Puerto Rico.[52] Circular

---

[50] "JOSE MARTINEZ GIL – Alleged Anarchist and Bolsheviki Propagandists among the Latin American Element in Ybor City, Florida," April 22, 1919. 366867 RG60, Department of Justice, Old German Files, United States National Archives (hereafter cited as RG60 OG USNA); "Memo on Bolshevik, Anarchist, and Socialist Newspapers." War Department Memo. May 3, 1919, 44. 10010-1276. Index Number 142232. United States National Archives.
[51] "Manifiesto a los Trabajadores de Puerto Rico," November 5, 1919. MPOP.
[52] Shaffer, *Black Flag Boricuas*, 160–161.

FIGURE 4.2 Launched on May Day 1920 in the midst of growing worker radicalism, the Bayamón-based *El Comunista* was the longest-running anarchist newspaper in Puerto Rico until it was closed under US government repression in early 1921.
Center for Puerto Rican Studies (New York)

migration saw anarchist labor leaders like Ángel María Dieppa, Alfonso Torres, Luisa Capetillo, Ventura Mijón, Emiliano Ramos, Herminio Colón, and José Alicea moving back and forth between the island and New York over the decade. For instance, Ventura Mijón worked with anarchists in New York as early as March 1910, Tampa Wobbly radicals in 1912, and Spanish, Puerto Rican, and Cuban anarchists in New York publishing *El Corsario* in 1919.

On May Day 1920, the Bayamón anarchists launched their newspaper *El Comunista*, edited by Mijón, who had recently returned from New York (Figure 4.2). They turned the paper into perhaps the most strident voice advocating revolutionary transformation that Puerto Rico had ever seen. The timing for such radicalism seemed perfect. In 1920, FLT membership had grown to 28,000, up from 8000 a decade earlier. Throughout that year, workers launched over 160 strikes across the island. The surge in labor militancy even prompted the island government to outlaw the flying of red flags during strikes and demonstrations.[53] Through their newspaper, the Bayamón anarchists capitalized on this labor militancy and urged Puerto Ricans to move even further to the left politically.[54] *El Comunista* offered Puerto Rican solidarity with Salinas and Penichet, who had been arrested by police while attending a conference to choose delegates for the Communist Third International.[55] Mijón urged "the Puerto Rican proletariat to make common cause with the American Communist Party and to adhere to the Third International in Moscow." He and the Bayamón anarchists celebrated the ACP declaration that it would no longer accept legalistic approaches to change the United States because "its program strives for the complete abolition of the State as a governmental institution ... With this declaration, the American Communist Party affirms the idea that inspires anarchist communism that we value as part of our own written and spoken propaganda." With that, the paper declared that the ACP was "the only true and real political party of the workers."[56]

Meanwhile, they offered uncritical support for the Bolsheviks. The position emerged from a series of local commentaries and international articles reprinted in *El Comunista*. In a reprinted column titled "Comunismo y Parlamentarismo," the author claimed that "revolutionary elements" around the world were "adhering to the communist movement ... under the battle cry of Soviet Power. Anarcho-syndicalist groups and groups simply calling themselves anarchist are also incorporating themselves into this general current." Anarchists now rejected their previous total opposition to government, seeing the "dictatorship of the proletariat" as beneficial to the anarchist cause because it consolidated working-class violence against the capitalist class. "Such violence – violence against those who oppress the millions of working masses – isn't bad violence: it is sacred violence."[57] As one author concluded, the dictatorship of the proletariat would lead to "establishing the ideal of Libertarian Communism" as Soviet Power abolished the last dregs of capitalism.[58]

Culture could be used for the cause as well. In July 1920, the Bayamón-based José Vallón Fuentes published two connected poems. The first, "Russia Redeemed," celebrates the hard-fought victory over tsarist

---

[53] Juan Ángel Silén, *Apuntes: Para la historia del movimiento obrero puertorriqueño*, 2nd edition (Río Piedras, PR: Norberto González, 1995), 82–83.
[54] *El Comunista*, May 8, 1920, 3–4.   [55] Ibid., May 29, 1920, 3.
[56] Ibid., November 13, 1920, 1 and 3.   [57] Ibid., July 10, 1920, 3.
[58] Ibid., August 14, 1920, 3; August 28, 1920, 2; June 19, 1920, 2; July 17, 1920, 1.

tyranny, and then a sovereign Russia's efforts to build a new society: "Oh sovereign Russia! That your government reflects / The most grandiose work that your people contemplated / The colossal work embraced by the people / That was fervently idealized by Nicolas Lenine." But, why aren't more countries following the Russian example, the poem continued? "Why are the rest of the world's peoples enchained by Despotism / Not imitating your rage, oh righteous Russia? / Why don't they forcefully throw into the Abyss / The cruel regime like the one that Trotsky reduced to ashes?" In the adjacent second poem titled "And you, gentle Borinquen?" the poet turns those questions specifically to Puerto Rico (Borinquen being the pre-Spanish name for the island). "The Hispanic Bourgeoisie with its squalid egoism / Is united with the same from Yankilandia / And together they make the most odious abject despotism. / Why does that damn chaos that Russia shook off / Inspired by the Cause of a higher Socialism / In an enormous struggle, not lead you to shake off your Nemesis?"[59] In their eyes, Bolshevism and anarcho-communism were fully compatible.

THE RED SCARE IN THE ANARCHIST CARIBBEAN

What we call the "Red Scare" from 1919 to 1920 was merely an extension of an antianarchist campaign dating to the turn of the century, in which authorities targeted La Resistencia in Tampa, forced Pedro Esteve to flee Florida, arrested Tampa anarchists for supposedly plotting to kill world leaders, and arrested radicals while shooting up union halls in Puerto Rico. This new wave of antiradical repression, though, used the full weight of Washington's legal and security apparatus to root out Caribbean anarchists. In June 1917, the United States passed the Espionage Act that prevented antiwar material from being mailed during wartime, but the government continued to enforce the act after the Armistice. The law became a key tool in the concerted US government effort to prevent Marxist and anarchist groups from cheaply using the US mail as a means of disseminating propaganda after the Russian Revolution. In its September 18, 1920 edition, *El Comunista* reported to its readers that the US Postal Service had denied it second-class status.[60] The government clampdown on *El Comunista* occurred just as global anarchists produced their most deadly assault: the September 16, 1920 Italian anarchist

---

[59] Ibid., July 10, 1920, 1.   [60] Ibid., September 18, 1920, 4.

bombing of Wall Street that killed thirty-eight people and shocked the nation. Thus, from Washington's perspective, Reds had brought war to the homeland, and they considered *El Comunista* to be on the frontlines of that global campaign.

In the wake of the new mailing prohibitions, the editors appealed for more financial contributions to sustain the newspaper. The effect was twofold. First, contrary to what one would expect, distribution throughout the United States increased after the mail prohibition. Copies were now carried from city to city by hand, surreptitiously mailed inside packages, and secreted away inside the luggage of migrating anarchists. Second, unlike most anarchist newspapers, *El Comunista* ran a financial surplus as a result of this increased surreptitious distribution and contributions from around Puerto Rico, Cuba, New Jersey, New York, and Florida.[61]

However, these surpluses could not save the newspaper. In December 1920, the US Bureau of Investigation opened a two-month-long case into the Bayamón anarchists. On January 31, 1921, Special Agent Hubbard submitted his report, highlighting the group's call for violent revolution and its desire to form "a Soviet government controlled by the laborers." Though "as yet their membership is not large ... they have already created considerable trouble and disorder." Hubbard identified seventy-one editors, writers, and members. He suggested that the group could take advantage of growing labor strife to agitate among the largely illiterate, black, and unemployed workers, "a great majority being of the ignorant laboring or 'peon' class, propaganda such as these people are turning out, is bound to obtain converts and cause trouble in the end." Hubbard concluded that this "outspoken adherent of the Third International of Moscow" sought to "incite the working classes of Porto Rico to destruction of all existing forms of government, and society."[62]

As so many in the intelligence agencies of the Americas did, he blurred the line between anarchists, communists, and Bolsheviks. Nevertheless, Hubbard was not entirely wrong in his characterizations of the Bayamón bloc. After all, anarchists supported the Bolsheviks, called for alliance with the ACP to support a revolutionary movement and urged a non-conciliatory awakening in Puerto Rican workers that would lead them to a Bolshevik-style uprising. His investigation ultimately led authorities to

---

[61] Ibid., December 11, 1920, 4; February 2, 1921, 4.
[62] "Information for General Intelligence Bulletin: The Communist Party of Porto Rico," January 31, 1921. 202600-40 RG65 OGF USNA.

close *El Comunista* in early 1921 and with it the demise of the Bayamón anarchist organization.⁶³

While US counterintelligence efforts against pro-Bolshevik anarchists in Puerto Rico led to the decline and near-death of anarchism on the island, the Red Scare activities of US officials in Washington and Tampa did the same in Florida. Between 1919 and 1920, federal officers, local officials, and the Anglo establishment worked diligently to uproot pro-Bolshevik, pro-anarchist sentiment across the United States, but especially in immigrant enclaves like Tampa. Even before the 1917 Revolution, US officials feared anti-American, pro-revolutionary literature was reaching the United States from Latin America. One of the first concerns emerged in summer 1917. In 1902, Colombian writer and activist José María Vargas Vila published a series of articles under the title *Ante los Bárbaros: el Yanki. He ahí el enemigo* (Confronting the Barbarians: The Yankee. Behold, the Enemy) in his New York-based *Némesis* magazine. Existentialist and anticlerical in tone, he defended freedom and justice in Latin America as the United States began its neocolonial expansion. The articles' blatant anti-Americanism led to his deportation. In 1917, a European publisher printed the articles in book form. Of the 5000 copies printed, apparently most went to Argentina, but over 100 copies were distributed between Philadelphia, Puerto Rico, and Cuba. The books soon appeared in Tampa. Justice Department officials there labeled it "seditious" and "pro-German." Afraid of a crackdown on their union, the Cigar Makers International Union (CMIU) told its *lectores* in the city's tobacco factories not to read it.⁶⁴

---

[63] In late 1928, while living in Tampa, Ángel María Dieppa wrote a seven-part series on the history of Spanish-speaking anarchists in North America. In Part Five, he reminisced about the relationship between *El Comunista*, Santiago Iglesias, and Bolshevism. Dieppa falsely claimed that Iglesias was a Marxist and State Communist (essentially a Bolshevik). Iglesias and his associates "invented a sewer full of infamous slanders against that handful of sincere comrades and not only that but he also denounced them before the government so that the group broke up, the newspaper ceased publishing, and all came to see that they had to abandon that island." In fact, *El Comunista*'s group was the one sympathetic to the Bolsheviks. *Cultura Proletaria*, December 1, 1928, 2. The seven-part series ran from November 3, 1928 to February 9, 1929 and helped to fuel a feud between the anarchist newspaper and the IWW's *Nueva Solidaridad*.

[64] See "'Ante los Barbaros,' and Other Seditious Matter from T. S. Marshall in Tampa," July 19, 1917; July 21, 1917; July 31, 1917; August 5, 1917. Also see "Letter from Department of State to A. Bruce Bielaski (Chief, Bureau of Investigation, Department of Justice) in Washington, DC," October 8, 1917 for publishing information. All are in 33988 RG60 OGF USNA. See also "Anarchistic and Bolsheviki Pamphlets Published in Spanish and Circulated in Ybor City, Tampa, Fla.," February 3, 1919. 342696 RG65 OGF USNA.

Vargas Vila's book was just the tip of the cultural iceberg. Ever-increasing amounts of Latin American radical literature began to arrive in Tampa, causing patriots no shortage of trepidation. Anarchists in Cuba and Puerto Rico moved in and out of Tampa or shipped propaganda to the city. In this context, Antonio Penichet – the indefatigable Bolshevik supporter in Havana – published his short novel *El soldado Rafael*. In the book, soldiers (who come from the working class) refuse orders to violently repress strikers and instead join strikers against the government and capitalists – anarcho-Bolshevism 101. The Cuban government tried to stop the book's distribution and have Penichet arrested.[65] Word of Penichet's story and its incendiary subject matter reached the United States in mid-1919, when the Cuban secret police forwarded a series of reports on IWW activity in Cuba and the United States to the Department of Justice's Jacksonville, Florida office. Cuban investigators had found copies of *El soldado Rafael* "on many of the soldiers of the [Cuban] Army and also on my investigation I found out that a few of the books were sent to the states [sic] to be translated into English." Undoubtedly, even if the books were not translated – and no English-language copy is known to exist – intelligence agents still had to be nervous, fearful that the book and other propaganda like it tapped into a growing theme of pro-Bolshevik solidarity among US Latin radicals. Because it was in Spanish, naturally intelligence agents feared its possible use within US Latin communities like Tampa.[66] Then, Penichet attempted to make his fiction a reality. In June 1919, he traveled from Havana to the central Cuban city of Camagüey to persuade Cuban soldiers to resist orders from their leaders when called to put down labor disputes.[67] The last thing transnational authorities wanted was radical life imitating radical art.

In the Red Scare climate, officials saw the potential for Bolshevik conspiracies everywhere. Anarchists and Wobblies linked with Cuban radicals seemed to be part of that global conspiracy in southern Florida. Anarchist and "Bolshevik" material continuously arrived in Tampa, much to the consternation of officials. Agent Byrd Douglas wrote to Washington in May 1919, noting that he thought "Bolshevik propaganda circulated in this country has been sent into Tampa among the Spanish

---

[65] *Crónicas cubanas*, 112; Antonio Penichet, *El soldado Rafael; páginas de la vida real* (Havana: Grupo Germinal, 1919).
[66] "Report from Angel Corugedo in Havana to C. B. Treadway in Jacksonville, July 7, 1919." 064523 RG65 OGF USNA.
[67] "Weekly Situation Survey for Week Ending February 18, 1920, Military Intelligence Division, General Staff, Section M.I.4.," 8000-377098 RG60 OGF USNA.

element," including two circulars addressed to "Soldiers and Workmen" and the New York-based anarchist newspaper *El Corsario*.[68] According to Douglas's informants, radicals strong-armed store owners into distributing radical literature. He conjured a mafia-like scenario whereby someone distributing radical pamphlets or newspapers "picked out some innocent party, either a restaurant owner or a coffee shop owner, and sent a bundle of papers and pamphlets to him requesting that he distribute them to the patrons who came to his place of business." If the owner refused, he faced a boycott with the result that he either submitted or had to go out of business.[69]

Circulation of radical literature was bad enough. But US authorities' bigger fears were what such circulation implied: a radical network stretching from the Caribbean through Tampa and to New York – a network that officials knew had existed in the 1890s during the Cuban War for Independence and again with the 1912–1913 episodes surrounding the supposed international anarchist assassination conspiracies. This network's continued existence took on greater importance in the context of feared Bolshevik global aspirations. The Justice Department's key concern in early 1919 was no small matter. It involved a supposed anarchist assassination plot against President Wilson and a Latin Red conspiracy stretching between Spain, New York, Philadelphia, Tampa, Cuba, and Puerto Rico.

On February 23, 1919, the president's ship was to land in Boston Harbor as Wilson returned from the Paris Peace Conference ending the Great War. According to Secret Service informants, a group of Spanish-speaking anarchists conspired to throw a bomb at the presidential party as it made its way through the city the following morning. On February 24, acting on this intelligence, Secret Service agents arrested fourteen anarchists associated with the New York City newspaper *El Corsario* and raided two homes of suspected anarchists there. Believing that two of the plotters had recently arrived in New York from Philadelphia, Justice Department agents swept through Philadelphia and arrested ten more anarchists. In both cities, all the anarchists were from Spain, Cuba, and Puerto Rico. No bombs were found, and the defendants claimed the

---

[68] "Letter from Tampa, Department of Justice/FBI to W. E. Allen, Acting Chief, Bureau of Investigation, Washington, DC from Byrd Douglas, May 27, 1919," 8000-353595 RG60 OGF USNA.

[69] "'Anarchist Pamphlets Written in Spanish: Distributed among the Latin American Element at Tampa, Florida, by Parties Unknown' from Byrd Douglas, Tampa, February 29, 1919," 342696 RG60 OGF USNA.

arrests were done on the pretense of looking for more information about anarchists throughout the country.[70]

The bomb scare in February might have been just that – a scare and not a real plot. The Justice Department had watched the group for some time. The New York office was suspicious of *El Corsario*. The Department's Tampa office, with its growing surveillance of anarchists in that city, came to New York's aid – and with the help of Tampa-based Luis Fabregat, a Cuban Socialist labor leader. Fabregat fled Cuba and the antiworker administration of President Mario Menocal after a 1917 strike wave. In the United States, he traveled to New York and other US cities, including Chicago, where he stood trial (but was acquitted) for working with the IWW. Then, he traveled to Tampa with hopes of returning to Cuba.[71] Fabregat came to Agent Douglas's attention when he distributed a Spanish-language pamphlet to soldiers on guard duty in Tampa's shipyards early in January 1919. The pamphlet called for workers and soldiers to unite and fight for a democratic revolution. For Douglas, this was further proof that the city was

> infested with an element of anarchists who are not only a great menace to this country but are fearless and insidious in their insidious work, and further Agent believes this same element is the brains of a crowd of Cuban and Spanish Bolshevists working throughout the country in close harmony with Italian, Mexican, Russian and I.W.W. despoilers who would cast political ruin over the country.

While Douglas could not confirm who published the propaganda, it was "probable that this pamphlet was published in Cuba and smuggled into the States, where it was later distributed by some of one of hundreds of Cuban and Spanish and Italian Anarchists."[72]

The following week, Douglas questioned a cooperative Fabregat, who readily supplied him with Spanish-language newspapers circulating among Tampa workers, information about local anarchists, and background on the publications they were reading – information that Douglas told his superiors "is very valuable in an investigation to determine

---

[70] *New York Times*, February 24, 1919, 1–2; February 25, 1919, 5; February 26, 1919, 11; *La Nueva Solidaridad*, March 1, 1919, 1.

[71] "Key West, Fla. U.S. Postal Censorship Report on Letter from Writer Unknown to Sr. Director Artistico de La Caricatura, Habana, Cuba Regarding 'LOUIS FABREGAT PEREZ,'" February 13, 1919. 342696 RG60 OGF USNA.

[72] "Anarchistic Pamphlet Written in Spanish and Distributed among the Latin American Element at Tampa Florida, by Parties Unknown," January 6, 1919. 342696 RG65 OGF USNA. Underlines in the original.

whether or not there is a concerted effort to arouse the spirit of Bolshevickism among the Latin American people in Tampa, Florida." In return, Fabregat hoped to gain a passport and a seaman's identification card that would allow him to leave the United States. However, Douglas refused to expedite either document.[73]

Agent Douglas informed his superiors about the circulation of one of the papers provided by Fabregat: *El Corsario*. On January 25 and 28, Douglas and Fabregat again met, with the subject bringing more propaganda to the office, including more issues of *El Corsario*. Douglas wanted to know the identities of the paper's publishers. While the paper did not list an editor, Fabregat suggested that it was "J. Gallart," a signatory to one of the paper's articles. Gallart was in fact a nom de plume of Cuban anarchist Marcelo Salinas – one of Fabregat's Cuban rivals.[74] This report led to a growing coordination between the Tampa and New York offices, with even more help from Fabregat. By early February, the New York field office began investigating the *El Corsario* anarchists, determining that the editor was "A. Sopelana," but Fabregat informed the agents that Sopelana was José Grau, a Spanish anarchist who had been in the United States for over one year.[75]

If true – and government authorities lacked this information before Fabregat's collusion – then one must ask just what Fabregat was up to. Fabregat was more than just desperate to flee the United States. He consciously helped the government expose anarchists. In fact, Fabregat would be no friend of anarchists when he returned to Havana. Throughout 1920, as editor of the Socialist *Rumbos Nuevos*, he regularly attacked anarchists as weak and spineless. He claimed that Havana's anarchists kicked out Socialists from anarchist-dominated unions, acted cowardly for not accepting responsibility for bombings in Havana, and had been strikebreakers in Tampa.[76] There was little love lost between Fabregat and anarchists on both sides of the straits. By identifying people

---

[73] "Anarchistic Pamphlets Written in Spanish and Circulated in Ybor City, Florida, January 14, 1919," 342696 RG65 OGF USNA; "Sr. Luis Fabregat y Perez – Application for Passport to go to Cuba," January 15, 1919, 342696 RG65 OGF USNA.

[74] Avrich, *Anarchist Voices*, 397–398; "Anarchistic Pamphlets – Published in US in Spanish Language and Circulated in Ybor City, Tampa, Florida," January 25, 1919, 342696 RG65 OGF USNA; "Anarchistic Pamphlets Written in Spanish and Circulated in Ybor City, Tampa, Florida, January 28, 1919," 342696 RG65 OGF USNA.

[75] "Anarchistic and Bolsheviki Pamphlets Published in Spanish and Circulated in Ybor City, Tampa, Fla.," February 3, 1919. 342696 RG65 OGF USNA.

[76] *Rumbos Nuevos: Semanario de la Vida Internacional*, July 3, 1920, 7–8; July 17, 1920, 12; August 7, 1920, 8.

associated with *El Corsario*, he assisted US government efforts to thwart the supposed assassination attempt on President Wilson. Or, at the very least, his information helped to give authorities a reason to raid these men's homes and arrest them on February 24.

Arrests of the *El Corsario* anarchists did not lessen Douglas's concerns about anarchism and Bolshevism in Tampa's Latin population, nor broader Justice Department concerns about anarcho-Bolshevism. The continued possibility of radicalism in the Tampa area grew in Douglas's eyes when he discerned that Grau had been neither charged nor deported. He feared that Grau would travel to Tampa and asked the New York office for any information on his whereabouts. Douglas reported "that every radical in this city when asked if he knows the El Corsario, invariably replies affirmatively. The mails have been watched but no one has yet been found to whom the delivery is made."[77] For an intelligence officer infused with the idealism and xenophobia of the Red Scare, such a situation bred fear and frustration.

The US Justice Department saw the February "bombing" plot and the *El Corsario* episode as part of a growing anarchist initiative across the United States that had international support. In response, the Justice Department announced new efforts to purge all foreign anarchists from US shores. This effort intensified when anarchists sent homemade bombs to numerous public figures – including Attorney General Palmer – between April and June 1919 at the exact time that Cuban radicalism increased and warnings of Penichet's novel *El soldado Rafael* began to concern authorities on both sides of the Florida Straits.

By late 1919 and early 1920, the notorious Anglo citizens were growing as agitated as US officials. The level of hatred and vitriol among the "patriots" concerned Agent Douglas, who raised the history of the shanghaied anarchists of 1901: "It will be remembered that some time ago the citizens of Tampa took matters into their own hands when a series of strikes among the cigar makers took place having been fomented by so called professional agitators." He feared "the same thing will happen in the near future" unless the government acted.[78] Tampa Mayor McKay also pressed local agents and Washington to do something about

---

[77] "Anarchistic Pamphlets Written in Spanish and Distributed among the Latin American Element of Tampa, Florida," February 25, 1919. 342696 RG65 OGF USNA; "A. Sopelano, alias Jose Grau – alleged anarchist. Editor El Corsario," July 26, 1919. 342696 RG65 OGF USNA.
[78] "Circulation of Reports of Bolsheviki Meetings Being Held in Tampa, Fla.," April 15, 1919. 8000-353595 RG60 OGF USNA.

anarchists and Bolsheviks infesting his city. Not content to wait for the federal government, McKay – who also owned the *Tampa Daily Times* – hired his own Pinkerton detective to find anarchists throughout the city.[79]

In October 1919, Tampa workers, frustrated with the high cost of living, boycotted merchants for ninety days to demonstrate their own economic power. By mid-November, merchants estimated they had lost between 15,000 and 20,000 customers. The Anglo establishment was livid. The result, wrote Douglas, "has caused a great loss of money and has likewise stirred up an unusual amount of friction." The merchants remained united against the boycott because "there has always been a certain amount of animosity between the American and the Latin-American element in this city."[80] Local residents began compiling their own lists of anarchists. One letter sent to the Justice Department in Washington, signed "A. Citizen," included a list of twelve Wobblies who continued affiliating with anarchists from "Spain, Cuba and New York in the early part of this year when they were intenting [sic] to do bodily harm to the President of our Great Nation."[81]

The Tampa American Legion also approached the US Attorney's office to help fight against "any work which might be instigated by Anarchists, I.W.W.'s and Bolsheviks in this city." Immediately, the Department of Justice and the American Legion coordinated efforts. F. M. Williams, chairman of Tampa's American Legion Post #5, wrote to US Attorney General Palmer that the Legion had appointed three members to help the District Attorney's office and the Department of Justice "round up violators of the law" in order to "rid this community of undesirable aliens and enemies of the government."[82]

Other Tampans became involved. M. E. Gillett was not your ordinary citizen. In the 1890s, he was Tampa's mayor. Since then, he had become

---

[79] "Letter from US Attorney General's Office to US Senator Duncan Fletcher," July 8, 1919; "Letter from Byrd Douglas to J. T. Suter, Acting Chief, Bureau of Investigation, Washington, DC," July 14, 1919. 8000-362112 RG60 OGF USNA.

[80] "Merchants' Boycott – Tampa, Florida by the Cigar Makers and other Latin-American People," November 12, 1919. 8000-382470 RG60 OGF USNA.

[81] "Letter from Tampa to Department of Justice," October 15, 1919. 362112 RG65 OGF USNA. The strike was linked to a fight against manufacturers pushing for an open shop rather than a union shop. See Durward Long, "The Open–Closed Shop Battle in Tampa's Cigar Industry, 1919–1921," *The Florida Historical Quarterly* 47, no. 2 (1968): 101–121.

[82] "Anarchists and Bolsheviki in Tampa, Florida," November 15, 1919; "Letter from the American Legion State of Florida to Attorney General Palmer," November 15, 1919. 8000-362112 RG60 OGF USNA.

the owner of the world's largest citrus nursery and general manager of the Florida Citrus Exchange. His son, D. C. Gillett, had managed the Gillett Lumber and Transportation Company, which operated ships between Tampa and the Caribbean.[83] Consequently, the Gilletts were prominent Tampa elite whose word carried considerable weight. In his letter, M.E. Gillett concluded that the strikes were creating "(a)n intolerable and unbearable condition" in Tampa. Then he recalled "they are dissatisfied just as they were years ago when as you may recollect, we deported a bunch of agitators to an island off the coast of British Honduras. Would to God that the rest of them were all in the same place." Gillett implied that if the government did not do something soon, the citizens would again step in to quell the "bunch of anarchists, I.W.W.'s, and Radical Socialists" because "these foreign-born agitators propose to eliminate all Americans wherever it is possible." He urged the bureau to send a spy – "preferably a Latin who can get into the good graces of the ring leaders here and get us a correct list of the undesireables [sic]. We will do the rest."[84]

Agent A. V. French seemed concerned. He wrote in early December 1919 that "the Italian-Spanish colonies of West Tampa and Ybor City, Florida are the most advanced towards the 'Social Revolution.' I could say they have established a Soviet on a small scale."[85] In response, the Justice Department sent Dante di Lillo undercover into the world of Tampa anarchism. Sometimes posing as a circus musician, other times as a Red Cross employee, and still other times as a linotype operator, di Lillo provided concise biographies of twenty-seven radicals. One anarchist was an editor, others were shop and food service employees. Most, not surprisingly, were tobacco workers who were members of the recently created Sociedad de Torcedores (Cigar Rollers Society). The Sociedad was just three weeks old in mid-December 1919, but already claimed to have 1126 members, including Wobblies. Just as important as their occupational diversity, the suspected anarchists were identified as Spaniards, Cubans, and Mexicans, and included at least two whites.[86] The anarchists on the lists reflected, again, what the government feared, and which

---

[83] Walter Hines Page and Arthur Wilson Page, *The World's Work, Volume XX, May to October 1910* (Garden City, NY: Doubleday, Page, & Co., 1910), no page numbers.

[84] "Letter from M.E. Gillett & Son to Mr. Frank Burke," November 15, 1919. 362112 RG65 OGF USNA.

[85] Report by Agent A. V. French. "Re: Anarchists and Bolsheviks in Tampa, Florida, December 2, 1919." 362112 RG65 OGF USNA.

[86] "List of Suspects Active in Anarchistic Movements," December 13, 1919. 362112 RG65 OGF USNA.

anarchists had labored to create: that Tampa was part of a regional and even global anarchist network.

One of di Lillo's anarchists was Luis Díaz, a baker who had been deported from Spain to Canada before arriving in Tampa to work in the cigar factories. As anarchists always did, they raised money for political prisoners. In Tampa, Díaz oversaw the fund and kept records of contributors and their locations. Obviously, this made him a prime target for government anti-Red initiatives. When Justice Department officials raided Tampa radicals, Díaz burned the records just before the authorities arrived, thus saving potentially dozens of sympathizers from governmental harassment.[87]

A constant vexing issue facing antiradical crusaders was how anarchist newspapers continued to arrive into and circulate within Tampa. Through his sleuth work, di Lillo reported that "[a] large number of radical newspapers are coming in from Cuba."[88] Thus, the constant flow of workers between Tampa and Cuba, and the continued influence of anarchist ship workers plying the waters from New York to Florida to Cuba seemed to be responsible. In short, the maritime commerce that fueled economic growth for the Anglo business community in Florida also provided the communication lifeline for Tampa's anarchists.

Ultimately, heightened surveillance and cooperation between private citizens and government officials at both the local and federal levels effectively undermined Tampa's anarchists. They were jailed, deported, or just dropped out of activism to avoid further repression. Two decades earlier, Barcia had urged anarchists to be prepared to take up arms to defend themselves against local capitalists and vigilantes. But two decades earlier, the anarchists did not face the concerted efforts of the whole US government trying to root them out of existence due to worries of Bolshevik infiltration. As difficult as organizing had always been, by 1920 it had become almost impossible. While individual anarchists like Luis Barcia continued to send money and the occasional word of support to the global anarchist press, by the early 1920s, anarchism in Florida was almost dead. In fact, one of the oldest Tampa anarchists – Ramón Colmé, who had been active since the beginning of the century – died from a prolonged illness in Tampa in December 1922.[89] His death was a fitting symbol for the demise of Florida anarchism. The strength of the radical Latin unions from the 1890s had been crushed but not destroyed after

---

[87] "Anarchists and Bolsheviki," January 27, 1920. 362112 RG65 OGF USNA.   [88] Ibid.
[89] *Cultura Obrera*, December 23, 1922, 3.

1901. The emergence of the IWW resurrected anarcho-syndicalist activism in the 1910s and during the Great War. But it would take the triumph of the Bolshevik Revolution and the resulting anti-Red hysteria in the United States after 1917 to eliminate the movement all but for good.

CONCLUSION

Without a doubt, Caribbean anarchists were not unique in the trials and tribulations they faced after the Bolsheviks came to power in late 1917. Around the region, they struggled to comprehend just what was going on in Russia and whether they would have to abandon their traditional anti-statist, anti-centralization principles in order to join the working-class revolution. In the smaller anarchist enclaves in Tampa, Panama, and Puerto Rico, anarchists tended to accept the Bolsheviks as the best game in town. While not perfect, it made more sense to support Moscow's agenda rather than oppose it and thus end up on the side of the global capitalist class that was set on ending the Russian experiment. In Cuba, though, the larger and older anarchist movement was split. While most anarchists supported the Bolsheviks early on, by the early and mid-1920s, a growing number of anarchists refused to accept a dictatorship of the proletariat as the means to an anarchist end. Nevertheless, until the unleashing of wholesale government repression against the Cuban left in mid-1925, many influential anarchists like Antonio Penichet and Alfredo López remained supportive of the Russian Revolution and cooperated with Marxists in new labor and educational initiatives.

Growing regional cooperation between anarchists increased in the years following 1917. The eastern edge of the network (Puerto Rico, Cuba, and Tampa) was increasingly linked to that "Continental Caribbean" city of New York via migration and media. Anarchists, Socialists, and Communists cooperated in New York City, Havana, and Panama. Puerto Rican anarchists moved to and interacted with anarchists and Communists in New York while maintaining links with their comrades on the island. Wobblies and anarchists (many who called themselves "communists") plotted transnationally between Florida, New York, Cuba, and Puerto Rico, including possibly coordinating an assassination plot against President Wilson.

But this plot (whether real or a US intelligence agency fiction) reflected fears in the region's capitals that a transnational anarchist network linked to the Bolshevik agenda was operating in the Caribbean and along the US East Coast. Radicalism was surging throughout the region at the same time as it was growing in the United States: strikes and bombings in Havana overlapped bombing campaigns across the United States; Wobblies linked New York, Tampa, Cuba, and Puerto Rico; radical literature flowed out of Cuba and into the US ethnic enclaves in Florida and up the US East Coast as well as across the Caribbean. It must have seemed that the Reds were everywhere ... and many of them were coming from the Caribbean.

Intelligence agencies unraveled the network as part of their Red Scare initiatives to root out radicalism in the late 1910s and early 1920s. As a result, the Red Scare radiated out of Washington and spread throughout the United States and the Caribbean – wherever Spanish-speaking anarchists were plotting. The Red Scare was twofold. It was a legitimate fear that pan-sectarian Reds in the hemisphere would continue to create new revolutionary societies in the face of international capitalist and US expansion in the Caribbean Basin. At the same time, the Red Scare reflected the fact that anarchists were cooperating in a regional network of radicalism to a level unlike what officials had seen before. Sure, there was cooperation in the 1890s regarding the Cuban War, the early 1900s labor actions, and in the early 1910s around strikes and a supposed global assassins network, but this was different, larger, and – from the view of governments, capitalists, nativists, and the like – more dangerous due to the threatening image that the Bolsheviks posed. Ultimately, US authorities using the full weight of the federal government largely uprooted anarchists in Tampa and Puerto Rico. But it would take longer to bring the Panamanian and Cuban anarchists in line.

5

Anarchists versus *Yanquis* II

The Canal, the Great War, Puerto Rico's Status, and Banana Republics, 1916–1926

> You want independence, but you can never forget your obligations to *Yanquilandia*; that is, you will always be disposed to giving life and all that you (don't) have for the existence and glory of the great nation to the North.
>
> Sandalio Marcial, Bayamón, Puerto Rico, 1920

As Europe devolved into conflagration following the assassination of Archduke Ferdinand in 1914, the Western Hemisphere seemed content to let the Old World murder itself. And while anarchists in Europe had to figure out how to navigate the increasingly treacherous political landscape, Caribbean anarchists were free from these concerns – at least until 1917. On April 6, 1917, the US Congress declared war on Germany. Suddenly, men in the United States were eligible for the military draft and undeclared aliens were required to register or face a year in prison. In Puerto Rico, islanders became US citizens that spring, just in time for adult males to be drafted into the US military. Cuban President Menocal followed Washington's lead and Cuba declared war on Germany on April 7. The Cuban Congress passed an obligatory military service law modeled on the US law, and Cuban men likewise became eligible to fight in Europe. Showing loyalty to the United States, the Republic of Panama also declared war on Germany within twenty-four hours of the US declaration. Then, US President Wilson issued an executive order excluding undesirable persons from the Canal Zone that practically mirrored the 1904 exclusions by again placing anarchists in the category of those with diseases, felonies, and people seeking to "incite insurrection."[1]

US entry into the Great War brought the Cuban and Puerto Rican economies even more firmly into the US trade orbit. Meanwhile, Washington used the Panama Canal – now in operation for more than two years – to transit military personnel and convoys to the European theater. The US military and a new National Guard solidified their presence in Puerto Rico, and Puerto Rican units helped guard the Canal Zone. US troops – which had invaded Cuba in 1906 and 1912 – did so again in 1917. That same year, the United States purchased the Danish Virgin Islands. Meanwhile, the US military had invaded and occupied Haiti since 1915 and the Dominican Republic since 1916. The Caribbean had become the US military's testing grounds for the European conflict, forcing anarchists to respond.

Anarchist anti-imperialism that began in the 1890s against Spanish colonial rule extended thirty years into the 1920s against US neocolonialism. This chapter examines the multiple ways and the numerous fronts on which Caribbean anarchists fought against US expansion in the region beginning in 1916. In Panama, they launched the first general strike against the US-run canal on the eve of US entry to the war. In Tampa, Cuba, and Puerto Rico, they led strikes to disrupt ramped-up war production, helped men avoid conscription, and used fiction to oppose militarism generally and the war specifically. In Puerto Rico, US citizenship merely escalated the debate within all sectors of the island's population on the question of Puerto Rico's political status. Anarchists rejected both nationalism and colonialism while developing a radical, Bolshevik-inspired alternative. Finally, anarchists throughout the Caribbean began condemning "banana republics" – dictators propped up by the United States who repressed workers radicalizing against US agricultural export companies; such repression allowed dictators to proclaim themselves to be "nationalists" and thus prevent US military interference, though of course it was about repressing radicalism and preserving security for US interests.

---

[1] Ricardo J. Alfaro, *Medio siglo de realaciones entre Panamá y los Estados Unidos* (Panama City: Secretaria de Información de la Presidencia de la República, 1959), 30–31; "The Panama Canal Executive Office: Exclusion of Undesirable Persons," RG185 1914–1934, 2-P-59/16.

THE 1916 GENERAL STRIKE ON THE PANAMA CANAL

As his ship docked in Colón, Panama on the western shores of the Caribbean, José María Blázquez de Pedro must have been reflecting on the odyssey that had brought him back to the region (Figure 5.1). He had last seen the Caribbean as a young war veteran when he and his fellow Spanish soldiers boarded their troop transports for the return trip to Spain at war's end in late 1898. Disillusionment with the war led him to anarchism in Spain, where for over a decade he worked in literary and educational radicalism. Now in mid-1914, just prior to the formal opening of the Panama Canal, he returned to the Caribbean as a thirty-nine-year-old veteran of Spanish government repression – a man who had seen waves of political abuses levied against his comrades and where he himself served time in Spanish jails. Upon landing in Panama, Blázquez de Pedro embarked on an eleven-year political journey that included reviving his radical literary work, but just as importantly included his growing labor militancy – a militancy that he soon put to work against US rule in the isthmus.

By July 1916, the Panama Canal had been operating for almost two years, and anarchists continued their long complaints about poor conditions. For instance, since the canal's opening, silver-roll workers saw their

FIGURE 5.1 José María Blázquez de Pedro in 1913 on the eve of leaving for Panama.
Author's personal collection

wages stagnate while costs of living rose over 60 percent.[2] Jorge de Borrán captured the essence of this environment in July when he wrote to the New York-based *Fuerza Cerebral* from his home in Colón. While appreciating the magnificence of the canal, the press and the US government failed to acknowledge the tremendous sacrifices made by "workers of all races" who "have left behind pieces of their flesh, their dreams, their sweat. There are many cemeteries and they are full." Meanwhile, Panama was crowded with those "who have been unable to return to their homes to see their families" and others who "lost their muscles and limbs under the brakes of a locomotive or crushed by a landslide or from a hasty powerful dynamite explosion that went off too early." US health officials claimed that 80 percent of all injuries in the Canal Zone were related to alcohol consumption, but de Borrán argued this was just a way for authorities to cover up deaths resulting from negligent oversight and errant explosions throughout the zone while money and ambition were being made by "the bandits of Wall Street in New York."[3] Limbs lost and profits gained.

On October 3, the newly formed Maritime Workers Association, headed by Peru-born anarchist Víctor Recoba (Figure 5.2), called a strike.[4] Recoba had been in the Canal Zone at least since May 1914 when he joined the anarchist group "Unión Libertaria" in Balboa. He worked on the canal first as a helper on a dredger, then as a fireman on a tugboat, and finally as a wiper (a low-level maintenance worker) on another tugboat. He quit his last job the first day of the strike.[5] In a letter to the Canal Zone's Acting Governor Chester Harding, Recoba wrote that "we have on this date taken the advantage granted by our constitution to every free person, and have retired form [sic] work, organixed [sic] ourselves into a body called the Maritime Association of Workmen, for the purpose of obtaining our rights," while demanding more pay and better food. The local press reported widespread sympathy for the strike among nitrate workers, Latin workers, American foremen, and others who were ready to call a general strike if necessary.[6]

---

[2] Zumoff, "Black Caribbean Labor Radicalism in Panama," 436.
[3] *Fuerza Cerebral*, July 15, 1916, 3.   [4] Conniff, *Black Labor on a White Canal*, 50–53.
[5] *¡Tierra!*, May 2, 1914, 4; Memorandum for Captain Mitchell, October 4, 1916 in RG185 ICC 1914–1934, 2-P-59.
[6] Letter from Victor Recoba to Colonel Harding; "La huelga de los trabajadores de la zona," *La Estrella*; Manifesto "A todos los Trabajadores. Al Público imparcial," RG185 ICC 1914–1934, 2-P-59.

FIGURE 5.2 Víctor Recoba from Peru (seated on the left) began his transnational anarchist activism in the Canal Zone in 1914, led the first general strike against the Canal Zone in 1916, and ventured around the Americas in the following decade, including Cuba, Mexico, Peru, and the United States.
Fundación Anselmo Lorenzo (Madrid)

The union's meetings were truly transnational affairs. One undercover policeman reported how hundreds of men "representing many nationalities" were beginning to attend meetings. Whites and mestizos from throughout Latin America and Europe, as well as black West Indians, filled the union's headquarters to hear speeches. West Indian speakers addressed audiences in English, others spoke in Spanish, and the union issued bilingual manifestos. The union leadership was equally international, including Spaniards, Peruvians, Panamanians, Costa Ricans, and Argentineans. The symbolism of this international strike contingent concerned Panamanian and US authorities, especially when people arrived at meetings and heard the featured speaker: the Spaniard Blázquez de Pedro. Isthmian Canal Commission (ICC) informants at union meetings described him as "a dyed-in-the-wool socialist, well-educated, a smooth talker, and capable of hoodwonking [sic] the class of people that compose the Maritime Union Society." In his talks, he called on those in attendance to persuade those still working to join the strike, and threatened violence if the Canal Zone authorities maintained their intransigence. Blázquez de Pedro's speeches, the manifestos, and reports that in fact strikers were preventing workers from boarding labor trains that took them from Panama to work in the Canal Zone incensed Governor Harding. He refused to meet union demands and in turn warned the union leaders that "[n]o interference on the part of the individuals of their association with our employees will be permitted." The Canal Zone government further refused to negotiate with the union because Harding claimed that since the leadership had quit work, "they have no present standing and are entitled to no consideration."[7]

By October 8, Harding still refused union demands. That day, the union launched its most visible effort yet: a demonstration and march throughout Panama City. In a bilingual manifesto distributed throughout the capital, the union reformulated its goals in less economic and more freedom-oriented language: "We intend to continue struggling for our partial and total liberty in spite of all obstacles, against all opposition, and above all vicissitudes." The manifesto now escalated the rhetoric and called workers to prepare a general strike. In a show of force, the union marched through the city. Some 200 sympathizers began the march, but as demonstrators made their way past Santa Ana Park the crowd swelled to over 1500 supporters marching behind the union leadership and three red flags bearing the union's name. Chants and speeches called out the strikers' demands, attacked US control of the canal, and denounced the threatened use of strikebreakers.[8]

With each passing day, the union was encouraged by reports that more and more workers of all nationalities refused to report to their jobs. Then, Blázquez de Pedro called on workers throughout the zone and the republic to launch a general strike on October 15. Harding pressured

---

[7] Memorandum for Capt. Mitchell, October 6, 1916; Manifesto "A todos los que trabajan/ To all who work," October 7, 1916; Memorandum to Captain Mitchell, October 10, 1916 and Colonel Harding's Statement to "Strike" Committee, RG185 ICC 1914–1934, 2-P-59; Memorandum to Captain Mitchell, October 12, 1916, RG185 ICC 1914–1934, 2-P-59; Memorandum for Captain Mitchell, October 4, 1916 and Letter from Resident Engineer to Acting Governor, October 5, 1916, RG185 ICC 1914–1934, 2-P-59; Re: Maritime Union Society, October 9, 1916, RG185 ICC 1914–1934, 2-P-59.

[8] Manifesto "A todos los que trabajan/To all who work" and "Dredging Division Strikers Denounce Canal Treatment," in *Star and Herald*, October 9, 1916, RG185 ICC 1914–1934, 2-P-59. Julio Carrasco, a longtime Argentinean anarchist in the zone, asserted that "[n]o American would stand for [scabs taking strikers' jobs], and no real American would wish for any human being to be treated like it, either, no matter what their color or nationality might be."

Panamanian authorities to help suppress the union and deport its leaders. In a letter to Panamanian president Ramón Valdés the day before the general strike was to begin, Harding stressed that any and all strikes threatened not only the canal but also Valdés's republic. He demanded Panamanian cooperation to protect the US canal, namely that "these individual agitators be expelled from the Republic," persons threatening violence "be promptly arrested," and "sufficient police protection be given" to those not on strike.[9]

Harding's demand for action from the Panamanian police was more than just a call for Pan-American cooperation against radical subversion; it was a recognition that local police forces seemed reluctant to quell the strike. Harding had reason to be concerned about the fealty of Panama's police toward upholding US interests. Tensions between US soldiers and Panamanian police had escalated over the years. Since 1912, there had been occasional flare-ups between US military personnel and Panamanian police. Sometimes these flare-ups resulted in each shooting at the other. So, it should not come as a surprise if some Panamanian policemen sympathized more with striking workers than with the dictates of *yanqui* bosses.

Still, US Canal Zone police were dismayed at how many Panamanian police seemed to be in solidarity with the strikers. Panamanian cops stood by as strikers positioned themselves in front of the labor trains each day to dissuade workers from boarding. This was not some nationalist stand-off between "Panamanians" and "Americans," but rather an act of transnational class solidarity. In fact, many Panamanian policemen were members of the "Central Obrero" union, the treasurer of which was a Panama City police captain. Though the union did not participate officially in the strike, many of its police members were clearly sympathetic to the international strikers.[10] What a scene! Anarchists and police working together against imperialist privilege. Undoubtedly, even the anarchists must have been as dismayed as Governor Harding.

On October 15, when 10,000 workers did not report to work, the Panamanian government arrested much of the union leadership. Union vice president Eliberto Segura (from Peru, like Recoba) protested the detentions. In the middle of the afternoon, Segura and the strikers

---

[9] Letter to His Excellency, Don Ramon M. Valdes, October 14, 1916, RG185 ICC 1914–1934, 2-P-59.
[10] Statement of Sydney King, October 14, 1916 and Memorandum for the Acting Governor, October 16, 1916, RG185 ICC 1914–1934, 2-P-59.

assembled once again in Santa Ana Park, hoping to make speeches and launch another street parade designed to pressure the government to release union leaders. Government officials had refused to issue a permit for either the meeting or the march, and when Segura began to speak, police loyal to the government arrested him. Chaos ensued as strikers fought back, leading to twenty strikers being arrested. But the turmoil was not over. As police led Segura and other detainees to the police station, a striker pulled out a gun and shot three times at the police captain – all shots missed. The Panamanian government responded by closing all saloons, boarding up the union meeting hall, and banning parades throughout the city.[11]

Then, the large West Indian population became a focal point for both strikers and authorities. The union urged Antilleans to continue with the strike and encourage their friends who were still working to stop. "West Indian Comrades, bear in mind that with *your* cooperation we will be victorious," read one manifesto. Strikers increased their presence at rail stations, trying to dissuade all workers (especially Antilleans) to stay away from work. Harding grew increasingly worried about Panama's ability to control the strikers and warned in a cable to the US War Department that he might have to invoke his rights under the United States–Panama Treaty to send US troops into Panama. Meanwhile, the British government offered its aid to US authorities by enticing British West Indians back to work.[12]

These joint government efforts ultimately proved too much for the union. By October 18, fewer strikers arrived to prevent workers from boarding trains. West Indians led the return of workers to the Canal Zone, but union activists continued to push their case. In a last gasp for the isthmus's international workforce to remain loyal to the strike, the union issued manifestos attacking the joint United States–Panama governmental efforts to suppress workers: "The insults and abuses offered by the authorities of the Republic of Panama are without doubt in obedience to the orders issued from the Government of the Canal Zone and which have now passed the limits of injustice and tyranny." The union urged workers to remain committed against "agents of the Panama Canal" in

---

[11] Manifesto "¡Adelante! Siempre adelante!" and Memorandum for the Acting Governor, October 16, 1916, RG185 ICC 1914–1934, 2-P-59.
[12] Manifesto "¡Alerta Compañeros!/Be on the Alert Comrades!, October 16, 1916, italics in the original; Cablegram sent no. 36, October 17, 1916; Memorandum for File, October 16, 1916, RG185 ICC 1914–1934, 2-P-59.

the republic. These were the union's last communications, and they ended not by promoting the strike's original economic goals but promoting the international union as the only bulwark against US imperialism in Panama.[13] Did the strike work? Not entirely, but there were some important consequences. On the one hand, Governor Harding established a board that raised silver-roll worker pay by 11 percent by January. That was good for workers. But the governments in the zone and the republic also discovered the benefits of dividing black and Latin workers.[14]

Meanwhile, the Panamanian government had to deal with the strike leaders. The Panamanian government arrested most of the union's international leadership and arranged to load them on the Peruvian ship *Urubamba* for deportation. The deportees included Recoba (Peru), Carlos Rodríguez (Costa Rica), Juan Perich (of undetermined origin), Arturo Walker (St. Vincent), Angelo Blajes (Greece), Segura (Peru), and César Lascarre (of undetermined origin). Those from Panama, like Manuel Garrido C. and Rafael Fori, were arrested, and orders were given to arrest the Argentinean anarchist Julio Carrasco and Blázquez de Pedro. However, much to the consternation of canal authorities, Garrido C. and Fori were released and never stood trial, while the arrest orders for Carrasco and Blázquez de Pedro were never executed. All remained free. Then, the captain of the *Urubamba* declined to load the deportees after the Peruvian government refused to grant passports to them.[15] In the end, some labor radicals stayed in Panama, some were eventually deported, and others left on their own. One union leader was deported twice. Segura, the former vice president of the union, was deported to Peru in October, arrested again in Panama in February 1917 when he was found living in Colón's Red Light District, and this time deported to Colombia.[16] As for Blázquez de Pedro: Though regularly labeled a "radical" and a "socialist" by informers, and while both the Canal Zone and Panamanian governments called for his arrest and deportation, the anarchist survived unscathed, working and agitating openly in Panama City for the next nine years.

---

[13] Memorandum to the Acting Governor, October 17, 1916; Manifesto "To All Nationalities of Colon"; Manifesto "Viva la Huelga! Abajo los tiranos!," RG185 ICC 1914–1934, 2-P-59.

[14] Zumoff, "Black Caribbean Labor Radicalism in Panama," 437.

[15] To the Chief of Police at Balboa, October 19, 1916; Memorandum for the Acting Governor, October 20, 1916 and Letter to Lt.-Col. Chester Harding from the District Attorney in Ancón, Panama Canal, October 25, 1916, RG185 ICC 1914–1934, 2-P-59.

[16] Memorandums for Chief of Division from Sgt. #4 Zone Police, February 20, 1917 and March 30, 1917, RG185 ICC 1914–1934 2-P-59.

CARIBBEAN ANARCHISTS AND THE GREAT WAR

Less than six months after the Canal Zone strike, anarchists in Puerto Rico, Florida, and Cuba confronted a very different dilemma related to US control: the military draft for the Great War. Fearing any anarchist interference in wartime preparation, the April declaration of war led to a concerted antianarchist campaign by Washington. The 1917 Espionage Act and the 1918 Sedition Act considered anarchists and any antiwar advocates as disloyal to the United States and undermining the US war effort. When combined with rampant American nationalism that swept the country from 1917 to 1920, the acts generated a sense of vigilante entitlement among some US citizens. Blessed by the US Justice Department, the American Protective League mobilized a quarter of a million volunteers to keep tabs on suspected troublemakers. Besides these vigilante operatives, the Justice Department itself deployed spies and informants in radical communities across the United States.

Despite such these Red Scare initiatives, anarchists spoke out and worked against conscription. Such defiance led authorities to raid Wobbly and anarchist offices across the United States, confiscate files, and deport foreign-born activists like Manuel Rey – a leader of the Maritime Transport Workers (MTW) in Philadelphia, with its large Spanish-speaking radical membership – who was arrested for violating the act and interfering with the draft.[17] Florencio Romero spoke out on a street corner in Caguas, Puerto Rico against the draft and claimed "that the United States had no right to compel Porto Ricans to fight for it as they were not Americans and it was an injustice to compel them to go to war," so Puerto Ricans "should resist the law." Throughout 1917, the authorities arrested several Puerto Ricans for violating wartime draft laws, including the anarchist José María Alicea, who was charged with draft dodging. Earlier that year, his anarchist brother Ángel ran afoul of authorities for not being registered for the draft.[18]

Throughout the war, US officials grew concerned about a conspiracy stretching throughout Spanish-speaking communities in the United States

---

[17] Alonso, "Spanish Anarchists," 95.
[18] "US vs. Florencia M. Romero, Violation of Section 3, Title 1 Espionage Act," November 13, 1917. Department of Justice, 98083 RG60 OGF USNA; "United States vs. Jose Alicea, et al. Viol. Sec. 5, Act," May 18, 1917. 92908 RG60 OGF USNA; Memo from Special Agent Johnson to A.B. Bielaski, August 7, 1917. 50181 RG60 OGF USNA. In Ángel's case, ultimately he produced a registration card.

and Puerto Rico, whereby draft-eligible men were devising ways to evade registration. The Department of Justice's (DOJ) John Haas, based in San Juan, reported "that Spanish residents on this Island have been carrying on a propaganda against the obligatory military service, and making statements derogatory to the President of the United States." DOJ agent H. S. Hubbard named three "Spaniards" in Puerta de Tierra, Puerto Rico who "talked against the draft and the U.S."[19] Washington interpreted such antidraft actions as part of a larger transnational network of Spanish-speaking radicals aiding and abetting Puerto Ricans to avoid conscription. Puerto Rican men were disembarking from Spanish ships, having obtained Spanish passports "usually given to them by Spanish Consuls at Central and South American Countries."[20]

In 1917, a small number of Wobblies remained active in Tampa, engaging in antimilitarist actions to help workers avoid the draft just like anarchists were doing in Puerto Rico. Anglo officials from Tampa Mayor McKay to the DOJ's Byrd Douglas noted that throughout the war years Wobblies actively campaigned against enlistment. As one anonymous writer to the DOJ in Washington put it, the Tampa Wobblies aided "those who were of draft age by furnishing them with everything that was necessary for them to leave this country causing quite a number to leave here."[21] One DOJ agent agreed, citing "the number of men who have evaded the draft law by leaving the United States and going to Cuba, Spain, and South American countries" despite the combined efforts of the immigration, customs, and justice officials.[22] Thus, US administrators in both Puerto Rico and Tampa were seeing the same thing: Wobblies and anarchists enabling draft-eligible men to avoid conscription by fleeing US territory.

While US authorities took precautions to monitor foreign radicals within US borders, they also viewed with rising concern growing radicalism and labor unrest in Cuba, and, again, Wobblies were involved. From 1917 to 1920, strikes stretched into every sector and across the

---

[19] "Informants," January 16, 1918; "In Re: Alleged Propaganda against Military Service, etc.," February 9, 1918, and "En re Vio. Espionage Act," September 26, 1918. 8000-16638 RG60 OGF USNA.

[20] "Navy Department, Office of Naval Intelligence: Evasion of the Selective Service Act," November 29, 1918. 16638 RG60 OGF USNA.

[21] "Letter from 'A. Citizen' to Department of Justice, Washington, DC," from Tampa, October 15, 1919. 8000-362112 RG60 OGF USNA.

[22] "Letter from Byrd Douglas to J. T. Suter, Acting Chief, Bureau of Investigation, Washington, DC," from Tampa, July 14, 1919. 8000-362112 RG60 OGF USNA.

island.[23] Because the strikes threatened US-owned businesses on the island, Washington believed that growing instability could force it to invade Cuba under the terms of the Platt Amendment – something that the United States clearly would prefer not to do as it built up for and then waged war in Europe. Still, a wave of local insurgencies, strikes, and banditry against sugar plantations forced the hands of Washington and Havana. President Menocal suspended constitutional guarantees and invited US Marines to "train" in Cuba. From August 1917 to December 1918, over 3000 Marines arrived to protect the sugar economy. But Washington had another fear. In March 1918, a US State Department cable declared that sugar sector strikes in 1917 were led by Industrial Workers of the World (IWW) agitators.[24] A dockworkers strike in Havana in late 1918 had Washington further convinced that the IWW was leading the charge to destabilize Cuba.[25] Thus, the IWW seemed to be reaching across the Florida Straits to undermine US security at home and abroad, and Washington was determined to use US troops in Cuba to suppress the radicals – even if it drew them away from the European conflict.[26]

ANARCHIST FICTION, ANTIMILITARISM, AND THE GREAT WAR

While anarchists resisted the draft and engaged in wartime labor actions, they also used another strategy to fight the militarist surge: literary anarchism. In their fiction, anarchists attacked militarism in general and the draft laws in particular. Havana-based anarchist labor leader and author Antonio Penichet placed antimilitarism and a critique of draft laws central to his novels ¡Alma Rebelde!, novela histórica (Rebel Soul: A Historical Novel) and La vida de un pernicioso (Life of a Dangerous Man).

[23] Cabrera, Los que viven por sus manos, 157–164.
[24] Cable from American Minister at Havana, March 11, 1918, RG59, Records of the Department of State Relating to Internal Affairs of Cuba, 1910–1929, United States National Archives, College Park, MD.
[25] La Nueva Solidaridad, December 7, 1918, 3.
[26] Panama had declared war against Germany the day after the United States, placing the republic as a loyal ally in protecting the Panama Canal against German espionage and U-boat activity. But what effect did this have on the average Panamanian resident who was now part of the war effort, asked Martín de Río. Food prices were soaring, but wages were not. He blamed the soaring prices on wartime demand and profiteering by private businessmen. Where were the food banks to help people in times of crisis? Why was the government doing nothing to protect its "working people"? See Verbo Rojo, August 26, 1917, 4 and August 30, 1917, 2.

¡*Alma Rebelde!* traces the life of Rodolfo from his boyhood in Cuba during the 1895–1898 War for Independence to the late 1910s. As a child during the war, his mother told him that Cubans were fighting to have their own government, like Spain. When the child asked why Cubans would want a government that ordered people to kill other people, his frustrated mother sent him out to play.[27] This questioning of the militaristic aspects of governments arises again midway through the novel. By 1917, Rodolfo is an anarchist organizer. When the government creates the new draft law, Rodolfo leads workers in a general strike. Penichet portrayed the draft law as an egregious assault on workers by a government that not only abused them and made them cower, but also wanted workers to put their lives on the line for that very state and bourgeoisie in order to kill other workers. "Rodolfo remembered again his mother's words: 'Governments oblige one to be a soldier,' 'governments order one to kill'."[28]

While Rodolfo emerges relatively unscathed from this ordeal, Penichet's character Joaquín in *La vida de un pernicioso* is less fortunate. Joaquín arrived in Cuba as a Spanish soldier before tearing off his uniform and joining the independence forces.[29] Thus, unlike Rodolfo, Joaquín experienced warfare as a young man. At war's end, Joaquín remains in Cuba and becomes an anarchist labor organizer. After Cuba declares war in April 1917, Joaquín is arrested and put on trial. The government charges him with urging workers to desert the military and speaking out against the draft. In his defense, Joaquín asks the court "Is there anything more inhumane, more criminal than to create obligatory service in order to put on uniforms, removing men from their factory jobs and the warmth of their homes?" Not persuaded, the court finds Joaquín guilty and sends him to jail for his antipatriotic activities.[30]

Most anarchists opposed the Great War as one more conflagration pitting the wealthy against each other for material and territorial gains while employing workers as cannon fodder in the trenches of Europe. To support either side was to support one imperial power over another. Thus, most agreed "that this fight was about, and against, empires," writes Kenyon Zimmer.[31] But not all anarchists supported neutrality,

---

[27] Antonio Penichet, *¡Alma Rebelde!, novela histórica* (Havana: El Ideal, 1921), 14.
[28] Ibid., 85.   [29] Penichet, *La vida de un pernicioso*, 27.   [30] Ibid., 115.
[31] Kenyon Zimmer, "At War with Empire: The Anti-Colonial Roots of American Anarchist Debates during the First World War," in *Anarchism, 1914–1918: Internationalism, Antimilitarism, and War*, eds. Matthew Adams and Ruth Kinna (Manchester: Manchester University Press, 2017), 176.

causing a worldwide dispute that centered around one of the most respected anarchists, Peter Kropotkin. While most anarchists believed in neutrality, some anarchists supported the Central Powers as a way to halt French and British imperialism. Others supported the Triple Entente to stop Prussian aggression. "The protection of 'small nationalities' from militaristic states would later be one of Kropotkin's core arguments for supporting the Allies," Zimmer observes.[32] Kropotkin feared that if left unchecked, the Germans would sweep through Europe, destroy Western civilization's progressive march toward freedom, and in the process conquer and subdue diverse nationalities. He called on people to join the military effort against Germany.[33] In short, he favored a militarist action to halt imperial Prussian militarism.

Kropotkin's stance created discord in the international anarchist movement, and the resulting dispute reached Caribbean shores in late 1914. In August that year, ¡Tierra! began covering the war, hoping that "after the fratricidal war that today covers Europe in blood, perhaps then the liberating revolution will emerge."[34] In one of ¡Tierra!'s last issues, a front-page editorial rejected Kropotkin's rationale and published a critique of Kropotkin's position by Alexander Berkman. Cultura Obrera likewise rejected Kropotkin and ran a multi-issue debate between its editor, Pedro Esteve, and Kropotkin.[35] Esteve rejected Kropotkin's idea that "invaders" (in this case supposedly Germans) should be opposed because, as Esteve reminded Kropotkin, both sides of this war were imperial invaders. While Kropotkin might have held a special place in his heart for France's revolutionary tradition, Western European liberal political values, and an England that had given him and other anarchists refuge, this did not warrant abandoning antimilitarist principles. Whether one country was more liberal than another did not matter, argued Esteve, if both sides were imperialists and workers everywhere continued to be abused.[36]

In the Caribbean, no anarchists came to Kropotkin's defense. Throughout 1915 and 1916, Blázquez de Pedro wrote a series of antiwar columns, publishing them in Barcelona's Tierra y Libertad and the Gijón,

---

[32] Ibid., 181.
[33] Peter Marshall, *Demanding the Impossible: A History of Anarchism* (London: Fontana Press/Harper Collins, 1993), 332; George Woodcock, *Anarchism: A History of Libertarian Ideas and Movements* (New York: World Publishing, 1971), 217.
[34] *¡Tierra!*, August 13, 1914, 1.
[35] See Ibid., November 26, 1914, 1; *Cultura Obrera*, December 12, 1914, 1–2; December 19, 1914, 1–2; January 2, 1915, 1–2.
[36] Zimmer, "At War with Empire," 182–183.

Spain-based *Acción Libertaria*. Blázquez de Pedro opposed Kropotkin's pro-war stance, believing that anarchist war supporters were surrendering to sentimentality. Blázquez de Pedro could understand why one might sympathize with countries like England and France while hating Germany. After all, there certainly seemed to be more liberal politics and political tolerance in France and England. Blázquez de Pedro also sympathized with these countries, but just in a "purely platonic" way. Still, that was no reason to "pick up a rifle in order to defend them." If these liberal countries were to fall to Germany and its allies, so be it. But if they were to win the war (as Kropotkin and his associates hoped), "I am convinced the triumph of France, England, and Belgium will be the beginning of a new French, English, and Belgian militarism much greater, more arrogant, and more aggressive than that of Germany."[37] Ultimately, Blázquez de Pedro believed that Kropotkin was committing a serious violation of anarchist ethics. He and others allowed their passions and sentiments to win out over their reason. As he put it, war supporters were guilty of a very Spanish word: *corazonado* – following one's heart and not one's head. "Kropotkin has been, on this issue, the man who is all heart."[38]

In Havana, Kropotkin's position also troubled Adrián del Valle. For del Valle, it was one thing to pick up arms to fight for a people's liberation as anarchists in Cuba did in the 1890s and in Mexico in the 1910s, but he was less sure that choosing sides in the current conflict would advance the anarchist cause. He confronted this dilemma in his novel *Jesús en la guerra*. He began the work in late 1914 after Europe began descending into madness. Del Valle's 224-page novel was not completed and published in Havana until 1917, just as the Cuban government declared war on Germany and initiated the draft. In the novel, del Valle's Jesus Christ roams the cities and countryside of war-ravaged Europe, meeting soldiers, mothers, anarchists, and even Kaiser Wilhelm. Early in the novel he meets Pablo, who hates all Germans. German soldiers had killed his son, who died "defending the fatherland." They ransacked his possessions, raped his wife and two daughters, and then burned his home to the ground. He tells Jesus that he would rather die than try to forgive and love those who destroyed his life. When a French mother prays to Jesus to help her son – a French soldier – to kill Germans, Jesus is aghast and implores the mother to think about what if a German mother prayed to him to do the same. "That's not important. Jesus is able to distinguish those who truly follow

---

[37] *Tierra y Libertad*, March 10, 1915, 2. [38] Ibid., May 12, 1915, 3.

him," the mother replies.[39] When a German official acknowledges that he was taught to love all as brothers, he tells Jesus that he was also taught to love his country above all others: "God cannot prohibit a good patriot from defending his fatherland."[40] In the end, most people Jesus meets lampoon and reject him. But the state has the last word. Just as Pontius Pilate and the Roman State crucified Jesus of Nazareth, del Valle's Jesus meets a similar fate at the hands of Kaiser Wilhelm. In a face-to-face confrontation, the Kaiser claims that Germans are God's new chosen people, justifying his quest to assert German supremacy across Europe. When Jesus rejects this, he is thrown in jail and put on trial, charged with being a French spy, being complicit in the deaths of German pilots, and attempting to assassinate the Kaiser. Jesus is found guilty and executed.[41]

Anarchists had a tradition of interpreting Jesus's teachings as supporting their message of revolution against inequality, wealth, militarism, and tyranny. To this end, anarchists "liberated" the symbol of Jesus from organized Christianity and put it to use in the anarchist cause.[42] In *Jesús en la guerra*, Jesus and anarchists help one another. As Jesus travels through the war zones, he attracts a series of disciples, including a cadre of anarchists who want to protect him as "he went from town to town denouncing the abominations of war and the divisions of men by country, condemning excesses of power and wealth, and predicting the arrival of an era of peace, based on loving one another and respecting human life."[43] However, Jesus's pacifism begins to alienate the anarchists. Published in 1917 in the months following the tsar's overthrow in Russia, del Valle's anarchists increasingly see violence as the only way to stop state-sanctioned murder. "We long for a peaceful and loving society," says one anarchist, "but we need to conquer that society by revolution, by violence since it will never arrive by persuasion and passive sacrifice ... And before picking up a rifle to defend a bourgeois fatherland, I prefer to be armed as a traitor to the fatherland."[44] Del Valle's anarchists conclude that violent struggle against all imperialism and all patriotism – Prussian or otherwise – is the only answer.

While anarchists rejected state-sanctioned militarism, they rarely shied away from violence in the name of liberation. They fought for Cuban

[39] Adrián del Valle, *Jesús en la guerra* (Havana: Escuela de la Casa de Beneficencia y Maternidad, 1917), 27–28.
[40] Ibid., 30.   [41] Ibid., 199–222.
[42] See, for instance, Blaine McKinley, "'A Religion of the New Time': Anarchist Memorials to the Haymarket Martyrs, 1888–1917," *Labor History* 28, no. 3 (1987): 386–400.
[43] Del Valle, *Jesús en la guerra*, 123–125, 128.   [44] Ibid., 173.

independence, called to arm themselves against Florida vigilantes, fought in Mexico, aided the Bolshevik cause, and more. These were not pacifists, and they did not hesitate to advocate armed insurrection to bring forth a new era of anarchist-defined justice – exactly what governments in Washington and across the Caribbean feared. Puerto Rican anarchists, inspired by the Bolshevik Revolution, would take up this pro-insurrection stance in the postwar Red Scare years, when they began calling for a revolutionary independence from US control.

ANARCHISTS AND PUERTO RICAN INDEPENDENCE

By the late 1910s, the debate over Puerto Rico's political status divided people across the island. Since its founding, the Federación Libre de Trabajadores (Free Federation of Workers, or FLT) leadership had officially rejected independence for Puerto Rico and instead promoted the island's special relationship with Washington that facilitated Americanization. In 1914, the new FLT newspaper *Justicia* made American citizenship one of its first causes. The editors claimed that since 1898, "Puerto Ricans have been unanimously soliciting American citizenship" because it was the right thing to do, and citizenship would undermine growing calls for independence.[45] In 1915, the newly formed Socialist Party led by Iglesias continued the call for US citizenship – something that eventually arrived in early 1917.

Anarchists generally rejected Americanization, US citizenship, and colonialism; yet, most were cautious about a nationalist independence movement too. As early as 1906, anarchists publishing *Voz Humana* rejected US rule of the island but did not see political independence as a viable answer under the nose of Washington, where the island would have a bourgeois state and capitalist system linked to the United States.[46] Almost a decade later, Ángel María Dieppa made the same point: The core of the argument was that political independence (the so-called Status Question) would not solve the Social Question. Capitalists would devise a post-independence system whereby they ran the government and restricted the working masses. As Dieppa put it, "If Puerto Rico would have its own government composed of natives of the country, what

---

[45] *Justicia*, November 8, 1914, 1.
[46] Jorell Meléndez-Badillo, "Los ecos del silencio: Dimensiones locales y aspiraciones globales del peródico *Voz Humana*," *La Brecha: Revista Anarquista de Historia y Ciencias Sociales* 2, no. 3 (2016): 26.

injustices and crimes would be committed!" Protestors would be jailed, and slavery would return. Independence meant returning to a backward time. To Dieppa, the US system was the best government people had yet encountered and in that there was hope for improving workers' situations – even if the system were not ideal. The United States was not tsarist Russia, the Spain of Alfonso XIII, or Sodom and Gomorrah. Rather, the US democratic system allowed space for socialistic ideas to advance peacefully against capitalism. As a result, Puerto Ricans should not strive for political independence but instead expand socialist ideals peacefully within the US political framework on the island.[47]

At the Socialist Party 1919 convention, Alfonso Torres pushed the Status Question. A longtime anarchist now vying for a leadership role within the party, Torres reflected the rationale that led anarchists in Spain, Cuba, and the United States to side with independence fighters in Cuba in the 1890s: The fight for freedom had to oppose oppression against both individuals and collective peoples. In other words, how could you fight for freedom and not fight against colonial rule? How could you fight for freedom in Puerto Rico and not fight against US control? Wasn't collective (even "national") liberty as important as individual liberty? Torres argued that an independence struggle should be part of a larger struggle "to advance the cause of the working classes." In this sense, independence propaganda would "create an environment of civic valor, power, and domination of the working class over the capitalist class."[48] At the convention, Torres continued to call for a formal vote on the issue, but the pro-American Iglesias refused to let the matter come to the convention floor, claiming that the party did "not need to define the Political Status in order to implement our ideal system."[49]

In 1920, anarchists publishing *El Comunista* in Bayamón took a revolutionary view of independence. The newspaper's editor, Ventura Mijón, firmly rejected the idea that leftist causes could be advanced if some worked within the system while others worked outside it. Running for office, serving in the government, and cooperating with the bourgeoisie were "counterproductive," bordered on "abandoning one's principles," and made one a colluding political lackey of Washington.

---

[47] *Justicia*, March 13, 1915, 2. See a similar point of view from José Dieppa in *Justicia*, July 17, 1915, 2.
[48] Programa Constitución Territorial y Actuaciones del Partido Socialista, 1919, 45–46. CDOSIP, Folder Programa del Partido Socialista. 1919. Fondo SIP
[49] Ibid., 47–49.

He rejected Dieppa's earlier position of working within the US system. But independence was not an end-goal either for Mijón, who thought the island's dispossessed had to take advantage of the global moment and radicalize, join in an alliance with the Bolsheviks, and "make common cause with the American Communist Party." The time was ripe for revolution, and only through revolution could true independence emerge. Thus, he agreed that the current colonial status had to end but only with a soviet republic guiding Puerto Rico to independence.[50]

Sandalio Marcial agreed. He challenged the bourgeois orientation of most nationalists and pro-independence advocates, claiming they would never do anything for the rural or urban poor once American vigilance was removed. Once the US flag was lowered, they would not give the order to end exploitation, be humane toward workers, make sure that money did not leave the island, or that wealth was distributed evenly. "If this is not your ideal for independence, then we would say to you that you are deceiving the people." The problem was that while the bourgeois nationalists claimed to be for independence, they would owe their power (and their economic livelihoods via trade relations) to the United States. "You want independence," Marcial wrote, "but you can never forget your obligations to *Yanquilandia*; that is, you will always be disposed to giving life and all that you (don't) have for the existence and glory of the great nation to the North." But who would be the ones called upon to sacrifice the most? The workers, who "you are disposed to sacrifice in the holocaust of honor and life to both capitalisms, that on the other side of the sea and that in this miserable island."[51]

Ultimately, anarchists did not speak with one voice on the contentious issue of Puerto Rican independence. Dieppa despised US colonial rule but thought American democratic institutions would be better than seeking independence where Puerto Rican capitalists would just take the island backward. Torres tried to get the Socialist Party – an official promoter of Americanization – to advocate for Puerto Rican independence but linked to workers' liberation. Marcial and Mijón argued that even if Washington granted independence to Puerto Rico – and under US law it would have to be the US Congress to do so – then it would be a bourgeois independence where workers were subservient to the interests of capitalists both on the island and abroad.

---

[50] *El Comunista*, August 28, 1920, 1 and 4; June 26, 1920, 6.
[51] Ibid., July 17, 1920, 2 and 4.

El Comunista was inspired by the Bolsheviks and would be satisfied only with an overly optimistic proletarian revolution that would free the island not just from Washington's political rule, but also from Anglo and Puerto Rican capitalist control. Maybe they had a point – even if a bit myopic. After all, in the 1890s, anarchists supported the independence cause in Cuba, mistakenly believing that political independence would lead to a social revolution. However, that never materialized and now Cuba was ruled by US and Cuban capitalists under Washington's gaze. Those who supported political independence alone or as a first step were deceiving islanders because independent or not, capitalists would run the island, and their future would always be linked to pleasing *Yanquilandia* and solidifying the ever-expanding US presence in the "American Mediterranean." Anarchists were not going to be fooled again. By the late 1910s and early 1920s, most anarchists in Puerto Rico believed that only a proletarian social revolution could lead the way to political independence, not vice versa.

ANTIMILITARISM, ANTI-IMPERIALISM, AND BANANA REPUBLICS

By 1920, Puerto Rico, Cuba, and Panama increasingly played an important role in US military and economic designs on the Caribbean Basin. Cuba's Guantanamo Bay was a Caribbean base for the US Navy. Panama was key to US influence in the Pacific and Atlantic worlds. The opening of the Panama Canal in 1914 meant that the Mona Passage between Puerto Rico and Hispaniola increased in geopolitical importance as a key access route from the Atlantic Ocean to the canal. And, as US citizens since 1917, Puerto Ricans were now eligible for military service in the US armed forces to protect the canal. Coupled with ongoing occupations of Haiti, the Dominican Republic, and Nicaragua, Washington had militarized the Caribbean.

US troops on the ground were coupled with other militarist activities launched by Caribbean governments. For instance, anarchists attacked how the US-imported public-school systems were being used to teach militarism. In Puerto Rico, Sandalio Marcial was the opening speaker at the May Day 1920 rally in Bayamón that launched *El Comunista*. Speaking before 200 people in the Plaza de Hostos, Marcial condemned the state of Puerto Rico's public education system, where children went to school to receive a "mostly military education. A child who obtains his Eighth Grade Diploma knows better how to kill a person than to solve an economic problem."[52] The following week, Antonio Álvarez echoed Marcial's sentiment and tied it to the emergence of the Puerto Rican National Guard, founded in 1919. For Álvarez, the public education system – financed by and supposedly serving the state – taught loyalty to the government as well as skills and desires in youth that would lead them to kill in the name of the state. He feared students would become mere servants of the military, and he knew why the Guard existed: to help the police repress striking workers and agitators for freedom.[53] Manuel García agreed. He had been watching the creation of a Guard unit in Bayamón. Most disconcerting was how workers made up the unit. He urged working-class soldiers to "refuse to form this over-praised 'National Guard'" that will protect the propertied class "by machine-gunning and subjugating the people."[54]

Anarchists in Cuba saw the same patriotic militarization of the school system. The 1910 government decree that students pledge allegiance to the flag and a 1914 requirement that curricula include patriotic education were but two examples. By the 1920s, when Cuban Marxists and anarchists worked together to launch a wave of rationalist schools across the island, they continued an antipatriotism critique of Cuban public education. In 1923, one writer to *Nueva Luz* protested the pledge of allegiance to a flag "that only serves to divide humanity." That same year, anarchists were disgusted when school children marched in the hot sun in a patriotic parade to honor José Martí. But, as one anarchist wondered, was the children's parade really to honor Martí – the father of Cuban independence – or to honor Marte (Mars), the god of war?[55]

While anarchists condemned the patriotic militarization of the islands' education systems, this was not just an assault on "nationalistic militarism." They knew that Cuban, Puerto Rican, and Panamanian military units protected capitalists, preserved US hegemony in the region, and were tools to control the region for Washington. Such militarism was about keeping peace in an American empire. But anarchists also saw how the United States regularly used American troops in the region and thus also condemned the growing US military presence throughout the Caribbean Basin. Between 1898 and 1930, the United States militarily intervened in one form or another in this region nearly twenty times. These included brief military excursions like that which helped to liberate Panama from Colombia in 1903 in order to build the Panama Canal; large-scale, multi-year

[52] Ibid., May 8, 1920, 4.   [53] Ibid., May 15, 1920, 3.   [54] Ibid., July 10, 1920, 2.
[55] Shaffer, *Anarchism and Countercultural Politics*, 70, 171–188.

interventions in Cuba, Haiti, the Dominican Republic, and Nicaragua; the 1914 intervention along Mexico's Gulf Coast; a 1925 occupation of Panama City; and the 1920s US Marines intervention in Nicaragua against Augusto César Sandino. This did not count the purchase of the Danish Virgin Islands in 1917 or the control of Puerto Rico.

In Puerto Rico, Manuel García and Amelio Morazín condemned the inherent hypocrisy in Wilsonian foreign policy – a policy invoked in early 1917 as Wilson embarked on his new term as US president. While the United States supposedly fought the Great War to protect and expand democracy, US troops were undermining democracy in the Caribbean. García condemned Wilson. He said Wilson wanted "to spread freedom and democracy in the world, and now you are like a blood-thirsty hyena sucking from Santo Domingo, Honduras, Costa Rica, Puerto Rico and Mexico."[56] Morazín added that Washington "talks to us about 'small countries' having the right to self-determination and yet such unfortunate countries planted right under the giant cry out" because they are under US domination. Puerto Rico suffered too under the giant, like an "unfortunate and miserable American Sicily, a kind of Cinderella of the Atlantic," that was unjustly despised and ill-treated.[57] Imagine, if you will, the Statue of Liberty as the wicked stepmother.

Panama was no stranger to US intervention. The United States militarily intervened in Panama in 1908, 1912, and 1918, plus occupied the Chiriquí region bordering Costa Rica for two years in order to protect US interests.[58] Anarchists in Panama decried possible US intervention in Mexico under the guise of "law and order" when it would really be for "oil, coal, copper, gold, sisal, silver, and many other very succulent items" that long had lured "many foreign exploiters" in Mexico.[59] Meanwhile, Cuba, the Dominican Republic, Panama, Mexico, and Nicaragua had become "economic colonies" of the United States. As one *Cuasimodo* columnist concluded, "[t]he Monroe Doctrine protects America against all European intervention, but not against the intervention of the United States in the rest of the American nations."[60]

Cuasimodo's editors especially attacked US support for authoritarian regimes throughout Latin America. In June 1920, Julio Barcos described US aid to caudillos who robbed their own countries, set up attractive business arrangements with US corporations, and armed these same

---

[56] *El Comunista*, May 8, 1920, 4. [57] Ibid., July 31, 1920, 2.
[58] Ivan Quintero, *El Sindicato General de Trabajadores* (Panama City: CELA, 1979), 6.
[59] *Cuasimodo*, October 1919, 21–22.   [60] Ibid., December 1919, 55.

caudillos when they cracked down on the opposition. These despots were criminals "of all of America" and they should not be sustained. Such strongmen were everywhere in the Caribbean Basin. Ironically, said caudillos justified their repression as necessary to preserve stability and thus prevent US intervention. By doing so, they proclaimed themselves to be nationalists, but really they were protecting their own wealth and that of US corporations.[61] In August, the editors urged the United States to stop helping Caribbean dictators and suggested that Washington should instead use its might to overthrow dictators. At least that way Washington could say it was truly on the side of Latin American people.[62] Latin Americans might even believe them.

The author Adrián del Valle found ample fodder here, too. In his short novel *Camelanga*, the longtime Havana anarchist described the fictional country of Camelanga as "a model republic, generally. She had as many uprisings as general elections." The country was the classic two-party state in which both parties represented the same people and generally offered the same policies. When one lost an election, it rose in rebellion rather than accept its defeat. During one such uprising, the rebellious dissident army officer General Tinajas gains power, executes the president, and deports his former military superior. For over twenty years, Tinajas rules the country single-handedly. With no political opposition, the country has no rebellions and so is peaceful and stable. Del Valle's satirical pen describes what comes next: "With the guarantee of peace, foreign capitalists had come, generously spending their money to exploit the natural riches of the country. The Camelangans had the opportunity to work for the capitalists' benefit, drawing a wage suitable enough to nourish themselves on beans and not acquire any cheap trinkets from

---

[61] Ibid., June 1920, 39–48.
[62] Ibid., August 1920, 43. US authorities became increasingly cautious about publications like *Cuasimodo*. Not only did American authorities fear their influence in Panama, but also beyond. In line with the times and the Red Scare sweeping the United States, postal officials banned *Cuasimodo* from the United States and Canal Zone postal systems. Still, due to the constant movement of people and goods through the canal, *Cuasimodo* found its way into the hands of anarchists outside of the isthmus. When US authorities raided the home of anarchist Julio Blanco in 1920 in Globe, Arizona in the southwestern United States, they found two issues of *Cuasimodo*. "Weekly Situation Survey for Week Ending June 9, 1920. Military Intelligence Division, General Staff, Section M.I.4.," 8000-377098 RG60 OGF USNA. Like most of its counterparts in the hemisphere, the magazine was short-lived. In late 1920, *Cuasimodo* folded and Barcos returned to Argentina to continue his activism. There, he launched an Argentinean version of *Cuasimodo* in April 1921. See Alexandra Pita González, "De la Liga Racionalista a Cómo Educa el Estado a Tu Hijo: El Itenario de Julio Barcos," *Revista Historia* 65–66 (2012): 130.

abroad." New buildings arise, inhabited by foreigners and the dictator's sycophants, while the president "permitted the people to continue living in their comfortable shacks in the worst neighborhoods where they could freely enjoy their poverty without offending the sense of smell and the view of the upper classes."[63]

During the first half of the 1920s, anarchists in Cuba saved some of their harshest criticism for both the US and Cuban governments working to enslave Cuban workers for the benefit of US corporate interests. During the Alfredo Zayas administration in the early 1920s, anarchists claimed that the Cuban republic was being transformed into a North American feudal estate. For instance, in early 1923, M. Cuervo drew an image of Cuba carved into "small States formed by foreign companies" and "constituting new feudalisms." A year later, Cuervo described the sugar *centrales* owned by the Cuba Cane Company around the city of Morón, where he lived and worked. What particularly bothered him was the readiness of so many working-class men to turn against their fellow workers by becoming part of "that army of guards that sustains the feudal vileness" of the owners. In both cases, Cuervo charged that such actions – whether made by foreign companies for profit or desperate workers seeking wages – proved how hollow were the cries of *Cuba libre* as those who support abuses "are also sons of the Liberators. Look at how they honor their ancestors!"[64]

By 1924, the Cuban economy had been hit by several years of economic decline, spurred mainly by the collapse of sugar prices from their war-era highs. In 1920, sugar prices hit twenty-two cents per pound, but fell drastically to under four cents per pound in late 1921. Companies could not pay their debts and became owned in large numbers by the US banks that held their loans. Workers suffered extraordinarily as they found their wages sliced. Anarchist-led unions responded. Strikes erupted throughout the island and in all economic sectors, especially sugar, railroads, and manufacturing.[65]

In November 1924, the Federación de Grupos Anarquistas de Cuba (Federation of Cuban Anarchist Groups, or FGAC) issued a manifesto seeking to organize all sugar plantation workers – meaning Cubans, Spaniards, and Antilleans. The federation blamed poor working

---

[63] Adrián del Valle, *Camelanga* (Barcelona: La Novela Ideal, n.d.), 17–18.
[64] *Nueva Luz*, February 15, 1923, 11; *El Progreso*, May 8, 1924, 4.
[65] Robert Jackson Anderson, *A History of Organized Labor in Cuba* (Westport, CT: Greenwood Publishing Group, 2002), 28–30.

conditions on collusion between Cuban and American elites. Cuban troops defended "the interests of those people, the majority of whom live outside of Cuba, under the pretext of the need to protect Cuban riches, put in danger by striking workers." The result was that workers in Cuba – regardless of whether they were Cuban, Spaniard, Haitian, or Jamaican – were "humiliated by Cuban authorities, placed unconditionally at the service of the large American businesses." Ultimately, concluded the manifesto, "the influence of capital is stronger than the sentiment for the homeland and for humanity, stronger than law and justice." The FGAC image of Cuba was clear: Over the course of thirty years the Spanish yoke of colonialism had been firmly replaced by the yoke of North American capitalism. The 1924 manifesto noted how "the liberating revolution [of 1895] had been falsified" by the Cuban government's conduct, that the government had sold out to North American imperialism, and workers' conditions "differed little from those of former slaves." Another anarchist compared the estates to the 1890s war-era concentration camps of Spanish General Weyler.[66]

In mid-1925, Gerardo Machado succeeded Zayas as president of the republic. Machado was elected in part on pledges that he would protect Cuban independence. What he meant was that he would control labor militancy, calm the industrial scene, and thus negate any need for the United States to send troops to Cuba under the terms of the Platt Amendment. Few were ready for the ruthlessness of his initiatives. Soon after taking the presidency, the government went on the offensive against the island's labor organizations. To Machado, eliminating radical speech, press, organizations, and strikes was central to his goal of "regeneration." The government banned the anarcho-syndicalist Sindicato Fabril, shut down its newspaper *El Progreso*, and deported 150 workers. Anarchists were murdered: Enrique Varona of the railroad workers in 1925, Alfredo López in 1926, and Margarito Iglesias of the Sindicato Fabril in 1927. José Miguel Pérez, a Spaniard who taught in the rationalist schools and worked with Julio Antonio Mella in educational and political initiatives, was deported in 1925. Other anarchists left the island, went into hiding, dropped their anarchist rabble-rousing, or were deported. The government repression also crushed the anarchist press.[67] In short, Machado's

---

[66] *¡Tierra!*, November 27, 1924, 1; *El Progreso*, November 29, 1924, 3 and 5.
[67] Shaffer, *Anarchism and Countercultural Politics*, 7, 58–59, 191–193; Casanovas Codina, *Bread, or Bullets!*, 227–228; *Cultura Obrera*, January 16, 1926, 4; May 1, 1926, 2; April 16, 1927, 3.

government was ruthless in attacking militant labor, especially anarchist organizations.

This became the storyline: Cuban independence had been betrayed by the island's own government at the expense of the working masses and for the benefit of North American capitalism. While nationalists proclaimed their patriotism, their crackdowns on leftists turned Cuba into a feudal colony of the Havana–Wall Street–Washington nexus. Under Zayas, the state "ordered the rural police to deal with workers with the blow of a machete. So is how the servant of Wall Street" dealt with sugar strikers, claimed the anarchist Jesús Louzara (aka Rudolf Lone). Machado followed, treating workers with more acts of violence, all for merely seeking the eight-hour day. Ultimately, "workers were murdered by the rural guard; others were found hanging from trees and many more were arrested and deported" by "the servants of the industrial fortresses that Wall Street established in this colony of *Yanquilandia*."[68]

Machado was merely the latest – and most brutal – tyrant to serve this nexus while using state violence to stave off further US military interventions. The leading anarchist newspaper in Buenos Aires, *La Protesta*, echoed this line in late 1926 and applied it more broadly to the wave of US military interventions in the Caribbean Basin over the previous quarter-century. Since the time of McKinley, the "recommendation was to deport from the island of Cuba and from all the rest of the small republics that today the Americans dominate, all of the Spaniards and descendants of Spaniards" – a common US reference to "pernicious foreigners," meaning dangerous anarchists – because "these people constituted a threat to the thieving ambitions of Uncle Sam." Ultimately, warned the writer, Machado's actions were part of a larger Yankee plot. The rest of Latin America needed to do something before Wall Street turned them into another Cuba.[69] So, here it all was – the total image of the moment that anarchists desperately used to frame their understanding of Cuban and by extension Caribbean reality: betrayed independence, North American imperialism, and tyrants instilling fear in the masses while the rich got richer. While sugar was the main export, Cuba nevertheless was still a "banana republic."

---

[68] "El martirologio del pueblo cubano." R. Lone Collection. Artículos Publicados (hereafter referred to as R. Lone Collection) IISG, Amsterdam.
[69] "De Estados Unidos: Un sirviente de Wall Street." R. Lone Collection.

CONCLUSION

By 1915, a new era in anarchist and US global politics was emerging. Anarchists in Cuba had suffered their greatest wave of repression. In Puerto Rico, some anarchists and potential supporters were lured to the new Socialist Party as one of the leading anarchist voices – Juan Vilar – died. In Panama, the canal had opened a year before and with it construction jobs disappeared, which reduced the number of anarchists in the isthmus. Yet, anarchists did not disappear; a transnational assortment of anarchists unified in late 1916 to launch the first general strike against the US-run canal. Meanwhile, US agribusiness expanded as the Great War in Europe resulted in agricultural profits skyrocketing. The canal served as a major transshipment point for US goods to now circumnavigate the globe. The US entry into the Great War in April 1917 resulted in Caribbean countries declaring war alongside Washington. The war linked ever more tightly the security arrangements of Puerto Rico, Cuba, Panama, and the United States. With this spike in militarism, anarchists launched new waves of anti-imperialist, antimilitarist agitation to challenge the regional war effort. When anarchists resisted, intelligence units throughout the Caribbean believed that such opposition was linked – and it was. Anarchists employed not only literary attacks and newspaper columns against the United States, but also direct action through strikes, marches, and helping others avoid military service. Through direct action, they hoped to stop or slow down the capitalist and imperialist systems extending throughout the Caribbean in the 1910s. But these were not nationally rooted forms of direct action. Rather, multinational radicals acted across international borders to lead protests, war-era labor strikes, and antidraft initiatives.

These lands were ruled by elected officials, but such elected officials still kowtowed to Washington's demands. If in Cuba by 1925 the feudal estate was ruled by a democratically elected tropical fascist, it was easy for him to order destruction and killings in the phony name of "Cuban nationalism" in which he acted to prevent another US invasion. Such patriotic rhetoric had a special meaning in Puerto Rico, where new voices were calling for Puerto Rican independence. However, the island's labor movement was officially pro-American and anti-independence. Anarchists – some of whom worked in the official wings of the labor movement and others of whom rejected it completely – never developed a unified line on independence, but most agreed that a political independence without working-class leadership and benefits would have few positive results. Inspired by the Russian Revolution, many believed that the island had a right to determine its own destiny and would do so, but only after a Bolshevik-style revolution toppled the ruling class – just as Lenin and Trotsky had done in Russia.

Generally, the anarchist antiauthoritarian impulse saw through the charades of "democracy," "patriotism," "independence," "making the world safe for democracy," and other empty words and phrases emanating from Washington, Havana, and elsewhere. In the era of the Great War and its aftermath, anarchists continued the previous decades' work to fight Spanish colonialism and US neocolonialism. They struggled to create an anarchist ideal free of rule from *Yanquilandia* as well as free from the capitalists who benefited from that rule and US militarism. That is, Caribbean anarchists were the Latin American anti-imperialist left years – and even decades – before Caribbean Marxists took marching orders from Moscow to form anti-imperialist leagues. By the 1920s, anarchists built on these decades of anti-imperialist initiatives to create their own notions of anarchist Pan-Americanism that would link anarchists throughout the Americas to battle states, capitalists, reformist unions, and the United States.

6

Bolivarianismo anarquista

Anarchist Pan-Americanism in the Heart of the Hemisphere

> The Fiesta de la Raza will be the day in which the American *hacendados* (large landowners) stop usurping the sweat of both American nationals and foreigners. It will be when the peoples of America are no longer divided as Spaniards and Galicians, Indians and Blacks, the exploited and the exploiters. And the Fiesta de la Raza will be when the sons of America receive the sons of old Europe with smiles on their lips and peace in their hearts, and they will say in a friendly way: Welcome, brother, to you who has come to help me work these lands that belong to everyone.
>
> Jorge de Borrán, New York, 1923

Something had gone horribly wrong. The airplane was losing altitude over the South American jungle. The young flight steward had already been sucked out of the open door, the plane had gone terribly off-track in a storm, and it was about to crash. The passengers were a mixed lot – a young, single woman fleeing a past life, a pair of eloping lovers, and an elderly professor and his wife. Among the others, two stood out: Crimp the bounty hunter, who boarded the flight in southern California with his prisoner, Vásquez, an anarchist from Panama who was being extradited to stand trial for murdering a high-ranking Panamanian politician. The small number of passengers, the pilot, and the co-pilot miraculously lived through the crash, and now plans were underway to survive in the jungle. As cooperation and mutual aid become the driving forces for survival and life, the anarchist is pleased to see his ideals playing out. But soon this experiment in anarchist cooperative living is threatened when our survivors begin to hear drumming that grows ever closer. According to the professor, these were "headhunters." When the bounty hunter Crimp is killed by a poison dart, the pilots make a mad scramble to repair one of the plane's engines. Unfortunately, flying with just one engine, the plane can only carry five people. The elderly professor and his wife stay behind, as does the anarchist, sacrificing for the common good as the plane lifts off from the trees and the drums grow louder. Believing that they would be killed slowly by headhunters, the three decide to take their lives. The anarchist knows that the one pistol they have has just two bullets. He shoots the professor and his wife. Vásquez is left to his grisly fate.

Welcome to Hollywood circa 1939, when a bilingual Panamanian anarchist could be a hero on the silver screen in John Farrow's film *Five Came Back* (Figure 6.1). The North American fictionalized anarchist hero from Latin America came at an interesting time. Anarchists had been virtually nonexistent in Panama for a decade. The year 1939 also marked Franco's fascist victory in the Spanish Civil War. Meanwhile in the United States, the rise of anti-Red persecutions – persecutions that heavily targeted Hollywood studios – were still a decade away. In fact, the screenplay for *Five Came Back* was written by Dalton Trumbo, a member of the Communist Party USA and one of the famous Hollywood Ten banned from working in Hollywood as a result of Red Scare persecutions after World War II.

Besides the curious timing of the movie, *Five Came Back* exemplified a remarkably accurate portrayal of anarchist cultural productions. Anarchist fiction, for instance, often played on the idea of survivors creating a new society modeled on anarchist ideas of living with nature along cooperative lines, reflective of Peter Kropotkin's evolutionary theory of mutual aid. *Five Came Back* also reflects a theme that has been little

FIGURE 6.1 Joseph Calleia (far right) as "Vasquez" – an anarchist on the run from Panama, caught in the United States, deported to Panama, and leader of plane crash survivors in a Latin American jungle in the 1939 movie *Five Came Back*.
RKO Radio Pictures

explored in the historiography of Latin American anarchism: Pan-Americanism. The Pan-American ideal had existed for over 100 years, perpetrated by both Latin American and US governments. Yet, *Five Came Back* – whether Farrow or Trumbo intended or not – reflected an anarchist Pan-Americanism. Vásquez is bilingual. When he flees Panama, he heads to the United States. There, it is presumed, he has anarchist contacts and comrades who will support him. The governments of the United States and Panama collude to extradite Vásquez. In the jungle, people from the Americas and from all classes cooperate. And in the end, the anarchist from Panama sacrifices himself for North Americans.

In this chapter, we examine the anarchist concept of Pan-American activism in the heart of the Americas and the western edge of the Caribbean network – Panama. In truth, the whole book thus far has reflected this concept: anarchists from throughout the Americas joined in common efforts with non-Latin American anarchists on the ideological battlefields and the violent streets of Florida, Cuba, Puerto Rico, and Panama when they came together to fight for Cuban independence, the Mexican Revolution, labor rights in the Panama Canal (especially in 1916), and in efforts to resist the Great War. The chapter begins by first examining the original state-defined versions of Pan-Americanism in the nineteenth century. Then, we explore anarchist Pan-Americanism in education and decidedly anarchist interpretations of Columbus Day/*Día de la Raza*. Next, as the 1920s unfolded, anarchist Pan-Americanism moved to the labor front again as radicals from around Latin America created workers organizations in Panama and launched the 1925 rent strike. The strike in October 1925 revealed another element of anarchist Pan-Americanism below the surface: plans for the first hemisphere-wide anarchist congress scheduled for Panama City in November 1925.

PAN-AMERICANISM: THE UNITED STATES
AND SIMÓN BOLÍVAR

Expressions of Pan-Americanism arose almost simultaneously in the United States and Latin America. In 1823, Washington announced the Monroe Doctrine. Seeing visions of grandeur and concerned about the future foreign policy of the new nation, US officials talked of the Western Hemisphere as a distinct entity from the "Old World." This was a hemisphere filled with countries newly liberated from European colonialism that were creating republics as opposed to monarchies. US President James Monroe warned Europe during his December 1823 speech to the

US Congress that if any European country tried to impose its political system in the Americas, the United States would stand with the hemisphere's new republics to oppose it.

While Washington held out this vision of mutual political defense, Simón Bolívar had a different idea. Coming on the heels of defeating Spanish colonialism throughout northern South America, Bolívar turned his attention to uniting former Spanish colonies. A year after Monroe's address, Bolívar wrote to Latin American heads of state that "it is time the interests and relations uniting the American Republics, formerly Spanish colonies, should have a fundamental basis that shall perpetuate, if possible, those Governments."[1] To this end, Bolívar called for a congress of the new Latin American countries to create a Pan-American alliance of mutual aid and defense. From June 22 to July 15, 1826, delegates from Mexico, Central America, Peru, and Gran Colombia discussed mutual defense and Bolívar's goal of liberating Cuba and Puerto Rico from Spanish rule. In the short term, little came from the meeting.[2]

By the late nineteenth century, the United States's newfound industrial wealth and modernizing navy led political and economic elites to seek new markets and protection of those markets. In this environment, Washington returned to the ideals of Monroe to create a new wave of Pan-American sentiment in the Western Hemisphere. From October 1889 to April 1890, Washington hosted the First International Conference of American States – the first time that representatives from all independent countries in the Americas had met. Washington wanted to create a customs union and a system to settle international disputes; Latin American delegates rejected these. Instead, they proposed a strict policy of nonterritorial conquest. The United States rejected that idea. The conference failed to resolve much. Latin Americans suspected the conference was merely a US tactic to gain more access to Latin American markets. But it set the stage for new conferences.[3] As the twentieth century unfolded, the United States increasingly saw these conferences as key to

---

[1] "The Congress of Panama," in *Latin America and the United States: A Documentary History*, eds. Robert Holden and Eric Zolov (New York: Oxford University Press, 2011), 17.

[2] On the Congress of Panama, see Kyle Longley, *In the Eagle's Shadow: The United States and Latin America*, 2nd edition (Wheeling, IL: Harlan Davidson, Inc., 2009), 37–39; Alonso Aguilar, *Pan-Americanism from Monroe to the Present: A View from the Other Side* (New York: Monthly Review Press, 1968), 27–30.

[3] Longley, *In the Eagle's Shadow*, 93.

the spread of stable and nominally republican governments that protected US investment while repelling forces that threatened either.[4]

While little cooperation between Washington and Latin American states existed at the end of the nineteenth century, Latin American governments had cooperated with each other over the years – without the United States. This was especially true for Caribbean Basin governments' near-continuous support for Cuban and Puerto Rican independence struggles in the 1860s and 1870s. However, just as significant was a "below-the-state" form of Pan-Americanism. For instance, in the 1890s, Mexican President Porfirio Díaz reneged on Mexico's historic support for Cuban independence. Instead, average Mexican citizens rallied to the independence cause.[5] It would be this type of popular Pan-Americanism that anarchists also envisioned throughout the first decades of the twentieth century.

EDUCATION, CHRISTOPHER COLUMBUS, AND ANARCHIST PAN-AMERICANISM

Following the 1916 general strike against the canal – a truly Pan-American labor action – José María Blázquez de Pedro remained the most notable anarchist in Panama. He realized, though, that with a dearth of anarchists he would have to broaden his connections and work with liberals on various issues. Once again, fellow traveling was a necessity. His first forays into a broader sectarian alliance occurred from 1914 to 1919, when he wrote periodic columns (especially on education and aesthetics) for mainstream newspapers like *Diario de Panamá* and the liberal magazine *La Revista Nueva* that was published by Panamanian educator José Moscote. Blázquez de Pedro urged government education officials and the Instituto Nacional – where his colleague Moscote was vice rector – to adopt a ten-point curriculum on aesthetics that included placing statues and sculptures on school patios and in public plazas and gardens, not painting historic stone structures, creating school libraries with carefully selected books on the arts, inviting poets and knowledgeable speakers to recite and lecture publicly, and, straight from Ferrer y

---

[4] Aguilar, *Pan-Americanism*, 39; Gregory Weeks, *U.S. and Latin American Relations* (New York: Pearson Longman, 2008), 64–65.
[5] See Muller's *Cuban Émigrés* for a brilliant discussion of this phenomenon between Mexico and Cuba that reflected what the author refers to as *americanismo*, rather than Pan-Americanism.

Guardia's educational program, taking children on monthly field trips to the countryside.[6]

In 1919, the anarchist educator Julio Barcos arrived in Panama and began working alongside Blázquez de Pedro to reform Panamanian education. Both recognized that Ferrer-style, independent rationalist schools were not feasible in Panama due to low working-class consciousness and workers' reluctance to donate money to the cause. As a result, both men attempted to inject as much Ferrerian-inspired educational theory as they could into reforming the Panamanian education system. Barcos was especially well-suited for this endeavor. Before leaving Argentina, he had been a central participant in education debates and the anarchist-led rationalist school movement in Buenos Aires. Between 1908 and 1909, he headed the Escuela Moderna de Buenos Aires.[7] After leaving Argentina, he traveled to the United States and Puerto Rico. He made his way to Central America, where he first met education reformers in El Salvador and Costa Rica. During a five-month stay in El Salvador, Barcos led efforts to create an Universidad Popular, a school for debate, and a new education law. Francisco Espinosa, one of Barcos's Salvadoran colleagues, explained how Barcos stressed that an education system that was in the hands of a government was an "instrument of servitude and degradation; in people's hands it would be an instrument of regeneration and freedom."[8]

Barcos's efforts in Costa Rica during the Federico Tinoco dictatorship in 1919 also earned praise from Costa Rican colleagues. In San José, he joined the opposition and maneuvered to liberate schools from dictatorial control. This angered Tinoco, who had him deported. Barcos went to Panama City from where he watched Costa Rica begin the return to democratic rule following the collapse of the dictatorship in August. In December, he wrote to Costa Rica's Secretary of Public Instruction Joaquín García Monge, praising new Costa Rican educational reforms and stressing his pleasure at seeing these reforms as "the art of emancipating education from politics."[9] Barcos's efforts made a broad impression on Costa Rican officials. In May 1920, it was announced – but later the

---

[6] Blázquez de Pedro, *Observaciones*, 25, 71–73. In mid-1917, Blázquez de Pedro supported a female organization known as "Las Hijas del Hogar" (Daughters of the Home) that offered night classes to anyone who attended. See Blázquez de Pedro, *Observaciones*, 115–118.

[7] Dora Barrancos, *Anarquismo, educación y costumbres en la Argentina de principios de siglo* (Buenos Aires: Editorial Contrapunto, 1990), 70–71.

[8] *Cuasimodo*, March 1920, 82–84.   [9] Ibid., December 1919, 24.

announcement rescinded – that the Costa Rican Congress would make him an honorary citizen of the country, joining several Costa Rican anarchists celebrated for their democratic achievements as *beneméritos* (distinguished citizens).[10] Barcos's ideas – born in Argentina and developed in El Salvador and Costa Rica – spread to Panama when he joined forces with the Panamanian Moscote, the Puerto Rican Nemesio Canales, and Blázquez de Pedro. Moscote – certainly no anarchist as vice rector of the National Institute, the first high school in the country – praised Barcos's ideas, believing they should be applied in Panama.[11]

Such educational Pan-Americanism reflected unity in purpose among radicals and progressives from Spain and Latin America. Blázquez de Pedro explored one way to nourish such unity. In an October 1917 talk celebrating the Fiesta de la Raza – a day celebrating Latin America's Hispanic heritage – he praised Latin culture as "the most experimental, the most philosophical, and the most refined of all the *razas*." Celebrating this day was a way to "foment the bonds of fraternity between Spaniards and Latin Americans." The Raza Latina would one day lead a revolution to reform humanity. "Then, the Raza Latina will succeed at pacifying the World, transforming weapons into tools of labor, ending wars for eternity, making reason and not force guide all human actions."[12] In 1919, he returned to this issue in a more direct labor and anarchist context in a column on the state of the "social movement" in Spain, which he believed had implications for Latin America. Since 1898, the "Spanish proletariat stands above the other progressive elements" in Spain. Spanish laborers had been working throughout the Americas, collaborating effectively with workers in their host countries. Because of this, governments in Argentina, Chile, Peru, and Cuba were quick to deport Spanish workers, like recent deportations in Cuba.[13] Thus, Spanish radicals collaborating alongside their American comrades would increase working-class consciousness and bring forth a new dawn for the American hemisphere. But this would not be at the exclusion of Anglo-Saxons. For instance, he was pleased to have witnessed a physical fitness competition between schools in the Republic and the Canal Zone. He praised the Panamanian students who nearly swept the competitions but noted that what was most important was this example of "fraternity between the two peoples," and that

---

[10] Ibid., April 1920, 81; May 1920, 80. See David Díaz Arias and Kirk Shaffer, "El ciudadano anarquista," *La Nación* (San José, Costa Rica), April 15, 2010, 34.
[11] *Cuasimodo*, March 1920, 88–90.   [12] Blázquez de Pedro, *Observaciones*, 128–130.
[13] *Cuasimodo*, October 1919, 34–40.

more activities between Anglos and Latinos were necessary to "convert Humanity into one single *Raza* of true brothers."[14]

In 1916, on the eve of the October strike against the canal, Jorge de Borrán was working and agitating in Panama and the Canal Zone. Afterward, he moved to Tampico, Mexico to work with Wobbly organizations and help create a Tampico branch of the New York group Germinal.[15] In 1923, he lived in New York City, edited the anarchist biweekly *Aurora*, and wrote the introduction to the Spanish version of Emma Goldman's *My Two Years in Russia*. That October, he offered his own Pan-American perspective about the Fiesta de la Raza, or Columbus Day as it was known in Anglo America. He complained that it was bourgeois Hispanics and Hispanic Americans in New York who celebrated by taking the day off and arguing about nationalism – was Columbus "Spanish," "Italian," etc.? But what is important about the day is not who discovered what or whether Columbus was Spanish. The importance of the day is that it began a new era. "We see in the discovery of the New World the realization of an idea and the fruit of an effort. A man of progressive ideas who investigates the truths of the era and who through logical consequence deduces that far beyond what is known there is something unknown and he has the determination to go to this far beyond." The day symbolized that just because we know something and live in this moment in time does not mean that something else does not or cannot exist – like maybe a future anarchist world. "And in order to reach these yet unknown worlds, we must have valor and perseverance, intellectual strength and will, and a great contempt for what is considered truth and reason in these miserable times in which we live," he wrote. Let this day be celebrated, but not by the bourgeoisie.

The Fiesta de la Raza will be the day in which the American *hacendados* [large land owners] stop usurping the sweat of both American nationals and foreigners. It will be when the peoples of America are no longer divided as Spaniards and Galicians, Indians and Blacks, the exploited and the exploiters. And the Fiesta de la Raza will be when the sons of America receive the sons of old Europe with

---

[14] Blázquez de Pedro, *Observaciones*, 136–137. There was no mention of blacks or Indians. In fact, as rural conflicts between the Panamanian government and the Kuna Indians erupted in the early 1920s, anarchists and their immigrant radical brethren in the port cities remained silent.

[15] Kevan Antonio Aguilar, "The IWW in Tampico: Anarchism, Internationalism, and Solidarity Unionism in a Mexican Port," in *Wobblies of the World: A Global History of the IWW*, eds. Peter Cole, David Struthers, and Kenyon Zimmer (Chicago: Pluto Press, 2017), 126–127.

smiles on their lips and peace in their hearts, and they will say in a friendly way: Welcome, brother, to you who has come to help me work these lands that belong to everyone.[16]

These anarchists imagined a world where people from North and South, East and West could unite and where labels, ethnicities, and national origins meant nothing as all "Americans" came together to work the earth with one another. They did not denounce Columbus for bringing death, destruction, and slavery to the Americas. Rather, they praised him as someone who questioned the truths of his time, ventured into a grand project, and helped to launch a new era joining together different peoples. Wasn't that what anarchists wanted too? Isn't that how they saw themselves?

Cuasimodo: Magazine Interamericano reflected this new Pan-Americanism – not the least by its very name. Barcos said he was neither pro- nor anti-US. He contrasted his ideas about the United States and Latin America with one of the hemisphere's most important voices on the subject – the Uruguayan essayist José Enrique Rodó. Rodó painted the United States as a brutish, action-over-thought Caliban and Latin America as Ariel (Figure 6.2). However, Barcos wrote, the United States/Caliban was spending over one million dollars a year on public education, while Latin America/Ariel spent "hardly one twentieth of that amount." This explained why "*el pueblo yanqui*" [the American public] progressed rapidly while "our 'glorious people' advanced at a turtle's pace." He concluded that while the United States may in fact be too keen to use military force, it nevertheless engineered the canal. "We should emulate the practical talent and enterprising audacity," noted Barcos (Figure 6.3).[17]

Ultimately, anarchists had no faith in their governments, Washington, or intergovernmental dialogue – a growing ideal in the early months of the League of Nations founded in January 1920. To anarchists, hemispheric unity had to exist among the people, not governments. As Barcos pointed out, one could not leave such an important development to "the politicians of capitalism who forged [the Great War] and now claim to be the apostles of the union of nations to end all war." No purely political body could artificially unite the Americas. A true Pan-Americanism had to unite average people: teachers, students, and workers. "The tendency and the doctrine of workers is to form regional federations within each country and unite them into international confederations," Barcos concluded. People at the grass roots, not politicians, were key to anarchist Pan-American unity.[18]

---

[16] *Aurora*, October 15, 1923, 1–2. [17] *Cuasimodo*, June 1919, 32–33.
[18] Ibid., August 1920, 46–47.

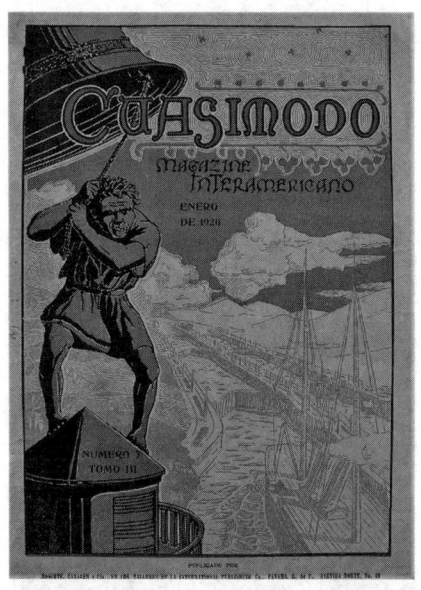

FIGURE 6.2 The anarchist Pan-American magazine *Cuasimodo: Magazine Interamericano* published in Panama City, complete with Cuasimodo ringing the steeple bell overlooking the Panama Canal, 1920.
International Institute of Social History (Amsterdam)

PAN-AMERICAN LABOR AND THE GRUPO COMUNISTA

In 1920, Panamanian voters reelected Belisario Porras as president. Through a series of new laws, infrastructure for healthcare, a railroad and telegraph, a nationalized lottery, and the inclusion of nationalist ideals taught in the public schools, Porras went far in creating a sense of Panamanian nationalism via populist measures that sought to improve working people's lives. Nevertheless, control over organized labor remained outside his grasp.[19] While few workers' organizations had existed in Panama by the 1920s, there was a history of mutual aid societies. By 1921, sixteen societies could be found in the country, some like the Sociedad del Socorros Mutuos dated to 1903.[20] The first nationwide labor organization in Panama since the 1916 general strike emerged in July 1921 when workers from a diverse array of ideological perspectives created the Federación Obrera de la República de Panamá (the Workers Federation of the Republic of Panama, or FORP) with its

[19] Soler, *Panamá*, 42.   [20] Quintero, *El Sindicato General de Trabajadores*, 8.

FIGURE 6.3 In 1919, Argentinean anarchist Julio Barcos arrived in Panama and published *Cuasimodo*.
Author's personal collection

newspaper *El Obrero*.[21] While the FORP's members were diverse politically, anarchists and Marxists controlled both the union and paper, while denying the government control over the union. These leftists were led by José González Rodríguez, Jorge A. Brower, Manuel Garrido C., and Blázquez de Pedro, who had been elected to the FORP's Central Executive Committee.[22] Especially interesting was their observation that "the communist [needed] to work in all labor associations whether republican, liberal, or socialist, because in those centers one can cleanse impure ideas and extol our principles, and it is there where their activities and intelligence are most necessary."[23] In July 1921, to consolidate and further their leftist agendas, Blázquez de Pedro and his comrades formed a separate entity known as the Grupo Comunista.

---

[21] Ibid., 9. Throughout 1920, black workers led by William Preston Stoute and affiliated with Marcus Garvey's United Negro Improvement Association struck in the canal, but this was neither Pan-American nor nationwide in scope.
[22] Ibid., 10. Garrido C. and Blázquez de Pedro were veterans of the 1916 general strike.
[23] *El Obrero*, August 20, 1921, 1.

For the next three years, the Grupo Comunista guided the FORP in Panama City while César Caballero and Segifredo Domínguez launched a chapter on the Caribbean coast in Colón in 1922.[24] The radicals began to make common cause with radicals in the United States. In their first international project, they joined global anarchists to condemn the July 1921 murder convictions of Nicola Sacco and Bartolomeo Vanzetti. *El Obrero* also reached out to the US-based Industrial Workers of the World (IWW) (Figure 6.4). In December 1921, the editors published the Basic Principles of the IWW – an act that clearly suggested where the FORP paper rested politically.[25]

By late November 1921, the Grupo Comunista's Pan-American flavor was clearly discernible: Colombian Leopoldo Amaya was president, the Panamanian Garrido was secretary, and other positions were filled by workers from Venezuela, Puerto Rico, Spain, and Panama. At least one woman played a key role in the group throughout 1921. The thirty-one-year-old Panamanian Julia Palau de Gámez was a notable radical who spoke regularly at meetings and attempted to launch various education projects. Panamanian and Ecuadorean students from the National Institute of Panama also joined the Communist Group – students who, as one informer described, "are supporters of T.M. Blasquez de Pedro [sic] in particular." In fact, the informer warned, the greatest danger came not from this group's cables to Washington protesting the Sacco and Vanzetti case or from their cultural activities, but from Blázquez de Pedro and these students. "The real danger is the inculcation of radical ideas in the minds of the schoolboys that it seems it is the particular endeavor of Blasquez de Pedro to ensnare in his schemes and ideas."[26]

Because the FORP was ideologically diverse, there were tensions between members. While leftists sought to align the FORP along anarcho-syndicalist or even Bolshevik lines, reformers wanted to link the union to Porras's populist government and associate with the American Federation of Labor's (AFL) Latin American initiatives. The Grupo Comunista insisted that the union in no way align with Porras: "we condemn all submission to any politics; we well know that no government has been nor will be a loyal friend of workers. While private property and

---

[24] Ibid., January 28, 1922, 3.
[25] Ibid., October 29, 1921, 2; December 3, 1921, 1; December 17, 1921, 1.
[26] Meeting of the Communist Group, October. 26, 1921 and Letter to William Jennings Price, United States Minister to Panama from Governor Jay Morrow, November 17, 1921. RG185 ICC 1914–1934, 2-P-70; Memorandum for the Governor from Inspector George Vraff, November 17, 1921. RG185 ICC 1914–1934, 2-P-8.

FIGURE 6.4 The anarchist–Marxist led FORP launched *El Obrero* in 1921 in Panama City. It included advice for workers to look to the IWW and radical workers rising up in the United States: "With a formidable momentum, the whole world is witnessing the advance and unquestionable progress of the worker. In the North, where the worker is beginning to test his power, he has quickly put Uncle Sam in a headlock. And in this social struggle they will be victorious – they have to be. The worker over the owner, labor over capital."
Biblioteca Nacional de Panamá (Panama City)

capitalism persist, governments by any name will never be more than just servants ... of the wealthy and influential classes."[27] The multinational character of the Grupo Comunista and the FORP (both the rank-and-file and leadership) contributed to this mistrust of the government. After all, to vote for the government one had to be a Panamanian citizen; yet, large numbers of the Grupo and the FORP were not.

[27] *El Obrero*, August 27, 1921, 1.

By 1923, reformers aligned with Porras began to gain control of the union and *El Obrero*. Increasingly shut out of the newspaper, Panama-based anarchists resorted to transnational anarchist media, specifically Havana's *Nueva Luz*. Vicente Barilla informed the networks of a new group of radicals in Panama: the Grupo Renovación Social, led by the Marxist Jorge Brower and anarchists Carlos Céspedes and Blázquez de Pedro. Of importance to the network were Barilla's notes on events in Ecuador, Peru, and Colombia. Because of Panama's geographic location, it was not only the western node of the Caribbean network but also the northern node of the South American Pacific Coast network stretching from Panama to Chile. As such, news about Colombia and Peru was often heard in the isthmus first and then passed on to Havana for regional dissemination.[28] Thus, as anarchists found themselves being pushed out of the FORP, they turned once again to the transnational network to deride, inform, and mobilize.

There was no clearer sign that control of the FORP had shifted than Samuel Gompers's 1924 visit to Panama. On January 1, Porras and FORP reformers warmly welcomed Gompers.[29] The AFL had a complicated history in the isthmus. During canal construction, the AFL helped white US workers like steam shovel operators and machinists win better conditions.[30] But the union also played racial politics by refusing to organize West Indian workers in the Canal Zone. In a sense, the AFL's attitude was pro-US worker and signaled the beginning of the AFL's ever-decreasing criticism of US foreign policy initiatives.[31]

The AFL's racial and ethnic politics disgusted anarchists. Regularly, the radical-dominated FORP had reached out to English-speaking West Indians in Panama to bring them into the union. For instance, in the second half of 1921, the FORP addressed problems faced by Antillean workers. The FORP claimed that mulattoes caused some of the problems. While acknowledging that they knew people of color in Panama who were better role models than many whites, mulattoes aped whites and denigrated black culture. Blacks should embrace and be proud of their

---

[28] *Nueva Luz*, March 8, 1923, 5; May 7, 1923, 7; June 14, 1923, 3. Barilla also sent money from Panama to Spanish-speaking anarchist newspapers abroad, including *Cultura Obrera*. See, for example, December 2, 1922, 4.
[29] Gandásequi, *Las luchas obreras en Panamá*, 52.
[30] Greene, *The Canal Builders*, 25–26.
[31] J. A. Zumoff, "The 1925 Tenants' Strike in Panama: West Indians, the Left, and the Labor Movement," *The Americas* 74, no. 4 (2017): 520–525; Conniff, *Black Labor on a White Canal*, 52–60.

culture and customs, yet at the same time all people "can end for good racial prejudices and everything deriving from such beliefs."[32] When it came down to it, though, if Antilleans were in miserable straits in Panama, one had to blame the Panamanian and American governments. The newspaper asked what the government intended to do about the roughly 2000 black workers and their families living in squalor. While the American government brought the Antillean workers to the isthmus to build the canal, they now lived in the Republic and it was up to Panama City to act. A consequence of this situation was that now some workers in Panama saw Antillean workers as the enemy and "the worker from this country wages war against the 'foreign worker,'" that is, the Antillean. Meanwhile, other foreign workers, whether "Spaniards, Puerto Ricans, Cubans, etc., etc., will be received with open arms, but not the Antilleans."[33] Thus, recognizing the diversity of the working class, *El Obrero* not only blamed the government for the deteriorating conditions of labor but also reminded Panamanian workers that black workers were their allies. Anarchist labor Pan-Americanism had to include all Americans ... including Black West Indians.

If Gompers's visit drove a large wedge between the FORP's two main ideological camps, the lead up to the December 1924 pan-AFL meeting in Mexico City solidified the split. FORP reformers argued that delegates to this AFL-organized meeting should be Panamanian citizens – a move designed to thwart the inclusion of immigrant migrant labor, but also to minimize the risk of sending representatives who held radical ideas.[34] Leftists walked out of the FORP and formed the Sindicato General de Trabajadores (General Union of Workers, or SGT). Among the founders was an assortment of Panamanian activists as well as Blázquez de Pedro, his brother Martín, and the Polish anarchist Sara Gratz, who had recently arrived from Peru with her nine-year-old daughter. Throughout 1925, the SGT led a wave of actions by workers from throughout Latin America and the Caribbean working in Panama. Among these radical actions, the most famous – and disastrous for anarchists – was the rent strike of 1925.

THE 1925 PANAMA RENT STRIKE

Eleven years after the canal's opening, unemployment, poor pay, deteriorating conditions, and expensive living made life in Panama difficult for

---

[32] *El Obrero*, September 24, 1921, 2.   [33] Ibid., October 8, 1921, 4.
[34] Quintero, *El Sindicato General*, 12–14.

working-class families. Populations in the main cities of Colón and Panama City had risen dramatically since canal construction began. From 1905 to 1920, Colón's population more than doubled from over 11,000 to nearly 27,000 people. Panama City's population almost tripled from approximately 22,000 to over 60,000.[35] Limited housing and high rents contributed to the cost of living outpacing wages. From 1920 to 1925, rents rose as much as 50 percent.[36]

The Grupo Comunista recognized that rent issues were not just a Panamanian concern but also a regional issue as a rent strike movement had been building in neighboring Colombia, led by the Peruvian-born anarchist Nicolás Gutarra. Gutarra was a cabinetmaker and former secretary of Peru's Federación Obrera Regional de Perú, who in 1919 helped organize Peruvian chapters calling for cheaper necessities.[37] In July 1921, Gutarra arrived in Barranquilla, Colombia. By late August 1923, he worked with over a dozen labor radicals to organize the city's Tenants League. Over the coming months, the League launched a wave of protests. In November, the local mayor and the regional governor condemned the League for "offenses against private property, rebellion against the laws of the country, [and] the suspension of construction projects due to their constant haranguing." In response, the League launched a 3000-person rent strike. Recognizing Gutarra's key role in the League and the strike movement, Colombian authorities declared him a "pernicious foreigner." Soon, troops armed with bayonets crushed the rent strike and arrested strikers. Authorities deported Gutarra to Panama at the end of January 1924 under a 1920 law allowing the government to deport foreigners for – among other things – professing anarchism.[38]

Meanwhile, the Barranquilla-based Grupo Libertaria called on Havana's anarchists to help publicize their plight: "you know that the workers without internationalizing ourselves will never realize the most beautiful, most noble and grandest aspiration that is our ideal."[39] Blázquez de Pedro, writing for Panama's Grupo Comunista, called on the president of Colombia to rein in the abuses being waged by the governor of Barranquilla against the Tenants League. He reminded the Colombian president that this was in no way a "Colombian" issue,

[35] Ibid., 4.
[36] *El Obrero* had attacked the emerging housing crisis as early as September 1921. See *El Obrero*, September 10, 1921, 1–2.
[37] Hirsch, "Peruvian Anarcho-Syndicalism," 233–235.
[38] Flórez Pinzón, "Anarquismo y anarcosindicalismo," 49–56.
[39] *Nueva Luz*, January 20, 1924, 3.

noting that the Grupo Comunista de Panamá represented more than just Panamanians. The Grupo "also included sons from Spain and various Hispano American Republics, including Colombia. We don't understand absurd and capricious borders because we know that the human species is at its base identical, and because of that we combat unjust authoritarian excesses wherever they manifest themselves." This was a transnational cry. Blázquez de Pedro sent the protest letter – as his Colombian comrades had done earlier – to Havana, where anarchists published it in *Nueva Luz* for distribution around the Caribbean Basin.[40] Because Gutarra was deported to Panama, it is reasonable to conclude that he interacted with Blázquez de Pedro, inspired the latter's protest letter, and used his Colombian experience to aid Panamanians as they began organizing tenants.

By mid-1925, the SGT formed Panama's own Liga de Inquilinos y Subsistencias, with Blázquez de Pedro playing an important propaganda role within the organization. Their newspaper *El Inquilino* reflected a Pan-American sensibility. For instance, below the masthead, there were two quotes, one on the left by the first US President George Washington ("It is preferable that the plains are covered with cadavers than inhabited by slaves") and the other on the right by anarchist Peter Kropotkin ("Society like the individual has its hours of cowardliness but also has its minutes of heroism"). Articles appeared mostly in Spanish, but sometimes in English to appeal to West Indian residents. In August, the editors asked West Indians to help write for *El Inquilino* since it was an arduous task for those with limited English skills to write or translate articles for the newspaper.[41]

In response, US and Panamanian authorities began to mobilize. In mid-August, they colluded to deport Rodolfo von Wedel. Von Wedel had been an activist in the Colombian labor movement, but in mid-1925 Colombian authorities deported him to Panama due to his anarchist radicalism in the city of Cali.[42] Upon arriving in Colón, he quickly renewed his activism by joining the city's SGT and Liga, radicalism that caught the attention of authorities. Panamanian police arrested von Wedel and turned him over to US officials in the Canal Zone, from where he was deported. In a three-hour meeting to protest von Wedel's arrest and transfer, speakers condemned the United States for violating Panamanian sovereignty. They asked: If von Wedel was agitating in the Republic, why

---

[40] Ibid., March 25, 1924, 2 and 7.   [41] *El Inquilino*, August 23, 1925, 4.
[42] Flórez Pinzón, "Anarquismo y anarcosindicalismo," 60 and 74.

had he been held in jail in the US Canal Zone and deported from there?[43] This would not be the last such transfer of radicals from the Republic to the US zone for deportation.

The local Panama City government attempted to deal with renters' demands in late September; however, Mayor Mario Galindo met with representatives of the reformist FORP, not the radical SGT or the Liga. The meeting outraged SGT and Liga leaders, who claimed the mayor should be meeting with them since they were coordinating the protests, had a newspaper, operated branches in Colón and Panama City, had held ten meetings in the capital city alone, and represented thousands of members. They warned that the SGT/Liga would ignore any agreement between the city and the FORP. When the mayor refused to put the SGT on any commission, SGT leaders appealed for help from President Rodolfo Chiari, claiming again that they were "the exclusive voice of the poorly treated tenants." Chiari ignored the appeal.[44]

On October 1 – the day after Governor Archibaldo Boyd warned "foreign agitators" to stop involvement with the Liga or face deportation as "pernicious and undesirable Aliens" – 4000 SGT renters went on strike in Panama City. They protested the landlords for unjustly raising rents and the government for imposing a real estate tax in February 1925 – a tax that landlords passed on to renters. On October 9, renters in Colón joined the strike. As the strike materialized, worker support networks went into action. Women played supportive roles in the strike, as they had in rent strikes elsewhere in the Americas. They used their familiarity with the neighborhoods to establish social networks, circulated petitions, mobilized residents, banged pots, and swept streets in symbolic protests.[45] Female *ligistas* organized community kitchens where they used their limited funds and collaborated on mass meal preparation to feed strikers.[46] *Ligistas* were preparing for a long strike.

"THE SANTA ANA MASSACRE"

Within days, the Liga began organizing a rally for Panama City's Santa Ana Park. However, on October 6, Mayor Galindo banned meetings in

---

[43] *El Inquilino*, August 23, 1925, 1–2.
[44] *La Estrella de Panamá*, September 22, 1925, 10–11; September 23, 1925, 11–12.
[45] *Star and Herald*, October 1, 1925, 11; Andrew Wood and James Baer, "Strength in Numbers: Urban Rent Strikes and Political Transformation in the Americas, 1904–1925," *Journal of Urban History* 32, no. 6 (2006): 869.
[46] Marta Matamoros, *El camino es la organización: la mujer en las luchas populares, 1925–1982* (Panama City: Unión Nacional de Mujeres Panameño, 1982), 8.

public places.[47] Two days later, *El Inquilino* urged readers to ignore Galindo. On October 10, the Liga issued the flyer "Sí Hay Mitin" (Yes, There Is a Meeting), calling on members and supporters to meet in the park at eight o'clock that night and "exercise their constitutional rights to free assembly."[48] Apparently not all activists believed Galindo's ban was in effect. Jorge Turner thought it had been reversed and that President Rodolfo Chiari had given his blessings to the meeting. "Nobody thought that the mayor would persist in opposing the desire or authorization of the President of the Republic," Turner claimed later.[49]

But they were wrong and misinformed. As strikers and supporters arrived on the evening of the tenth, they found the park peppered with red flags and the Liga leadership on the park's bandstand preparing to address the growing crowd. Then confusion erupted. The 29-year-old journalist Gavino Sierra Gutiérrez, standing on the bandstand between the flags of the Liga and the SGT, looked out on the crowd, saw approaching armed police led by Commander Ricardo Arango, and whistled to warn the crowd of the ensuing danger. As the crowd began to disperse, Mayor Galindo, who had come with the police, climbed onto the bandstand with a revolver in his hand, strode to Samuel Casís – a thirty-five-year-old painter and Liga Central Committee leader – and pointed the revolver at Casís's chest. Casís fled, Galindo jumped down, but then climbed back up – this time without his gun. Meanwhile, some *ligistas* began fighting the police, and at least one cop found himself spiraling downward through the air as Liga members picked him up and threw him off the bandstand.[50] Sierra Gutiérrez lingered until "a police force armed with rifles and led by Eduardo Chiari, Mayor Galindo, and Governor Boyd" charged the bandstand. They ordered him to get down and then Boyd pistol-whipped him in the face several times.[51]

The coordinated repression involved not just the police and the mayor's office, but also the fire department and US military. Police units

---

[47] Statement by Diógenes de la Rosa, October 21, 1925. Junta de Inquilinato 1925 (hereafter referred to as JdI 1925), Box 41, Tomo 1. Archivo Nacional de Panamá, Panama City, Panama; Jorge Boyd, Prosecutor General of the Nation Statement to Supreme Court, March 10, 1926. JdI 1925, Box 41, Tomo 1.
[48] Documentos Sueltas. *El Inquilino*, October 8, 1925; "Sí Hay Mitin" (flyer). JdI 1925, Box 42, Tomo 3.
[49] Statement by Diógenes de la Rosa, October 21, 1925. JdI 1925, Box 41, Tomo 1; Quintero, *El Sindicato General*, 17.
[50] Ibid.; Statement by Dr. Alejandro Vásquez D., n.d. JdI 1925, Box 41, Tomo II.
[51] Declaration of G. Sierra Gutiérrez, n.d. JdI 1925, Box 41, Tomo II.

had arrived with the local fire brigade. When the police charged, according to a Colombian Liga member, Antonio Landazuli, many officers leveled their guns and indiscriminately fired into the crowd. A Lieutenant Correa, as well as Chief Arango, fired into the demonstration. Strikers fled the park, but not before the fire brigades shot them with water hoses to impede their flight from arrest.[52] Meanwhile, US Commander MacDonald watched from the sidelines. Arango had been in touch with MacDonald earlier in the day and asked the American if he would bring a "detachment of armed US soldiers and station them in front of the Variedades Theater with the goal of giving protection in case the police would need it." MacDonald agreed to cooperate any way he could. But what MacDonald saw that night in Santa Ana Park pretty-well freaked him out. He had arrived on a motorcycle to oversee the rally and repression from the nearby theater. The sight of red flags everywhere, the fire department hosing down demonstrators, and workers throwing cops off the bandstand did not sit well.[53]

By next morning, the Chiari government had detained at least thirty men and prepared deportations of Carlos Céspedes (a Colombian journalist), Arsenio Gómez (a Colombian schoolteacher), and Peruvian schoolteachers Nicolás Terreros, Luis Fernández Bustamante, and Esteban M. Pavletich. In Colón, the government arrested Liga members from Peru, Chile, Mexico, and Colombia. Soon, rumors flew wildly through the country and contributed to government paranoia. One of the most influential rumors was that *ligistas* all along intended to attack police and then take over a police station, supposedly with the intention of capturing weapons. This rumor was joined by another: The *ligistas* might have had allies among the police. Apparently, not all police and firemen were pleased to be on the side of repression. After all, many of them were also poorly paid renters and sympathetic to the goals of the Liga – a dynamic like Panamanian police sympathy with general strikers in 1916. In addition, numerous fire fighters quit the force in the days immediately following the Santa Ana Park events, many out of sympathy for the strikers, though the government claimed it was because they had been threatened by *ligistas*. Into an environment in which the

---

[52] Declaration of Felipe López, October 11, 1925. JdI 1925, Box 41, Tomo I; Declaration of Antonio Landazuli, n.d. JdI 1925, Box 41, Tomo II; *Star and Herald*, October 11, 1925, 1 and 19; Declaration of Carlos C. Espinosa, n.d. JdI 1925, Box 41, Tomo I.
[53] Declaration of Comandante Ricardo Arango, J. n.d. JdI 1925, Box 41, Tomo II; Declaration of US Commander MacDonald. n.d. JdI 1925, Box 42, Tomo III.

government could no longer count on unanimous and unquestioning support from the police or fire departments, more rumors began circulating. President Chiari was concerned about a rumored plot in which policemen who belonged to the Liga intended to stage an armed uprising and topple him. This rumor, coupled with facts about the Pan-American character of the strikers, leadership, and deportees, raised an alarm. Thus, from the government's perspective, this had been a foreign operation designed not to reduce rents but for a Communist takeover of Panama.

Tensions were still high the next afternoon for the funeral of Marcial Mirones – a *ligista* shot dead during the violence in Santa Ana Park. Some 4000 people attended the funeral procession. *Ligistas* carried Mirones's casket to the cemetery, where numerous speeches were made. After the burial, marchers pushed shoulder-to-shoulder from the cemetery to DeLesseps Park for a meeting, where they heard more speeches praising the Liga and condemning government violence. However, mounted police soon arrived and broke up the park rally. After regrouping, marchers headed for Santa Ana Park, but police stopped their advance. A tense stand-off ensued. Then, out of the blue, someone shot a gun; nobody knows who. The police – fearing a shoot-out – broke ranks and marchers continued toward the park where they encountered yet another police line. At that point, taking stock of the heavily armed police presence, with machine guns stationed strategically around the park, the mourners headed home.

The government was scared. Chief of Police Leonides Pretelt published a call for volunteers. Pretelt planned to deputize citizen vigilantes because, as he put it, the Liga "threatens the security and rights of peaceful citizens," "attacks the legally constituted government," "threatens property and life," and because the government could not guarantee that the police were with them. Answering the call was the Veterans of Independence, who volunteered to assist the security services against foreign radicals if necessary.[54] Then, Chiari played his last desperate card: On October 12, he invoked the United States–Panama Treaty of 1903 and requested US military assistance to crush the rent strike.[55]

October 12: The *Día de la Raza* in Latin America (Columbus Day in the United States). The date's irony cannot be missed, because on that day

---

[54] *La Estrella de Panamá*, October 12, 1925, 10; *Star and Herald*, October 12, 1925, 1.
[55] *Star and Herald*, October 12, 1925, 1, 2, and 4; October 13, 1925, 1; *La Estrella de Panamá*, October 12, 1925, 9–10.

three battalions of the US Army invaded the Republic.[56] They included the recently reorganized Forty-Second Infantry Regiment – a unit composed of Puerto Rican soldiers under US officers and which had been in the Canal Zone since 1917.[57] But US soldiers immediately encountered resistance and defiance. That day, the Liga's Central Committee circulated a flyer written by detained Liga leaders. They urged Chiari to acknowledge that the meeting ban was unconstitutional, reaffirm the constitutional right to assemble, immediately release all detainees, and suspend deportations of foreign strikers. The flyer condemned the government and the bourgeoisie for "calling on help from foreign forces to silence the pained cries and the hunger of the proletariat." The writers signed the flyer with that old but true anarchist closing: "SALUD Y REVOLUCION SOCIAL" (Cheers and Social Revolution).[58]

But if Chiari and the Americans thought that three battalions of US troops would immediately quiet the storm, they misread the situation. The same day that troops poured into Panama, merchants, artisans, and public service providers launched a general strike to protest US actions, Chiari's abandonment of national sovereignty, and abuses against the *ligistas*. A crowd of several thousand in Panama City tried to prevent US troops from marching into the city, but they were dispersed when soldiers lowered bayonet-fixed rifles at the crowd. Elsewhere, strikers cut telephone cables laid out by troops, and occasionally militants confronted soldiers when they rode past on motorcycles and side cars waving red flags. The same day, a second dead striker – Ferdin Jaén – was laid to rest. When thousands of strikers carrying more red flags followed the body to the cemetery, Panamanian police with bayonets charged the procession while US troops shot and killed two young Panamanian men.

That night, the Liga met at their headquarters in defiance of a military order prohibiting such gatherings. The US Army raided the meeting and arrested fifty. But during the raid, one of the attendees – Damian Cabrera – died. Again, rumors flew throughout the city. The government claimed that Cabrera had tried to avoid arrest by leaping off a balcony, but misjudged the jump, landed wrong, and broke his neck. The SGT and

---

[56] Muñoz, *Blázquez de Pedro*, 189–191; Soler, *Panamá*, 53; "Arango Blamed for First Shot, October 23, 1925," RG185 ICC 1914–1934, 80-H-5/clippings; *Star and Herald*, October 13, 1925, 1.
[57] Thanks go out to Micah Wright for information on the Puerto Rican-manned units in the zone.
[58] Documentos Sueltos. "Desde la Cárcel: Al Proletariado Panameño," October 12, 1925. JdI 1925, Box 42, Tomo III.

Liga were incensed, claiming that US troops killed him. The next day, an SGT flyer called on all to join forces and attend the funeral of Cabrera, who was "victimized last night by foreign bayonets with the consent of our government." Fearing an increasingly radicalized city, authorities banned a public funeral for Cabrera, limiting attendance to just family and close friends. The government also closed the Henry Printers press in the city for "irresponsibly" printing the flyer that claimed Cabrera had been killed by a *yanqui* bayonet.[59]

Ultimately, the disturbances were short-lived. By October 14, US troops and Panamanian police brought a semblance of calm to the capital. The general strike ended that day and public services returned to normal operation. Some troops left the city. But the remaining troops stayed largely to guard working-class areas – areas, as the press puts it, "susceptible to disturbances because of the elements there residing."[60] On October 23, the rent strike had been suppressed throughout the Republic, and the remaining US troops returned to the Canal Zone. President Chiari banned the flying of red flags and ordered the deportation of "dangerous" foreigners. The climate of fear worked. Printing shops refused to print anything publicizing the strike or the strike's main issues for fear that the government would close them like it had closed Henry Printers.[61]

Part of the calming effect resulted from overtures made by President Chiari as well as the detention or deportation of most of the radical leadership of the Liga and SGT. Chiari announced that there was clear evidence that landlords had charged unfairly high rents and pledged that the government would roll back rents to January levels. Meanwhile, the Liga – now under moderate Panamanian leadership – issued a manifesto urging Liga cooperation with the government to find solutions. The manifesto betrayed the internationalist dimensions of the SGT and the earlier Liga leadership by stressing that the organizations were patriotic. It concluded that "the popular classes of the Isthmus have always been respectful of the law and the constituted authorities" – a statement

---

[59] "SINDICATO GENERAL DE TRABAJADORES, Compañeros! Hay que asistir al sepelio del compañero DAMIAN CABRERA." JdI 1925, Box 41, Tomo II; *Star and Herald*, October 13, 1925, 1; October 14, 1925, 1 and 4; *La Estrella de Panamá*, October 14, 1924, 10.

[60] *New York Times*, October 13, 1925, 1; October 14, 1925, 1; Quintero, *El Sindicato General*, 17; *Star and Herald*, October 15, 1925, 1.

[61] Soler, *Panamá*, 54–55; "Order Restored in Panama," October 14, 1925. RG185 ICC 1914–1934, 80-H-5/clippings.

woefully devoid of historical accuracy.[62] At the same time, the government began purging policemen who had defied orders to pursue and abuse *ligistas*.[63]

By the end of December, the authorities had deported at least sixteen radicals, including José María Blázquez de Pedro, his brother Martín, and Sara Gratz with her daughter, as well as others from Spain, Mexico, Ecuador, Peru, Guadeloupe, and more. All were deported for their relationship to events at Santa Ana Park or "for making communist propaganda in the country."[64] Meanwhile, Panamanian Liga members were arrested, and statements taken to prepare for trial. Attorney General Jorge Boyd charged detainees with "crimes against the country" and/or crimes "against the freedom of industry and work." The government argued that because the Liga held the meeting in defiance of the mayor's ban, the Liga was responsible for all deaths and injuries.[65] As the charges read, "according to statements and documents issued under the flag of the rent strikers, several Panamanians and foreigners were planning a revolutionary coup with communist tendencies and a goal of imposing on our Republic a governmental regime rejected today in all civilized countries."[66]

The charge about a communist coup was based on three documents. First, the Panamanian National Assembly had passed legislation in April 1925 "banning the immigration of persons who seek to transform society by violent means such as communists, socialists, and anarchists" while at the same time pledging to not recognize the Soviet Union.[67] The second document was an October 23, 1925 letter from District Attorney Martínez about an anonymous letter outlining how the Liga "threatened to subvert the public order of the Nation." The letter compared Panama with "modern Russia," noting that while conditions were not quite the same "we nevertheless have men of character who are willing to die for our cause of liberty, justice, and rights. In just causes, there are always

---

[62] *Star and Herald*, October 14, 1925, 1 and 4; *La Estrella de Panamá*, October 18, 1925, 19.
[63] *La Estrella de Panamá*, October 13, 1925, 11; *Star and Herald*, October 19, 1925, 1.
[64] To the Superior Court of the Republic. List of Deported from Panama and Colón. December 22, 1925 and December 26, 1925. JdI 1925, Box 41, Tomo 1; *Star and Herald*, October 30, 1925, 1; November 2, 1925, 1; November 6, 1925, 5; November 7, 1925, 1; *La Estrella de Panamá*, November 9, 1925, 9.
[65] Jorge Boyd Statement to the Supreme Court, March 19, 1926. JdI 1925, Box 41, Tomo 1.
[66] Defense Statement of Eugenio L. Cossáni, March 16, 1926. JdI 1925, Box 41, Tomo 1.
[67] Letter from President Chiari on Antibolshevik Measures in Panama, February 11, 1927. Administración del Estado. 1925–1927. Exp. 52. #208.1.2.1. Presidente Rodolfo Chiari. Correspondencia. Folio 107. Archivo Nacional de Panamá, Panama City, Panama.

martyrs ... and our cause is the same justice and rights" found in the USSR.[68] The third document was a ten-page report listing the detained as "known communists" who for years had "successfully fomented rebellion against the right of private property, which is the basis for the communist doctrine," and they found an issue (high rents) that they could use to gain sympathetic followers among the poor. In addition, the Liga had printed *El Inquilino* at the El Laborista print shop, which housed a library of "communist works and propaganda magazines." Meanwhile, one *ligista*, Samuel Casís, had a "large library of communist books and signs of a subversive nature."[69] "Anarchist," "Communist," it really didn't matter to the authorities. In mid-1920s Panama, anyone railing against capitalism, the state that protected it, and the foreign army that safeguarded both was a "communist" in this post–Bolshevik Revolution world.

Of course, the defendants saw all this rather differently. The thirty-eight-year-old radical lawyer and friend of Blázquez de Pedro, Manuel V. Garrido C., stated that the Liga had held only peaceful meetings to protest a real and severe grievance. But some police officials were spooked by the growth and militancy of the Liga's statements. "Under this panic and false alarm, the mayor, violating the categorical disposition of the constitution, wanted to stop the rent strikers' meeting."[70] Cristóbal Segundo, the lawyer for several arrested *ligistas*, argued to the court that what we had here was little more than the government doing what governments always seemed to do: "defending the egoistic interests of the capitalist classes and maintaining completely their state of economic dominance while appearing to be working in the community's interest, i.e., the need to conserve social order and respect for the principle of authority."[71] Sierra Gutiérrez represented the standard defense: the government was really the entity undermining the country by issuing unconstitutional orders. This was the true *lèse-majesté* – the real act of subversion against the country – "the crime against individual rights." And when it came down to it, it was the violence perpetrated by the police that night at the park that was illegitimate ... acts that were the true cause of the injuries and deaths.[72]

---

[68] Letter from Fiscal Martínez to Superior Court, October 23, 1925. JdI 1925, Box 41, Tomo I.
[69] Documentos Sueltos. Untitled letter, n.d. JdI 1925, Box 42, Tomo III.
[70] Defense of Manuel V. Garrido C., March 16, 1926. JdI 1925, Box 41, Tomo I.
[71] Statement by Lawyer Cristóbal L. Segundo for Defendants Sucre, Casís, and Brower, March 12, 1926. JdI 1925, Box 41, Tomo iI.
[72] Defense Statement of Gavino Sierra Gutiérrez, n.d. JdI 1925, Box 41, Tomo I.

Ultimately, the rent strike suffered the same defeat as most working-class rent strikes in Latin America. Housing conditions were wretched in Havana in 1900, and anarchists had tried organizing a rent strike there, but to no avail. Police felt little sympathy with Argentine strikers in 1907 and forcibly crushed that movement. In Havana in 1919, anarchist-led demonstrations to lower the costs of basic goods and rents by 50 percent met with police violence in which one striker died. When police attacked the dead striker's funeral procession, groups organized by anarcho-syndicalist Alfredo López fought back, killing two policemen and wounding others; however, rent prices did not come down. Mexican tenants in Veracruz suffered police evictions in 1922.[73] In Colombia, Barranquilla's police used bayonetted rifles to attack and put down rent strikers in 1923. The outcome for Panama's strikers was the same as for their counterparts in Latin America – jail or deportation with little success.

Yet, two things made the defeat of the rent strikers in Panama unique. First, unlike elsewhere, the US military joined in the repression. This Pan-American repression led to a second consequence. As US soldiers moved into the Republic from the Canal Zone and Panamanian police arrested strike organizers for trial or deportation, the repression prevented the holding of the Inter-Continental Congress of Anarchists – the first hemispheric attempt to bring forth a formal anarchist Pan-Americanism.

THE PAN-AMERICAN ANARCHIST CONGRESS

Throughout 1925, anarchists across the Americas planned the congress, which was scheduled to open in Panama City on November 1, 1925, and with anarchists sailing into Panama in October. Which anarchist was key to organizing the meeting in Panama? José María Blázquez de Pedro. But while he and his brother Martín were the Panama organizers, it was Mexico-based José C. Valadés (Figure 6.5) and Buenos Aires-based Julio Díaz representing the Federación Obrera Regional Argentina (Argentina Regional Workers Federation, or FORA) who initiated the congress.[74] Valadés had joined the Mexican Confederación General de Trabajadores

---

[73] Sánchez Cobos, *Sembrando Ideales*, 303; Wood and Baer, "Strength in Numbers," 871–873.

[74] I'm indebted to Steven Hirsch who – unknowingly – led me not only to Valadés but also the 1925 anarchist congress when he asked me to look for some material in the IISG in Amsterdam years ago. One historian writes that "the government conjured up the specter of an anarchist invasion" of Panama. While it wasn't a "conjuring" or "invasion," it certainly was very real. See Zumoff, "The 1925 Tenants' Strike," 520.

FIGURE 6.5 The Mexican-born José C. Valadés joined with Julio Díaz from Argentina to coordinate a 1925 anarchist conference in Panama with the cooperation of the Blázquez de Pedro brothers.
Author's personal collection

(General Confederation of Workers, or CGT) and became its secretary general in 1921. The CGT promoted itself as "libertarian communist." Valadés helped to organize the Federación de Jóvenes Comunistas (Young Communists Federation) in August 1922 with twenty-four other people influenced in the early 1920s by a wide range of leftist radicals, including Kropotkin, Flores Magón, Lenin, and Stirner. In his memoir, Valadés confessed that at this time, even though he admired the Bolshevik Revolution, his anarchist ideas of liberty

> were not compatible with the dictatorship of the proletariat ... I believed in the heroism of Nicolás Lenin but feared he was a tyrant. Would the Russian people obtain some benefit with this innovator's rise to power? Would the caudillo of the proletariat be just like any other political caudillo? ... I began to feel like I was walking the tightrope: Russia or freedom.

It was a group of Spanish anarchists fleeing repression in Cuba, especially José Rubio, that helped Valadés see that modern-day revolutionaries "were walking with two obligations: to help the Revolution of the Russian people and to not divide the world's revolutionary forces."[75]

In January 1923, Valadés attended the funeral of Ricardo Flores Magón, who had died in December in a US federal penitentiary in Leavenworth, Kansas. The Mexican government gave Flores Magón a full state funeral – an oxymoronic move to be sure, a state funeral for an anti-state anarchist – where Valadés spoke. The funeral also mended a somewhat tattered relationship between Valadés and Alejandro Montoya, aka Víctor Recoba. Recoba had become one of those anarchist migrants that the networks needed for their survival and to flourish. After leading the 1916 strike against the Panama Canal, Recoba returned to Peru, but in 1919 he was in Philadelphia working for that city's Centro de Estudios Sociales (Social Studies Center, or CES) around the time that Spanish-speaking anarchists there had been accused of the plot to assassinate President Wilson.[76] By 1920 he was in Havana, serving on the credentials committee of the labor congress that year where Antonio Penichet and Marcelo Salinas helped to create the friendship committee with Bolshevik Russia.[77] Soon, he returned to Peru, but then fled the dictatorial rule of Augusto Leguía. He ended up in Mexico, going by the name Alejandro Montoya. His hardcore stances against Communists had led to friction with Valadés, but the two met at Flores Magón's funeral and embraced one another as old comrades. In March 1923 – two months after the funeral – the Mexican government deported Recoba.[78] That same year, Valadés was in Tampico, Mexico, where he aligned himself with the city's emerging IWW.[79] In September 1924, he lured Librado Rivera – Ricardo Flores Magón's main aide – to Tampico, where they agitated for anarchist causes, building on a

---

[75] José C. Valadés, *Memorias de un joven rebelde. 2a. parte. Mis confesiones* (Sinaloa, Mexico: Universidad Autónoma de Sinaloa, 1985), 84–85, 94; Aguilar, "The IWW in Tampico," 129.

[76] "Memorandum on Bolshevist, Anarchist and Socialist Newspapers in the United States with a Partial List of Individuals." 10110-1276. War Department Memo. May 3, 1919, 38. US Military Intelligence Division Reports, Surveillance of Radicals in the United States, 1917–1941. From Military Agency Records RG 165. United States National Archives.

[77] Jeifets, et al., *La internacional comunista y América Latina*, 229.

[78] Valadés, *Memorias de un joven rebelde*, 129; Ricardo Melgar Bao, "Redes del exilio aprista en México (1923–1924)," in *México, país refugio: la experiencia de los exilios en el siglo XX*, ed. Pablo Yankelevich (Mexico City: Plaza y Valdes, 2002), 248.

[79] Ibid., 139.

Tampico organization launched earlier in part by Recoba, who was operating under the name F. Ríos at the time.[80]

Valadés optimistically saw hope for the embryonic anarchist cause throughout Central America. In a letter to Diego Abad de Santillán (with whom he kept in regular contact) he wrote that throughout the region "we should be able to accomplish much through our anarchist propaganda." As a result, he and Julio Díaz initiated a propaganda tour through Central America, making contacts especially in San Salvador and Guatemala City.[81] In the former, Díaz contacted the Salvadoran anarchist Virgilio Alvarado Chacón before being deported.[82] In February 1923, a group of Guatemalan teachers organized themselves into a revolutionary syndicate. In a column published in Havana's *Nueva Luz*, they proclaimed that nothing would improve the state of education until "the teachers themselves rebel against State exploitation." They declared "a war to the death versus both capitalist and state education while supporting rationalist education that proclaims the principles of the Social Revolution." The group joined "in solidarity with the libertarian centers of Europe and America," including the Communist Youth of Mexico.[83] That the union linked itself to the Mexican Communist Youth – of which Valadés was still a member in early 1923 – suggests that Valadés knew of like-minded souls in the country who could help him and Díaz. One such comrade was Antonio Méndez Paz, an anarchist member of a group who created Guatemala's first revolutionary syndicalist organization – the Unificación Obrera Socialista (Socialist Worker Unification) in 1921. When Díaz arrived in Guatemala in 1925 to help plan the Panama congress, it was Méndez he sought out.[84]

---

[80] Donald C. Hodges, *Mexican Anarchism after the Revolution* (Austin: University of Texas Press, 1995), 19–21; Jeifets, et al., *La internacional comunista y América Latina*, 229; Valadés, *Memorias de un joven rebelde*, 142.

[81] Letters dated August 19, 1924 and August 15, 1925. Diego Abad de Santillán Archive, IISG, Amsterdam (hereafter cited as DASA. Correspondence.) J. C. Valadés, 1924–1926. Folder 282.

[82] Letter dated August 15, 1925. DASA. Correspondence. J. C. Valadés, 1924–1926. Folder 282; María Migueláñez Martínez, "El proyecto continental del anarquismo argentino: resultados y usos de una propaganda transfronteriza (1920–1930)," *Revista de Historia Contemporanea* 94 (2014): 7–8.

[83] *Nueva Luz*, April 5, 1923, 7; Arturo Taracena Arriola, "Presencia anarquista en Guatemala entre 1920 y 1932," *Mesoamerica* 15 (1988): 5–9.

[84] Omar Lucas Monteflores, "El anarquismo en Guatemala: El anarcosyndicalismo en la Ciudad de Guatemala, 1920–1932" (PhD dissertation, Universidad de San Carlos de Guatemala, 2011), 56, 108–114; letter dated August 15, 1925. DASA. Correspondence. J. C. Valadés, 1924–1926. Folder 282.

By August 1925, Valadés was excited to secure the cooperation of Blázquez de Pedro to host the Panama congress. Meanwhile, delegates from Nicaragua, Colombia, Argentina, Uruguay, Chile, Guatemala, El Salvador, Panama, and Peru pledged to attend. The Ecuadorean delegation likely would include Antonio Santo Maldonado, a Catalán who fled Spain in 1909, went to Cuba and Puerto Rico, then to Venezuela, the Dominican Republic, Colombia, and more. Each time, he was deported for his anarchist activities.[85] The Cubans at this time were fighting for their lives – literally – against Machado and could not send representatives. Valadés built on his IWW contacts in Tampico and invited the IWW executive committee in Chicago to send representatives as well, though costs prevented Wobblies from doing so.[86] Valadés and Díaz's initiative was ambitious, to say the least, but Panama – as a central point in the hemisphere – was a perfect location, with access made easier thanks to the surge in passenger ships to and through the Panama Canal.

However, the congress failed to materialize. On October 31 – a week after the US Army crushed the rent strike and returned to the Canal Zone – anarchist delegates from Peru, Chile, Uruguay, Argentina, and Mexico began to arrive in Panama, having no idea about events that had transpired in the previous two and half weeks.[87] But US and Panamanian authorities had been tipped off about the congress, which is why they were prepared to look for Latin American anarchists arriving by ship. After the US withdrawal from Panama on October 23, Panamanian authorities began arresting all "communist" leaders of the Liga. Congress secretary Martín Blázquez de Pedro (José María's younger brother) and his colleague Sara Gratz were preparing for their comrades' arrival. However, both were detained. When authorities arrested Martín, they discovered in his possession letters concerning the upcoming congress from anarchists in Germany, Peru, Nicaragua, and

---

[85] Letter from Delfín González to Abad de Santillán, September 10, 1925. DASA. Correspondence. J. C. Valadés, 1924–1926. Folder 282.
[86] Letters dated August 20, 1924; May 25, 1925; August 15, 1925; September 8, 1925; September 25, 1925; October 16, 1925; October 17, 1925. DASA. Correspondence. J. C. Valadés, 1924–1926. Folder 282.
[87] Letter dated November 4, 1925. DASA. Correspondence. J. C. Valadés, 1924–1926. Folder 282. This wasn't the first anarchist call for a hemispheric congress. For instance, in 1923, Elias Catellano – who had worked in the Canal Zone in 1911 with M. D. Rodríguez's Federation group in Gorgona – was in New York by 1923 when he urged comrades to hold a congress where "we invite all of our comrades from North, Central, and South America to cooperate in our work." *Aurora*, November 1, 1923, 12. *Aurora* was published by one of Catellano's Canal Zone comrades, Jorge de Borrán.

Argentina. The found correspondence gave authorities a clear picture that anarchists from around the Americas were mobilizing and heading to Panama right at the very moment that the Liga had chosen to launch its rent strike. The group La Protesta in Lima had written to Martín and accepted the invitation. On October 11 (as Panama-based radicals fought authorities and the US military authorities were on the verge of moving into Panama City), La Protesta's anarchists met to select delegates. One confiscated letter from the group raised a few eyebrows among isthmian authorities. The letter noted that Oscar Alforo and – incredibly enough – Víctor Recoba had been designated as the Peruvian group's delegates to the Panama congress. In May 1925, Recoba was supposed to meet the European anarchists Buenaventura Durruti and Francisco Ascaso in Chile to rob a bank, which they did, but he did not because he was not yet in Chile. The bank robbers took the nearly 47,000 pesos back to Spain to help fund resistance to dictator Miguel Primo de Rivera.[88] By late 1925, Recoba was in Lima and ready to depart for Panama, where his anarchist labor activism had begun a decade earlier when he led the 1916 canal strike.[89] With information from the letters, officials in Panama and the Canal Zone quickly mobilized and intercepted the incoming anarchist attendees. After all, authorities had the names and countries of origin. It was easy to pick them up when they arrived in port.

As authorities denied entry to those anarchists coming for the congress, they also began deporting non-Panamanian radicals and the Blázquez de Pedro brothers were prime targets. Panamanian authorities had quickly linked the Blázquez de Pedro brothers with the organizing, not just because the letters were found on Martín, but also some communications were addressed to their Panama City residence, like a telegram from Nicaragua that went to Calle 13 Oeste 45 Panama – the Blázquez de Pedro home and regular meeting place for leftists.[90]

---

[88] Abel Paz, *Durruti in the Spanish Revolution* (Oakland: AK Press, 2007), 75–76.
[89] Letter "Comrada, Secretaria de la Ia Conferencia Intercontinental. Panama," October 17, 1925. JdI 1925, Box 41, Tomo 1; "Panama Congress Planned by Reds," October 30, 1925. RG185 ICC 1914–1934, 80-H-5/clippings; US State Department Weekly Country Report from Panama for 10/31 to 11/7 on Communist Leanings of Inquilinos with Enclosures, November 14, 1925. 819.00B RG59 General Records of the Department of State. Panama. General Conditions (hereafter cited as RG59 Panama. General Conditions). United States National Archives, College Park, MD; Jeifets et al., *La Internacional Comunista y América Latina*, 280.
[90] Telegram from Managua. JdI 1925, Box 41, Tomo 1.

José María was deported twice. On September 24 – one week before the Liga launched the rent strike – he was standing in the doorway of the Tipografía Moderna in Panama City. President Chiari and his cabinet had determined that Blázquez de Pedro was an "undesirable" foreigner who advocated communism. They ordered Governor Boyd to arrest and deport him.[91] Because Panamanian authorities feared that his followers would attack the Panama City jail where Blázquez de Pedro was being held, officials transferred him to a US jail in the Canal Zone. Under cover of darkness, they put him on a train to Cristóbal with the intention that he would be put on a ship and deported the next day. Within hours of Blázquez de Pedro's transfer, incensed radicals held a protest meeting at the Sociedad Hijos del Trabajo. The SGT hired a North American lawyer – Felix E. Porter – to file a writ of *habeas corpus* on Blázquez de Pedro's behalf with the US District Court for the Canal Zone. Porter claimed that the anarchist was being held in US territory without having broken any law in the Canal Zone or even being arrested there – not unlike the von Wedel case a month earlier. Thus, the detention was illegal.[92]

Unfortunately, minutes mattered. The writ was presented to the Acting Inspector of Police of the Canal Zone at 10:55 a.m. on September 25. But two hours earlier at 8:45 a.m., US Lieutenant Kallay had handed the anarchist back to Panamanian authorities, and they put him on the *Manuel Calvo* bound for Spain. The ship left for Spain at 10:34 a.m. As Blázquez de Pedro by then was no longer in US custody, his lawyer had no recourse. Canal Zone authorities justified this act to facilitate the deportation of someone who had not violated a Canal Zone law, claiming that the United States was in the right because zone authorities were performing "an act of comity—the performance of a moral duty to a sister nation, with whom we are on friendly terms," that is, international cooperation against transnational anarchists in the name of Pan-Americanism.[93]

---

[91] *Star and Herald*, October 25, 1925, 1 and 3.
[92] Ibid., September 25, 1925, 1 and 3; *Estrella de Panamá*, September 25, 1925, 10 and 11; September 26, 1925, 11.
[93] Report on Tenants League from Charge d'Affaires, Panama Canal to Secretary of State, October 3, 1925. 819.502/3 RG59 Panama. Labor. Unions and Organizations; Report on Pedro, Jose B de from Charge d'Affaires, Panama Canal to Secretary of State, October 3, 1925. 319.5224 RG59 General Records of the Department of State. Relating to Political Relations between the US and Panama, 1910–29; Report with Enclosure on US District Court for the Canal Zone on Blázquez de Pedro's Writ of Habeas Corpus, November 10, 1925. 319.5224 RG59 General Records of the Department of State. *Canal Zone Reports.* Vol. 3, 1927, #728 de causas civiles brought before court between May 1,

As the US-based anarchist Rudolfo Lone, who had been an anarchist in the zone between 1912 and 1913 before going to Cuba and then Steubenville, Ohio, put it: "this is like saying that [Panamanian authorities] are simply an agent of Uncle Sam" and that Chiari and his collaborators are little more than "puppets" of Wall Street bankers.[94]

But this was not the end of José María's anarchist wanderings. As the Liga launched the rent strike, he was on his own transnational deportation odyssey. Though he had been deported, he managed to jump ship when it docked in the Dutch Caribbean island of Curaçao. He then boarded another ship bound for Limón, Costa Rica, but authorities denied him permission to disembark. He then headed to Puerto Colombia but was also refused permission to land. Finally, he returned to where his journey began a month before – to Cristóbal, Panama. There, authorities arrested him again in the midst of the US occupation and held Blázquez de Pedro in jail, with the media barred from interviewing him.[95] He was loaded onto the Italian ship *Bologna* with his brother Martín, who was being deported after authorities found the anarchist congress letters on him. The brothers' ship set off for the Canary Islands on October 30.[96] They never arrived, having instead left the ship when it docked in Havana.

However, late 1925 was a bad time to be an anarchist of any kind in Cuba. Cuba's labor left was at that very moment under assault from the Machado government. Anarchists and Marxists were being jailed, deported, and disappeared. Others fled the island into exile as the government closed anarchist publications. The Blázquez de Pedro brothers lived out the remainder of their lives in a Cuba where anarchists were regularly repressed. These were more than just trying times politically for the brothers. Exiled from a land where they had devoted so much Pan-American anarchist organizing for a decade, they now found themselves not only politically isolated but also ill. Havana had long been a breeding ground for tuberculosis, which both brothers soon contracted. After a year-and-a-half in forced exile in a land that was anything but a reprieve,

---

1914 and January 1, 1926, 588–592. United States National Archives. College Park, MD. See also, C.H. Cuestas, "Las últimas horas de Blázquez de Pedro en Panamá," *Tareas* 98 (1998): 115–120.

[94] "La doctrina de Monroe" and "La deportación de J.M. Blazquez de Pedro." R. Lone Collection, IISG. Amsterdam.

[95] *Estrella de Panamá*, October 16, 1925, 9.

[96] US State Department Weekly Country Report from Panama for 10/31 to 11/7 on Communist Leanings of Inquilinos with Enclosures, November 14, 1925. 819.00B RG59 Panama. General Conditions.

the fifty-two-year-old José María died from tuberculosis on May 11, 1927. Seemingly bound to follow his brother's fate in life and death, Martín also died of tuberculosis in Havana on December 6, 1927.

CONCLUSION

So, there it is. If those violent events in Santa Ana Park had not occurred that warm October evening, and if the Liga had respected the denial to hold a rally, then the police assaults and arrests would not have occurred. There would have been no widespread crackdown on radicals, and police would not have found the letters in Martín's possession. Authorities would not have realized hemispheric anarchists were converging on the city directly under their noses. Víctor Recoba probably would have returned to the city. Other anarchists from the Americas would have disembarked and made their way to central Panama City. And, José María Blázquez de Pedro – the key to organizing the conference until his untimely departure a month earlier – possibly would have returned since there would not have been a heightened awareness on the part of authorities to be on the alert for him. He could have been in his Panama City home with his brother Martín and welcomed the arriving anarchists to the first international anarchist congress of the hemisphere. What if the Liga had refrained from the Santa Ana meeting? But no. The Liga had to defy the mayor.

Still, one wonders what the Blázquez de Pedro brothers were thinking. While their colleagues in the Liga prepared for the rent strike in September and October, these radicals knew that international anarchists would at that very time be heading to the isthmus. Perhaps they thought that the October rent strike would galvanize Panama, creating a radicalized critical mass of people that international anarchists would arrive and find at month's end. Would the congress, then, be a culminating event for the strike – a way to impress both foreign visitors and local strikers alike? A dual radical strike that would have been heralded throughout the Americas to organize hemispheric support for anarchism? Or, and this is some crazy thinking to be sure, maybe the Chiari government was right. José María Blázquez de Pedro knew the international anarchists were arriving just as workers and tenants in Panama were radicalizing. Did he and his anarchist comrades have a secret plan ... a plan to bring forth a strike that was about more than just rents? Did they envision the confluence of the rent strike and the congress as a secret plan to mobilize the national and international masses in Panama to topple the government?

Maybe. It's just speculation. After all, there is no indication that Valadés or Díaz knew about the rent strike issues or possibility of a rent strike just before the planned congress. But Blázquez de Pedro did! Doesn't it seem like a rather intriguing possibility – a potentially revealing coincidence – considering the actors involved and the timing? But if this was the secret plan, the anarchists seriously underestimated their US counterparts, who, seeing the Chiari government on the ropes, mobilized their own Pan-American strike force with the Panamanian government to crush the strike, ultimately undermine the congress, and drive foreign radicals out of the isthmus.

While Bolívar and the United States had developed different ideas about Pan-Americanism, their projects and goals linked independent nation-states together into a hemispheric union. In the 1910s and 1920s, anarchists in both actions and thoughts saw a new Pan-American project: hemispheric unity of workers, students, teachers, and anarchists (not governments) throughout the Americas centered on anti-imperialist, antipolitics ideas. Panama became a crossroads for anarchists connecting Central America with both the Caribbean islands (especially Cuba) and South America (especially Colombia and Peru). The 1916 general strike was the first organized labor attempt to place this ideal into action. The magazine *Cuasimodo* criticized US imperialism and false Pan-Americanism, calling for greater unity between not only Latin Americans but also Latins and Anglos. By 1921, Blázquez de Pedro and others developed a "communist" group composed of workers and activists from throughout Latin America to guide a new labor movement in Panama – a movement that was soon taken over by forces loyal to the US-based AFL and its conservative form of labor Pan-Americanism. But leftists continued to fight, formed a new Pan-American union, and called a multinational rent strike while international anarchists planned the first hemispheric congress.

It is true that anarchists failed in almost all these attempts. The strikes were suppressed, non-anarchists took over the labor movement, the international congress never materialized, and anarchists were deported far and wide. Some deported transnational radicals found new theaters to fight the social revolution. For instance, the Blázquez de Pedro brothers worked with anarcho-naturists and the group Pro-Vida in Havana following deportation from Panama.[97] Nicolás Gutarra would end up

---

[97] Del Valle published some of José María's works posthumously in the early 1930s. See Soriano Jiménez and Íñiguez, *José María Blázquez de Pedro*, 289–295.

in Guatemala, helping Manuel Bautista Grajedo found the Comité Pro-Acción Sindical (Pro-Action Union Committee, or CPAS) in 1928.[98] The nineteen-year-old Peruvian radical Esteban Pavletich and his Peruvian comrade Nicolás Terreros were deported to Puerto Barrios, Guatemala on October 15, 1925. There they met the Cuban Julio Antonio Mella, who had been part of the anarchist–Marxist alliance in Cuba in 1925 until his exile. Mella first went to Honduras and then Guatemala on his way to Mexico. In Guatemala, he worked with Pavletich and Terreros to help lead a bakers strike and to form a branch of the Liga Anti-imperialista in Guatemala City. The three foreigners were soon deported.[99] Mella made his way to Mexico, where he supported anti-Machado movements. Meanwhile, Pavletich made his way to Nicaragua, where he continued his radical anti-imperialism and fought alongside Augusto César Sandino in 1928.[100] Between 1923 and 1926, Sandino himself had been radicalized in the anarcho-syndicalist dominated oil fields of Tampico, Mexico with Recoba and Valadés.

The failed rent strike proved one of the last efforts of anarchists working in Panama. In 1926, there was no May Day celebration because, according to J. G. Smith of the US legation in the Canal Zone, the deportations from the previous year "eliminated" any Bolshevik or Communist presence in the country. But that wasn't quite right. The SGT issued a manifesto in September 1926 calling for a commemoration on October 10 to "remember the martyrs," to "renew adherence to workers' ideals and to strengthen the bonds of the exploited." However, the Panamanian government prohibited any commemorations of the "massacre of October 10" – as radicals called it – and mobilized police units around Panama City just in case members of the SGT defied the government – again.[101]

---

[98] Monteflores, "El anarquismo en Guatemala," 105–108.
[99] 819.00B RG 59. Internal Affairs of Panama. General Conditions; *Cultura Obrera*, March 6, 1926, 3; Tarcena Arriola, "Presencia anarquista en Guatemala," 9.
[100] Pavletich was a young university student in Peru before journeying to Panama and beyond. His politics seemed fluid – as was typical for the time – with some writers calling him an APRISTA (follower of the anti-imperialist, pro-working-class APRA party in Peru) and others an anarchist. Considering the fluidity of politics at this time, both might very well have been true. See Cappelletti, *Hechos y figuras del anarquismo hispanoamericano*, 43; Carr, "Pioneering Transnational Solidarity in the Americas," 148; Barry Carr, "Radicals, Revolutionaries, and Exiles: Mexico City in the 1920s," *Berkeley Review of Latin American Studies* (2010): n.p.
[101] Report from J. G. South, May 4, 1926; Report from J. G. South, October 11, 1926; Flyer "TRABAJADORES, A LA UNION!" September 25, 1926 from US Legation in the

By 1928, fears of Reds had subsided, and the government sanctioned a commemoration of the October events on the third anniversary. Some 2000 people peacefully paraded to Amador Cemetery. After laying flowers on the tombs of the martyrs – including an artificial flower bouquet sent by former president Belisario Porras! – representatives from the SGT, those arrested in 1925, and the newly formed Panama Labor Party spoke solemnly. In 1929, to mark the fourth anniversary, the Panama Labor Party began to publish the newspaper *El Mazo*. US intelligence was worried, claiming that it was a "communist journal of the most radical type." And it was the most radical thing published in Panama since the Liga's *El Inquilino*. Its bilingual (English and Spanish) pages praised the Russian Revolution, attacked US imperialism, and celebrated the 1925 martyrs. The party was made up of a wide array of leftist groups, including the SGT, the Juventud Proletaria (Proletarian Youth), La Unión de Obreros y Campesinos (The Union of Workers and Peasants), and the Sindicato Femenino (Women's Syndicate).[102]

The party organized the "Fourth Anniversary of the Santa Ana Massacre," at which 3000 people marched to the cemetery and parks. Speakers called for the end to *yanqui* imperialism and support for prisoners in Argentina, Colombia, Venezuela, and Cuba. From signs at the march, it was clear that what began as a call for lower rents in 1925 had morphed into an anarchist–communist movement denouncing imperialism and urging "solidarity of the soldiers, sailors and marines with the workers and peasants of Panama!"[103] Though the masthead of the newspaper included a hammer and sickle while being the official voice of the Panama Labor Party, the language of some writers and their actions clearly reflected a lingering anarchist influence. For instance, when critics

Panama Canal, Panama to Secretary of State, Washington, DC. 819.502/13 RG59 Panama. Labor. Unions and Organization (hereafter cited as RG59 Panama. Labor). United States National Archives, College Park, MD. The Catholic Church did see lingering radicalism though. Fr. José Suárez, priest of Santa Ana parish – whose church sits just steps from the bandstand that was the focal point of violence the previous year – and editor of the newspaper *El Pueblo*, sent a list of suspected socialists, Communists, and anarchists working in the public education bureaucracy to the US legation in the Canal Zone. Of the twenty-five names he listed, only two were specifically identified for their political ideology: Azecar (a Chilean anarchist) and Federico Calvo (a Colombian anarchist). See J. G. South to Secretary of State in Washington Noting Enclosed "Memorandum of a Conversation" between Munro and Fr. José Suárez, Priest of Santa Ana Parish. 819.502/15 RG59 Panama. Labor.

[102] Report from J. G. South, December 17, 1929, from US Legation in the Panama Canal, Panama to Secretary of State, Washington, DC. 819.911 RG59 Panama. Labor.

[103] *El Mazo*, October 24, 1929, 4 and 6; October 27, 1925, 1–6.

attacked *El Mazo* as a threat to the Panamanian government, Leopoldino Cabrales B. replied that "we—secure in our libertarian ideals—attack without half measures every bourgeois and *yanqui* imperialist servile institution in Panama that tries to crush us."[104]

The newspaper's anarchist sensibilities perhaps were reflected most at the end of October, when the paper announced that the Blázquez de Pedro brothers' remains were coming home to Panama. "Eternal praise to those like J. M. Blázquez de Pedro who know how to be loyal to and sacrifice themselves for their ideals." The paper, along with "the revolutionary working-class organizations of this capital city" publicly welcomed and commemorated the return of their fallen heroes.[105] The two men were buried in Havana until 1929, when their remains were exhumed and transported to Panama City. There, they were buried in the same grave as their brother Bernave, who had died in late 1921 when the brothers had embarked on a new wave of radical union activism in the newly formed FORP – a wave of radicalism that led to this unhappy end.[106]

Ten years after José María Blázquez de Pedro's reburial in Panama City, Hollywood would immortalize an anarchist from Panama in *Five Came Back*. But the fictional anarchist Vásquez from the movie represents something quite real in the history of transnational anarchism in Panama and the Panama Canal Zone – a hemispheric sensibility, multinational in membership, bilingual in message and audience, and thus Pan-American in scope, deeds, and goals.

---

[104] Ibid., October 27, 1929, 6.   [105] Ibid.
[106] Franco Muñoz, *Blázquez de Pedro*, 199. Precise death dates are found on the tombstone in Panama City's Amador Cemetery.

7

Down but Not Out

Confronting Socialists, Communists, and Tropical Fascists, 1925–1934

> Everything has its end. Discontent is spreading. The political opposition to Machado is rising. And the worker, the one who has paid the most, is coming to the fore with his rebellious, devastating, iconoclastic spirit. And what happened yesterday to the Bourbon Dynasty perhaps is repeating itself tomorrow, even more so, with Machado and his republic.
>
> *Cultura Proletaria*, August 1931

The year 1925 could have been a pretty good year to be an anarchist in the Caribbean. True, anarchists in Puerto Rico and Florida were in decline, but they were rising in Cuba, Panama, and even in Venezuela and Colombia. In the latter, anarchists launched two newspapers in 1925 and 1926 – *Organización* and *Vía Libre* – and J. M. Gutiérrez Posada began communicating with Havana by sending articles to a new era of ¡*Tierra!*.[1] In Venezuela, by the mid-1920s, anarchists and syndicalists launched labor organizations in the Venezuelan oil fields.[2] Meanwhile, in Cuba, anarchists and Marxists joined forces to form the first truly islandwide labor organization – the Confederación Nacional de Obreros Cubanos (National Confederation of Cuban Workers, or CNOC). Rationalist schools with Marxist and anarchist cooperation existed around the island, and in Havana between 1924 and 1925 there

---

[1] ¡*Tierra!*, April 16, 1925, 3.
[2] Montes de Oca, *Contracorriente*, 103–105. See also, Paredes Goicochea, Diego, "El anarcosindicalismo colombiano de 1924–1928: hacia la claridad ideológica, táctica y organizativa" in *Pasado y presente del anarquismo y del anarcosindicalismo en Colombia*, ed. CILEP (Bogotá: CILEP, 2011), 115–129.

were six anarchist newspapers. Plus, anarchists and Marxists in Panama succeeded in organizing workers to challenge the Federación Obrera de la República de Panamá (the Workers Federation of the Republic of Panama, or FORP), the government, and the landlords. To top it all off, anarchists from throughout Latin America had plotted to land in Panama at the end of the year to form the first hemispheric anarchist congress. It could have been a good year.

But it wasn't. In the network's eastern node of Cuba, Gerardo Machado became president in May. He quickly unleashed a fascistic wave of terror against anarchists. Meanwhile, in the western node of Panama, the joint operations of the Panamanian government and the US Canal Zone authorities crushed the rent strike, undermined further anarchist organizing, and led to deportations of key international radicals. In September, more bad news arrived around the network: Pedro Esteve – a central figure in Spanish-speaking anarchist organizing in New York and Tampa since the 1890s and whose *Cultura Obrera* linked the Caribbean Basin with New York City – died.[3] With the deaths of Peter Kropotkin in 1921, Luisa Capetillo in Puerto Rico in 1922, and now Esteve in 1925, leading intellectual and activist lights were extinguished. It almost set the funereal stage for what was coming.

By the end of 1925, things had never looked grimmer for anarchists in the region. Yet, despite the disheartening events sweeping the Caribbean, signs of life remained, and the struggle continued. By 1926, Guatemalan anarchists led by Manuel Bautista Grajedo founded "Grupo Nueva Senda," organized indigenous sugar workers on the southern coast, and linked themselves to Cuba. Guatemalan anarchists led by Bautista Grajedo formed the Comité Pro-Acción Sindical (Pro-Action Union Committee, or CPAS) by 1928, drew eight of fourteen unions away from the Communist-dominated Federación Regional Obrera de Guatemala (Regional Worker Federation of Guatemala), and published *Orientación Sindical*. They reached out to the Caribbean network, informing comrades of their often-failed attempts to battle the United Fruit Company or organize workers.[4] In Costa Rica, the group "Vanguardia Proletaria" in Heredia, led by Joaquín Calvo Z., contacted the network in June 1928. In San José, the Agrupación Obrera de Estudios Sociales (Social Studies Labor Group) "Hacia la Libertad" published short-lived newspapers like

---

[3] *Cultura Obrera*, September 19, 1925, 1.
[4] *Cultura Proletaria*, May 12, 1928, 3; February 8, 1930, 3; Taracena Arriola, "Presencia anarquista en Guatemala," 10–13.

Germinación in late 1929.[5] That same year, a small group of leftists published *El Mazo* in Panama City. In Colombia, María Cano and Torres Giraldo worked within the labor movement in the country's oil and banana sectors, where they maintained contact with international anarchists and shaped growing militancy in these vital economic areas.[6]

In June 1929, anarchists like Álbin García and Rudolfo Lone in the United States launched a campaign to create a Federation of Spanish-Speaking Anarchists in North America. Both men worked with the Steubenville, Ohio group "Los Iconoclastos," but seventeen years earlier they had also worked together in the Canal Zone with M. D. Rodríguez. Using *Cultura Proletaria* as their organizing vehicle, they linked groups across the geographical reach of North America. Luis Barcia in Tampa and anarchists in Bayamón regularly sent money to the newspaper.[7] Money and columns arrived from Costa Rica, El Salvador, Mexico City, and Guatemala throughout the end of 1929.[8] Even Maximiliano Olay – the thirty-two-year-old, Spanish-born radical who had worked with Cuban and Puerto Rican anarchists in Tampa and who roomed with Manuel Pardiñas (the assassin of Spanish Prime Minister Canalejas in 1912) – was back in the transnational picture, working with the new federation.[9] In December 1931, Emiliano Ramos called on workers from the Panama Canal to Canada to join forces during the Depression in order to sustain *Cultura Proletaria*, better fund and support each other, and become a united front against the AFL.[10] The spirit of Pan-American anarchism continued.

This chapter focuses on the lingering anarchist presence in Puerto Rico and Cuba into the early years of the Great Depression. In Puerto Rico, longtime anarchist Emiliano Ramos did what he could to preserve an anarchist presence against the strengthening Socialist Party and the nationalist cause led by Pedro Albizu Campos while maintaining ever-dwindling linkages with the remaining anarchist network. In Cuba, anarchists suffered through years of the *machadato*, never relinquishing their hatred for the dictator, his US allies, and a growing number of foes in the Cuban Communist Party.

---

[5] *Germinación*, November 1929; *Cultura Proletaria*, June 16, 1928, 3.
[6] Mauricio Flórez Pinzón, "El final del movimiento autónomo: el anarquismo entre 1928–1930" in *Pasado y presente del anarquismo y del anarcosindicalismo en Colombia*, ed. CILEP (Bogotá: CILEP, 2011), 144–150.
[7] *Cultura Proletaria*, March 9, 1929, 4; July 6, 1929, 4; September 28, 1929, 4.
[8] Ibid., September 5, 1929, 4; October 26, 1929, 4; November 2, 1929, 4.
[9] Ibid., June 1, 1929, 3.   [10] Ibid., December 5, 1931, 2.

ANARCHISM IN PUERTO RICO

By 1923, numerous people who had flirted with anarchism to varying degrees in previous decades had become leading Socialist Party functionaries in Puerto Rico, including Alfonso Torres, Prudencio Rivera Martínez, José Ferrer y Ferrer, Epifanio Fiz Jiménez, and Pablo Vega Santos.[11] Despite the collapse of *El Comunista* in early 1921 and the gradual slide of many anarchists into the Socialist Party during the 1920s and early 1930s, several anarchists remained committed to the struggle. Emiliano Ramos not only was an elder statesman (if anarchists can be called "statesmen") of Puerto Rican and Caribbean anarchism. He had moved to Tampa at the beginning of the century, where he raised money for Havana's *¡Tierra!* in mid-1903 and sold copies of the paper to his Tampa colleagues.[12] In January 1904, Ramos moved to Havana, where he continued his militancy.[13] Two decades later in 1926, Ramos was living in Cayey, Puerto Rico when he began submitting regular columns to *Cultura Obrera*.

Over the years, Ramos repeatedly attacked the impact of the Socialist Party on the island's labor movement. While the party was not in political power, the fact that it engaged in electoral politics was enough to call it a sham representation of working people's desires. Ramos condemned the Socialists for not more vociferously attacking the dire state of the island's economy. The party did not want to bite the hand that fed it, that is Washington, illustrating how the Socialists "have been and are the most fervent Americanists on the island ... sanctioning all of the clumsiness and errors committed by the government in Washington."[14] Any anti-Americanism on the island sprang from the people responding to Yankee domination, not the Socialists who had conspired in that domination.[15] Instead, "Socialist methods have defrauded the hopes of the working people; they have converted the working class into a submissive, distrustful beast," Ramos argued.[16]

He then contrasted the Cuban labor movement in which anarchists and Marxists often worked together with the Puerto Rican movement. He

---

[11] *Partido Socialista: Comité Ejecutivo Territorial, San Juan, Puerto Rico. Actas desde Julio de 1923 hasta Diciembre de 1926.* See 161 and 174, for instance. CDOSIP, Fondo SIP.
[12] See, for instance, *¡Tierra!*, June 27, 1903, 4; August 1, 1903, 4; September 5, 1903, 4.
[13] *¡Tierra!*, July 16, 1904, 4; August 6, 1904, 4.
[14] *Cultura Obrera*, March 13, 1926, 3-4.   [15] *Cultura Proletaria*, April 23, 1927, 3.
[16] *Cultura Obrera*, March 20, 1926, 3.

noted that Cubans invited workers of different political and ideological tendencies to their meetings in the early 1920s. But such pan-leftist unity was absent in Puerto Rico. He recounted how in 1918 his local tobacco workers union voted to have Ramos represent them at a labor congress in Ponce. Yet, when he arrived at the congress, some delegates began murmuring about his presence. When he rose to challenge a proposed vote of confidence in the labor leadership, delegates voted to expel Ramos. Two tobacco workers picked him up by the arms and threw him into the street. "These Puerto Rican ideological sycophants are disciples of an ex-anarchist who here they call Iglesias; they are worse than the most bourgeois reactionaries; they have the appetites of [Spanish leader] Primo de Rivera and the cruelty of Mussolini."[17]

Ramos also confronted the Socialist Luis Muñoz Marín. Muñoz Marín's father had been an important political leader in the late 1800s, and the son followed his footsteps into politics so that in 1949 he would become Puerto Rico's first popularly elected governor. But long before then, he flirted with Socialist politics, supported and encouraged the Argentinean anarchist Julio Barcos on his way from Buenos Aires to Panama City, praised anarchists in *El Comunista*, and openly supported the Bolshevik Revolution.[18] As Ramos recalled, "we accepted this young man's revolutionary propaganda, reached out our hand of rebellion, and offered him our friendship. I was the only one who distrusted him a little," fearing he would be like so many "anarchists" who go on to abandon the cause. And now, just five years after the collapse of *El Comunista*, Muñoz Marín seemed to have abandoned all his radical views too and become a mainstream politician.[19]

In short, the Socialist Party and the Federación Libre de Trabajadores (Free Federation of Workers, or FLT) were parts of the problem, not a solution. For goodness's sakes, they even convinced federationists to raise money for a statue to Samuel Gompers for, in Ramos's words, "his meritorious work having consolidated the exploitation of national industrialism to benefit American industrialism."[20] Iglesias? Muñoz Marín? The island was increasingly home to traitors to social revolution and Puerto Rico's masses suffered as a result. Fed up with the Socialists, Ramos suggested in 1927 that what Puerto Rico really needed was the Industrial Workers of the World (IWW). While he was not overly pleased about what he saw as the centralizing tendencies of the IWW, "it is the

---

[17] Ibid., May 29, 1926, 3.   [18] Shaffer, *Black Flag Boricuas*, 161–166.
[19] *Cultura Obrera*, August 21, 1926, 3.   [20] *Cultura Proletaria*, April 20, 1929, 3.

labor organization of the North that I like best. Likewise, I am disposed to accept the creation of a branch of the IWW in the country and work for it." Did Puerto Ricans in the United States agree, he asked? If so, then a Wobbly organizer needed to be sent to the island soon – something that does not seem to have occurred.[21]

In 1930, Ángel María Dieppa – working with other leftists in New York – joined his old colleague Ramos to bemoan what Puerto Rico had become over three decades following the end of Spanish rule. In a series of columns to *Cultura Proletaria* titled "The Two Puerto Ricos," he described an island of wealth and tourism that lived side-by-side with immense poverty. And what had the Socialists done about this? Nothing. They had worked for over a decade in the government alongside bourgeois parties, but there was no socialism on the island. Rather, during this time "Puerto Rico has been converted into a vast Yankee factory. Churches of every sect and belief stand out in each barrio or municipality," while the Catholics seem to have spread everywhere faster than during the Spanish era. Why was this? He blamed the Socialist Party and Iglesias. Their role in helping to undermine anarchism in the 1910s removed the biggest anticlerical roadblock to the spread of Catholicism.[22]

In late July 1931, Ramos traveled to the old anarchist stronghold of Bayamón at the invitation of Ventura Mijón – an anarchist in Puerto Rico, New York and Tampa for over two decades and an original founder of *El Comunista* in 1920. After meeting with several comrades, they decided to create a new anarchist group – the first in five years – to spread propaganda among workers who, while already poor, were beginning to feel the added impact of the Great Depression. In August, the group formally met and claimed supporters across eastern Puerto Rico in San Juan, Caguas, and Humacao. Ramos urged supporters to hold public meetings and spread the word of rebellion against the complacent politicians.[23] The time for a new wave of anarchist organizing seemed right. Neither citizenship nor Socialists in the government had done anything to relieve Puerto Ricans' suffering. But by 1934, anarchism's long, if not very successful history had come to an end on the island. Perhaps no better symbolic event marked this death than the founding that year of the Puerto Rican Communist Party, where the

---

[21] Ibid., July 23, 1927, 3.   [22] Ibid., January 11, 1930, 3; February 1, 1930, 1.
[23] Ibid., August 15, 1931, 2. In June 1926, a group of twelve anarchists in Mayagüez sent money to *Cultura Obrera* for copies of the paper. *Cultura Obrera*, June 19, 1926, 3.

life-long anarchist Mijón signed the official communiqué announcing the party's formation.[24]

WITHER CUBAN ANARCHISM

Nine years earlier, a handful of Marxists organized the Partido Comunista Cubano (Cuban Communist Party, or PCC) in Havana. By 1925, the Comintern began to focus on Cuba and sent former Mexican anarchist Enrique Flores Magón to Havana. In August, and at Flores Magón's urging, radicals formed the PCC. Though Julio Antonio Mella – a fellow traveler with numerous anarcho-syndicalists – was chosen to be one of the PCC Central Committee's thirteen members, conflicts emerged, and Mella's independent streak led to conflict. In December, he began a hunger strike after Machado's government arrested him and several anarchist comrades, charging them with planting a bomb in the Payret Theater to protest the increasing government repression. The PCC opposed the hunger strike. In January 1926, Mella was released but his colleagues, like the anarchists Rafael Serra, Alfredo López, and Antonio Penichet, remained behind bars. Joint Communist and anarchist protests eventually saw the release of all other detainees later that month. But Mella was not in the clear. Because the PCC had opposed his hunger strike, it expelled him from the party – a move they reversed in 1927, but by that time Mella and a host of other Cuban radicals were in exile in Mexico City.[25]

If anarchists in Puerto Rico suffered from lack of working-class interest and the pull of political parties like the Socialist Party, anarchists in Cuba had very different concerns. They struggled not only for the life of the movement but also their very physical lives. Machado argued that his crackdown was part of a larger campaign to regenerate Cuba – regenerate it by "keeping the worker submissive and the Yankee imperialist owners of Cuba content," claimed *Cultura Obrera*.[26] While the role of Machado as a surrogate for Wall Street and Washington was a central theme in late-1920s anarchist portrayals of the island, some anarchists added one more feature to the mix: the haunting rise of European fascism. Transatlantic anarchists began fearing the specter of fascism as yet another in the seemingly endless waves of tyrannous ideologies out to destroy freedom.

---

[24] Silén, *Apuntes*, 98.
[25] Christine Hatzky, *Julio Antonio Mella (1903–1929), una biografía* (Santiago de Cuba: Editorial Oriente, 2008), 154–161, 188–189.
[26] *Cultura Obrera*, August 21, 1926, 3.

Between Mussolini's Fascist Italy, Primo de Rivera's fascism in Spain and Stalin's Communist Soviet Union, the global tide of freedom seemed to be in retreat. The emergence of Machado and his brutality against the left resulted in the inevitable associations of Machado with fascism. Once, Washington came to Cubans' aid against the murderer Weyler, wrote one columnist. But thirty years later, "the crimes of the new Cuban Weyler are without parallel in history while Washington sits by and does nothing." Meanwhile, the "fascist terror" of the "Cuban Mussolini" helped to hide Wall Street's crimes as "Cuban workers labor under the yoke of Wall Street's representative in the Antillean fiefdom and in poorer conditions than slaves in the Roman era."[27]

Nothing prepared the movement for the viciousness of the state's antiradical campaign. To escape violence befalling him, Domingo Mir – an anarchist active in Havana since the founding of the original *¡Tierra!* in 1902 – fled the capital in July 1925, moved across the island to Santiago de Cuba, and began communicating with anarchists in New York.[28] Native reporters on the island like Mir risked their safety to send columns abroad. After reading this coverage, the nascent Guatemalan movement professed solidarity with Cuba's anarchists and aligned with *Cultura Obrera*. From October to at least April the following year, Guatemalan anarchists sent money and columns from Quetzaltenango and Coatepeque in the western part of the country.[29] In a cry for fraternity, one Guatemalan writer drew a parallel with Cuba's War for Independence. What Machado had unleashed was no different than Weyler's butchery in the 1890s, when comrades were sent to Africa to perish in political prisons or "died tragically in the streets and jungles of Cuba."[30] It makes one wonder how an anarchist in the middle of Central America knew so well this nearly thirty-year-old Caribbean anarchist story.

One of the island's best-known anarchists was Alfredo López. In May 1926, he and his Socialist colleague Alejandro Barreiro were detained for distributing a pamphlet called "Los Obreros Cubanos y el Primero de Mayo" (Cuban Workers and May First).[31] Being arrested was nothing new for López. In the past, he had always been released. But in July, he

---

[27] Ibid., January 16, 1927, 4; "El Brazo Acusador de Bouzon: Las Víctimas del General Gerardo Machado." Centro Internacional, Amigos Internacionales de La Libertad. New York, July 1928. Max Nettlau Collection. Regions and Countries. Central and South America. Other Countries. Cuba, 1892–1928, folder 3404. IISG, Amsterdam.
[28] *Cultura Obrera*, July 24, 1925, 3.
[29] Ibid., October 16, 1926, 4; November 6, 1926, 3; April 9, 1927, 3.
[30] Ibid., November 20, 1926, 3. [31] Ibid., May 29, 1926, 3.

was again detained and disappeared for good. Soon, word of his disappearance spread to the transnational movement. *Cultura Obrera* ran a full front-page story on the disappearance, placing it in the context of an entire year's attacks on Cuban anarchists. The story included a photo of López and another of his wife Inocenta Betancourt with their young children.[32] International outrage soon followed. S. F. Marat offered some of the first on-the-ground anarchist reporting of López's disappearance, arguing that it wasn't just Machado who was to blame but also the "yellow unionists" like Juan Arévalo, Luis Fabregat, and Augustín Pérez who were government collaborators selling out anarchists. Oh, and was he angry! It was now time "to join our forces and our passions and practice an eye for an eye and a tooth for a tooth … When the autocracy plants terror and uses force to suppress the people's freedom, then the people must make use of these same weapons in order to demolish the tyranny and bring forth freedom. There is no other solution."[33]

From Puerto Rico, Emiliano Ramos became almost mystical about the repression in Cuba and López's fate. On October 20, 1926, a category 4 hurricane descended on Cuba, making landfall twice that day with winds reaching 240 km/h (150 mph), devastating Havana, destroying thousands of homes, killing as many as 600 people, and sinking numerous vessels in Havana's harbor. The steamer *Máximo Gómez* broke its moorings and crashed into other ships.[34] This steamer was important because the government was filling it with anarchists and Communists to be deported. For Ramos, something almost preternatural seemed to be happening. There was no doubt that workers suffered most from the devastation because their workplaces and homes were most likely to be destroyed. But maybe, just maybe, there was something more at work. "Perhaps the body or spirit of Alfredo López, thrown into the sea by Machado's goons, with a wire wrapped around his neck, agitated the waters to produce the catastrophe and claim vengeance on his murderer. Who knows?"[35] López had gone missing three months earlier, but his remains had yet to be found. Speculation was rife that he had been thrown into shark-infested waters, but no anarchist knew for sure.

---

[32] Ibid., August 28, 1926, 1 and 4.   [33] *Solidaridad*, September 18, 1926, 4.

[34] "Cuba Hurricanes Historic Threats," www.cubahurricanes.org/history-hurricanes-chronicles.php; "Documentation of Tropical Cyclone Changes," www.aoml.noaa.gov/hrd/hurdat/metadata_dec12.html.

[35] *Cultura Obrera*, November 27, 1926, 3. For examples of later descriptions of the expulsions of foreigners onto the ship, see *Solidaridad*, August 18, 1928, 1; January 19, 1929, 1.

Despite the anarchist near-universal hatred for all things spiritual, Ramos's tongue-in-cheek suggestion was one of the few bits of humor that anarchists enjoyed. The laughter didn't last long.

Perhaps the best-known anarchist labor leader on the island (and still alive, remarkably) was Antonio Penichet. In December 1926, he was sentenced to six months in jail for slandering Machado. Jail time wasn't the anarchists' worst fears for Penichet. What worried them more was that he was to serve his time not in Havana, but in the central Cuban city of Santa Clara. Anarchists feared that if such a transfer occurred, then Machado's men would shoot Penichet, claiming that he was trying to escape. With no witnesses around to claim otherwise, there would be no accountability and Penichet would be dead. They urged the international community to appeal to consulates and embassies to protect Penichet from such a fate. "Although we could not stop the murder of Varona or López or so many others who fell riddled with bullets or were hung in plain sight, at least we can try to stop this new crime against Penichet."[36]

Because of Penichet's stature in the history of the Cuban labor movement, even non-anarchists protested his arrest. Now in exile in Mexico City, Julio Antonio Mella urged his readers in *El Machete* to come to Penichet's rescue. Penichet and López had been instrumental in Mella's growth and understanding of working-class issues generally and anarchist ideas specifically when they worked together to create the Universidad Popular José Martí (José Martí Popular University) in Havana in 1923.[37] Writing for the Liga Internacional Pro-Luchadores Perseguidos (International League for Persecuted Combatants), Mella condemned Penichet's arrest. "Comrade Penichet should not be incarcerated; his life and activity are necessary for Cuban workers." He urged readers to protest until Penichet was released.[38] They did; he was.

It was not just the labor anarchists who fell victim to Machado; so did naturists. Naturism had a long life in Cuba. It had emerged in the early 1900s, largely intertwined with the anarchist movement and those who believed in the healing powers of nudism, vegetarian diets, and alternative health treatments. While some naturist doctors had been persecuted by the law for practicing medicine without a license, by and large the

---

[36] *Cultura Obrera*, December 18, 1926, 3; December 25, 1926, 4; January 8, 1927, 2.
[37] Hatzky, *Julio Antonio Mella*, 121–127.
[38] Raquel Tibol, *Julio Antonio Mella en EL MACHETE: Antología parcial de un luchador y su momento histórico* (Mexico City: Fondo de Cultura Popular, 1968), 322.

movement was popular enough to attract even non-anarchist figures. The naturist newspaper *Pro-Vida* published regularly in Havana, with little interruption for well over a decade.[39] But to Machado and his paranoia about all things anarchist, even naturists were possible targets for repression, as Aquilino López and Miguel Talens found out in May 1927 when they were jailed for one year for practicing medicine, naturism, and vegetarianism.[40] That same month, José María Blázquez de Pedro, who was working with the group Pro-Vida after his deportation from Panama, died from tuberculosis.

Sometimes anarchists got lucky. Since the early 1900s, a regular anarchist activist was Rafael Serra – El Abuelo (The Grandfather) as he came to be known. One of the few Afro-Cubans to play a key role in the movement, Serra had escaped the early years of Machado's persecution by hiding out in Santiago de las Vegas on the outskirts of Havana. This time, being known by a cop was a good thing for an anarchist. The town's police chief had once been a tobacco worker and had been friends with Serra since they were children. Knowing the plight of Cuba's anarchists, the police chief offered Serra his protection and helped to hide him ... a deception that worked until Machado's Secret Police found Serra and arrested him in mid-1928. He spent a week in jail before miraculously being released – possibly thanks to the intervention of his policeman friend.[41]

As years went by, Machado's government stopped at little to prevent the anarchist press from reorganizing on the island and international anarchist newspapers from arriving. Cubans were jailed merely for possessing copies of newspapers like *Cultura Obrera* and *Cultura Proletaria*.[42] Despite this, in 1931 *Cultura Proletaria* still found its way into places like Holguín in eastern Cuba, where anarchists were imprisoned for having it. While the paper criticized Machado endlessly, it also played the role of a transnational anarchist counterintelligence tool by publishing letters from Cuba about possible spies in their midst. When the paper reached Cuba and circulated surreptitiously, it alerted readers to be on their guard for certain *agents provocateurs*. For instance, in August 1931, the writer "Nijota" clarified for readers that a man who had been killed recently, and who was thought to be an anarchist, was a police informant.

---

[39] Shaffer, *Anarchism and Countercultural Politics*, 126–161.
[40] *Solidaridad*, May 14, 1927, 4.   [41] Ibid., July 21, 1928, 1.
[42] *Cultura Proletaria*, November 2, 1929, 1; November 16, 1929, 1; December 21, 1929, 1–2.

Nijota alerted anarchists to be on their guard as more spies were likely among them.[43]

Within this climate of state repression, Machado hosted the Sixth Pan-American Conference in 1928. On the eve of the conference, leftists attacked the absurd idea that all countries in the hemisphere were equal. How could they be if one (the United States) regularly used military force against its Latin neighbors? The regional anti-imperialist movement condemned both the conference and US actions in Nicaragua, where US Marines were combating the anarcho-syndicalist-inspired Augusto César Sandino. For the United States to promote Pan-Americanism in a country ruled by a vicious dictator (Cuba) while simultaneously using its military to attack a Latin American freedom fighter (Nicaragua) was the height of hypocrisy for the great democratic republic of the United States. From Mexico City, Julio Antonio Mella reported on an event at the opening of the conference in Havana's National Theater. As the conference got under way, groups throughout the theater shouted "Viva Sandino!" and "Death to imperialism!"[44] Throughout the conference, Mella railed against Machado and his repression in critiques identical to those made by anarchists still on the island or in exile in Mexico, Spain, and New York.[45]

Luis Aurelio, editor of the IWW's New York-based *Solidaridad*, attacked the conference too. Regional leaders professed their nationalism, but nationalism was a lie in the Caribbean, where the United States ruled supreme. What could reasonably come from this conference or any notion of Pan-Americanism? "Do you have any hope," asked Aurelio, "that the Conference celebrated in Havana would suggest some new political formula that would change the lives of their peoples?" While some might attack the Monroe Doctrine with a "racial political formula of *hispanoamericanismo* [i.e., Hispanic America vs. North America] in these same countries," too often those proclaiming a *hispanoamericano* sentiment were those who used force against their own countrymen just to gain power – and then become Wall Street lackeys; in short, the banana republic syndrome. Ultimately, neither "Monroe-ism, Pan-Americanism, nor Hispano-Americanism will solve the problems of oppression and

---

[43] Ibid., January 31, 1931, 1; August 8, 1931, 2.
[44] Tibol, *Julio Antonio Mella en EL MACHETE*, 190.
[45] A good place to see this is in the section on Mella's writing about "El Imperialismo Norteamericano" and the AFL's pan-Americanism in Tibol, *Julio Antonio Mella en EL MACHETE* (Mexico City: Fondo de Cultura Popular, 1968), 169–251.

tyranny that Hispanic-Americans face at the hands of their directors and their foreign directors." Rather, "the people have to orient themselves along another path contrary to the political one" that "has no limitations based on borders or races ... Humanism."[46]

Meanwhile, some anarchists labeled the meeting the "VI Conference of Pan ... of Wall Street." Writing from Santiago de Cuba, "John Smith" lamented that the rest of the Americas continued to play this game of Pan-Americanism with Washington even while knowing the reality. In Puerto Rico, Emiliano Ramos noted how one attendee after another spoke in "elevated tones of cordiality," but in the end "Nicaragua, Cuba, Santo Domingo, Haiti, and Puerto Rico are just glorious trophies of the Northern vandals."[47] Of course, anarchists knew full well what was happening. This was a meeting of collusion between imperial power, native lackeys, and transnational corporations ("Wall Street," in anarchist parlance then as today) that operated in the region. "We know all of the outrages committed by the sugar trust in Cuba, the oil trust in Mexico, Venezuela, and Colombia, the fruit trust in all of the Central American nations" and expect nothing beneficial to come from the conference, concluded *Solidaridad*.[48]

Transnational capitalist and governmental collusion were bad enough. But it was even worse when former radicals for the anarchist cause had become central supporters of this brand of Pan-Americanism. Take, for instance, Orestes Ferrara. As one recalls from earlier chapters, the former Italian anarchist based out of Tampa and who went to Cuba to fight against Spain had after the war become a lawyer and politician. In 1908, he defended anarchist Abelardo Saavedra in a Havana court against charges that he defamed Mexican President Díaz. Yet, look at Ferrara in 1928. What was one to make of him? A Cuban correspondent to *Cultura Proletaria* called Ferrara the chief proponent of US interventionism – someone who "considers Yankee intervention in Latin American countries as a cordial act of charity." The charge seemed reasonable, since the former anarchist was now Machado's ambassador to Washington and both were Liberal Party leaders who acted like "two debt collecting mannequins for Wall Street."[49]

---

[46] *Solidaridad*, July 9, 1927, 2; February 18, 1928, 1 and 4.
[47] *Cultura Proletaria*, February 4, 1928, 1.   [48] *Solidaridad*, January 21, 1928, 1.
[49] *Cultura Proletaria*, March 10, 1928, 3. The Cuban diatribe against Ferrara mirrored Ramos's attack against Santiago Iglesias as a former anarchist who sold out the movement and its men and women to become "a colonial Senator [in the island legislature] for the socialist gang" and a "perpetual delegate of the American Federation of Labor."

Throughout all of this, anarchists resorted to a campaign they had been forced to practice too often over the decades: raising money for the wives and children of anarchist victims of oppression. By late 1928, *Cultura Proletaria* was experiencing something like a financial boom. By December it was doing something that anarchist newspapers rarely did: running in the black and significantly so. This could only happen if lots of money was arriving. This had implications for their Cuban comrades. The editors opened a "Pro-Prisoner and Persecuted" fundraising campaign to help those suffering under the *machadato*. By year's end, they had raised over $463.[50] Meanwhile, Antonio Penichet again was harassed by authorities. The Secret Police arrested him, and before he could say goodbye to his wife and children he was whisked to a boat and deported to Mexico. Establishing himself in the home of Latin American political refugees – Mexico City – he began to live in exile with other Cuban anarchists and Marxists like Mella. Penichet's *compañera* wanted to go with the couple's children to Mexico. In August, New York's anarchists began raising money to help her and other spouses leave Cuba to be with their partners abroad.[51]

Over the next couple of years, Penichet involved himself in exile politics in Mexico City. He worked with Mella in the Asociación de Nuevos Emigrados Revolucionarios de Cuba (Association of New Revolutionary Emigrants from Cuba, or ANERC), an organization that Mella had founded in early 1928 and that included a range of Communists and anarchists from the island. The work against Machado and imperialism was reminiscent of their work a few years earlier when the two, along with Alfredo López, had brought together students and workers into a growing force for radical leftist change on the eve of Machado's election. Inspired in part by Sandino's anti-imperialism in Nicaragua and the history of Cuba's War for Independence, Mella hoped to lead an exile invasion of Cuba to overthrow Machado and by extension beat back US imperialism. His colleagues in ANERC became the leaders of this initiative, including Penichet, Penichet's old friend and Socialist ally in the

---

Cultura Obrera, May 1, 1926, 2. And Iglesias had no love lost for the anarchists like Ramos. In September 1922, Iglesias attacked anarchism in Cuba, blaming anarchists for capitalism's success in Cuba, then suggesting that their old, ineffective tactics had led to "the surrender of the laboring classes" in Cuba. See "'Cuba and Porto Rico Are...' Letter that Should be Read by Socialists and Anarchists," September 4, 1922. Erick José Pérez Collection. Box 1, Folder 1. IISG, Amsterdam.

[50] *Cultura Proletaria*, December 22, 1928, 1.

[51] *Solidaridad*, August 4, 1928, 3; *Cultura Proletaria*, August 25, 1928, 1.

Cuban labor movement Alejandro Barreiro, and Sandalio Junco (an Afro-Cuban syndicalist and secretary of the PCC before fleeing to Mexico in 1927). In May 1928, they claimed in their newspaper *Cuba Libre* that they embodied the spirit of the 1895 revolutionaries: "*¡Cuba Libre, para los trabajadores!* [Free Cuba, for the workers!]. This is the only way to apply the principles of the Revolutionary Party of 1895 to 1928. For the rural and urban workers, for the intellectual and manual workers, for all those who are exploited and struggle to improve their condition."[52] As historian Christine Hatzky concludes, "with the ANERC, Mella ... was looking to link national liberation with social revolution."[53] Of course, this was exactly the anarchist rationale and goal for supporting the War for Independence in the 1890s: Transnational anti-imperialism would liberate the island and create a free, egalitarian working-class Cuba. It wasn't working any better in 1928 than it did in 1898.

Late in the evening of January 10, 1929, as Mella walked home with his companion Tina Modotti, one of Machado's goons assassinated him. His Mexico City funeral two days later brought forth the entire Cuban exile community. Speaking on behalf of ANERC, Penichet recalled Mella's life in Cuba, especially his enlightened years as a university student when he ventured into the Workers Centers, "never again returning to the bourgeois class from which he had come." Linking Mella to recent Cuban history, Penichet called him "the successor of Martí" who "not only brought fear to Machado and his henchmen but also to the governing class of the United States because it knew that Mella was capable of leading the liberating movement against imperialism." But Mella was more than just the new Martí. Upon hearing the news of the assassination, Penichet had declared that "they have killed the Sandino of Cuba."[54]

In Puerto Rico, Emiliano Ramos feared that Mella's murder was part of a larger transnational plot against radicals that he suspected involved his own planned demise. Years later, he recalled how two days after Mella's assassination, he was walking home late one night in the rain. As he crossed the street toward his house, he believed someone tried to murder him. The timing and method, he claimed, were designed to make it look like an accident, but he was convinced that the "rural *caciquismo*

---

[52] Hatzky, *Julio Antonio Mella*, 288–293. Quote included in Hatzky, 293.
[53] Ibid., 295.
[54] Quoted from a reproduction of speeches in Tibol, *Julio Antonio Mella en EL MACHETE*, 359; Hatzky, *Julio Antonio Mella*, 208, 243.

[local political despotism] of this municipality attempted to stop my life as a fighter."[55]

The repression unleashed by Machado made organizing nearly impossible in Cuba. But anarchists kept trying. By mid-1928, the Federation of Tobacco Leaf Strippers was publishing *Trabajo* while anarchists in Havana began publishing the magazine *Inquietud*. The publications were sent around Cuba and abroad, reaching Ramos in Puerto Rico. Both publications also issued calls for renewed opposition to the government; both seemed to have survived only a little while.[56] Víctor Muñoz admitted that organizing was difficult since it was almost impossible to publish any anarchist material in Cuba.[57] On occasion, small anarchist groups did announce their organization – a move that always carried considerable risk, especially when people listed their names. In 1929, activists formed the Comité Revolucionario Proletario de Cuba (Cuban Revolutionary Proletariat Committee) in Havana and two years later there emerged a Comité Pro-Presos Libertarios (Pro-Anarchist Prisoners Committee).[58]

By 1931, widespread outrage against Machado began to spread across Cuba. Perhaps the end was near, or, so hoped the editors of *Cultura Proleteria*, who reminded readers – especially those in Cuba who were somehow still getting the paper – that even Weyler's butchery had come to an end.

Everything has its end. Discontent is spreading. The political opposition to Machado is rising. And the worker, the one who has paid the most, is coming to the fore with his rebellious, devastating, iconoclastic spirit. And what happened yesterday to the Bourbon Dynasty perhaps is repeating itself tomorrow, even more so, with Machado and his republic.[59]

In February 1932, the anarchist group Alba Roja organized in the central Cuban city of Camagüey. Soon after, the group Pensamiento y Acción, based in Havana and Casablanca, announced their affiliation with the Federation of Cuban Anarchist Groups (FGAC), while the anarchist-led Ateneo Popular began to coordinate actions by April.[60] The Federation spent equal time attacking the Cuban Communist Party, fascism, and Machado – linking all three together as they did in mid-1932 when their definition of fascism included the "hateful, antihuman, true tyranny" in

---

[55] *Cultura Proletaria*, January 30, 1932, 4.   [56] Ibid., May 12, 1928, 3.
[57] Ibid., September 28, 1929, 1; January 11, 1930, 2.
[58] Ibid., November 16, 1929, 1; April 11, 1931, 3.   [59] Ibid., June 6, 1931, 1.
[60] Fernández, *Cuban Anarchism*, 57–58; *Cultura Proletaria*, February 2, 1932, 1; April 16, 1932, 2; November 12, 1932, 2.

Moscow.[61] Like Ramos's constant attacks on the Socialist Party in Puerto Rico for deceiving the working class, Havana's anarchists followed suit and blamed the PCC for much of the workers' ills, not the least of which was the way the PCC now supposedly dominated the CNOC while purging anarchists from the organization: "According to the communist-fascist philosophical concept or conception of those who plunder the CNOC and the Soviet government's theories as well, the worker can be nothing more than a slave, cannot nor should be free ... *Compañeros*, Cuban workers, if you want to perpetuate your condition as slaves, join and vote for the Communist Party."[62] They argued that the Communists could only do this if Machado let them, implying something resembling collusion.

Machado's government tried to shut down wide-scale opposition from 1931 to 1933, caring little about the scale of violent repression. Anarchists of course tried to resist, but the violence was overwhelming. While acknowledging they wanted to do more to fight back, "they are ferociously persecuted ... and fully expect to be jailed on even the slightest pretext," wrote one sympathizer.[63] By 1933, Machado was losing favor with both the United States and the Cuban military. Organized labor stepped into this new opening and launched a series of strikes. Antonio Penichet had returned from exile and been elected to the general strike committee of the Federación Obrera de la Habana (Havana Workers Federation, or FOH). With Cuba in full rebellion during the 1933 Revolution, workers throughout the island employed direct action. Striking sugar workers led mill occupations, converting many into soviets – decentralized organs of power and decision-making that were a far cry, in anarchist eyes, from the centralization of the modern Communist movement rooted in Moscow. The rapid spread of these occupations and calls for decentralized decision-making across the sugar zones illustrated the continued anarcho-syndicalist influences of direct action and local autonomy in Cuba – even if widespread anarchist organization was lacking.[64]

In mid-1933, the United States attempted to reconcile tensions between Machado and the capitalist class. Many hoped this would lead to peace,

---

[61] *Cultura Proletaria*, May 21, 1932, 2.
[62] Ibid., November 26, 1932, 2; Fernández, *Cuban Anarchism*, 57.
[63] *Cultura Proletaria*, August 27, 1932, 2.
[64] Sam Dolgoff, *The Cuban Revolution: A Critical Perspective* (Montreal: Black Rose Books, 1977), 48; Barry Carr, "Mill Occupations and Soviets: The Mobilisation of Sugar Workers in Cuba 1917–1933," *Journal of Latin American Studies* 28 (1996): 156–157.

an end to the repression, and a return of certain constitutional liberties. But anarchists urged caution: Was this little more than a way for Machado to pacify the bourgeois opposition who had begun to abandon him? Was this just another way to deceive workers? "Cuban workers need to take advantage of their acquired experiences and from this moment continue the true struggle against the man and the government that had spilled so much innocent blood." Anarchists needed to reclaim their leading roles in the labor organizations to fulfill this revolutionary duty.[65] There could be no compromise that allowed Machado to stay in power or that equally benefited the bourgeoisie.

Soon, widespread strikes began to destabilize the government. In late July 1933, anarchists supported a transportation strike called by the CNOC. The economy stopped, and now Machado found himself increasingly reviled and isolated by most sectors of the Cuban economy. But anarchists soon found themselves victimized by both old enemies (Machado) and old allies (the Communist Party and the CNOC). With a general strike holding in early August, Machado sought a militarized solution. On August 8, he issued Decree 1147, creating a national militia. Strikers were machine-gunned on the streets of Havana. Meanwhile, Communists and anarchists, who had been precarious allies and persecuted together during the Machado years, now attacked each other. In the waning days of the *machadato*, anarchists accused members of the PCC of working clandestinely with Machado's Secret Police to end the strike and purge all anarchist presence from the unions. As a result, Communist–anarchist tensions and suspicions increased.[66]

On August 11, a military revolt forced Machado's hand. Anarchists greeted Machado's fall in August 1933 with ambivalence. On one hand, dating back to the Bolshevik Revolution, here was – at least to some degree – a unity of purpose that joined the Cuban Army and the working class against a dictatorship. Yet, while happy to see their old enemy gone, his fall had resulted from the connivance of Washington and Wall Street, which believed that Machado had outlived his usefulness as a ruler. The editors of *Cultura Proletaria* likened the events to the Cuban War for Independence. In both instances, Cubans had revolted against a barbaric government that butchered the island's residents. Then, the United States became involved to satisfy its own interests. "Those today who praise the

---

[65] *Cultura Proletaria*, June 24, 1933, 1.
[66] Mirta Rosell, ed., *Luchas obreras contra Machado* (Havana: Editorial de Ciencias Sociales, 1973), 273; Fernández, *Cuban Anarchism*, 58.

people as heroes of the moment are nothing more than the unconscious instruments of the spectacular handiwork of Roosevelt and the Wall Street bankers." They particularly took US President Franklin Roosevelt to task. After all, he had pledged repeatedly that the United States would refrain from engaging in the internal affairs of Latin America. Now, Cubans had risen to determine their own fate as they had in 1895, but Roosevelt had stepped in to control the day as did the United States in 1898, making sure that the popular insurrection did not go too far. Roosevelt's actions, like those in 1898, illustrated "that the interest of American bankers and their imperialist aspirations are of higher interest than the interests of independence and freedom of Hispanic peoples." Anarchists had to continue to fight. "In Cuba there has not been a revolution but a reaction to the intolerable state of things ... Anarchists in Cuba, CONTINUE TO FAN THE FLAMES. The Cuban land is prepared, the furrow is open for intense, systematic, and tireless propaganda."[67]

Following Machado's departure on August 12, the anarchists and Communists ratcheted up their antagonistic rhetoric against one another. Soon, though, the two camps called a truce. On August 24, the remains of Alfredo López and other labor leaders were found in the stables at the Atarés Castle in Havana. Radicals from all camps filed through the streets to Colón Cemetery to bury López. At the cemetery, representatives from different labor organizations spoke. Antonio Penichet spoke as the family's representative.[68] However, the truce was temporary. Communists accused anarchists of being "reformists" and willing to work with the interim government: The "Executive of the Havana Workers Federation, has helped and is helping the leaders of the bourgeois opposition and its provisional government, in conjunction with the anarchist rats of the Ateneo Popular ... and the rest of the traitors to the interests of the working class who are colluding and trying to destroy" the CNOC.[69] On August 27, armed Communists shot up the anarchist-dominated FOH. One anarchist was killed, and several were wounded. Such actions, argued the anarchist FGAC, were devised to purge anarchists from the labor movement as well as to provoke a US military intervention that could prop up the provisional government with which the PCC was

---

[67] *Cultura Proletaria*, August 19, 1933, 1. Most historians now call the fall of Machado the "1933 Revolution." Anarchists would question what was so "revolutionary" about it.
[68] Evelio Tellería Toca, "Alfredo López," *Bohemia*, October 27, 1972.
[69] Rosell, *Luchas obreras contra Machado*, 277–280.

colluding. Anarchists responded on August 28. The FGAC issued a manifesto detailing its version of a treacherous alliance between the PCC and Machado during the strike. Anarchists claimed that the Bolshevik takeover of the CNOC was to be feared by all who "have an interest in surmounting the current social state, who struggle sincerely for a society free of tyrants from above and below" because the PCC and CNOC's "slanderous propaganda" was full of lies designed to get workers to turn on anarchists.[70] In short, both anarchists and Communists used the charge of government collaboration to justify their actions against the other.

From September 1933 to January 1934, Ramón Grau San Martín ruled as the new Cuban president. Anarchist elements who had survived continued to organize in small groups but with little impact around the island. A short-lived edition of ¡Tierra!, now in its third phase and edited by Fausto Ballagas, began publishing as the official voice of the FGAC in October 1933.[71] Anarchists old and new continued to associate with the newspaper, including Penichet. Penichet was still revered among colleagues and praised in late 1933 when he refused a distinguished position as director of the *Boletín de la Secretaría del Trabajo* in the new government. In fact, his short novel *El soldado Rafael* – which had so concerned government intelligence officers in the United States and Cuba fifteen years earlier – was still in print and sold through the pages of ¡Tierra!.[72]

Through its pages, anarchists continued to make their case and attempted to deprive the PCC of one of its own when ¡Tierra! coopted – or should we say "liberated" – Julio Antonio Mella from the Communists. ¡Tierra! ran a biography of Mella with the subtitle "Libertarian Communist," recalling how Mella always worked well with and respected his anarchist colleagues, even if they did not always agree on the role of the Third International or the dictatorship of the proletariat. As Juan de Alcántara concluded, when Mella was in Mexico, he wrote to Havana's anarchists and praised them for "always being the first." While the Communists now remembered Mella in authoritarian terms as their "leader," their "chief," their "caudillo," the anarchists remembered Mella in egalitarian terms as a "brother, a cordial friend, a fraternal *compañero*."[73]

---

[70] "Manifiesto" August 28, 1933 published in *Cultura Proletaria*, September 9, 1933, 1–2; Fernández, *Cuban Anarchism*, 58–59.
[71] *Cultura Proletaria*, October 23, 1933, 1; ¡Tierra!, November 10, 1933, 1, for example.
[72] ¡Tierra!, November 10, 1933, 1; January 10, 1934, 3.
[73] *Cultura Proletaria*, March 10, 1934, 2.

But anarchists suffered again. In January 1934, a coalition of right-wingers and Cuban soldiers led by Fulgencio Batista overthrew the Grau government. When the United States recognized the new government, anarchists again found themselves on the wrong end of history, and those old refrains about Cuba–United States governmental cooperation for the interests of capital – refrains dating to the immediate post-Independence War writings of Luis Barcia, Adrián del Valle, and Errico Malatesta – retained their historical significance and continued accuracy. To anarchists, the year's events that saw the end of the tyrant, the rise of the rival PCC to some level of political acceptance, a new coup showcasing the military's strength, and the US oversight of it all was too much. What Cubans really wanted, wrote one anarchist, was "rice and beans with the least amount of politics possible and without dictators in the kitchen."[74] No luck. ¡Tierra! folded, and the same year Ventura Mijón joined the Communist Party in Puerto Rico.

[74] Ibid., November 4, 1933, 1; December 2, 1933, 1.

A Literary Epilogue
Marcelo Salinas and Adrián del Valle, 1920s–1930s

> For him, seeing your work, there was something that was obvious: art is power. Only that, or especially that: power. Not to control countries and change societies, to cause revolutions or oppress others. It is the power to touch the souls of men and, incidentally, place there the seeds of their improvement and happiness.
> Leonardo Padura's *Heretics*

> Rational Culture disseminated among the working class by means that facilitate knowledge and truth will emancipate all who fall under tyranny and bring complete individual sovereignty rooted in collective freedom.
> Jaime Vidal, *Risveglio* (Tampa), October 1916

If by the late 1920s and early 1930s Caribbean anarchists were on the ropes in political and labor struggles, anarchists in Cuba remained quite active in at least one realm: the literary struggle. In fact, anarchist authors Marcelo Salinas and Adrián del Valle saw their publishing careers thrive. And they did so at the very moment that their comrades were being hunted down, exiled, jailed, or murdered. As the *machadato* was bent on destroying anarchists throughout Cuba, del Valle and Salinas continued to live, write, and publish in Havana. They kept alive an anarchist sensibility for readers in Cuba and abroad by publishing their nonfiction, fiction, and plays, even receiving widespread recognition for their literary exploits.

Since the 1890s, the Catalonian-born del Valle had been a leading voice in the anarchist movement as a columnist, advocate for naturism, editor, playwright, and fiction writer. Two years into Machado's regime in mid-1927, del Valle was feted at a literary conference in Havana – an

FIGURE E.1 Marcelo Salinas (circa 1928 with the publication of *Alma Guajira*). He and Adrián del Valle (in the late *machadato* years) enjoyed literary success at the very moment their comrades in Cuba were under threat by the Machado government.
Biblioteca Nacional de Cuba (Havana)

event celebrated in the pages of New York's Industrial Workers of the World (IWW) newspaper, *Solidaridad*.[1] In September 1929, he won top prize from the Cuban Academy of History for a work of nonfiction. In early 1928, the Cuban-born Salinas (Figure E.1) received an award for his play "Alma Guajira" (Soul of the Peasant) – an award not without controversy. Third place went to the American Federation of Labor (AFL) representative in Cuba, Carlos Loveira, who said Salinas was a Spaniard and should be ineligible for the prize. It was probably more political than that. But the honor also divided anarchists when they discovered it was awarded at a luncheon attended by Machado himself.[2] Still, the play was so popular that it was turned into a screenplay and shortly thereafter in April 1929 converted to celluloid, when Mario Orts

---

[1] *Solidaridad*, July 9, 1927, 4.
[2] Ibid., March 3, 1928, 1; MLCE, ed., *Marcelo Salinas, Un ideal sublime y elevado* (Miami: Ediciones del Movimiento Libertario Cubano en el Exilio, 1977), 28–29.

Ramos directed the film version, making *Alma Guajira* possibly the first movie written by an American anarchist. Then, two years after the 1933 Revolution, Salinas again earned recognition for his literary achievements when the Ministry of Education acclaimed his now forgotten novel *Un aprendiz de revolucionario* (An Apprentice Revolutionary).[3]

These were men of immense imagination. One had to be to fight for a cause for so long that must have seemed hopeless more times than not. Imagination is a strong impulse. It must be in a revolutionary who fights (in word or action) to overturn so many forms of authoritarianism and create a radically imagined world of freedom, cooperation, and equality while under frequent duress. Anarchist cultural productions exemplified the anarchist revolutionary imagination. In this imagining of the past, the present and the future, del Valle and Salinas created an art form – like Leonardo Padura's character – designed to empower people to understand their world, improve themselves, promote happiness, and lead more humane lives, the basis for sustained revolutionary change.

Del Valle's fiction was transnational as it was published and distributed throughout the networks. In addition, while he centered many of his stories in Cuba, he also created fictional settings any reader in Spain, Latin America, Tampa, or New York could envision, and thus the stories helped to create a transnational revolutionary imaginary for readers wherever they were read. Salinas's fiction, though, was thoroughly "Cuban." For a man who traveled along the US eastern seaboard, Spain, and Cuba, it strikes one that he would create such a Cuba-centered world. But his stories and plays take readers to specific rural Cuban locations or walk them through the streets, intersections, and parks of Havana. In addition, Salinas's dialogue is rooted in the vernacular of Cuban Spanish.

Salinas's "Alma Guajira" originally was staged by the Compañia Dramática Camila Quiroga on January 28, 1928 in Havana's Payret Theater. Eventually it was performed in Havana's National Theater – a great irony since anarchists had been arrested nearly a decade earlier for planting a bomb in that same theater during a performance of Verdi's *Aida* by Italian tenor Enrico Caruso. Why bomb the opera? To protest the arrest of anarchists, including Salinas, just weeks before. Salinas's play lacks any overt political statements, but that does not mean it wasn't political. In three acts, we witness a campesino family deal with love,

---

[3] MLCE, *Marcelo Salinas, Un ideal sublime y elevado*, 10; "Santiago de las Vegas en Líneas," http://sdlv.blogspot.com/2008/02/teatro-santiaguero-alma-guajira.html.

betrayal, and murder in the name of honor. Charito is a young woman adopted as a child by Don Lico. Don Lico's biological son, Juan Antonio, desires her, but she rejects any romantic relationship with him because he is essentially her brother. The spurned Juan Antonio accuses Charito of really desiring the Spaniard Zaragosa. Meanwhile, her closest friend and adopted sister Lolita desires Florencio, whom Don Lico despises. After a party, Florencio is murdered. Blame initially falls on Zaragoza, who earlier had been fighting with Florencio. But soon it is revealed that Don Lico had confronted Florencio after the party, accusing Florencio of bringing dishonor to his family for his pursuit of Lolita. When Florencio charged him with a knife, Don Lico shot him twice. Guilt, pride, and honor lead Don Lico to turn himself in to the rural guard. By the third act, with dad in jail, accusations fly around Charito, including that Juan Antonio had been her first boyfriend, but then abused her and she rejected him – maybe for Zaragosa. One day, Juan Antonio meets Zaragosa at a bar, and the former refuses to drink with the latter; both move to fight one another until the bar owner steps in. Charito later confronts Juan Antonio and says to let it go – Zaragosa is not the enemy here – but of course the jilted lover cannot do it. If he doesn't fight Zaragosa, then everyone would see him as a coward. The two men then confront each other, but when Charito tries to intervene, Zaragosa shoves her into the wall. In the end, Charito leaves to go far away and follow her destiny without these two macho yahoos holding her back.[4]

Some could read the story as a feminist work – maybe anarcho-feminism. Charito – originally the play was titled "Charito" – is strong, independent, and unwilling to play the game of domesticity or honor. When the two men who desire her the most begin to fight for her, she's had enough of the stupidity and rejects them both. Now, she's leaving to pursue her own life. Charito is a young woman who spurns a "Spaniard" and a "Cuban" to take an independent path that she decides for herself. Without doubt, there is an element of political allegory in that rejection and path forward. In another sense, as historian Mario Castillo observes, the play offers a realistic life of 1920s rural Cubans. Salinas neither portrays *guajiros* as a rural-peasant-for-comedy source (i.e., backward buffoons), nor does he put these peasants on a pedestal and offer them as noble rural Cubans who embody the essence of the island that all should follow. Rather, they suffer everyday challenges, exude unsavory

---

[4] Marcelo Salinas, "Alma Guajira" in *Teatro Cubano Contemporaneo*, ed. D. Martí de Cid (Madrid: Aguilar, 1962), 387–448.

characteristics, and live unremarkable lives – like most people. Nothing simple or boilerplate here; nothing honorific either.[5]

The question remains, how could an anarchist and his play be acknowledged publicly by Machado during this time of political persecution? There is little that directly cries "anarchist" about the storyline. One suspects Machado might have been playing the anarchist in order to prop up the dictator's own image. The play opened just twelve days after the 1928 Pan-American Conference of Foreign Ministers began. In late February as the foreign ministers' conference was concluding, Machado attended the awards luncheon. Was Machado trying to put on a civilized face by recognizing a play by the political opposition just at the time he was crushing anarchists? Was this a way to show the world that radical criticisms of his regime were overblown? Certainly, this is what Salinas's anarchist critics thought, and they accused Salinas of playing along and not saying anything by having lunch with the dictator.

If in 1928 Salinas refrained from an openly political play, by the 1930s after Machado fell, Salinas placed politics and ideology front-and-center. Completed in 1935, the novel *Un aprendiz de revolucionario* begins in the last years of the Machado dictatorship and places the political intrigues of various opposition forces both before and after Machado's fall at the center of the story. The novel opens with the two revolutionaries Facundo and Manolo Mesa hiding on a ranch in rural Santa Clara, trying to avoid Machado's security forces. The ranch overseer is Justo García, a former combatant in the War for Independence who is quick to disabuse his new guests about political ambitions of revolutionaries: Average men and women had gained nothing from the so-called revolution of the 1890s.[6] In the midst of this political story line is a sexual one. The married Mesa makes several awkward, though welcomed, advances on the young Emilia, who lives at the cattle ranch where our revolutionaries are hiding.[7] But another revolutionary – Nicolás – saw Mesa and Emilia kissing. He then blackmails Mesa to keep the secret – perhaps symbolic of the backstabbing by fellow revolutionaries during the *machadato*.[8]

Eventually, news arrives of increasing political repression in the capital, with constant fights between the police and the people.[9] The time has come, Mesa decides, and the two fugitives unite with three others,

---

[5] I want to thank historian Mario Castillo in Havana for sharing some of his insights into Salinas and his works.
[6] Marcelo Salinas, *Un aprendiz de revolucionario* (El Fígaro: Havana, 1937), 55–56.
[7] Ibid., 22–24.   [8] Ibid., 30–33.   [9] Ibid., 51.

including Nicolás, to join the struggle. But one night Nicolás gets drunk and begins talking about Emilia and Mesa, sparking a fight that leads to Mesa shooting and killing Nicolás.[10] Meanwhile, Mesa discovers that García has been arrested for wandering around rebel zones looking for Mesa after the old man found out about him and Emilia. Wracked by the guilt of pseudoadultery, García's imprisonment, and the murder of Nicolás, and coupled with a growing awareness that things are not going well for rebels in Santa Clara, Mesa makes plans to leave Cuba. By the end of part one, we find him on the coast, boarding a ship that takes him into exile in Mexico – not unlike many of Salinas's colleagues.[11]

Part two opens two years later in 1933, as Mesa returns to Cuba immediately after the fall of Machado's government in August when, from September 1933 to January 1934, the provisional government of activists, students, intellectuals, and low-ranking soldiers ruled the country.[12] Salinas describes the fake revolutionaries who want to shape the new government – people united in opposition to Machado but who now seem to have changed one set of leaders for another with no real changes for the people.[13] One day Mesa has lunch with former revolutionaries in a mansion in the ritzy Havana neighborhood of Vedado. Political power is all everyone seems to discuss. Ultimately, "this couldn't be the Revolution," concludes the narrator.[14] A frustrated Mesa attends a meeting of the political coalition responsible for taking down the dictatorship. The first speaker talks about the necessity of creating a bourgeois democracy for Cuba. A very small handful of men praise a Communist speaker. Mesa rejects both. Then an old, black anarchist named Sierra speaks. Salinas seems to have modeled the character after his friend and longtime Afro-Cuban anarchist Rafael Serra. The fictional Sierra attacks the idea that Cuba's future should be guided by the bourgeoisie or the dictatorship of the proletariat, and then launches into a verbal assault against Soviet-style governments. Communists in the audience shout at Sierra, calling him a "liar," "yellow," and a "reactionary." One cries out that once the Communists come to power, the anarchists' heads "would be the first to fall." To Mesa, Sierra's ideas didn't seem so bad.[15]

---

[10] Ibid., 71.   [11] Ibid., 99–104.
[12] For an excellent analysis of this time, see Robert Whitney, *State and Revolution in Cuba: Mass Mobilization and Political Change, 1920–1940* (Chapel Hill: University of North Carolina Press, 2001).
[13] Salinas, *Un aprendiz de revolucionario*, 109.   [14] Ibid., 115–119.
[15] Ibid., 120–126.

Salinas grounds Mesa's revolutionary disillusionment with the 1933 Revolution in an atmosphere that any anarchist must have understood: the roles of the military and the Communists, the non-revolutionary transformations of the so-called revolution, and more. The novel ends with Mesa attending an open-air meeting. Red flags, speakers, and a growing crowd fill an intersection in the working-class heart of Old Havana. Soon, soldiers arrive and start shooting into the crowd. As people disperse, an army bullet hits Mesa, who collapses. A man and woman take him by the arms calling, "Let's go, comrade. Get up!" But Mesa couldn't. "He would never rise again!"[16] Such was the state of anarchism in the mid-1930s, hounded by the government, military, and Communists.

Del Valle had a long literary career before the *machadato*. Early in Cuba's neocolonial era, del Valle published two short story collections: *Cuentos Inverosímiles* (Improbable Stories, 1903) and *Por el camino* (Along the Road, 1907). During the Great War he published *Jesús en la guerra*. But it was, ironically enough, during the Machado regime that del Valle launched into his most fertile and prolific literary years. From 1925 to 1933, he published fourteen short novels as part of the Barcelona-based La Novela Ideal and La Novela Libre series. During these years, he also published three novels: *Juan sin pan; novela social* (Juan without Bread: Social Novel, 1926), *Náufragos* (Shipwrecked, n.d. but after 1925), and *La mulata Soledad* (The Mulatta Soledad, 1929).[17] Thus, del Valle continued to create a fictionalized world from an anarchist point of view that kept the Ideal alive in words while the flesh and bones of the Ideal were being driven out and underground by Machado.

Del Valle's fiction from these years portrays horrendous and immoral capitalist societies that reflected the state of Cuban capitalism in the

---

[16] Ibid., 186. Much of Salinas's works are hard to find almost a century after they were published. But they had some importance beyond Cuba. For instance, his short story "The Protector" was anthologized in the United States in 1936. An unnamed father and son steal sweet potatoes from a plantation, only to be caught by a working-class private security guard. The guard refuses to shoot or arrest the father and walks away. The son promises his father that from now on the boy will protect his dad. The story was translated by renowned US author Langston Hughes, who might have known Salinas from Hughes's travels to Cuba in 1927, 1930, and 1931. See "The Protector," in *A Book of Contemporary Short Stories*, ed. Dorothy Brewster (New York: The Macmillan Company, 1936), 371–376.

[17] *Náufragos* was originally published in the La Novela Ideal series, where stories were usually about thirty pages long. In 1952, seven years after his death, a much longer 145-page novel was published in Toulouse, France.

1920s. Del Valle did not so much attack capitalism head-on as he did wealth, corruption, class conflict, and an exploitative mentality unleashed by capitalism. In *Náufragos*, the character Álvar is shipwrecked on the South Pacific island of Maruba. He discovers Polynesian culture and adapts to its precapitalist ways. But then Christian missionaries arrive, followed by a US phosphate mining company, Chinese laborers, gringo men chasing little island girls, alcoholism, and vice. Soon the New York-based Maruba Phosphate Company is the sole owner of the island and creates a modern capitalist extractive economy.[18]

Capitalism can both destroy and corrupt. In *Ambición* (Ambition), José arrives in Cuba from Galicia to work in his uncle Pablo's store in the central Cuban community of Morón. After ten years, Pablo has saved half of José's money for him. When Pablo is incapacitated by a heart attack, José does the unthinkable: He suffocates Pablo and takes the money.[19] In del Valle's world, the rich have many vices and almost no virtues. In *Aristócratas* (Aristocrats), the Marchioness of Manzanar speaks of how wonderful the aristocracy is. She and her husband spoil their pets while complaining about the poor. When her precious dog dies, she fills the void by pursuing sexual affairs. She finds a well-built chauffer because she needs a strong prole to fuck her since aristocratic men are weak and screw a bit too meekly. Meanwhile, her husband the Marquess gets drunk and rapes the maid. Both enjoy "deliciously plebian love."[20]

In some of del Valle's stories, the characters find respite from exploitation by de-linking themselves from the capitalism–politics–religion unholy trinity and recovering their humanity by "getting back to nature." We see this a bit in *Náufragos*, when Álvar admires the pre-phosphate era Marubans who live in harmony with the natural world, eat fresh food, and frolic nude with each other. He believes the natives are happier than they are because in capitalist society one "works much harder than those savages, with less useful return for yourself than they get; suffering privations and poverty as children, indignities and humiliations as men."[21] One might willingly escape capitalist society to do honest labor with your fellow humans. In *Cero* (Zero) and *El tesoro escondido* (The Hidden Treasure), two Cuban men do just that. One day Cero finds a lost, disoriented man who he names Cero-Cero. For the next thirteen years,

---

[18] Adrián del Valle, *Náufragos* (Toulouse: Ediciones "Universo," 1952), 57–102.
[19] Adrián del Valle, *Ambición* (Barcelona: La Revista Blanca, n.d.), 3–30.
[20] Adrián del Valle, *Aristócratas* (Barcelona: La Revista Blanca, n.d.), 7–18.
[21] Del Valle, *Náufragos*, 59–60.

they work side by side on Cero's farm in the hills. One day, Cero-Cero remembers his name is Alonso Castillejos and he is president of the Banco Intercomercial. He returns to his family in Havana. What he finds disgusts him: Family and friends reject him and his appearance, there is no authentic joy, a life of corruption, cut-throat competition, and exploitation. So he fakes his death and returns to the farm, where Alonso is dead and Cero-Cero lives.[22] Escaping to the regenerative countryside is central also to *El tesoro escondido*. Two veterans of Cuba's War for Independence lament how their country has been "converted into a nation of bureaucrats and proletarians."[23] When one man dies, his friend contacts the surviving grandsons with letters telling them that there is a treasure buried on his land. One day they find a box containing another letter that says their grandfather's land belongs to any and all of the grandsons who will leave behind their sick, urban lifestyles to cultivate the land themselves "as a natural source of life," not for profit.[24] Only one grandson accepts the offer.

While plenty of women have been documented in anarchist movements throughout the Americas, the truth is that most anarchists were men. This was especially true of migrant anarchists who regularly journeyed without families from workplace to workplace, country to country. Yet, anarchist fiction writers did not forget women. Del Valle frequently placed women, sexuality, and male–female relationships front-and-center in his Machado-era fiction that created several strong-willed working-class women. In *Mi amigo Julio* (My Friend Julio), "Julio" is a woman who left home as a teenager after problems with her stepfather and being raped by a cousin. For over two years she wondered around dressed as a man, but eventually meets Juvenal Arce – a young man in whom she confides, returns dressed as a woman, and with whom she makes love, living together happily unwed afterward.[25] The act of men and women living together outside of marriage became a regular feature of anarchist fiction and pops up repeatedly in del Valle's stories. In *Jubilosa*, an older black anarchist begins to live openly in free union with a young mulatta.[26] In *La mulata Soledad*, the heroine is a strong-willed mixed-race woman. She has a baby with a white doctor who has decided to work mainly with

---

[22] Adrián del Valle, *Cero* (Barcelona: La Revista Blanca, n.d.), 1–30.
[23] Adrián del Valle, *El tesoro Escondido* (Barcelona: La Revista Blanca, n.d.), 7–8.
[24] Ibid., 30.
[25] Adrián del Valle, *Mi amigo Julio* (Barcelona: La Revista Blanca, n.d.), 28–30.
[26] Adrián del Valle, *Jubilosa* (Barcelona: La Revista Blanca, n.d.), 30.

workers. Soledad the seamstress is responsible for helping him to see his true calling as they head off to live a life together in free union.[27] In a time when so many male labor leaders were being persecuted in Cuba, real wives and mothers had to be strong. We can think of these heroic female characters as del Valle's ode of love and respect for the women who did much of the unsung work that enabled their husbands and fathers to spread the anarchist Ideal – and who often were left behind when men were jailed, deported, forced into exile, or killed by Machado.

All these stories were "political" because they challenged the sociocultural norms of those in power. But several of del Valle's stories from the Machado era were more blatantly political. Some characters are heroic because they simply walked away from politics and began living an anarchist ideal – a prefigurative politics. For instance, del Valle's *Camelanga* features a "model republic" looking rather like Machado's Cuba: authoritarian rule, repression of even the slightest opposition, and the spread of foreign capital taking advantage of the new "stability." But the hero of the story is Marcial, who leads a revolution, topples the dictator, and kills him. After serving a term as president, Marcial moves to the mountains and lives a life of studying, farming, and taking care of his chickens. He simply refuses to play politics any longer.[28] Del Valle's Prince Filiberto in *El príncipe que no quiso gobernar* (The Prince Who Refused to Rule) follows a similar trajectory. Upon assuming the throne after his brother's death, Filiberto journeys on a listening tour disguised as a peasant. He hears men speak mainly of the lack of justice. When he returns to the palace, his ministers refuse to act on his suggestions to divide land, open free schools, help feed the poor, streamline the bureaucracy, and tax the rich. He has had enough, abandons the throne, and returns to the countryside to marry, have children, read, love, and cultivate the land.[29]

If the Prince and Marcial abandon politics to "live anarchism," other characters in these Machado-era stories rose up in arms against oppressors and abusers. There was of course the case of the Mexican revolutionary Sancho Canales from *De maestro a guerrillero*. Sancho's desire to exact revenge on the rich who had destroyed both his school and his young girlfriend leads him to put aside teaching and peaceful work. Now

---

[27] Adrián del Valle, *La mulata Soledad* (Barcelona: Impresos Costa, 1929), 158–159.
[28] Del Valle, *Camelanga*, 17–30.
[29] Adrián del Valle, *El príncipe que no quiso gobernar* (Barcelona: La Revista Blanca, n.d.), 24–30.

he picks up his gun, heads to the hills, and pursues armed revolutionary struggle against oppression – perhaps a not-so-subtle call to arms for Machado-era Cubans, too.[30] In *Náufragos*, as the phosphate company transforms the island from a tranquil land to the worst of capitalist-inflicted vice, corruption, and exploitation, Álvar decides to fight back. Working as a doctor in the company towns allows him constant contact with the workers. After a year, this Cuban doctor has organized a transnational cohort of young native and Chinese workers who revolt against the American company.[31] Del Valle's *Juan sin pan* is a two-part novel. In part two, titled "Revolución," workers protest war, capitalism, and patriotism. They launch a general strike and troops arrive to maintain order. Juan is a poor young man who lives and hangs out with numerous homeless men – some noble, some not so much. They are Marx's lumpen proletariat. But unlike Marx's view of them as apolitical or even counter-revolutionary, they join the general strike and the revolutionary multitudes that burn churches and houses of rich people, ransack warehouses looking for food, and march on the governmental palace.[32]

Del Valle's last short novel for the La Novela Ideal series was *Tiberianos*, written probably around 1930. The story is set in 1890s New York, where the young Cuban Joselillo sells contraband Cuban cigars. Soon, he is joined by Miguelillo, a Spaniard who fled political persecution in Cuba. In a bar one night, Miguelillo confesses to fellow patrons that he supports the War for Independence, but not as a patriot, rather as someone who believes that an "independent and democratic Cuba will realize the natural aspirations of a people that long to extract themselves from domination exerted by a faraway and foreign government." After casting off colonial rule, "conscientious Cubans" will continue to fight for "the true ideal of freedom, equality, and social solidarity. Far from the nationalist ideal of oppressed peoples is the human ideal of those longing for a society of truly free and equal men, united by the ties of solidarity."[33] While del Valle set the story in the 1890s, it would have resonated during the *machadato* too: an internationalist born in Spain, politically active in Cuba and now in exile, pursuing freedom and justice against a nationalist dictatorship dominated by "a faraway and foreign government." Cuba had not come very far in thirty years.

---

[30] Del Valle, *De maestro a guerrillero*, 25–30.   [31] Del Valle, *Náufragos*, 103–115.
[32] Adrián del Valle, *Juan sin pan; novela social* (Buenos Aires: B. Fueyo, 1926), 82–176.
[33] Adrián del Valle, *Tiberianos* (Barcelona: La Revista Blanca, n.d.), 21.

Del Valle was more than a fiction writer. In 1930, he published a curious work of history on the Gran Legión del Águila Negra (Grand Legion of the Black Eagle). As we look back 100 years or so at our Caribbean anarchists, we see that del Valle too was looking back 100 years at this conspiracy of a handful of Latin American radicals fighting for Cuban independence. The legion was founded in Veracruz, Mexico in May 1823 by Mexican President Guadalupe Victoria "with the objective of contributing to the success of freedom and independence in the Americas" and extending the revolutionary push for independence to Spain's last possessions in the Antilles. Cubans living in Mexico began to affiliate with the Mexican organization and "wanted to extend its activities to Cuba, hoping to help elements on the island who sympathized with independence" while expecting help from Águila Negra organizations in Mexico and Colombia.[34]

This was, in short, a transnational revolutionary movement for freedom against a tyrannous government in Cuba that operated exactly a century before the *machadato*. Del Valle took this historical moment from the late 1820s and published this history during the Machado repression of his fellow revolutionaries to – without explicitly saying so – highlight linkages between the two Caribbean freedom movements. For instance, the Mexico link in the 1820s had its 1920s counterpart with Cubans like Mella and Penichet as representatives of ANERC in Mexico, who publicly declared their desire to invade Cuba to liberate the island from oppression. And the story returned the focus to Cuba's wars for independence, allowing a reader to easily see that the fight against tyranny had not ended but continued through the late 1920s. There are many parallels to be sure, and for someone as gifted, knowledgeable, and articulate as del Valle, it is impossible to think that this was all somehow coincidental.

Ultimately, the anarchist nature of del Valle's historical overview of the Águila Negra conspiracy emerges on the last page of the book. Who does del Valle use to evaluate revolutionary movements? Peter Kropotkin. Del Valle quotes Kropotkin's study of the French Revolution to explain why the Águila Negra failed to catch on in 1820s Cuba: "it is essential that *revolutionary action*, arising from the people, coincide with the movement of *revolutionary thought*, arising from the educated classes. The

---

[34] Adrián del Valle, *Historia documentada de la conspiración de la Gran Legión del Águila Negra* (Havana: Imprenta "El Siglo XX," 1930), 94–95. See also Muller, *Cuban Émigrés*, 137–138.

union of the two is key." But this had not been the case in the 1820s. "The Cuban masses – whites and blacks – were in no condition to respond with revolutionary action to the revolutionary ideas of the select, progressive minority."[35]

Del Valle did not end on a negative note, however. In his concluding paragraphs, he again quoted Kropotkin: "But hoping is not enough. One has to work: the first rebels have given their lives to prepare the revolution ... Ideas always govern the world and great ideas, energetically presented, always determine wills."[36] As though writing to his anarchist comrades then in hiding or jail or exile, del Valle offered these final lines: "Freedom, whether for peoples or for individuals, is the great idea engine that moves all of them into action. The idea that inspired the Grand Legion of the Black Eagle ... worked for Cuba's liberation from Spanish dominion. It continued to live in the Cuban conscience."[37] The 1820s conspirators had not failed, but rather had seen their ideas live on until the revolutionary masses ultimately rose against Spanish colonial rule. His contemporary comrades might be hurting, but their efforts helped to reinforce the anarchist ideal of freedom in the island's collective conscience. It may not happen tomorrow, but it would come.

The prepublished manuscript about a transnational revolutionary movement that cited Kropotkin in its final pages was submitted to the prestigious Cuban Academy of History, whose president was the great historian of Cuban culture, and one of del Valle's friends, Fernando Ortiz. On September 21, 1929, the Academy held a literary competition in which members unanimously awarded the top prize to del Valle.[38] Here was yet another literary award to an anarchist right in the middle of Machado's repression of anarchists. And it quite literally brought us full circle: from the nineteenth-century Caribbean fights against colonial tyranny to the neocolonial *machadato*.

Anarchists continued to work over the decades. In 1937 and 1938, Cuba's Federation of Cuban Anarchist Groups (FGAC) organized against fascism and in support of the war against Franco in Spain. Relatedly, Maximiliano Olay had returned to the United States from Cuba. In 1937 the Spanish Republic's CNT–FAI revolutionary union appointed him to be the CNT's delegate in the United States to publicize its activities. The Asociación Libertaria de Cuba (Libertarian Association of Cuba, or ALC) formed in 1943. The popular Cuban magazine *Bohemia* even

---

[35] Del Valle, *Historia*, 98. Italics in original.   [36] Ibid., 98.   [37] Ibid.
[38] Ibid., xii–xiv.

featured the ALC in 1947 (two years after Adrián del Valle's death). Salinas was the ALC's secretary of culture by 1948. During the Cuban Revolution, anarchists worked in the urban underground resistance to the Batista dictatorship, but in the early 1960s their opposition to growing Marxist–Leninist command and control of the island led many of them to flee Communist repression.[39]

In Florida, almost no anarchism survived the Red Scare of the 1910s and 1920s. Luis Barcia eventually left activism, opened a cafeteria and a coffee roasting and distribution company in Tampa; then he opened what appears to be Florida's first chocolate factory, which he ran for over 25 years.[40] On occasion, Barcia still sent money to anarchist newspapers in New York City, but there was nothing much beyond that. In fact, in his 1957 unpublished autobiography, he discussed anarchists but never mentioned the word anarchism anywhere in the sixty-seven single-spaced typed pages. Decades later, Florida's Latin anarchism shifted to Miami. By the 1970s and 1980s, anarchists who had fled the Cuban Revolution established a base among the broader exile community and continued their antiauthoritarian critiques of US foreign policy, the Soviet Union, the Castro government, the Reagan Administration, and more. Meanwhile in Panama, an upstart "Labor Party" that blended Marxism and anarchism emerged by 1929. They commemorated the 1925 rent strike and its repression while welcoming the remains of the Blázquez de Pedro brothers. But little anarchist sensibility carried through after that.

In Puerto Rico, the Status Question remained a leading divisive issue as the Nationalist Party emerged with a powerful presence. In 1933, Emiliano Ramos denounced the nationalists. Anarchists feared that all the talk about Puerto Rican nationalism then emerging on the island thanks to the independence movement and Pedro Albizu Campos could be a slippery slope. "Although Puerto Rican Nationalism," Emiliano Ramos wrote, "has nothing in common with that of Hitler and Mussolini, Puerto Rican Nationalism nevertheless carries in it the virus that will cause death ... We suppose the Nationalist Party of Puerto Rico is merely political, that it seeks Puerto Rican independence from the tutelage of the United States." But if independence were achieved, would the party

---

[39] Ariel Mae Lambe, "Cuban Antifascism and the Spanish Civil War: Transnational Activism, Networks, and Solidarity in the 1930s" (PhD dissertation, Columbia University, 2014), 333–362; Zimmer, *Immigrants against the State*, 198; Shaffer, *Anarchism and Countercultural Politics*, 231–233.
[40] Barcia, "Autobiography of Luis Barcia Quilabert," 63–65.

abdicate power? Probably not, which was the problem. It was little more than another political party designed to exploit "national" sentiment for its own limited agenda. The people loved flags, hymns, parades, and the fetishistic trappings of nationalism, but those had to be avoided for a truly revolutionary society to emerge. And, perhaps above all, one had to stop the almost holy reverence for the words and person of Albizu Campos – another fetish bordering on a cult of personality, claimed Ramos.[41] It might not be fascism, but rabid nationalism coupled with a cult of personality looked a little too much like Mussolini and his black shirts for comfort.

Decades of Cold War-ism ensued, and few anarchist organizations emerged in the Caribbean – or elsewhere around the world. However, the collapse of the Berlin Wall, Eastern European Communist governments, and ultimately the Soviet Union ushered in a new wave of global anarchist and antiauthoritarian organizing. Anarchism spiked with the new millennium: the 1999 Seattle World Trade Organization meeting, the World Social Forums, the legacy of the 1994 Zapatista rebellion in Mexico, the factory occupations and horizontalist movement in Argentina, environmental and indigenous rights movements throughout the Americas, protests and movements against austerity and neoliberalism throughout Europe, the Occupy Movement based largely in the United States, and the Rojava anarchists in northern Syria/western Kurdistan. These were all movements based less around the notion of liberal human rights and more about decentralized power against modern capitalist globalization as activists pursued social justice.

Anarchists in the Caribbean became active too. In 2012 in Puerto Rico, they hosted the Third North American Anarchist Studies Network Conference bringing together scholars and activists from the Americas. Five years later, comrades in Mexico City held another iteration of the conference. Numerous anarchist groups appeared throughout the region in El Salvador, the Dominican Republic, Puerto Rico, Bonaire, Miami, and Cuba. In 2015, anarchists from around the Caribbean met in Santiago de los Caballeros in the Dominican Republic to form the Federación Anarquista Centroamericana y del Caribe (Central American and Caribbean Anarchist Federation). In 2018, the Taller Libertario Alfredo López (Alfredo López Libertarian Workshop) in the Havana suburb of Marianao launched ABRA – the first Centro de Estudios Sociales (Social Studies

---

[41] *Cultura Proletaria*, June 24, 1933, 4.

Center, or CES) and anarchist library on the island in a half-century.[42] Thus, as the spread of capitalist globalization and the ever-longer reach of US foreign policy engulfed the planet after 2000, people began to organize and think again in anarchist terms against hierarchy and authoritarianism in all its guises. These new counter-globalization responses hark back a century earlier when anarchists launched attacks on political systems, religious structures, the spread of global capitalism, and the expansionistic United States.

When we return our gaze to the first decades of the twentieth century, it is fascinating to consider how so much anarchist activism, organization, and survival in the Caribbean Basin can be attributed to a handful of longtime radicals active in the cause for decades. Sure, there were hundreds and maybe thousands of activists over the years. Some lost their lives in revolutions, police brutality, American military interventions, and more. Others abandoned their anarchism and became liberals, Socialists, or Communists. Meanwhile, several anarchists never wavered and remained active in the Caribbean network for decades. Their presence, their writings, and their repeated sacrifices reflected committed personal histories that shaped the network nodes that in turn anchored the Caribbean anarchist network. Luisa Capetillo's fifteen years of activism took her from Puerto Rico to New York, Havana, and Tampa until her death. Ventura Mijón spent two decades moving back and forth between Puerto Rico and Tampa before succumbing to the lure of Communism in the 1930s. Antonio Penichet worked most of his adult life in the Cuban movement but spent time in New York and exile in Mexico City. In Florida, Luis Barcia was still politically engaged into the 1920s after beginning his regional anarchist career in the early 1890s in New York, Tampa, and Havana. The same was true for Emiliano Ramos in Puerto Rico, who in the 1930s was completing nearly forty years of transnational anarchist activism. Of course, one cannot forget José María Blázquez de Pedro, who was an anarchist for twenty-five years. He spent the first half of his anarchist life in Spain and most of the last half in Panama, where, were it not for combined Panama–United States security efforts, he certainly would have lived for years to come and likely would have been in the capital city in early November 1925 to welcome his Latin American comrades for the first Pan-American anarchist congress. Then there was Adrián del Valle, who arrived in Cuba in the early

---

[42] "Cuba: Apertura del Centro Social y Biblioteca Libertaria ABRA en La Habana," www.alasbarricadas.org/noticias/node/39903.

1890s, left for New York during the Cuban War, returned in late 1898 and continued as the best-known anarchist via his writing and organizing until he died in 1945 – over fifty years of Caribbean anarchist engagement. And as for Marcelo Salinas, well, here was a man who began fighting for anarchism in Cuba in the first decade of independence from Spain, fought for the cause in Tampa, where he helped build the first IWW Local, agitated and edited newspapers in New York and Barcelona, spent the late 1910s and 1920s in the political hotbed of Havana, where he remained until the 1970s when he went to the United States and continued the struggle in the heart of Cold War Miami – some seventy-odd years fighting for anarchism.

Whatever we want to say about small groups, limited movements, short-term and small-scale newspapers and the like, these were men and women, husbands, sons, daughters, fighters, and lovers who devoted much of their adult lives to living out an ideal for themselves while struggling to create that ideal for others. They were not nationalists – something that put them in the minority as Cuba, Panama, and Puerto Rico were themselves coming out of centuries of outside control. And they did not just "go-it-alone." They organized locally with other anarchists and sometimes fellow travelers, whether Socialists, Communists, or liberals who didn't share all their anarchist views.

Their local organizing did not occur in a vacuum. These locales were interconnected, woven into a network – sometimes strongly, sometimes loosely – that linked them with comrades across the "Continental Caribbean" and which itself was linked to transatlantic networks in Southern Europe, a network across the United States–Mexico borderlands, and a Pacific network that especially connected to Peru. At this very moment in history, Washington was turning the Caribbean into its own "American Mediterranean," where Protestant missionaries swarmed in, agribusiness firms helped bring forth banana republics, political machinations emerged to provide the façade of republican political institutions (and thus the façade of "freedom"), and all were to be protected by US machine guns. Anarchists had a different internationalist romance and dream for the region.

It's worth remembering that anarchists were not apolitical. They opposed the authoritarian, top-down dynamics of all political systems, but that itself was a conscious political decision. Oh, they knew politics was about power. Yet, it was more than that. Politics was also about idealism and desire. The author John Blackthorn (aka, the former US presidential candidate Gary Hart) explains in his novel *I, Che Guevara*.

In the book, Che Guevara survived his 1967 Bolivian execution, and on the eve of the new millennium has returned to Cuba as the island is about to hold its first freely contested national elections thanks to an announcement by Fidel Castro. Through dialogue with average people, Che mobilizes a grass roots, community-based mass movement that rejects the politics of the state (the old Communists) and the politics of money (the Miami-based political party). People have the power to rule themselves at the local level, according to Che's *"república auténtica"* (authentic republic) movement. Like the new Che, anarchists recognized that below the surface of power politics was something else – "longing," says Blackthorn's Che. "Longing for something better. Now your materialist thinks that longing is about things. And, for the poor guy, there's something to that. Everybody longs for the basics for himself and his family – shelter, food, a job. But there is more. I mean the longing for peace, for healthy children, for clean air and water, for goodwill in the community, for hope for a better life for your children." In a sense, "pleasure" as José María Blázquez de Pedro might have seen it – more than just individual, physical pleasure, but instead having the time and conditions to enjoy the broader pleasures of existence with one's family and community. Only people with decentralized control over their own lives (an authentic republic?) could make this happen.[43]

Anarchists longed to create such a world. They tried to inspire it in themselves and their followers across the Caribbean – a prefigurative politics of living the revolution in the present until the longed-for social revolution would destroy the authoritarian institutions of states, religions, capitalism, and imperialism. In its wake, people themselves would at last be free to create a world of social and individual freedom. If anarchists ultimately failed to consummate that dream, they cannot be faulted for trying to create in the Caribbean – a region whose history was filled with crimes of slavery, tyranny, exploitation, and colonialism – a humane region of free, autonomous, egalitarian peoples devoid of militaristic, exploitative, and authoritarian aspirations.

---

[43] John Blackthorn, *I, Che Guevara* (New York: William Morrow and Company, Inc., 2000), 330.

Bibliography

ARCHIVES, INSTITUTES, AND LIBRARIES

Archivo General de Puerto Rico (San Juan)
Archivo Nacional de Panamá (Panama City)
    Secretaria de Relaciones Exteriores. Memoria 1911
    Presidencia de Maximiliano Valdés. Correspondencia a/por el Presidente
    Junta de Inquilinato 1925
    Junta Inquilinaria
    Administración del Estado. Presidencia Rodolfo Enrique Chiari Robles Correspondencia
    Administración del Estado. Presidencia Dr. Belisario Porras. Correspondencia.
Biblioteca Nacional José Martí (Havana)
Biblioteca Nacional de Panamá (Panama City)
Biblioteca Nacional de Puerto Rico (San Juan)
International Institute of Social History (Amsterdam)
    Diego Abad de Santillán Collection
    R. Lone Collection
    Max Nettlau Collection
    Erick José Pérez Collection
Instituto de Historia (Havana)
Instituto de Literatura y Lingüística (Havana)
Museo Municipal de Regla, Cuba
    Eduardo Gómez Luaces. "Monografía histórica del movimiento obrero en Regla (1833–1958)," unpublished manuscript
New York City Public Library
University of Florida
    Latin America and Caribbean Collection
    Album X rari nantis in gurgite vasto. Presidio August 1922–January 1923, Francisco Alonso, ed., unpublished manuscript

University of South Florida
"Autobiography of Luis Barcia Quilabert," unpublished manuscript
"Manifiesto a los Obreros y al Pueblo de Tampa en general," Tampa Microform Reel N53
United States National Archives, College Park, Maryland
RG 59. General Records of the Department of State
RG 60. General Records of the Department of Justice
RG 65. Records of the Federal Bureau of Investigation
RG 185. Isthmian Canal Commission Records
RG 199. Records of the Provisional Government: "Confidential" Correspondence, 1906–1909
US Military Intelligence Division Reports, Surveillance of Radicals in the United States, 1917–1941 (from Military Agency Records, RG 165)
Universidad de Puerto Rico – Humacao
Centro de Documentación Obrera Santiago Iglesias Pantín (CDOSIP)
Universidad de Puerto Rico – Río Piedras
Movimiento Obrero Puertorriqueño hojas sueltas 1898–1937, Microfilm
Periódicos Obreros Puertorriqueños, Colección Puertorriqueña

NEWSPAPERS AND MAGAZINES

Acción Consciente (Havana) 1922
Acción Libertaria (Gijón/Vigo/Madrid, Spain) 1910–1915
Archivo Social (Havana) 1894
Aurora (New York) 1922–1924
Brazo y Cerebro (New York) 1912–1914
Campana Misteriosa (Havana) 1905
Cuasimodo (Panama City) 1919–1920
Cultura Obrera (New York) 1911–1927
Cultura Proletaria (New York) 1927–1934
Diario de la Marina (Havana) 1900
Doctrina Anarquista Socialista (Paterson, New Jersey) 1905
El Audaz (Havana) 1912
El Centinela (San Juan) 1909
El Combate (Arecibo, Puerto Rico) 1910–1911
El Comunista (Bayamón, Puerto Rico) 1920–1921
El Dependiente (Havana) 1911–1917
El Despertar (New York) 1891–1902
El Eco de Torcedor (Bayamón, Puerto Rico) 1909
El Eco Proletario (San Juan) 1892
El Esclavo (Tampa) 1894–1898
El Inquilino (Panama City) 1925
El Internacional (Tampa) 1904–1946
El Libertario (Gijón, Spain) 1911–1913
El Libertario (Havana) 1905
El Mazo (Panama City) 1929

El Naturista (Havana) 1910
El Nuevo Ideal (Havana) 1899–1901
El Obrero (Panama City) 1921–1922
El Obrero Industrial (Tampa) 1911–1914
El Porvenir Social (San Juan) 1898–1899
El Productor (Havana) 1887–1890
El Productor Panadero (Havana) 1922
El Progreso (Havana) 1923–1925
El Rebelde (New York) 1898
El Sembrador (Havana) 1924
El Único (Gatún and Colón, Panama Canal Zone) 1911–1912
Ensayo Obrero (San Juan) 1897–1898
Estrella de Panamá (Panama City) 1925
Fiat Lux (Havana) 1911
Fuerza Cerebral (New York) 1916
Fuerza Consciente (Los Angeles and San Francisco) 1913–1914
Gaceta Oficial, Segunda Época (Panama City) 1904
Germinación (San José, Costa Rica) 1929
Germinal (Havana) 1904
Guángara Libertaria (Miami) 1980–1992
Hijos del Mundo (Havana) 1892
International Shipping Digest 1919
Justicia (San Juan) 1914–1926
Labor Sana (Havana) 1917
¡Liberación!: Periódico Libertario (Ybor City/Tampa) 1912
L'Idée Ouviere (Le Havre, France) 1887–1888
La Antorcha (Tampa) 1906
La Batalla (Havana) 1911
La Conciencia Libre (Ponce, Puerto Rico) 1909–1912
La Defensa (Havana) 1902
La Democracia (San Juan) 1911–1912
La Federación (Tampa) 1900
La Federación Libre (San Juan) 1899
La Lucha (Havana) 1915
La Miseria (San Juan) 1901
La Nueva Solidaridad (Chicago) 1918–1921
La Revista Blanca (Barcelona) 1932
La Revista Nueva: ciencias, literatura, y artes (Panama City) 1916–1919
La Sotana (Arecibo, Puerto Rico) 1912
La Voz del Dependiente (Havana) 1907–1911
La Voz del Esclavo (Tampa) 1900
La Voz del Obrero (La Coruña, Spain) 1913
Los Angeles Herald (Los Angeles) 1908
Los Tiempos Nuevos (Havana) 1921
Luz y Vida (San Juan) 1909
Luzbel (Havana) 1904
Memorandum Tipográfico (Havana) 1914–1916

New York Times (New York) 1906, 1911, 1919
Nueva Luz (Havana) 1922–1925
Nuevo Horizonte (San Juan) 1909
Porto Rico Workingmen's Journal (San Juan) 1905
Pro-Vida (Havana) 1915–1923
Rebelión!/Rebelión (Regla) 1908–1909/1910
Regeneración (Los Angeles) 1910–1918
Revista Lotería (Panama City) 1971
Risveglio (Tampa) 1913–1916
Rumbos Nuevos (Havana) 1920
Solidaridad (New York) 1926–1930
Star and Herald (Panama City) 1925
¡Tierra! (Havana), 1903–1915, 1925
Tierra y Libertad (Barcelona) 1907–1917
Tribuna Libre (Gijón, Spain) 1909
Unión Obrera (Mayagüez, Puerto Rico) 1903–1922
Verbo Rojo (Panama City) 1917
Vía Libre (Havana) 1911
Voz Humana (Caguas, Puerto Rico) 1906
Yo Acuso (Bayamón, Puerto Rico) 1918

ARTICLES, BOOKS, CHAPTERS, AND WEBSITES

Aguilar, A. (1968). *Pan-Americanism from Monroe to the Present: A View from the Other Side*, New York: Monthly Review Press.
Aguilar, K. A. (2017). The IWW in Tampico: Anarchism, Internationalism, and Solidarity Unionism in a Mexican Port. In P. Cole, D. Struthers, and K. Zimmer, eds., *Wobblies of the World: A Global History of the IWW*, Chicago: Pluto Press, pp. 124–139.
Albornoz, M. and Galeano, D. (2017). Anarquistas y policías en el atlántico sudamericano: una red transnacional, 1890–1910. *Boletín del Instituto de Historia Argentina y Americana "Dr. Emilio Ravignani,"* 47, 101–134.
Albro, W. (1996). *To Die on Your Feet: The Life, Times, and Writings of Práxedis G. Guerrero*, Fort Worth: Texas Christian University Press.
Alfaro, R. J. (1959). *Medio siglo de realaciones entre Panamá y los Estados Unidos*, Panama: Secretaria de Informacón de la Presidencia de la República.
Alexander, R. J. (2002). *A History of Organized Labor in Cuba*, Westport: Praeger.
Alonso Fernández, B. (2006). Migración y sindicalismo. Marineros y anarquistas españoles en Nueva York (1902–1930). *Historia Social*, 54, 113–135.
(2017). Spanish Anarchists and Maritime Workers in the IWW. In P. Cole, D. Struthers, and K. Zimmer, eds., *Wobblies of the World: A Global History of the IWW*. Chicago: Pluto Press, pp. 89–102.
Anderson, B. (2005). *Under Three Flags: Anarchism and the Colonial Imagination*, New York: Verso.

Arroyo, J. (2013). *Writing Secrecy in Caribbean Freemasonry*, New York: Palgrave Macmillan.
Atton, C. (1999). Green Anarchist: A Case Study of Collective Action in the Radical Media. *Anarchist Studies*, 7, 25–49.
Avrich, P. (2005). *Anarchist Voices: An Oral History of Anarchism in America*, Chico, CA: AK Press.
Bantman, C. (2009). The Militant Go-between: Émile Pouget's Transnational Propaganda (1880–1914). *Labour History Review*, 74(3), 274–287.
Bantman, C. and Altena, B. (2017). Introduction: Problematizing Scales of Analysis in Network-Based Social Movements. In C. Bantman and B. Altena, eds., *Reassessing the Transnational Turn: Scales of Analysis in Anarchist and Syndicalist Studies*. Oakland, CA: PM Press, pp. 3–22.
Barrancos, D. (1990). *Anarquismo, educación y costumbres en la Argentina de principios de siglo*, Buenos Aires: Editorial Contrapunto.
Barrera Bassols, J. (2011). Los rebeldes de la bandera roja: textos del periódico *¡Tierra!*, de La Habana, sobre la revolución Mexicana, Mexico City: Instituto Nacional de Antropología e Historia.
Bedford, J. (1995). Samuel Gompers & the Caribbean: The AFL, Cuba & Puerto Rico, 1898–1906. *Labor's Heritage*, 6(4), 4–25.
Berquist, C. (1986). *Labor in Latin America: Comparative Essays on Chile, Argentina, Venezuela and Colombia*, Palo Alto: Stanford University Press.
Blackthorn, J. (2000). *I, Che Guevara*, New York: William Morrow and Company, Inc.
Blázquez de Pedro, J. M. (1905). *Pensares*, Barcelona: Imprenta de Cuesta.
   (1905). *Rebeldías Contadas*, Bejar, Spain: Tipografía Silverio Sánchez.
   (1906). *El derecho al placer*, Barcelona: Biblioteca Vertice.
   (1910). *La agonía del repatriado: Poema-monólogo*, Lisbon: Typographia do Commercio.
   (1922). *Observaciones de un andariego en Panamá: crónicas y artículos, sin prólogo ajeno*, Panama City: Talleres Gráficos de "El Tiempo."
   (1924). De Antaño y Ogaño. In *Sangre de mi sangre (Poesias): Sin Ajena prologación*, Panama City: Impreso Talleres Gráficos "La Unión," pp. 116–118.
   (1924). *Sangre de mi sangre: (Poesias). Sin ajena prologación*, Panama City: Talleres Gráficos "La Unión."
   (1987). La Igualdad Anarquista. *Tareas*, 1987, 110–111. (Originally published in *Ecléctica: Revista mensual* 1(1), September 15, 1917.)
Bullard, A. (1914). *Panama: The Canal, the Country, and the People*, revised edition, New York: Macmillan Company.
Cabrera, O. (1985). *Los que viven por sus manos*, Havana: Editorial de Ciencias Sociales.
   (1979). Enrique Creci: un patriota obrero. *Santiago*, 36, 121–150.
Capetillo, L. (1992). *Amor y anarquía: Los escritos de Luisa Capetillo*, Julio Ramos, ed., San Juan: Ediciones Huracán.
Cappelletti, A. J. (1990). *El anarquismo en América Latina*, Caracas: Biblioteca Ayacucho.

(1990). *Hechos y figures del anarquismo hispanoamericano*, Madrid: Ediciones Madre Tierra.
Carr, B. (1996). Mill Occupations and Soviets: The Mobilisation of Sugar Workers in Cuba, 1917–1933. *Journal of Latin American Studies*, 28, 129–158.
  (2010). Radicals, Revolutionaries, and Exiles: Mexico City in the 1920s. *Berkeley Review of Latin American Studies*, http://clas.berkeley.edu/research/mexico-radicals-revolutionaries-and-exiles-mexico-city-1920s.
  (2014). "Across Seas and Borders": Charting the Webs of Radical Internationalism in the Circum-Caribbean. In L. Roniger, J. Green, and P. Yankelevich, eds., *Exile & the Politics of Exclusion in the Americas*. Brighton: Sussex Academic Press, pp. 217–240.
  (2014). Pioneering Transnational Solidarity in the Americas: The Movement in Support of Augusto C. Sandino, 1927–1934. *Journal of Iberian and Latin American Research*, 20(2), 141–152.
Casanovas Codina, J. (1990). *Bread, or Bullets! Urban Labor and Spanish Colonialism in Cuba, 1850–1898*, Pittsburgh: University of Pittsburgh Press.
Castañeda, C. J. (2017). Times of Propaganda and Struggle: El Despertar and Brooklyn's Spanish Anarchists, 1890–1905. In Tom Goyens, ed., *Radical Gotham: Anarchism in New York City from Schwab's Saloon to Occupy Wall Street*. Urbana: University of Illinois Press, pp. 77–99.
Cohn, J. (2014). *Underground Passages: Anarchist Resistance Culture, 1848–2011*, Oakland: AK Press.
Cole, P. (2007). *Wobblies on the Waterfront: Interracial Unionism in Progressive-Era Philadelphia*, Urbana: University of Illinois Press.
Congress of Panama. (2011). In R. Holden and E. Zolov, eds., *Latin America and the United States: A Documentary History*, New York: Oxford University Press.
Conniff, M. (1985). *Black Labor on a White Canal: Panama, 1904–1981*, Pittsburgh: University of Pittsburgh Press.
Craib, R. (2016). *The Cry of the Renegade: Politics and Poetry in Interwar Chile*, New York: Oxford University Press.
  (2017). Sedentary Anarchists. In C. Bantman and B. Altena, eds., *Reassessing the Transnational Turn: Scales of Analysis in Anarchist and Syndicalist Studies*. Oakland: PM Press, pp. 139–156.
Cruz, J. J. (2002). You Can't Go Home, Yankee: Teaching U.S. History to Canary Islands Students. *The History Teacher*, 35(3), 343–372.
Cruz, V. (1906). *Hacia el porvenir*, San Juan, PR: La República Española.
Cuba: Apertura del Centro Social y Biblioteca Libertaria ABRA en La Habana (n.d.). www.alasbarricadas.org/noticias/node/39903.
Cuba Hurricanes Historic Threats (n.d.). www.cubahurricanes.org/history-hurricaneschronicles.php.
Cuestas, C. H. (1998). Las últimas horas de Blázquez de Pedro en Panamá. *Tareas*, 98, 115–120.
Cuevas, A. (1980). *El movimiento inquilinario de 1925*, Panama City: Centro de Estudios Latinoamericanos.
Daniel, E. M. (2015). Cuban Cigar Makers in Havana, Key West, and Ybor City, 1850s–1890s: A Single Universe? In G. de Laforcade and K. Shaffer, eds.,

In Defiance of Boundaries: Anarchism in Latin American History. Gainesville: University Press of Florida, pp. 25–47.
De Laforcade, G. (2011). Federative Futures: Waterways, Resistance Societies, and the Subversion of Nationalism in the Early 20th-Century Anarchism of the Río de la Plata Region. *Estudios Interdisciplinarios de América Latina*, 22 (2), 71–96.
  (2017). Argentine Organized Labor: Culture, Representations, and Ideological Alignments in the Wake of the Bolshevik Revolution. Paper presented at the Latin American Studies Association meeting, Lima, Peru.
De Laforcade, G. and Shaffer, K. (2015). Introduction: The Hidden Story Line of Anarchism in Latin American History. In G. de Laforcade and K. Shaffer, eds., *In Defiance of Boundaries: Anarchism in Latin American History*. Gainesville: University Press of Florida, pp. 1–22.
De Lidia, P. (aka Adrián del Valle). (1898). *Fin de fiesta, cuadro dramático*, New York: np.
De Sárraga, B. (2015). *El clericalismo en América a través de un continente*, Lisbon: José Assis & A. Coelho Dias.
Del Valle, A. (n.d.). *Ambición*, Barcelona: La Revista Blanca.
  (n.d.). *Aristócratas*, Barcelona: La Revista Blanca.
  (n.d.). *Camelanga*, Barcelona: La Revista Blanca.
  (n.d.). *Cero*, Barcelona: La Revista Blanca.
  (n.d.). *De maestro a guerrillero*, Barcelona: La Revista Blanca.
  (n.d.). *El príncipe que no quiso gobernar*, Barcelona: La Revista Blanca.
  (n.d.). *El tesoro Escondido*, Barcelona: La Revista Blanca.
  (n.d.). *Jubilosa*, Barcelona: La Revista Blanca.
  (n.d.). *Mi amigo Julio*, Barcelona: La Revista Blanca.
  (n.d.). *Náufragos*, Toulouse: Ediciones "Universo."
  (n.d.). *Tiberianos*, Barcelona: La Revista Blanca.
  (n.d.) *Todo lo vence el amor*, Barcelona: La Revista Blanca.
  (1907). *Por el camino*, Barcelona: F. Granada.
  (1917). *Jesús en la guerra*, Havana: Escuela de la Casa de Beneficencia y Maternidad.
  (1925). *Kropotkin, Vida y obras*, Buenos Aires: Agrupación C. Cafiero.
  (1926). *Juan sin pan; novela social*, Buenos Aires: B. Fueyo.
  (1929). *La mulata Soledad*, Barcelona: Impresos Costa.
  (1930). *Historia documentada de la conspiración de la Gran Legión del Águila Negra*, Havana: El Siglo XX.
Del Vasto, C. (2003). "Verbo Rojo": Primer periódico liberal-socializante panameño. *Revista Panameño de Ciencias Sociales*, 1, 37–40.
Díaz-Arias, D. (2015). From Radicals to Heroes of the Republic: Anarchism and National Identity in Costa Rica, 1900–1977. In G. de Laforcade and K. Shaffer, eds., *In Defiance of Boundaries: Anarchism in Latin American History*. Gainesville: University Press of Florida, pp. 219–242.
Díaz-Arias, D. and Shaffer, K. (2010). El ciudadano anarquista. *La Nación (San José, Costa)*, April 15, 34.
Dieppa, A. M. (1915). *El porvenir de la sociedad humana*, San Juan, PR: El Eco.

Documentation of Tropical Cyclone Changes (n.d.). www.aoml.noaa.gov/hrd/hurdat/metadata_dec12.html.
Dolgoff, S. (1977). *The Cuban Revolution: A Critical Perspective*, Montreal: Black Rose Books.
Downing, J. D. H. (2001). *Radical Media: Rebellious Communication and Social Movements*, Thousand Oaks: Sage.
Emmer, P. C., Brereton, B., Higman, B. W., eds. (2004). *General History of the Caribbean: Caribbean in the Twentieth Century*, London: UNESCO Publishing.
Espina, R. R. (1923). Rebeldía. In F. Alonso, ed., *Album X rari nantis in gurgite vasto. Presidio August 1922–January 1923*, unpublished manuscript, University of Florida Libraries, pp. 42–43.
Esteve, P. (1990). *Memoria de la conferencia anarquista internacional: Celebrada en Chicago en septiembre de 1893. A los anarquistas de España y Cuba*, Paterson, NJ: El Despertar.
Fernández, F. (1994). *La sangre de Santa Águeda: Angiolillo, Betances, and Cánovas*, Miami: Ediciones Universal.
  (2001). *Cuban Anarchism: The History of a Movement*, Tucson: Sharp Press.
Five Came Back. (1939). John Farrow, dir., RKO Radio Pictures.
Flórez Pinzón, M. (2011). Anarquismo y anarcosindicalismo en Colombia antes de 1924. In CILEP, ed., *Pasado y presente del anarquismo y del anarcosindicalismo en Colombia*. Bogotá: CILEP, pp. 35–58.
  (2011). El anarcosindicalismo en Colombia de 1924–1928. In CILEP, ed., *Pasado y presente del anarquismo y del anarcosindicalismo en Colombia*. Bogotá: CILEP, pp. 59–113.
  (2011). El final del movimiento autónomo: el anarquismo entre 1928–1930. In CILEP, ed., *Pasado y presente del anarquismo y del anarcosindicalismo en Colombia*. Bogotá: CILEP, pp. 131–150.
Franck, H. A. (1913). *Zone Policeman 88: A Close Range Study of the Panama Canal and Its Workers*, New York: The Century Co.
Franco Muñoz, H. (1986). *Blázquez de Pedro y los orígenes del sindicalismo panameño*, Panama City: Movimiento Editores.
Galván-Álvarez, E. (2017). Anarchism and the Anti-colonial Canarian Imagination. *History Workshop Journal*, 83(1), 253–271.
Gandásequi, M. (1990). *Las luchas obreras en Panamá, 1850–1978*, Panama City: CELA.
García, G. L. and Quintero Rivera, A. G. (1982). *Desafío y solidaridad: breve historia del movimiento obrero puertorriqueño*, Río Piedras, PR: Ediciones Huracán.
García Osuna, A. J. (2003). *The Cuban Filmography: 1897 through 2001*, Jefferson: McFarland and Company.
González, A. P. (2012). De la Liga Racionalista a Cómo Educa el Estado a Tu Hijo: El Itenario de Julio Barcos. *Revista Historia*, 65–66, 123–141.
González, D. (1988). La inmigración española en Cuba. *Economía y Desarrollo* 1: 105.
González, J. (1907). *El tabaquero en Tampa: Impresiones personales*, Havana: Rambla y Bouza.

Gorman, A. (2010). "Diverse in Race, Religion and Nationality ... but United in Aspirations of Civil Progress": The Anarchist Movement in Egypt 1860–1940. In S. Hirsch and L. van der Walt, eds., *Anarchism and Syndicalism in the Colonial and Postcolonial World*, Leiden: Brill, pp. 3–31.

Greene, J. (2004). Spaniards on the Silver Roll: Labor Troubles and Liminality in the Panama Canal Zone, 1904–1914. *International Labor and Working-Class History*, 66, 78–98.

  (2009). *The Canal Builders: Making America's Empire at the Panama Canal*, New York: Penguin Press.

Grez Toso, S. (2012). Resistencia cultural anarquista: Poesía, canto y dramaturgia en Chile, 1895–1918. In C. E. Lida and P. Yankelevich, eds., *Cultura y política del anarquismo en España e Iberoamérica*. Mexico City: El Colgio de México, pp. 259–296.

Guiral Moreno, M. (1919). *La dictadura proletariado*, Havana: El Siglo XX.

Hatzky, C. (2008). *Julio Antonio Mella (1903–1929), una biografía*, Santiago de Cuba: Editorial Oriente.

Hernández, S. (2016). Chicanas in the Borderlands: Trans-border Conversations of Feminism and Anarchism, 1905–1938. In C. K. Blanton, ed., *A Promising Problem: The New Chicana/o History of the Twenty-First Century*. Austin: University of Texas Press, pp. 135–160.

Hernández Padilla, S. (1988). *El magonismo: historia de una pasión libertaria, 1900–1922*, 2nd edition, Mexico City: Ediciones Era.

Hewitt, N. (2001). *Southern Discomfort: Women's Activism in Tampa, Florida, 1880s–1920s*, Urbana: University of Illinois Press.

Hirsch, S. (2010). Peruvian Anarcho-Syndicalism: Adapting Transnational Influences and Forging Counterhegemonic Practices, 1905–1930. In S. Hirsch and L. van der Walt, eds., *Anarchism and Syndicalism in the Colonial and Postcolonial World, 1870–1940: The Praxis of National Liberation, Internationalism, and Social Revolution*. Leiden: Brill, pp. 227–271.

  (2017). Ripple Effects: The Bolshevik Revolution and the Decline of Peruvian Anarchism, 1917–1930. Paper presented at the Latin American Studies Association meeting in Lima, Peru.

Hodges, D. C. (1995). *Mexican Anarchism after the Revolution*. Austin: University of Texas Press.

Hoyt, A. (2018). And They Called Them "Galleanisti": The Rise of the *Cronaca Souversiva* and the Formation of America's Most Infamous Anarchist Faction (1895–1912). Ph.D. dissertation, University of Minnesota.

  (2018). Uncovering and Understanding Hidden Bonds: Applying Social Field Theory to the Financial Records of Anarchist Newspapers. In F. Ferretti, G. Barrera de la Torre, A. Ince, and F. Toro eds., *Historical Geographies of Anarchism: Early Critical Geographers and Present-Day Scientific Challenges*, London: Routledge, pp. 25–39.

Iglesias de Pagán, I. (1973). *El obrerismo en Puerto Rico: Época de Santiago Iglesias (1896–1905)*, Palencia de Castilla: Ediciones Juan Ponce de León.

Iglesias Pantín, S. (1929/1958). *Luchas emancipadoras (Crónicas de Puerto Rico)*, Vol. I, San Juan, PR: Imprenta Venezuela.

Instituto de Historia del Movimiento Comunista y de la Revolución Socialista de Cuba (1975). *El movimiento obrero cubano: documentos y artículos*, Vol. 1. Havana: Editorial de Ciencias Sociales.
IWW Local Unions (Database) (n.d.). http://depts.washington.edu/iww/locals.shtml.
Jeifets, L. S., Jeifets, V. L., and Huber, P., eds. (2004). *La Internacional Comunista y América Latina, 1919–1943: Diccionario Biográfico*, Moscow: Instituto de Latinoamérica de la Academia de las Ciencias.
Jensen, R. B. (2014). *The Battle against Anarchist Terrorism: An International History, 1878– 1934*, New York: Cambridge University Press.
Justiniani, N. (1971). Recuerdos imborrables Don José María Blásquez de Pedro y el Dr. José Llorent. *Revista Lotería*, 186, 69–70.
Kaltmeier, O. (2014). Inter-American Perspectives for the Re-thinking of Area Studies. *Forum for Inter-American Research*, 7(3), 171–182.
Kanello, N. (2011). *Hispanic Immigrant Literature: El Sueño del Retorno*, Austin: University of Texas Press.
Khuri-Makdisi, I. (2010). *The Eastern Mediterranean and the Making of Global Radicalism, 1860–1914*, Berkeley: University of California Press.
Lambe, A. M. (2014). Cuban Antifascism and the Spanish Civil War: Transnational Activism, Networks, and Solidarity in the 1930s. Ph.D. dissertation, Columbia University.
Leier, M. (2009). *Bakunin: The Creative Passion*, New York: Seven Stories Press.
Linebaugh, P. and Rediker, M. (2000). *The Many-Headed Hydra: Sailors, Slaves, Commoners, and the Hidden History of the Revolutionary Atlantic*, Boston: Beacon Press.
Llaguno Thomas, J. J. (2016). Acción Local y Auditorio Global: La Presencia Anarquista en América Central Según sus Fondos Documentales entre 1910 y 1930. *Diálogos*, 17(2), 33–51.
Long, D. (1965). "La Resistencia": Tampa's Immigrant Labor Union. *Labor History*, 6, 193–213.
 (1968). The Open–Closed Shop Battle in Tampa's Cigar Industry, 1919–1921. *The Florida Historical Quarterly*, 47(2), 101–121.
Longley, K. (2009). *In the Eagle's Shadow: The United States and Latin America*, 2nd edition, Wheeling, IL: Harlan Davidson, Inc.
López, J. J. (1910). *Voces Libertarias*, San Juan, PR: Tipografía La Bomba.
Loveira, C. (1923). *El socialismo en Yucatán*, Havana: El Siglo XX.
Marco Serra, Y. (1997). *Los obreros españoles en la construcción del canal de Panamá. La emigración española hacia Panamá vista a través de la prensa Española*, Panama: Editorial Portobelo.
Maritime Timetable Images (n.d.). www.timetableimages.com/maritime.
Marshall, P. (1993). *Demanding the Impossible: A History of Anarchism*, London: Fontana Press/Harper Collins.
Matamoros, M. (1982). *El camino es la organización: la mujer en las luchas populares, 1925–1982*, Panama: Unión Nacional de Mujeres Panameñas.
Mayol Martínez, J. (1899). Enrique Creci. Typewritten copy from his book Vibraciones. Museo Municipal de Regla, Cuba.

McKinley, B. (1987). "A Religion of the New Time": Anarchist Memorials to the Haymarket Martyrs, 1888–1917. *Labor History*, 28(3), 386–400.

MCLE, ed. (1977). *Marcelo Salinas, Un ideal sublime y elevado*, Miami: Ediciones del Movimiento Libertario Cubano en el Exilio.

Meléndez-Badillo, J. A. (2013). Interpreting, Deconstructing and Deciphering Ideograms of Rebellion: An Approach to the History of Reading in Puerto Rico's Anarchist Groups at the Beginning of the Twentieth Century, 1899–1919. In J. A. Meléndez-Badillo and N. Jun, eds., *Without Borders or Limits: An Interdisciplinary Approach to Anarchist Studies*. Cambridge: Cambridge Scholars Publishing, pp. 57–74.

  (2016). Los ecos del silencio: Dimensiones locales y aspiraciones globales del peródico Voz Humana. *La Brecha: Revista Anarquista de Historia y Ciencias Sociales*, 2(3), 23–27.

Melgar Bao, R. (2002). Redes del exilio aprista en México (1923–1924). In P. Yankelevich, ed., *México, país refugio: la experiencia de los exilios en el siglo XX*. Mexico City: Plaza y Valdes, pp. 245–264.

  (2009). Cominternismo intellectual: Representaciones, redes y practicas politico culturales en América Central, 1921–1933. *Revista Complutense de Historia de América*, 35, 135–159.

Migueláñez Martínez, M. (2014). El proyecto continental del anarquismo argentino: resultados y usos de una propaganda transfronteriza (1920–1930). *Revista de Historia Contemporanea*, 94(2), 71–95.

Miranda, M. M. (1903). *Memorias de un deportado*, Havana: La Luz.

Monteflores, O. L. (2011). El anarquismo en Guatemala: El anarcosyndicalismo en la Ciudad de Guatemala, 1920–1932. Thesis, Universidad de San Carlos de Guatemala.

Montes de Oca, R. (2016). *Contracorriente: Historia del movimiento anarquista en Venezuela (1811–1998)*, Caracas: El Libertario.

Mormino, G. R. and Pozzetta, G. E. (1986). Spanish Anarchism in Tampa, Florida, 1886–1931. In D. Hoerder, ed., *"Struggle a Hard Battle": Essays on Working-Class Immigrants*. DeKalb: Northern Illinois University Press, 170–198.

Muller, D. A. (2017). *Cuban Émigrés & Independence in the Nineteenth-Century Gulf World*, Chapel Hill: University of North Carolina Press.

Muriel, J. (1986). Este hombre generoso que no sabía odiar. *Guángara Libertaria*, Winter, 15–24.

Naranjo Orovio, C. (1992). Trabajo libre e inmigración española en Cuba, 1880–1930. *Revista de Indias* 52: 790.

Navas, L. (1979). *El movimiento obrero en Panamá (1880–1914)*, San José, Costa Rica: Editorial Universitaria Centroamericana.

  (1997). Tareas sobre la marcha: *Cuasimodo* y el movimiento obrero. *Tareas*, 97, 133–144.

Olay, M. (1941). *Mirando al mundo*, Buenos Aires: Impresos Americalee.

Padura, L. (2017). *Heretics*, New York: Farrar, Straus and Giroux.

Page, W. H. and Page, A. W. (1910). *The World's Work, Volume XX, May to October 1910*, Garden City, NY: Doubleday, Page, & Co.

Paredes Goicochea, D. (2011). El anarcosindicalismo colombiano de 1924–1928: hacia la claridad ideológica, táctica y organizativa. In CILEP, ed., *Pasado y presente del anarquismo y del anarcosindicalismo en Colombia*. Bogotá: CILEP, pp. 115–129.

Paz, A. (2007). *Durruti in the Spanish Revolution*, Oakland: AK Press.

Penichet, A. (1918). *Del ambiente proletario*, Havana: Avisador Comercial.

　(1919). *El soldado Rafael; páginas de la vida real*, Havana: Grupo Germinal.

　(1919). *La vida de un pernicioso*, Havana: Avisador Comercial.

　(1921). *¡Alma Rebelde!, novela histórica*, Havana: El Ideal.

　(1922). *Tácticas en uso y tácticas a seguir*, Havana: El Ideal.

Pérez, E. J. (1989). May Day 1899 in Puerto Rico. In A. Panaccione, ed., *The Memory of May Day: An Iconographic History of the Origins and Implanting of a Workers' Holiday*. Venezia: Marsilio Editori, pp. 679–685.

Pérez, L. A. (1988). *Cuba: Between Reform and Revolution*, New York: Oxford University Press.

Poyo, G. (1985). The Anarchist Challenge to the Cuban Independence Movement, 1885–1890. *Cuban Studies*, 15(1), 29–42.

Primelles, L, ed. (1957). *Crónica Cubana, 1919–1922*. Havana: Editorial Lex.

Procedimientos del sexto congreso obrero de la Federación Libre de los Trabajadores de Puerto Rico. Celebrado del 18 al 24 de marzo de 1910, en la ciudad de Juncos, Puerto Rico (1910). San Juan, PR: Tipografía de M. Burillo & Co.

Proceedings of the First Canal Commission. March 22, 1904 to March 29, 1905 (1905). Washington: ICC.

Putnam, L. (2009). Nothing Matters but Color: Transnational Circuits, the Interwar Caribbean, and the Black International. In M. West, W. Martin, and F. Wilkins, eds., *From Toussaint to Tupac: The Black International since the Age of Revolution*. Chapel Hill: University of North Carolina Press, pp. 107–129.

　(2013). *Radical Moves: Caribbean Migrants and the Politics of Race in the Age of Jazz*, Chapel Hill: University of North Carolina Press.

Quintero, I. (1979). *El Sindicato General de Trabajadores*, Panama City: CELA.

Ramnath, M. (2011). *Decolonizing Anarchism: An Antiauthoritarian History of India's Liberation Struggle*. Oakland: AK Press.

　(2019). Non-Western Anarchism and Postcolonialism. In C. Levy and M. S. Adams, eds., *The Palgrave Handbook of Anarchism*. London: Palgrave Macmillan.

Reyes Rivas, E. M. (2000). *El trabajo de las mujeres en la historia de la construcción del Canal de Panamá, 1881–1914*, Panama City: Universidad de Panama's Instituto de la Mujer.

Rosell, M. ed. (1973). *Luchas obreras contra Machado*, Havana: Editorial de Ciencias Sociales.

Salinas, M. (1936). The Protector. In D. Brewster, ed., *A Book of Contemporary Short Stories*. New York: Macmillan Company, pp. 371–376.

　(1937). *Un aprendiz de revolucionario*, El Fígaro: Havana.

　(1962). Alma Guajira. In D. Martí de Cid, ed., *Teatro Cubano Contemporaneo*, 2nd edition, Madrid: Aguilar, pp. 387–448.

Sánchez Cobos, A. (2008). *Sembrando ideales. Anarquistas españoles en Cuba (1902–1925)*, Madrid: Consejo Superior de Investigaciones Científicas.
Sandos, J. (1992). *Rebellion in the Borderlands: Anarchism and the Plan de San Diego*, Norman: University of Oklahoma Press.
Santiago de las Vegas en Líneas. http://sdlv.blogspot.com/2008/02/teatro-santia guero-alma-guajira.html.
Scaglione, J. (1992). City in Turmoil: Tampa and the Strike of 1910. *Sunland Tribune*, 18, 29–36.
Schmidt, M. and van der Walt, L. (2009). *Black Flame: The Revolutionary Class Politics of Anarchism and Syndicalism*, Oakland: AK Press.
Schwartz, R. (1989). *Lawless Liberators: Political Banditry and Cuban Independence*, Durham, NC: Duke University Press.
Selbin, E. (2016). Spaces and Places of (Im)Possibility and Desire: Transversal Revolutionary Imaginaries in the Twentieth Century Americas. *Forum for Inter-American Research*, 9(1), 19–40.
Shaffer, K. (2005). *Anarchism and Countercultural Politics in Early Twentieth-Century Cuba*, Gainesville: University Press of Florida.
  (2009). Havana Hub: Cuban Anarchism, Radical Media, and the Trans-Caribbean Anarchist Network, 1902–1915. *Caribbean Studies*, 37(2), 45–81.
  (2011). Contesting Internationalists: Transnational Anarchism, Anti-imperialism, and US Expansion in the Caribbean, 1890s–1930s. *Estudios Interdisciplinarios de América Latina y el Caribe*, 22(2), 11–38.
  (2013). *Black Flag Boricuas: Anarchism, Antiauthoritarianism, and the Left in Puerto Rico, 1897–1921*, Urbana: University of Illinois Press.
  (2014). An Anarchist Crucible: International Anarchist Migrants and Their Cuban Experiences, 1890s–1920s. In M. Font and A. Tinajero, eds., *Handbook on Cuban History, Literature, and the Arts*. Boulder: Paradigm Press, pp. 79–91.
  (2014). Latin Lines and Dots: Transnational Anarchism, Regional Networks, and Italian Libertarians in Latin America. *Zapruder World: An International Journal for the History of Social Conflict*, 1, http://zapruderworld.org/?s=latin+lines+and+dots.
Silén, J. A. (1995). *Apuntes: Para la historia del movimiento obrero puertorriqueño*, 2nd edition, Río Piedras, PR: Norberto González.
Smith, M. (1995). The Political Economy of Sugar Production and the Environment of Eastern Cuba, 1898–1923. *Environmental History Review*, 19(4), 31–48.
Soler, R. (1989). *Panamá: historia de una crisis*, Panama City: Siglo XXI.
Sonn, R. (1992). *Anarchism*, New York: Twayne Publishers.
Soriano Jiménez, I. C. and Íñiguez, M. (2017). *José María Blázquez de Pedro: anarquista de ambos mundos (en Béjar, Panamá y Cuba)*, Vitoria, Spain: Asociación Isaac Puente.
Sowell, D. (1992). *The Early Colombian Labor Movement: Artisans and Politics in Bogotá, 1832–1919*. Philadelphia: Temple University Press.
Struthers, D. (2017). IWW International and Interracial Organizing in the Southwestern United States. In P. Cole, D. Struthers, and K. Zimmer, eds.,

Wobblies of the World: A Global History of the IWW. London: Pluto Press, pp. 74–88.
  (2019). *The World in a City: Multiethnic Radicalism in Early Twentieth-Century Los Angeles*, Urbana: University of Illinois Press.
Sueiro Seoane, S. (2014). Prensa y redes anarquistas transnacionales: El olvidado papel de J.C. Campos y sus crónicas sobre los mártires de Chicago en el anarquismo de lengua hispana. *Cuadernos de Historia Contemporánea*, 36, 259–295.
Táctica, (Soler, R.). (1996). Cuasimodo: alba de la utopía. *Tareas*, 94, 9–38.
Taracena Arriola, A. (1988). Presencia anarquista en Guatemala entre 1920 y 1932. *Mesoamerica*, 15, 1–23.
Tellería Toca, E. (1972). Alfredo López. *Bohemia*, 43, 97–103.
  (1973). *Los congreso obreros en Cuba*, Havana: Editorial de Ciencias Sociales.
Tibol, R. (1968). *Julio Antonio Mella en EL MACHETE: Antología parcial de un luchador y su momento histórico*, Mexico City: Fondo de Cultura Popular.
Torres, A. (1905). *¡Solidaridad!*, San Juan, PR: Unión Tipográfica.
Turcato, D. (2007). Italian Anarchism as a Transnational Movement, 1885–1915. *International Review of Social History*, 52, 407–444.
  (2010). The Hidden History of the Anarchist Atlantic: Malatesta in America, 1899–1900. Paper presented at the European Social Science History Conference, Ghent, Belgium.
  (2012). *Making Sense of Anarchism: Errico Malatesta's Experiments with Revolution, 1889–1900*, New York: Palgrave Macmillan.
  (2017). Nations without Borders: Anarchists and National Identity. In C. Bantman and B. Altena, eds., *Reassessing the Transnational Turn: Scales of Analysis in Anarchist and Syndicalist Studies*. Oakland: PM Press, pp. 25–42.
Turner, J. (1982). *Raíz, historia y perspectivas del movimiento obrero panameño*, Mexico City: Editorial Signos.
Valadés, J. C. (1986). *Memorias de un joven rebelde. 2a. parte. Mis confesiones*, Sinaloa, Mexico: Universidad Autónoma de Sinaloa.
Van der Walt, L. and Hirsch, S. (2010). Rethinking Anarchism and Syndicalism. In S. Hirsch and L. van der Walt, eds., *Anarchism and Syndicalism in the Colonial and Postcolonial World*. Leiden: Brill, pp. xxxi–lxxiii.
Villanueva Martínez, O., ed. (1992). *Biófila Panclasta: El eterno prisionero*, Bogotá: Editorial CODICE LTDA.
Viñas, D. (1983). *Anarquistas en América Latina*, Ciudad de México: Editorial Katun.
Weber, D. (2016). Wobblies of the Partido Liberal Mexicano: Reenvisioning Internationalist and Transnationalist Movements through Mexican Lenses. *Pacific Historical Review*, 85(2), 188–226.
Weeks, G. (2008). *U.S. and Latin American Relations*, New York: Pearson Longman.
Wells, A. and Joseph, G. (1996). *Summer of Discontent, Season of Upheaval: Elite Politics and Rural Insurgency in Yucatán, 1876–1915*, Palo Alto: Stanford University Press.
Whitney, R. (2001). *State and Revolution in Cuba: Mass Mobilization and Political Change, 1920–1940*, Chapel Hill: University of North Carolina Press.

Wood, A. and Baer, J. (2006). Strength in Numbers: Urban Rent Strikes and Political Transformation in the Americas, 1904–1925. *Journal of Urban History*, 32(6), 862–885.

Woodcock, G. (1971). *Anarchism: A History of Libertarian Ideas and Movements*, New York: World Publishing.

Zimmer, K. (2015). *Immigrants against the State: Yiddish and Italian Anarchism in America*, Urbana: University of Illinois Press.

　(2017). A Golden Gate of Anarchy: Local and Transnational Dimensions of Anarchism in San Francisco, 1880s–1930. In C. Bantman and B. Altena, eds., *Reassessing the Transnational Turn: Scales of Analysis in Anarchist and Syndicalist Studies*. Oakland: PM Press, pp. 100–117.

　(2017). At War with Empire: The Anti-colonial Roots of American Anarchist Debates during the First World War. In M. Adams and R. Kinna, eds., *Anarchism, 1914–1918: Internationalism, Antimilitarism, and War*. Manchester: Manchester University Press, pp. 175–198.

Zumoff, J. A. (2013). Black Caribbean Labor Radicalism in Panama, 1914–1921. *Journal of Social History*, 47(2), 429–457.

　(2017). The 1925 Tenants' Strike in Panama: West Indians, the Left, and the Labor Movement. *The Americas*, 74(4), 513–546.

Index

Abad de Santillán, Diego, 242
Abello, Manuel Martínez, 81
ACP (American Communist Party), 174, 204
   and Puerto Rican anarchists, 170, 172
AFL (American Federation of Labor), 20, 65, 225
   anarchist conflicts with, 103
   anarchist cooperation with, 32
   in Canal Zone, 227
Albizu Campos, Pedro
   anarchist opposition to, 254
   and anarchist critiques of, 261
Albuquerque, Miguel, 26
Alicea, José María, 171
   anti-military draft actions, 195
Alicea, Juan M., 170
Alonsín, J., 67
Altena, Bert, 9, 23, 27
Álvarez, Antonio
   and anti-militarism, 206
American Legion, 181
American Tobacco Corporation, 14
Anarcho-Journalism, 25–26, 30–34, 88, 227
Anderson, Benedict, 26, 38, 41
ANERC (Asociación de Nuevos Emigrados Revolucionarios de Cuba), 264–265
Angiolillo, Michele, 60
Anti-Americanism, 65
   anarchist about Mexican Revolution, 129–130

anarchist in Cuba 1920s, 209–210
   and deportation of José María Blázquez de Pedro, 246
   Cuba 1898–1902, 66–70
   regional, 123–124
Anti-clericalism, 1, 112
   in Puerto Rico, 257
Anti-colonialism, 1, 65
Anti-imperialism, 20–21, 39, 65, 187
Antilleans, 14, 27, 112, 227
Anti-militarism
   and education in Cuba, 206
   and education in Puerto Rico, 205–206
Arévalo, Juan, 260
Ascaso, Francisco, 244
Asociación Libertaria de Cuba, 262
Assassination, 79
   of Cuban radicals, 210
   of European leaders, 134
   of President McKinley, 84
   plot vs. President Wilson, 177–180
   plots against radicals, 266–267
Ateneo Popular, 267, 270
Atton, Chris, 30
Aurelio, Luis, 263

Bakunin, Mikhail, 105
Baliño, Carlos, 164–165
Ballagas, Fausto, 271
Banana Republic, 40, 187
   Cuba as, 211
Banditry, 197
   anarchist support for, 71

Bantman, Constance, 9, 23, 27
Barcia, Luis, 100, 104, 183, 254
  in 1920s, 254
  and ¡Tierra!, 86
  during Cuban War for Independence, 81
  in Cuba, 66–67
  in Florida, 75, 81–82
  in New York, 81
  and post-anarchist era, 254
  radical biography of, 80–82
  shanghaiied, 82–84
  and trans-straits organizing, 75–76
  and violence, 84
Barcos, Julio, 26
  and anti-Americanism, 207
  and Bolshevik Revolution, 157
  in Central America, 219–220
  and Pan-Americanism, 222
Barilla, Vicente, 227
Barreiro, Alejandro, 259, 266
  and Marxist-anarchist alliance, 164
Barrera Bassols, Jacinto, 127, 130
Barrios, Francisca, 129
Barrios, Ramón, 170
Basora, Florencio, 109, 128
Batista, Fulgencio, 272
Bautista Grajedo, Manuel, 253
Berkman, Alexander, 199
Betances, Ramón Emeterio, 59–60
Betancourt, Inocenta, 260
Blajes, Angelo, 194
Blázquez de Pedro, José María, 262
  and 1916 general strike, 190, 194
  and anarchist congress 1925, 7, 239, 243
  anticlerical, 3
  arrival in Canal Zone, 110, 120–122, 188
  and Bolshevik Revolution, 158, 164
  burial of in Panama, 251
  and Colombian anarchists, 229–230
  and communism, 159
  Cuban War for Independence, 1–3
  death of in Cuba, 247, 262
  deportation from Panama of, 7–8, 245–246
  education, 3–4, 6
  and education in Panama, 218–219
  family, 5
  and Fiesta de la Raza, 220
  and the FORP, 224
  and Grupo Comunista, 158, 224
  and Grupo Renovación Social, 227
  labor, 7
  labor in Panama, 5
  and Pan-Americanism, 220–221, 225
  and planning for Inter-Continental Congress of Anarchists, 247–248
  and pleasure, 4–5, 262
  poetry of, 29
  and Russian Revolution, 157
  and SGT, 228
  versus democracy, 6
  versus Kropotkin on Great War, 199–200
Blázquez de Pedro, Martín, 239, 243
  and SGT, 228
Bolívar, Simón, 216–217
Bolshevik Revolution, 154
  and anarchist opposition to in Cuba, 163–167
  and anarchist support for, 164
  and anarchist support for in Cuba, 165–166
  in Cuba, 159–168
  in Florida, 182
  and impact on José C. Valadés, 240
  impact in Latin America, 155
  in Panama, 156–159
  in Puerto Rico, 170–173
Bombings
  by anarchists in Cuba, 72, 162, 263
  as assassination of President Wilson, 177
  during Cuban War for Independence, 55–56
  and Red Scare, 180
Bosch, Mayor Antonio (Regla, Cuba), 166
Boyd, Governor Archibaldo (Panama), 231
Brower, Jorge, 227
  and the FORP, 224

Caballero, César, 225
Campo, Salvatore "Sem," 141–142
Campos, J.C., 49, 81
Canalejas, Prime Minister José (Spain), 134
Canales, Nemesio, 220
Cano, María, 254
Canoura, Vicente, 165
Cánovas del Castillo, Prime Minister Antonio (Spain), 51
Capetillo, Luisa, 103, 171, 253
Carr, Barry, 18, 25, 37, 41
Carrasco, Julio
  1916 general strike in Canal Zone, 194

and anti-Americanism in Canal Zone, 118
Carrera Jústiz, Francisco, 161
Carrillo Puerto, Governor Felipe (Mexico), 153
Caruso, Enrico, 162, 275
Casa del Obrero Internacional, 150
Casellas, Pedro, 82
Casís, Samuel, 232, 238
Castillo, Mario, 276
Cerraí, J., 46, 50–52
Céspedes, Carlos, 227, 233
CGT (Confederación General de Trabajadores), 240
Chacón Uceda, Juan, 113
Chas, Enrique T., 143
Chiari, President Rodolfo (Panama), 231–232, 234
  and banning red flags, 236
  and deportation of José María Blázquez de Pedro, 245
  invites US military, 234
Citizens Committee (Tampa), 80, 82–84, 100
  Red Scare version, 180–182
CMIU (Cigar Makers International Union), 94
CNOC (Confederación Nacional de Obreros Cubanos), 167, 252
  anarchist attacks against in 1930s, 271
Cohn, Jesse, 27
Cole, Peter, 104
Colmé, Ramón, 183
Colombia, 36–37, 40
  anarchism in, 227, 231, 243
  anarchists in, 229–230, 252, 254
Colón, Herminio, 171
Columbus, Christopher
  anarchist interpretation of, 221–222
Comintern (Communist International), 21, 36, 172
Comité Pro-Presos Internacional, 115
Comité Pro-Presos Libertarios, 267
Comité Revolucionario Proletario de Cuba, 267
Congreso Nacional Obrero (Cuba), 162
Continental Caribbean, 289
Costa Rica, 36–37, 40
  anarchists in, 253
Craib, Raymond, 24
Creci, Enrique, 42–44, 61
Cruz, Venancio, 95, 97

Cuba libre, 118
  anarchist derision of, 74
  anarchist support for, 55
Cuban War for Independence, 38
  as allegory for *machadto* era, 283–285
  anarchist opposition to, 53
  anarchist support for, 51–60
  in anarchist fiction, 277, 283
  impact on anarchists, 62–63, 205
  as inspiration for 1920s exiles, 266
Cuervo, M., 209

Davis, Governor George (Canal Zone), 107
De Borrán, Jorge
  in Canal Zone, 189
  in New York, 159, 221–222
  and Pan-Americanism, 221–222
De Laforcade, Geoffroy, 10
De León, Daniel, 93
De Lidia, Palmiro, 54, 95
  support for Cuban War for Independence, 55
De Sárraga, Belén, 25
Debs, Eugene V., 46
Del Valle, Adrián, 25, 28, 38, 288
  Ambición, 280
  Aristócratas, 280
  Anti-Americanism, 66–67
  and Bolshevik Revolution, 168–174
  Camelanga, 282
  Camelanga and Banana Republics, 208–209
  Cero, 280
  De maestro a guerrillero, 138, 282
  death of, 286
  and *El Nuevo Ideal*, 66
  El príncipe que no quiso gobernar, 282
  El tesoro escondido, 280
  Fin de fiesta, 29
  and Great War, 200
  Historia documentada de la conspiración de la Gran Legión del Águila Negra, 283–285
  Jesús en la guerra, 200–201
  Juan sin pan, 283
  Jubilosa, 281
  and Kropotkin, 284–285
  La mulata Soledad, 281
  litarary prizes for, 273
  and *machadato*-era fiction, 279–284
  and Mexican Revolution, 137–139

Del Valle, Adrián (cont.)
  Mi amigo Julio, 281
  Náufragos, 280, 283
  and settings for stories, 275
  on a stateless Cuba, 70
  and trans-straits organizing, 75–76, 82
  Tiberianos, 283
  women in *machadato*-era fiction, 281–282
Delgado, Secundino, 53
Democracy
  anarchist attacks against in Cuba, 72
  anarchist attacks against in Florida, 48–51
  anarchist attacks against in Panama, 117–118
  anarchist attacks against in Puerto Rico, 96–98
Deportation
  and anarchist diffusion, 17, 248–249
  of anarchists during Cuban War for Independence, 56
  from Panama 1916, 194
  from Panama 1925, 230, 233, 236, 245–246, 248–249
  from United States, 135–136, 175
  in post-independence Cuba, 73, 160, 170, 210–211, 260
Día de la Raza
  and Panama Rent Strike, 234
Díaz, Julio, 239
  in Central America, 242
Díaz, Luis, 183
Díaz, Marcelino, 120
Díaz, President Porfirio (Mexico), 127
Dieppa, Ángel María, 171
  -and Bolshevism, 175
  and Mexican Revolution, 134
  and Puerto Rican independence, 202–203
  on 1930s Puerto Rico, 257
Díez, Paulino, 167
Domínguez, Segrifredo, 225
Downing, John, 31
Draft, military, 39
  anarchist opposition to, 195–196
  laws, 186
Duch, Antonio J., 127
Durruti, Buenaventura, 244

Ecuador
  anarchism in, 227
  anarchists in, 26

Education
  and anarchist anti-militarism, 205–206
  in Central America, 219–220
  and Mexican Revolution, 132–133, 138, 143
  and the Moncaleano Affair, 150–151
  rationalist, 219–220
El Grupo Soviet de Bayamón, 170
El Salvador, 36–37
Escabí, Paca, 97
Espina, R.R., 163
Esteve, Pedro, 25, 38
  death of, 253
  in Florida, 88, 131, 173
  linked to Puerto Rican anarchists, 169
  and Mexican Revolution, 131, 142, 147
  in New York, 103
  and Pardiñas obituary, 135
  versus Kropotkin on Great War, 199
Ethnicity
  and class conflict in Cuba, 69
  and class conflict in Florida, 76–78, 86–87, 101
  and race in Canal Zone, 111–113
  and race in Panama, 227–228

Fabregat, Luis, 178–180, 260
  anti-anarchism in Cuba, 179
Fascism, 40
Federación Anarquista Centroamericana y del Caribe, 287
Federación Anarquista de Cuba, 91
Federación Anarquista de Panamá, 114, 141, 145
Federación de Jóvenes Comunistas, 240
Federación de los Grupos Anarquistas (Cuba), 160
Fernández Bustamante, Luis, 233
Fernando Póo, 17, 70
Ferrara, Orestes
  and anarchism in Tampa, 57
  as Cuban ambassador during *machadato*, 264
  as Havana lawyer, 127
  opposition to Bolshevik Revolution, 161
Ferrer y Ferrer, José, 94–95, 255
Ferrer y Guardia, Francisco, 3, 146
FGAC (Federación de Grupos Anarquistas de Cuba), 267, 270
  and Spanish Civil War, 285

Index

Fiction, Anarchist
  and the Great War, 29
  approaches to, 27–30, 139
Fiesta de la Raza, 220–222
FII (Federación Individualista Internacional), 114, 120
Finlay, Dr. Carlos, 115
Five Came Back, 214–216, 251
Fiz Jiménez, Epifanio, 255
Flores Magón, Enrique
  and Moncaleano Affair, 150
  and PCC in Cuba, 258
Flores Magón, Ricardo, 240
  and conflicts in Los Angeles, 147
  funeral of, 241
  in St. Louis, 110
FLT (Federación Libre de Trabajadores), 171
FOH (Federación Obrera de la Habana), 167, 268
  anarchist criticism of, 167–168
FORA (Federación Obrera Regional de Argentina), 10, 239
Fori, Rafael, 194
FORP (Federación Obrera de la República de Panamá), 7
FORP (Federación Obrera Regional de Perú), 229
Freemasons, 14
Fuentes, Manuel, 88
Fueyo, José, 82, 88

Galindo, Mayor Mario (Panama City)
  and rent strike, 231–232
García, Álbin, 254
García, José
  in Cuban War for Independence, 52
  and rural anarchism in Cuba, 89–90
García, Manuel
  and anti-militarism, 206
  attacks Wilsonian foreign policy, 207
Garrido C., Manuel
  and the FORP, 224
  and 1916 general strike in Canal Zone, 194
  and rent strike prosecution, 238
Garvey, Marcus, 37
Gillett, M.E., 181
Globalization, 40
Goicoitía, Maximino, 45, 47
Gómez, Arsenio, 233

Gompers, Samuel, 85
  and Panama, 227–228
González Rodríguez, José, 224
González, Herminio, 103
González, Serafín, 141
  and Panama-Cuba link, 110
Gorgas, Dr. William, 115
Gratz, Sara, 243
  and SGT, 228
Grau San Martín, President Ramón (Cuba), 271
Grau, José, 180
  accused in Wilson assassination plot, 179
Great War, 39
  anarchist attacks on military draft, 195–196
  anarchist literature about, 197–202
  anarchist support for, 198–199
  Panama declaration of war (1917), 186
  and US militarization of Caribbean, 187
  US military draft for, 186
Grez Toso, Sergio, 28
Grupo Acción Libertaria (Cuba), 160
Grupo Comunista, 7
  and Bolshevik Revolution, 159
  formation of, 158
  and Pan-American labor, 223–226
  and rent issues in Panama, 229
  and transnational links, 159
Grupo Renovación Social, 227
Guatemala, 36–37, 40
  anarchism in, 259
  anarchists in, 253
Guerrero, Práxedis, 128
Guevara, Ernesto, 290
Guiral Moreno, Mario
  opposition to Bolshevik Revolution, 161
Gutarra, Nicolás, 17, 229–230
Gutiérrez Posada, J.M., 252
Gutiérrez, Sierra
  and rent strike prosecution, 238

Harding, Acting Governor Chester
  and 1916 general strike, 189–194
Hart, Gary
  I, Che Guevara, 289
Hatzky, Christine, 266
Haymarket Affair, 48–49, 51, 67, 83, 88, 129, 131
Haywood, Big Bill, 102
Hernández, Sonia, 152
Hershey, Milton, 15

Hirsch, Steven, 10, 20, 239
Horizontalism, 287
Hoyt, Andrew, 31
Hughes, Langston, 279
Hurtado, Braulio, 118, 120, 141

ICC (Isthmian Canal Commission)
  anti-anarchist law, 107
Iglesias Pantín, Santiago, 62
  anarchist attacks on, 256
  anarchist criticisms of, 96
  and AFL, 94
  and Americanization of Puerto Rico, 92
  and Bolshevism, 175
  in Cuba, 57
  and opposition to anarchism, 95–96, 264
  and Puerto Rican independence, 203
  and SLP, 93–94
Iglesias, Jesús, 102
Iglesias, Margarito
  assassination of, 210
Imperialism, 19–20, 34
Independence
  anarchist approaches to in Puerto Rico, 40, 187, 202–205
  anarchist critiques of Puerto Rican nationalists, 202–203, 286–287
  of Panama, 62, 64, 105
Inter-Continental Congress of Anarchists, 7, 239–247
  planning for, 239–243, 248
  suppression of, 243–247
Intervention, US Military, 206–207
  and *machadato*, 211–212
Italians
  anarchists in Florida, 57, 88
  anarchists in New Jersey, 147
  anarchists in Panama, 141
  and Mexican Revolution, 142
IWW (Industrial Workers of the World), 65, 178, 263
  in Cuba, 161, 169–170
  in Florida, 101–105, 134, 181–182, 184
  and Great War, 196–197
  and the Inter-Continental Congress of Anarchists, 243
  in Panama, 225
  in Puerto Rico, 169–170, 256
  and Red Scare, 181
  and transnationalism, 161, 169–170, 196–197

Junco, Sandalio, 266

Kelly, Charles, 82
Kropotkin, Peter, 47, 129, 163, 230, 240
  and Adrián del Valle, 284–285
  and Bolshevik Revolution, 155, 168–174
  death of, 253
  and Great War, 198–200
  and José María Bláquez de Pedro's Great War critique, 199–200

Labor Conditions
  in Florida cigar factories, 45–48
Landazuli, Antonio, 233
Lascarre, César, 194
Lectores, 28, 45
  and anarchism, 98–99
  and CMIU, 175
Lenin, Vladimir, 164–165, 240
  monument to in Cuba, 166
  and Puerto Rican anarchists, 173
Liga de Inquilinos y Subsistencias, 7, 230
  and lead up to rent strike, 231
  moderates in, 236
  and Pan-Americanism, 234
  and response to US invasion, 235
Liga Internacional Racionalista Sección de Cuba, 113
Linebaugh, Peter, 41
Lípiz, Vicente, 73
Llaguno Thomas, José Julián, 23, 39
Lone, Rudolfo, 246
  and anarchist Pan-Americanism, 254
López, Alfredo, 258, 265
  assassination of, 210
  and Bolshevik Revolution, 160, 184
  death of, 259–261
  and the FOH, 167
  remains of, 270
  repression against, 162
López, Aquilino
  in Canal Zone controversy, 142, 144–145
  in Cuba-Panama network, 140
  opposed to PLM, 143
  repression against for naturism, 262
López, Juan José
  and Mexican Revolution, 133–134
Lores, Marcial, 72, 89
Louzara, Jesús
  and the *machadato*, 211
  in Canal Zone, 145

Loveira, Carlos
 and Marcelo Salinas award controversy, 274
 and Mexican Revolution, 153–154

Maceo, Antonio, 59
Machadato, 258–270
 in Cuban anarchist fiction, 277–279
 fall of, 268–270
 José María Blázquez de Pedro in, 246
 and repression of leftists, 210–211
Machado, President Gerardo (Cuba)
 compared to General Weyler, 259, 267
 election of, 168
 as fascist, 258
 and repression, 210
 as US surrogate, 268–270
Madero, President Francisco (Mexico), 137
 anarchist opposition to, 128–130
 assassination plot against, 134–136
Magonistas, 39, 130
 in St. Louis, 128
Magoon, General Charles
 in Canal Zone, 107
 in Cuba, 72
Malatesta, Errico, 25, 38, 65
 in Cuba 1900, 123
 in Florida 1900, 76
Marat, S.F., 260
Marcial, Sandalio
 and anti-militarism, 205
 and Puerto Rican independence, 204
Martí, José, 42, 52, 59
 and militarism legacy, 206
Martínez Abello, Manuel, 87
Martínez Gil, José, 169
Martínez Ybor, Vicente, 44, 47
Marxism, 13, 39
 in anarchist fiction, 278
 in Cuba, 65, 164, 167, 258
 in Panama, 227
May Day
 and the Cuban War for Independence, 51
 in Cuba, 160, 166
 in Panama, 157, 249
 in Puerto Rico, 92, 95, 166, 205
McKinley, President William, 93, 211
 assassination of, 84
 and Cuban War for Independence, 59, 66
Meléndez-Badillo, Jorell, 28

Mella, Julio Antonio, 210
 and anarchist cooperation with, 167
 anarchist liberation of from PCC, 271
 assassination of, 266–267
 compared to Sandino, 266
 on 1928 Pan Am Conference, 263
 and PCC in Cuba, 258
 on Penichet persecution, 261
Mendoza, Francisca J., 146
Menocal, President Mario (Cuba), 73–74, 151, 178
 anti-radicalism, 162
 and declaration of war (1917), 186
 and US military 1917–1918, 197
Messonier, Enrique, 44
Mexican Revolution, 124
 and anarchist literature, 133–139
 and anarchist network policing, 139–153
 anarchist opposition to, 142–144
 anarchist support of, 130–133
 Caribbean anarchist money for, 131–133
 controversies around, 139–151
 impact on Caribbean network, 126
Mexico, 36–37
 Caribbean anarchists in, 126–128
 Cuban exiles in, 265–266
 exiles in, 40
Migration, 16
 anarchists to Canal Zone, 24, 105, 109–111
 of anarchists to Cuba, 24, 80, 89
 to Canal Zone, 108–109
 celebrity anarchist, 25–26
 rank-and-file anarchists, 27
 of Spanish anarchists, 17–18
Mijón, Ventura, 171, 272, 288
 and *El Comunista*, 166–175
 and Puerto Rican Communist Party, 257–258
 and Puerto Rican independence, 203–204
 in Tampa, 102, 134
 transnational migration of, 171
Miqué, Y.A., 67
Mir, Domingo, 110, 259
Miranda, Manuel María, 17, 93, 126
 and anarchist congress, 77
 and Bubis, 70
 deportation of, 56
 on Fernando Póo, 60
Mirones, Marcial, 234
Modotti, Tina, 266

Moncaleano, Blanca, 151
  in Los Angeles, 151
  in Mexico, 148–149
  and rationalist education, 147–148
Moncaleano, Juan Francisco
  child abuse claims, 151
  in Colombia, 147
  in Cuba, 116, 151
  death of (1916), 151
  in Los Angeles, 149–151
  in Mexico, 130, 148–149
  and the Moncaleano Affair, 147–151
  and rationalist education, 147–148
Monroe Doctrine, 216
Monroe, President James, 216
Morales, Eusebio A., 157
Morazín, Amelio
  attacks Wilsonian foreign policy, 207
Morera, Roque, 55
Moscote, José, 218, 220
Mouroa, Luis, 102
Moyano, Antonio, 165
MTW (Maritime Transport Workers), 103, 195
Muñoz Marín, Luis
  anarchist attacks on, 256
  and Bolshevik Revolution, 158
Muñoz, Víctor, 267

Napoleón, José, 156
Nationalism, 1, 13
Naturism
  repression against in Cuba, 261
Negrín, Alfredo, 170
Neocolonialism, 34–36, 65, 69, 73–74, 187
New York City
  and *El Corsario* plot vs. Pres. Wilson, 177
  and Puerto Rican anarchists, 170–178
  as part of the Caribbean, 36
  Puerto Rican anarchist migration, 170–178
Nodal Cities, 18–19, 22
Nogales Méndez, Rafael de, 130
North American Anarchist Studies Network, 287
Novo, José, 119, 141
Núñez, Civil Governor Emilio (Cuba), 68

Occupation, military
  of Cuba, 66, 72–73
  opposition to in Cuba, 66–70

Occupy Movement, 287
Olay, Maximiliano
  in 1920s, 254
  and assassination plot, 135–136
  and return to Americas, 135
  and Spanish Civil War, 285
  in Tampa, 102
Olivé, Salvatore, 113
Orts Ramos, Mario, 275
Owen, W.C., 119

P. de Araujo, Antonio, 146
  and Moncaleano Affair, 150
Padura, Leonardo, 275
Palau de Gámez, Julia, 225
Palau, Antonio, 170
Palmer, Attorney General A. Mitchell (US), 180
Panama Canal Zone
  anarchist anticlericalism in, 116–117
  and anarchist anti-Americanism in, 111–120
  anarchist organizing in (1905-1914), 109–122
  anti-Americanism 1916, 189
  anti-anarchist laws, 107, 186
  1916 general strike, 187–194
  Martime Workers Association, 189–194
  President Roosevelt's visit to (1906), 110–111
  Spaniards in, 108–109
  Víctor Recoba, 189
Pan-American Conference 1928
  anarchist critiques of, 263–264
Pan-Americanism, 40
  anarchist, 213, 219–220, 222, 248, 254
  and Bolshevik Revolution, 158
  and FORP in Panama, 223–228
  and the Grupo Comuista (Panama), 223–226
  of Latin American Masses, 218
  and Liga de Inquilinos y Subsistencias, 230, 234
  of Monroe Doctrine, 216–217
  of Simón Bolívar, 216–217
  and suppression of anarchist congress, 248
Panclasta, Biófilo, 118
Pardiñas, Manuel
  assassination of Canalejas, 134
Parilla, Manuel de J., 102

Pavletich, Esteban M.
 and fluid politics, 249
 in Guatemala with Mella, 249
 in Nicaragua with Sandino, 249
 in Panama, 233
PCC (Partido Comunista Cubano), 254
 anarchist attacks against, 267, 269
 anarchist conflicts with, 270–271
 organized 1925, 258
Peña Vilaboa, José, 164
Penichet, Antonio, 29, 258, 288
 and anti-Machado activities in Cuba, 268
 and antimilitarist fiction, 197–198
 and Bolshevik Revolution, 160, 164–166, 184
 and *El soldado Rafael*, 176, 271
 in exile in Mexico City, 265–267
 on Julio Antonio Mella's death, 266
 persecution of, 265
 repression against, 162, 261
 speaking at Alfredo López funeral, 270
Pérez Ponce, Tomás, 127
Pérez, Augustín, 260
Pérez, José Miguel
 deportation of from Cuba, 210
Peru
 anarchism in, 227
Philadelphia, 27, 37, 104, 195
 and *El Corsario* plot vs. Pres. Wilson, 177
Platt Amendment, 19, 64, 72–73, 105, 123, 168, 197, 210
Plaza, Enrique, 170
PLM (Partido Liberal Mexicano), 39
 anarchist opposition to, 142–144
 and Baja California, 128–130
Police
 in Cuba, 262
 in Panama 1925, 233–234
 Panama 1916 against strikers, 193
 Panama 1916 cooperation with strikers, 192
Populism
 in Panama, 117–118, 225
 in United States, 50
Porras, President Belisario (Panama), 117, 223
 and the FORP, 227
Post-colonialism, 34–36
Prats, Luis, 109–110
PRC (Partido Revolucionario Cubano), 52

Pretelt, Chief of Police Leonides (Panama City), 234
Pujal, José, 130, 150

Raíces, J., 54
Ramnath, Maia, 34–36
Ramos, Emiliano, 171, 288
 attacks on Santiago Iglesias Pantín, 264
 attacks on Socialist Party, 255–257
 in Cuba, 255
 and death of Alfredo López, 260–261
 on death of Julio Antonio Mella, 264
 in El Grupo Soviet de Bayamón, 170
 in the FRT, 1890s, 92
 and 1928 Pan Am conference, 264
 and Pan-Americanism, 254
 in 1920s and 1930s Puerto Rico, 255–257
 in Tampa, 255
Rebolledo, Teófila, 144
Reclus, Élisée, 105
Recoba, Víctor
 and 1916 general strike in Canal Zone, 189
 and anarchist congress 1925, 244
 deportation from Panama, 194
 in Cuba, 241
 in Mexico, 241–242
 in Peru, 241
 in Philadelphia, 241
Red Scare, 13, 208
 in Florida, 175–184
 post-McKinley assassination, 156
 pre-1917 in US, 173
 in Puerto Rico, 175
 and radical literature in Florida, 175–177
 in United States, 195
Rediker, Marcus, 41
Rent Strike
 in Colombia, 17, 229–230, 239
 commemorations in Panama, 249–251
 in Cuba, 71–72, 239
 and funerals in Panama, 234–235
 and government fear of Communism in Panama, 238
 in Panama, 7, 239
 and US military response in Panama, 233–236
 and women in Panama, 231
Rey, Manuel, 104
 anti-military draft actions, 195

Rivera Martínez, Prudencia, 255
Rivera, Librado, 241
Rodó, José Enrique, 222
Rodríguez, M.D., 34
   anticlericalism of, 116–117
   and Anti-Americanism, 113–117
   and *El Único*, 113–117
   against Flores Magón, 142–144
   and individualist anarchism, 114–115
   and the Moncaleano Affair, 149
   and network controversies, 145–146
   and race, 112
   transnational activism before 1910, 113
   transnational anarchism before 1910, 143–144
   versus *¡Tierra!*, 140–141
Roig San Martín, Enrique, 44
Rojava, 287
Romero Palacios, Rafael, 130, 150
   controversy in Los Angeles, 146–147
Romero, Florencio, 195
Roosevelt, President Franklin, 270
Roosevelt, President Theodore, 64, 105
   1906 Canal Visit of, 110–111
   anti-anarchist law in Canal Zone, 106–107
Ros Planas, Francisco, 127–128
Rubio, José
   and impact on José Valadés, 240
   exile to Mexico from Cuba, 160
Russian Revolution, *See* Bolshevik Revolution

Saavedra, Abelardo, 264
   and 1907 Cuba propaganda tour, 72, 89–90
   deportation of, 73
   and rural anarchism in Cuba, 73
   trial of, 127
Sacco and Vanzetti, 225
Salinas, Marcelo, 27, 289
   accused in Wilson assassination plot, 179
   and the ALC in 1940s, 286
   Alma Guajira and rural Cuba, 276
   Alma Guajira as anarcho-feminism, 276
   and *Alma Guajira*, 275–277
   and *Alma Guajira* controversy, 277
   and assassination plot, 134–136
   and Bolshevik Revolution, 160, 162
   El Protector, 279
   in Florida, 102–103, 134
   and IWW, 103
   and Langston Hughes, 279
   and literary awards, 30, 274
   and Mexican Revolution, 29, 128, 136–137
   and opposition to Bolshevik Revolution, 165
   and Pardiñas obituary, 135
   repression against, 162
   and settings for stories, 275
   Un aprendiz de revolucionario, 277–279
Sánchez Cobos, Amparo, 24
Sánchez, Santiago, 150
Sandino, Augusto César, 21, 263, 265
Santo Maldonado, Antonio, 243
Sanz, Antonio, 141
Seattle World Trade Organization meeting, 287
Sección Comunista de Cuba, 160
Segura, Eliberto
   and 1916 general strike in Canal Zone, 192
   deportations of, 194
Serra, Rafael, 258
   in anarchist fiction, 278
   repression against, 262
SGT (Sindicato General de Trabajadores), 7
Shipping, Passenger, 15–17
   and anarchist congress 1925, 243
Sierra Gutiérrez, Gavino, 232
Sindicato Fabril
   banning of under Machado, 210
Sirino, Severo, 92, 95
SLP (Socialist Labor Party of the United States), 93–94
Socialist Party
   anarchist attacks against in Puerto Rico, 255–257
   in Puerto Rico, 169
   in Puerto Rico and independence, 202
   in United States, 50
Sonn, Richard, 125
Statue of Liberty, 48
   as symbolism for anarchists, 48, 67
Stirner, Max, 114, 240
Strikes
   in Canal Zone 1916, 5, 39, 188–194
   Florida cigar workers 1894, 45
   Florida cigar workers 1894–1895, 47
   during Great War, 187
   Huelga de Pesa (Florida 1899), 75–76

in Cuba
  1917–1920, 196
in Florida
  1895 to 1896, 58
  1919 boycott, 181
  cigar workers (1910), 99–101
  1901 general strike, 79–85
in Puerto Rico
  1919, 171
  tobacco workers (1919), 169
Struthers, David, 24

Talens, Miguel, 262
Talía, Ángel, 111
Taller Libertario Alfredo López, 287
Tejera, Humberto, 158
Tenorio Aguilera, Juan, 150
Terreros, Nicolás, 233
¡Tierra!, 38, 65, 85
  and Canal Zone anarchists, 111, 120
  closing of, 74, 91–92
  circulation of, 91–92
  and conflict with Panama anarchists, 140–141
  as a Cuban paper, 88–92
  early Florida support of, 86–88
  and Florida support of, 98–101
  and Great War, 199
  in Mexico, 126–128
  as regional paper, 32–33, 86, 122–123
  and support for PLM, 128–130
Torres, Alfonso, 171
  and democracy, 96–97
  in FLT, 95
  and Puerto Rican independence, 203
  in Socialist Party, 255
Transnational
  and biography, 9
  and translocal, 22–23
Transnationalism
  anarchist network policing, 139–153
  and anarchist antimilitarism during Great War, 195–197
  and anarchist networks, 8–10, 22–23, 184–185, 227
  and circulation of radical literature during Red Scare, 175–177
  and IWW, 196
  and the IWW, 161, 196–197
  of labor in Panama Canal Zone, 190
  policing, 127, 193

surveillance, 13, 39, 135, 176, 180, 185, 196–197
Tur, Juan, 150
  deportation of from Cuba, 73
  and Moncaleano Affair, 149
Turcato, Davide, 21, 76

Uceda, Jorgonis, 118
UNIA (Universal Negro Improvement Association), 14, 37
  in Panama, 224
Unions
  CMIU (Cigar Makers International Union), 78–79
  in Canal Zone
    Maritime Workers Association, 189–194
  in Cuba, 44
    Círculo de Trabajadores, 68
    Junta Central de Trabajadores de la Región Cubana, 51
    Sindicato Fabril, 167
  in Florida
    CMIU, 85
    CMIU and anarchist oppostion, 101–103
    CMIU and anarchist support, 98
    La Resistencia, 100
    Sociedad de Torcedores, 182
  in Panama
    Central Obrero, 192
    FORP, 223–228
    SGT (Sindicato General de Trabajadores)
    origins, 228
    SGT and rent strike, 231
  in Puerto Rico
    FLT (Federación Libre de Trabajadores), 93–98, 169
    FLT (Federación Libre de Trabajadores) and anarchists, 94–98
    FLT and Puerto Rican independence, 202
    FRT (Federación Regional de los Trabajadores), 92–93
    La Liga Obrera de Tampa, 76–78
    La Resistencia (Tampa), 76
    Sociedad General de Trabajadores (Tampa), 75
United Fruit Company, 15

Valadés, José C.
  in early 1920s Mexico, 239–241
  and Pan-American anarchist congress, 242–243
  and Víctor Recoba, 241–242
Valdés, President Ramón (Panama), 192
Vallón Fuentes, José, 172
Van der Walt, Lucien, 155
Vargas Vila, José, 175
Varona, Enrique
  assassination of, 210
Vega Santos, Pablo, 95, 255
Vega, Carlos, 140
Venezuela, 36–37
  anarchism in, 243
  anarchists in, 252
Vidal, Jaime, 28, 104
Vilar, Juan, 95, 97, 212
Villar, Jovino, 67
Von Wedel, Rodolfo, 230

Walker, Arturo, 194
Weber, Devra, 152
West Indians, 27
  and anarchist in Canal Zone, 190
  and anarchists in Canal Zone, 111–113, 193
  and anarchists in Panama, 227–228
  in Canal Zone, 109
  in Panama, 106, 227, 230
West Indies, 37
Weyler, General Valeriano (Spain)
  and anarchist assassination attempt, 53
  1920s compared to Weyler's Cuba, 210
  and rule in Cuba, 55–56
Wilson, President Woodrow
  anarchist attacks on foreign policy, 207
  anarchist plot against, 177–180
Wood, General Leonard, 68, 72
World Social Forums, 287

Zapata, Emiliano, 137
Zapatistas, 287
Zayas, President Alfredo (Cuba), 209, 211
Zimmer, Kenyon, 61, 198